RIGHTS REMEMBERED

Rights Remembered

A Salish Grandmother Speaks on

American Indian History and the Future

Pauline R. Hillaire

Scälla — Of the Killer Whale

Elder of the Lummi Tribe

Edited by Gregory P. Fields

UNIVERSITY OF NEBRASKA PRESS

LINCOLN AND LONDON

Funding for this book and its companion media was
provided by Southern Illinois University–Edwardsville;
the Edwardsville (IL) chapter of the National Society of
the Daughters of the American Revolution; SoundWise
Studios, Bellingham, Washington; the Jack Straw Cultural
Center, Seattle; and the family of Pauline Hillaire.

Frontispiece: *Eagleman* by John A. Grant II (Colville
Confederated Tribes), Nespelem, Washington, b. 1930.

Library of Congress Cataloging-in-Publication Data
Names: Hillaire, Pauline, 1929– | Fields, Gregory P., 1961–
Title: Rights remembered: a Salish grandmother
speaks on American Indian history and the future /
Pauline R. Hillaire (Scälla of the Killer Whale, Elder
of the Lummi Tribe); edited by Gregory P. Fields.
Description: Lincoln: University of Nebraska Press,
2016. | Series: American Indian lives | Includes
bibliographical references and index.
Identifiers: LCCN 2015028638
ISBN 9780803245846 (cloth: alkaline paper)
ISBN 9780803285781 (epub)
ISBN 9780803285798 (mobi)
ISBN 9780803285804 (pdf)
Subjects: LCSH: Hillaire, Pauline, 1929– | Salish
Indians—Biography. | Salish women—Biography. |
Indian grandmothers—Northwest, Pacific—Biography.
| Salish Indians—Social life and customs. | Salish
Indians—Poetry. | Indians of North America—Northwest,
Pacific—Government relations—History. | Indians,
Treatment of—Northwest, Pacific—History. | Indians
of North America—Northwest, Pacific—Treaties. |
Northwest, Pacific—Race relations—History.
Classification: LCC E99.S2 H45 2016 | DDC 978.6004/979435—
dc23 LC record available at http://lccn.loc.gov/2015028638

Set in Charis by L. Auten.
Designed by N. Putens.

For my father
Joseph R. Hillaire
Kwul-kwul'tʷ: Spirit of the War Club
Lummi, 1894–1967

CONTENTS

ILLUSTRATIONS

FIGURES

As I wrote this book, I truly followed a desperate trail. Alone, I would never have made it. With the help of my sister, Mary Ellen Hillaire, my father, Joseph R. Hillaire, my grandfather, Frank Hillaire, my mother, and all my brothers and sisters, I remain encouraged, even at the end. You see, my entire family was with me, spiritually. Their words did not haunt me; they helped me. The Great Spirit played the most important role in this enormous task. There were times when I thought, no; this should not be done. But the messages began to sound better and better, so I continued. Friends and relatives in this world encouraged me. Never disregard heartfelt encouragement. It seems to clear the littered pathway to your goal as if by pure magic.

With this book, I reach out to those strong, healthy, and curious future generations and encourage them to never give up. The strength of our ancestors remains with us. All we have to do is discover it and continue to the end of the trail. My focus remains on our Indian youth: children, grandchildren, and great grandchildren. I see amongst them very talented people, surging forward with sacred curiosity. They have the qualities that our ancestors saw in earlier generations. Hope will help carry you, and persistence pays off—not that you will get richer and richer, but that your hearts maintain a steady path forward.

As you read my book, keep my message clear in your mind. My prayer is for more land and for the rights of Indian people across America. Please study the philosophy of our elders. In addition, study the philosophy of the few U.S. officials who cared, but who couldn't get very far with their hopes for us, because of Indian policy and law.

There are two sides to making a law strong for the people. One side is the character of the people who make the law; the other side is the strength of those who carry the law through barriers in behalf of the people. Setting policies and ensuring that policies are applied—nationally, and in your own locality—is a challenge. Some of us were born without that particular talent. Therefore, we must watch for the individuals who can face the challenge. We must review their strengths, courage, tenacity, and their capability to carry the ball, and like the champions they are, make the scores needed to get us to the right place.

I chose to investigate the U.S. government documents because of my father's encouragement. My sister followed in his footsteps; in her lifetime, she too conveyed important messages to, and on behalf of, our Indian people. I chose my father and my sister as role models because of their ability to communicate to relatives, friends, and the population at large. For over forty years, I carried my research documents with me from place to place—thinking about them, placing them in perspective, absorbing images of the past, present, and future, in my efforts to tie them together—trying to make sense of that world of words. And that took time and patience. Not once was I tempted to throw anything away. The messages were loud and clear: messages about land, law, survival, timidity, and questions about how things could be set right.

Our treaty rights are, first of all, rights that we have reserved. I hope that this book will help show how our Indian leaders have remembered our rights, and I hope it will help Indian and non-Indian citizens and leaders to remember our history and our rights. Laws and policies are extremely important, like gems and jewels in a treasure place. Perseverance is the key, and love is the light.

Pauline R. Hillaire
Lummi Indian Reservation
Bellingham, Washington

ACKNOWLEDGMENTS

In the preface of this book, Pauline Hillaire thanks the elder generations of her family, and here we thank the younger generations of the family who have helped her with her work and in so many ways. As Pauline completed this book, she was assisted at home by her daughter Debra Covington Paul (Hae'tel'wit, Lummi/Colville, 1952–2012; this Native name is a feminine form of the name of Pauline's paternal grandfather, Frank Hillaire, Haeteluk or Hae'tel'luk).

The Edwardsville (IL) chapter of the National Society of the Daughters of the American Revolution contributed generously to the production of this book and its companion media. We are thankful for what their support made possible, and for their encouragement of dialogue concerning American history and democratic principles. The Jack Straw Cultural Center (Seattle) and SoundWise Studios (Bellingham) made possible a number of studio recording sessions that provided material for the companion media. We are grateful for the kindness of audio engineers Tom Stiles at Jack Straw, and Tom and Nancy Jordan of SoundWise.

Genuine thanks to Southern Illinois University–Edwardsville for the Hoppe Research Professorship, which provided invaluable time for the completion of this book. Skillful assistance was provided by SIUE research assistants Jordan Blackhurst, Lauren Gibson, and Jenna Tucker.

University of Nebraska Press has our enduring thanks for bringing out this book. For their comments on the manuscript, we very much appreciate the time and expertise contributed by David R. M. Beck, Suzanne Crawford-O'Brien, Raymond J. DeMallie, Rowena McClinton, and our anonymous reviewer. We are ever thankful to our sponsoring editor, Matthew Bokovoy, for his good counsel. Our production editor Sara Springsteen, copyeditor Jane Curran, and the members of the press staff have our respect and appreciation for their expertise in the art and technology of producing books. Many thanks also to the editors of the American Indian Lives series for their work and their leadership.

Great thanks to Raymond DeMallie and Douglas Parks and the American Indian Studies Research Institute at Indiana University–Bloomington, for resources provided for the completion of this work. Special thanks to Jon Bowman, director of the AISRI's Center for the Documentation of Endangered Languages. Special thanks to Rebecca Chamberlain of the Evergreen State College for all her years of work and for her travel with Scälla, which helped make this book possible, and for this book's biographical essay, "Scälla—Of the Killer Whale: A Song of Hope."

For assistance with Lummi terms, we are thankful to Tsi'li'xʷ Bill James, Lummi Hereditary Chief; the late Brent Galloway, professor emeritus, First Nations University, Regina; and Professor Timothy Montler, University of North Texas.

The expertise of cartographers makes books much more than they would be without their science and art. The maps were made by Professor Charles Yeager of Snow College (UT) and Zach Schleicher of Southern Illinois University–Edwardsville, in consultation with Professor Randall Pearson, director of the Laboratory for Spatial Analysis at SIUE. Cartography and the abstract for map 9 were done by Tim Wahl of Bellingham, Washington.

Two individuals warrant recognition for their research assistance, and for being strong praying people in behalf of this book: Pat Rasmussen in Washington, and Jay W. Kemp in Illinois.

We are ever thankful to our families and friends, and for their help through long years.

RIGHTS REMEMBERED

2. Pauline R. Hillaire, Scälla—Of the Killer Whale (Lummi, b. 1929). Portrait for the 1996 Washington State Governor's Heritage Award. Arts Washington, photo by J. Frederick (Fritz) Dent, 1996.

Introduction

American Indian History and the Future

Gregory P. Fields

This book is a contribution to ethnohistory carried out by a Native investigator. It is grounded in Native experience and oral tradition, and the author's analysis of primary source documents of the U.S. government. *Rights Remembered* offers a Native elder's analysis of U.S./Indian relations in the Puget Sound region of Washington, particularly in the mid-nineteenth century, when treaties and reservations were established there. *Rights Remembered* presents the results of Lummi elder Pauline Hillaire's analysis of documents from the U.S. Congressional Serial Set, in particular, the Reports of the Commissioners of Indian Affairs. This book reconstructs, from a Native viewpoint, the history of Anglo-European relations with the first people of North America and the Pacific Northwest. The fundamental messages of *Rights Remembered* are that Indian rights have always existed, that those rights must be remembered, and that remembering those rights means restoring and respecting them in policy and practice.

Scälla, Pauline Hillaire, was born in Bellingham, Washington. In her understanding, she was born in 1929; some U.S. records list her birth year as 1931. She was raised by parents and elders for whom ancestral lifeways, the arrival of Euro-Americans, and changes of postcontact life were fairly recent, in both memory and in fact. The author, over eighty years old when this book was completed, began writing it nearly fifty years ago. It comes to press about a century and a half after the signing of the Treaty of Point Elliott and the other Pacific Northwest treaties. Woven throughout the book is the author's commentary on her life, the lives of her family, and the lives of Lummi and Coast Salish people generally, since the time that treaties and reservations were imposed. The author also looks to the future and calls for people—Native and non-Native—to create a better future: a nation of citizens living in a sociopolitical system that is more functional and just, rather than a future conditioned by continuing failures to respond to the events and the lessons of history.

As the author completes the work of her life in the early twenty-first century, there remain living relatively few U.S. Native elders who are immediate descendants of the generations who experienced the arrival of settlers, traders, missionaries, governmental officials, treaties, and reservations. The Treaty of Point Elliott (1855) initially established four reservations in the Puget Sound region of Washington Territory, including that of Scälla's Lummi Tribe. Among the leaders who signed the Point Elliott Treaty, along with the well-known Chief Seattle (Si?ał), was Scälla's great-great grandfather, on her mother's side: Tseleq (Tsi'li'xʷ). The main Lummi leader who signed the treaty was Tseleq's brother, Chowitsut. Scälla speaks to us now as a Native person who was educated in ancestral traditions that were still strongly in place in the lifetimes of her parents, Joseph Hillaire and Edna Scott Hillaire Price, both born in 1894. She speaks as an American Indian who has lived through America's twentieth-century history, paying careful attention to patterns and connections of historical events.

In *A Forest of Time: Native Ways of History*, anthropologist Peter Nabokov speaks of comments made by Cherokee historian Rachel Caroline Eaton (1869–1938) about the challenges faced by Native historians, who must "somehow combine and contextualize raw materials from an alien archival tradition, honor the authority of a specific geography, and interweave their own oral tradition's multiple genres." This is the challenge that Pauline Hillaire has undertaken in *Rights Remembered*. Explicit and implicit in Pauline's analysis is the observation that the ahistoric nature of American Indian history is a consequence of two significant factors: (1) the oral and lived (as distinct from written) nature of Indian knowledge, values, and culture, and (2) the dominant culture's tendency to disregard the traces of history, owing to influences of, and benefits derived from, its own interpretations and values. As Nabokov observes, crediting Eaton, "The special burdens placed upon the creative Indian historian to command cross-cultural genres and multiple voices would seem to have made them proto-postmodernists, before the term was ever coined."[1]

Rights Remembered has three main sections: Part 1, "The Nineteenth Century and Before," covers the treaty era and the time of Pauline's grandparents and earlier generations (chapters 1–5). Chapters 1 and 2 deal with colonization and the Indian experience in the founding of the United States, so readers who want to begin with Indian history in the Pacific Northwest might prefer to begin with chapter 3. Part 2, "The Twentieth Century and After," covers Puget Sound Indian history in the lifetimes of Pauline, her parents, and her descendants (chapters 6–9). Part 3, "Oral History and Cultural Teachings," is introduced by a short biography of the author, titled "Scälla—Of the Killer Whale: A Song of Hope" (chapter 10). Part 3 contains Pauline's commentary on spiritual and philosophical foundations of Lummi and Coast Salish life (chapter 11), followed by poetry by Pauline and by her father, Joseph Hillaire (chapter 12). The book's final chapter (chapter 13), "History in the Time of the Treaty of Point Elliott," is a transcription of an oration given by Joe Hillaire and recaps the history that Pauline accounts and analyzes in the preceding chapters. Appendixes provide (1) the Treaty of Point Elliott (1855), (2) the United Nations Declaration on the Rights of Indigenous Peoples (2007), and (3) a chronology of events in U.S. Indian history and policy (fifteenth to twenty-first centuries), emphasizing the Point Elliott Treaty tribes.

The name *Scälla* is pronounced *Skahla*, which could also be spelled *Skālla*, with a bar (macron) above the first *a*, pronounced as in the word "call." Scälla has for many years spelled her Native name with two dots (an umlaut) over the first *a*, so we have maintained that spelling.

Scälla—Of the Killer Whale[2] has carried many responsibilities as a cultural historian: She has learned and taught cultural traditions and philosophy through song, dance, legends, genealogy, and oral history. Following her father and grandfather, she has labored to help young people at Lummi learn and perpetuate their ancestral knowledge, traditions, and values. Like her father, Joseph Hillaire, Kwul-kwul't^w: Spirit of the War Club, and his father, Frank Hillaire, Haeteluk: Bad/Formidable Man, Scälla has educated the public about aspects of Lummi and Coast Salish culture, and she has done so in a spirit of generosity and cultural cooperation. In the tradition of the forbears in her family's chiefly line, Scälla takes seriously the responsibility of speaking in behalf of her people, and she does so with humility and diplomacy.

Rights Remembered carries a message to people of the United States and to people of the world. It is a book for indigenous and non-indigenous readers: researchers, teachers and students, policy makers, tribal leaders and U.S. leaders, and citizens of all cultures. It calls for restoring the truths of history concerning what happened for Indian America when Europeans arrived and established the United States, how Indian policies were conceived and carried out, and how Indian lands, livelihood, and lives were lost in the Northwest. *Rights Remembered* calls for cultural reconciliation based on a solid foundation of the truths of history. The book contains a sustained argument for land rights. The author's fundamental call is for respecting the rights of Native people: rights to resources for that which is required for a good life, rights to nonprejudicial treatment and dignity, and rights under treaties, agreements, policies, and law. Significantly, the book calls for remembering the rights that already exist for sovereign peoples to manage their national affairs, and for remembering the human rights that exist for each individual.

Scälla is very straightforward about the injustices, losses, suffering, and deaths suffered by Indian people, but her way is one of reconciliation, healing, and justice. Chapter 1 carries the title "Forgotten Genocide." The question may arise as to whether "genocide" is too strong a term in this book, with its focus on the Pacific Northwest, given that the Pacific Northwest tribes were not subjected to the degrees of physical genocide suffered by many Native peoples. Scälla is writing about, and in behalf of, Native America as a whole, with her Lummi and Coast Salish homeland as a focus. In chapter 1 Scälla provides the criteria of genocide articulated in the United Nations "Declaration on Genocide," and she states her position on why "genocide" is the appropriate term for the various methods of extermination of Indian life that have taken place in the United States from before its founding—some of which continue in the present day. In addition to deaths by disease, execution by the state, military action, and civilian violence, ongoing cultural genocide occurred in the Pacific Northwest, much of it stemming from loss of lands and from federal policy efforts, which caused deprivations in both physical livelihood and spiritual relationships with the lands and waters. Native ceremonies and traditional cultural practices were prohibited by U.S. Indian policy, and these were further compromised by loss of lands and lives, resulting in a cycle of damage to cultural and personal identity and wholeness. In her youth, Scälla experienced her mother Edna's speaking only in a whisper when she spoke her Native languages, because after Edna was punished in boarding school for speaking them, she never again spoke them aloud. That was the point in history where a link was broken and particular dialects died in a family.

I met Scälla in 2007 at a memorial service on the Tulalip Reservation near Seattle. Over the years we have worked together on a number of projects in Washington State and in Illinois. In Illinois, Scälla visited Cahokia Mounds, the most populous precontact settlement north of Mexico, and she was happy to be in the homeland of an Indian leader whom she especially respects, the Sauk Chief Black Hawk. In 2008 Scälla asked me to help her secure publication for this book, and it has been the greatest honor to do so. In the autobiography that Scälla wrote for this book, she explains how she wrote it. My work in editing this book has been to verify sources, to discuss with Scälla the intent of particular passages, to organize material in terms of sequence and the presentation of ideas, to verify and add references, and to prepare the manuscript for publication. It has been a genuinely collaborative effort. Scälla and I worked together from 2008 through 2011 on her two manuscripts, *Rights Remembered* and *A Totem Pole History: The Work of Lummi Carver Joe Hillaire*.[3] Scälla suffered a stroke in November 2011, which impaired her speech. I continued to visit Scälla and to remain in consultation with members of her family as I completed the editing of *Rights Remembered*. In September 2013, Scälla was honored by the National Endowment for the Humanities with a National Heritage Fellowship. The award was accepted by her daughter Audrey Chicone, who spoke in the family's tradition of orators on her mother's behalf at the Library of Congress. Seventeen members of a Lummi song and dance group, Children of the Setting Sun, representing four generations, sang and danced in Scälla's honor at the NEA Concert that week in Washington DC, led by her grandson, Benjamin Covington — Cuth Sells (Lummi/Colville, b. 1980). Among the nine fellows honored in 2013, Scälla was the one designated as the Bess Lomax Hawes National Heritage Fellow, in recognition of her lifetime contributions to cultural heritage preservation. She stayed strong, and in December 2013, the month that *A Totem Pole History* was published, she attended — with members of the group Children of the Setting Sun — three of the seven presentations held in Washington State to announce the book.

Scälla's topics and tone in this book are serious, punctuated by her wonderful, occasionally humorous or wry turns of phrase — as readers acquainted with her will appreciate. She wrote this book informed by the U.S. government's official records of Indian history and policy, and by her knowledge of the history, oral tradition, and lived tradition of her people. The life experience that underlies her knowledge base grew from many relationships with elders, contemporaries, and young people in her family, Lummi tribal community, and other Native communities of western and eastern Washington where she lived and worked. She was assiduous with the bibliographic notation of the many government documents that she quotes and refers to. The U.S. Congressional Serial Set is not easy to work with, even in an online, searchable format, but in the 1960s Scälla managed with unwieldy microfiche copies at the

University of Washington library. Scälla and I did most of our research consultation by phone and email, along with our mailing books, articles, and drafts back and forth. We worked together in person when conditions for travel permitted, at least once per year.

One time, Scälla and I were talking on the phone. She was talking about some Coast Salish philosophical ideas. I was on my porch, looking out at the sky, reflecting in the back of my mind about how she and I were under the same sky, in Washington and Illinois, respectively. I thought I had an insight about something she had said about matter and spirit, and the idea seemed to be exemplified by how the phone allows us to communicate distantly by voice. I said, "Like the phone; we can talk, even though we're thousands of miles apart." "But that's of the white man," Scälla said.

Rights Remembered is not primarily a biography, yet it has strong biographical elements. I encouraged Scälla to add more detail about her very interesting life, even though she did not set out to write an autobiography, and she did not consider the particulars of her life that important. As I grew to know Scälla better, and as I grew to know this book, I came to understand that Scälla's biography is not so much about the stories of her individual journey. Her story is, in large measure, a story of her people: her ancestors, her family and descendants, her tribe—the Lummi or xwlemi (*xʷlə'mi*), also known as Lhaq'temish ("LAHK-tem-ish"): *People of the Sea*. Her story—those aspects that she chooses to tell here—is also a story of, and for, Coast Salish people and the First People of all this land. One way that this book is biographical is in the sense that a web of historical factors in the twentieth century Northwest contributed to the particulars of the life of Pauline Rose Hillaire, Scälla, Of the Killer Whale. The historical circumstances of Scälla's life are among the factors that influence her analysis of the Indian Affairs reports and other government documents, which provide a record of white people's attitudes and U.S. policies and actions concerning Indians. Her life-experience in the Indian and white worlds, the ancestral history and cultural traditions passed down to her, and her examination of pertinent U.S. records, all influence the way that she analyzes history and policy. These sources, along with the historical conditions in which those influences were transmitted and received, affect her observations and the recommendations she makes for the future. As readers, we are privileged to observe Scälla's mind in action, working on a range of issues concerning history, sociology, policy, and law. We can observe her mind at work on problems of our past, and of the current age—and this is part of our appreciating her biography.

Scälla began the research for this book in the mid-1960s: roughly a century after the Treaty of Point Elliott was ratified in 1859. Now, in the early twenty-first century, Scälla speaks as an engaged citizen of the Lummi Nation and of the United States. She looks to the future for her grandchildren and great-grandchildren, for Salish and other indigenous tribes and peoples, for U.S. citizens and leaders, for the world's nations, and for the earth, air, rivers, and oceans.

HISTORICAL CONTEXT OF THE PACIFIC NORTHWEST TREATIES

In eastern North America, Native people began experiencing the arrival and influx of Europeans in the fifteenth century, after the expeditions of Columbus. The Spanish soon colonized land in Florida and in New Mexico, and the French claimed the midsection of what is now the United States, from the Great Lakes south to present-day Louisiana, along with extensive territory in present-day Canada. Starting in the seventeenth century, numerous colonies began to grow on the eastern seaboard, established by immigrants from Great Britain and other European nations. By the time the thirteen American colonies declared their independence in 1776, European immigrants to America had been causing various impacts on Indian life for nearly three centuries. On the Northwest Coast, however, the 1770s was the decade when most Native people were encountering non-Indians for the first time.

Earlier in the eighteenth century the Russians, interested primarily in the profits of the fur trade, had become a presence in British Columbia and Alaska. A number of Spanish and English expeditions had taken place along the Northwest Coast as early as the sixteenth century (see appendix 3). Along with Russia, both Spain and Britain laid claim to large areas of the Northwest Coast. Navigators—geographic explorers, military officers representing their nations, and entrepreneurs—sailed the Pacific coast and into the Northwest's bays, straits, and rivers. Some of these navigators charted the region's geography, and several of them asserted claims of national ownership. Often these claims were made by merely sighting land, and there was little or no communication with Native residents. In the 1770s, relationships based on trade became established between Europeans and Native people of the North Pacific Coast. The Europeans also brought smallpox and other diseases that soon began to decimate Native populations, who had no previous exposure or immunity.

In the early eighteenth century, a number of corporations were established on both sides of the present-day U.S./Canada border, seeking to profit from the region's natural resources. The British Hudson's Bay Company (HBC) was dominant among the companies that operated trading posts: There were HBC posts at Victoria on Vancouver Island, at Fort Langley on the mainland of British North America (in present-day British Columbia), and one at Fort Nisqually, in the southern Puget Sound area. Commerce provided conditions for Native people to interact with the newly arrived white residents, through trade, employment, and intermarriage. In the 1830s and 1840s several major missionary initiatives were launched in the Northwest, with the aim of "civilization" of Native persons. In the minds of the colonizers, "civilization" meant Christianization and adoption of agriculture and the "settled" life. These aims were reprised with variations in future years, as the United States proceeded with taking over Indian lands and other resources.

The story told in this book centers on the land losses of the Lummi and other tribes who are parties to the 1855 Treaty of Point Elliott. Thus the heart of the story begins in the 1840s, when U.S. land holdings expanded dramatically, and the rapid acquisition of the western and southwestern regions of the United States had major impacts on U.S. Indian policy. From 1803 until the 1840s the nation's western border stopped at the eastern side of the Rocky Mountains. This was the western border of the lands that the United States had acquired from France by the Louisiana Purchase in 1803. In 1844 James K. Polk was elected U.S. president, running on a platform of territorial expansion. Westward expansion came to be called "Manifest Destiny" in the national consciousness of the time: The bringing of Euro-American type civilization and settlement to the western wilderness was said to be endorsed by God himself. In 1845 the independent republic of Texas was annexed to the United States as a state. The acquisition of Texas, and a year later the Oregon Territory, added an enormous region of valuable land to the nation. Acquisition of the Oregon Territory instigated events in the Northwest that are addressed in this book.

The United States and Great Britain had jointly occupied the Oregon Territory since 1818. In 1846 the Oregon Treaty established an international border at the 49th parallel, between present-day Washington State and British Columbia. This added to the U.S. land base the future states of Washington and Oregon, plus portions of Idaho, Montana, and Wyoming (see maps 3–5). Finally, in 1848, at the end of the Mexican War, the United States acquired, by the Treaty of Guadalupe Hidalgo, the regions that Americans would call California, New Mexico Territory, and Utah Territory.[4] The acquisitions of Texas, the Oregon Territory, and the southwestern lands (by annexation, treaty, and war, respectively) added 1.2 million square miles to the U.S. land area, increasing its size by over 60 percent. Many Indian tribes and persons inhabited these regions now controlled by the United States: lands to which non-Indian Americans began flocking for residential and business interests.

The first major influxes of non-Indian settlers to the desirable lands of the Oregon Territory occurred in the 1840s. Most of the new residents arrived by wagon train.[5] However, at that time, Indian policies in the Oregon Territory were both lacking and contradictory, and the injustice and suffering that resulted for tribal people had effects that extend into the present time. In the 1840s there was rapid erosion of the Indian removal policies of the 1830s, in particular, erosion of the government's stated aim of a permanent "Indian frontier" to ensure that Indians would retain, or be relocated to, homelands west of the

Mississippi River. Non-Indian residences, farms, ranches, and industries rapidly surrounded the land that remained in Indian Country. Settlers, miners, traders, and missionaries heading west disturbed Indian homelands and damaged ecosystems as they traveled. New Indian policy was needed to solve what the United States regarded as the latest forms of "the Indian problem": (1) non-Indian citizens needed military protection as they traversed, and took over, lands occupied by indigenous residents; (2) Indian claims had to be "extinguished" for lands desired by (or already in use by) non-Indians; and (3) plans were needed for relocation of displaced Indian people, now that the "permanent Indian Frontier" was seen as the illusion and the deception that it was.[6]

In the first of several public talks that I heard Pauline Hillaire give about this book when she was writing it, it was significant to me that she commented on the personalities and approaches of various Indian officials who were involved with Indian Affairs at the time that her tribe's treaty was enacted in the mid-nineteenth century, such as Commissioner of Indian Affairs George W. Manypenny. Manypenny, in Hillaire's words, "commended the survival of Indian people," yet it was he who negotiated in 1876 an illegal agreement with Lakota leaders, whose people the United States had placed under duress to surrender the sacred Black Hills: lands that could be very lucrative to non-Indians and that were part of the reserved lands of the Sioux Nation, according to the 1868 Treaty of Fort Laramie.[7] The narrative and the citations in this book provide names and titles of Indian Affairs officials, U.S. presidents, and others who were involved in treaty era events in Puget Sound. Reflection on the actions and interactions of the individuals who were involved with the Washington State treaties illuminates Indian policy as a product of personalities, as well as a product of ideologies. Although individuals are affected by the ideologies and policies of their time, it remains the case that a fairly small number of Indian Affairs officials were directly involved with Indian people and exchanged correspondence and policy recommendations concerning Indian Affairs, and that Congress relied heavily on the information and judgments that these officials provided.

Examination of events and themes in Indian policy during the Pacific Northwest treaty era affords insight for the future—and suggests both caution and hope.

A few words about the structure and function of the Indian Affairs Office in the mid-nineteenth century may help the reader appreciate the government documents that are analyzed in this book. The commissioner of Indian Affairs was the main officer to whom communications concerning Indian Affairs were transmitted. Superintendents and agents in the field submitted reports and correspondence to the commissioner, and the commissioner responded to them with relevant replies, orders, and instructions. (In 1849 Commissioner Orlando Brown noted in his annual report that there were only five superintendents and nine agents for the entire nation.)[8] The commissioner also sent correspondence to the Office of Indian Affairs (OIA), and items were returned from the OIA to the commissioner for action. Agents had duties including the making of treaties (when authorized by the secretary of the interior or the commissioner of Indian Affairs), licensing of traders, supervision of Indian education, and the promotion of missionary work.[9] Agents also had the responsibility of distributing annuity goods or funds, which left open the possibility of withholding annuities from Indians and cheating them for personal gain. Superintendents could, and sometimes did, perform the duties of agents, but superintendents' assignments were more administrative, usually covering several Indian agencies. The superintendent was the central figure of communication between agents and the commissioner of Indian Affairs. In sum, superintendents received reports from field agents and orders from Washington DC, and they provided reports on tribal conditions, financial statements, and recommendations for appropriations.[10] In the territories, the post of superintendent of Indian Affairs was sometimes combined with that of governor, which could result in neglect of Indian issues or the subjection of Indian affairs to partisan politics.[11]

Reports of the commissioners, superintendents, and agents, along with related documents, formed the *Annual Report of the Commissioner of Indian Affairs* (*ARCIA*), which is published in the United States

Congressional Serial Set, as part of the *Annual Message of the President of the United States*, or as Department of the Interior responses by the secretary of the interior.[12] (The title "commissioner of Indian Affairs" went out of use in 1981. From 1981 to 2003 the title "deputy commissioner" was used, and in 2003 the title was changed to "director of the Bureau of Indian Affairs.")[13]

Before 1849 the commissioner of Indian Affairs reported to the secretary of war. In 1849 the Office of Indian Affairs was transferred from the Department of War to the Department of the Interior; therefore, after 1849 the Indian commissioner reported to the secretary of the interior. This change produced conflict between military and civilian leadership concerning Indian affairs. The change occurred slightly before the United States entered into treaties with the nations of the Pacific Northwest. The change helps to account for some of the steps and missteps in U.S. relations with the tribes of the Northwest. Therefore, it is a significant factor to consider in analysis of the delay of the treaties' ratification, which had long-term effects on the conditions of life for Native people there.

During the final few years that the Oregon Country was still jointly occupied by the United States and Great Britain, Dr. Elijah White was Indian sub-agent, serving from 1842 to 1845. His efforts helped prevent violence on the part of the Cayuse and Nez Perce, but opponents forced him out of office. No official representative of Indian Affairs was appointed for the Oregon Territory until 1848, when the Oregon Territory was formally established by an act of Congress. In 1849, Joseph Lane was appointed territorial governor and ex officio superintendent of Indian Affairs; he served until 1850. Serious problems in Indian/non-Indian relations existed when Lane arrived. Increasing numbers of white immigrants were streaming in and taking over Indian lands, utilizing the Oregon Land Donation Act, which allowed settlers to gain title to parcels of land, one-half to one square mile in size, in order to establish homesteads. However, no treaties had yet been enacted in the Oregon Territory (the northern part of the Oregon Territory was the land that would become Washington Territory; it was subdivided from the Oregon Territory in 1853). The government was giving away land that still belonged to Indian people.

An important event in Lane's term was the trial and execution of five Cayuse held responsible for an attack that had far-reaching consequences for Indian/non-Indian relations in the Northwest. In 1849 Indians east of the Cascades killed a missionary couple, Dr. and Mrs. Marcus and Narcissa Whitman. The Whitmans operated a mission and medical clinic at Waiilatpu, near Walla Walla. The mission was also a resting point for people traveling on the Oregon Trail. Dr. Whitman's treatment of white patients was statistically more successful than was his treatment of Indian patients, more of whom died owing to lack of immunity to newly introduced diseases. Indian people already had reason to question whether the whites intended to exterminate them entirely, and during a measles outbreak suspicion arose that the missionaries were giving poison, not medicine, to sick Native people. On November 29, 1847, the Whitmans were killed by Cayuse and Umatilla, along with about a dozen other whites, with dozens more whites taken captive. The Cayuse War began the following year. The war amounted to an unsuccessful attempt by white Americans to bring the killers to account. A peace commission was appointed, led by the level-headed Joel Palmer, but eventually he resigned, for reasons including his disgust with the actions of militia leader Cornelius Gilliam, who pursued a policy of exterminating Indians and attacking innocent Cayuse who had not been involved in the killings. Gilliam, with his volunteer army, provoked the Columbia Basin tribes (Wallawalla, Umatilla, Palouse, and Nez Perce) nearly to the point of their uniting in war.[14] Two and a half years after the incident, the Cayuse offered to surrender the five men said to be responsible. The five were executed, and this brought an end to the tribe's needing to stay on the run to avoid capture. The Cayuse War left bitterness and doubt that extended long after. These events figured into the reluctance of the U.S. Congress to immediately ratify the treaties made in the Washington Territory.

Despite the fact that settlers in the Puget Sound region experienced relatively little conflict—and a good deal of cooperation—with Indians of that region, the "Bostons," or white American residents, became insecure when they learned of these events involving the Cayuse. This insecurity, along with events around Puget Sound that Euro-Americans regarded as threatening, led settlers there to appeal to the newly established territorial government for protection. Under Governor Joseph Lane, fortified buildings and an army fort were constructed, and the first Indian agent for the region, J. Q. Thornton, was appointed in 1849. One of Thornton's first tasks was to arrange the trial of six Snoqualmie, who earlier had an altercation with whites at Fort Nisqually. This is one of the events that Pauline Hillaire discusses in chapter 4, "Reservation Creation": the immediate execution of two of the accused, which she cites as an example of the harshness of the newly imposed U.S. administration. Historian Alexandra Harmon also examines this event, in connection with the new government's efforts to impose law to establish its dominance. Harmon considers how the United States uses the event in an effort to demarcate two unitary groups: all whites, as distinct from Indians as a homogenous group. This division failed to capture Indian people's experience of the interrelated and porous Native groups in which they participated; it also oversimplified the diversity of "non-Indian" groups and persons.[15]

The territorial governor who succeeded Joseph Lane was John P. Gaines, appointed in 1850, when Zachary Taylor replaced James K. Polk as U.S. president. In 1849 the Oregon Territory had sent its first delegate to Congress: Samuel R. Thurston. Congress adopted Thurston's resolution to extinguish the land title of coastal Indians and to relocate them to east of the Cascades. In chapter 8, "Aboriginal Fishermen," the failed relocation plan is accounted according to oral history and the records of Congress. Even though the relocation failed, the congressional act that endorsed it (June 5, 1850) set in motion the colonization of the region. The commissioner of Indian Affairs in 1850 was Luke Lea, who appointed Anson Dart to be superintendent of Indian Affairs for the Oregon Territory. Dart resigned, effective June 1853 (citing the high cost of living and low salary). Dart was replaced by Joel Palmer

(1810–81).[16] Palmer negotiated eleven treaties in the Oregon Territory (nine of them ratified) and served as superintendent of Indian Affairs during another war that was significant for Northwest Indian history: the Rogue River War. Palmer was forced out of office in 1856, owing to his support for Indians in a climate where many white citizens advocated their extermination. In 1853, when the Washington Territory was divided from the Oregon Territory, the first governor of Washington Territory was appointed: Isaac I. Stevens, who served simultaneously as superintendent of Indian Affairs for the new territory.

Governor Isaac Ingalls Stevens (1818–62) had enormous influence on the establishment of Washington's treaties and reservations, as well as its early relations with Indian nations. Stevens was a graduate of West Point Military Academy, a brevet major of the U.S. Army, and a veteran of the Mexican War. Trained as an engineer and geographer, he resigned a post with the U.S. Army Corps of Engineers for greater challenges: to assume the post of governor of Washington Territory (under the Department of State) and superintendent of Indian Affairs (under the Department of the Interior) and to supervise the exploration and survey of a route for a Pacific railroad (under the Department of War). Over the fourteen months from December 1854 to January 1856, Stevens transacted ten treaties with Indians of the Pacific Northwest (see chapter 5, note 55). The commissioner of Indian Affairs during Stevens's tenure as governor and superintendent of Indian Affairs was George W. Manypenny (1808–92), who served as commissioner from 1853 to 1857. Manypenny had negotiated the Omaha Treaty and eight other treaties with tribes immediately west of the Missouri River. He provided treaty texts for Stevens to review in preparing to negotiate treaties in the Northwest. The first two of Stevens's treaties were signed in the Puget Sound area. The first was the Treaty of Medicine Creek, in the south, and the second—the focus of this book—was the Treaty of Point Elliott, in the north (see map 6).

The U.S. Congress did not ratify eight of Stevens's ten treaties, including the Treaty of Point Elliott, until four years after they had been signed by Native "chiefs, headmen, and delegates" and by representatives of the

U.S. government. Stevens left Washington Territory in 1857, with those treaties still unratified, to become a territorial delegate to Congress, where he worked for their ratification. The delay of ratification left Indian tribes and persons without homelands, without payment for their lands, in many cases without adequate means of subsistence, and, to varying degrees, without sufficient conditions for stable communities and lives. Even so, Native people, overall, survived using what remained of their aboriginal resources and by means of employment in industries such as logging. In the years that passed between the signing and ratification of the western Washington treaties, Indians could hope that their new arrangements with the United States would provide adequate conditions, even without access to all the resources that their lands and waters had formerly provided. They could hope also that ratification would help free them from harassment by non-Indians. Non-Indians could hope to be freed of conflict with Indians over land-claims, and in some cases, of having to interact with Indians at all.

On the eastern side of the Cascade Mountains prospectors, merchants, and other travelers were streaming across lands belonging to the tribes of the plateau and the Columbia River Basin. A main attraction was that gold had been discovered on the upper Columbia River. Not only did these trespassers violate Native space, they usurped game animals and firewood essential to Native economies. The hooves of their heavily laden pack animals damaged the earth and plants essential to the food chain and the stability of eco-systems on which human and other life depended. Under threat of more permanent encroachment, an alliance led by Yakama Chief Kamiakin fought a war, known as the Yakama War, from September 1955 until April of 1856.

West of the Cascades, a series of conflicts known as the Puget Sound War involved sporadic raids and killings. Armed conflict was conducted in the town of Seattle for only one day. Chief Seattle did not participate in "the Battle of Seattle" (January 26, 1856). The dates of the Puget Sound War (1855–56) are marked by events concerning the Nisqually subchief Leschi. In chapter 5, "After the Treaty," Hillaire writes about the Indian wars in the Northwest. She examines the delay of the ratification of the

Point Elliott Treaty as a case study for learning from the patterns of the past. She remarks, "In the government's thinking, and in the public mind, it seems that the Rogue River War, the Yakama War, and the conflicts in the Puget Sound area 'were dwelt upon, to create an image of warlike tribes.'" Hillaire's observation conveys a great deal and raises an issue treated in Alexandra Harmon's analysis of how settlers in the Puget Sound area variously hypothesized the causes of conflicts, in order to support various preferred agendas for relations among Indian and non-Indian peoples.[17] Hillaire's perspective gives current voice to the historical experience of many Native people of the coast. In Hillaire's case we can observe that, in oral history from her area of northern Puget Sound, "the Indian Wars of the Pacific Northwest" were not, for the most part, experiential and impactful events. Yet in the minds of government officials and congressional delegates, a wide swath of culture areas was encompassed in a unitary concept of Northwest Indians: an "image of warlike tribes" was both magnified and generalized across the nation.

The focus of U.S. Indian policy during the decades between 1880 and 1920 was the assimilation of Indian people into the dominant society. The government aimed to destroy Native cultural life and unity by means such as Indian boarding schools, which attempted to eradicate Native identities and languages, and by BIA policies that made it a punishable offense to carry out spiritual practices and ceremonies. Federal policy regarding Indian lands remained a major threat to Indian life and culture. Frederick Hoxie discusses the case of the Puyallup, Coast Salish people of southern Puget Sound, to exemplify an early instance of a problem that tribes faced in the decades following the establishment of the reservations, as non-Indian settlements and industry grew. As the city of Tacoma expanded, urbanization reached the borders of the Puyallup Reservation in 1886, just thirty-two years after the signing of the Treaty of Medicine Creek. Settlers began to insist that the reservation lands should be reduced and that the treaty had run its course. Delegates from Washington Territory introduced legislation in Congress to terminate the treaty and the trust titles by which the Puyallup held their allotted lands. The measures did not pass, but the Puyallup's experience would occur for other tribes around the turn of the century. By 1920, U.S. Indian land policy took a form that Hoxie calls *colonial land policy*: "Like an imperial power, the American government would 'develop' Native property, by opening it to white farmers and businessmen, thereby 'freeing' Indians to participate in the process as they could."[18]

One of U.S. Indian policy's main weapons in that era was the allotment of Native lands into individually owned parcels, by means of the General Allotment Act or Dawes Act (1887). Many non-Indians, both elected officials and citizens who worked to defend Indians rights, had good intentions regarding allotment; they thought that private land ownership would help Native Americans fit in to the larger society and to prosper. But allotment policies were applied in violation of treaty provisions, and they were written to give the U.S. government license to take back "surplus" Indian lands. Allotment had two underlying aims for the United States: (1) the weakening of tribal unity and (2) the nation's usurpation of much of the Native land base. As a result of the Dawes Act, about two-thirds of Indian reservation lands became non-Indian owned lands. Moreover, the allotment system, with its faulty and lacking provisions for land inheritance, produced endless complications regarding heirship. Heirship problems severely and tragically compromised the ability of Native families to retain their lands from one generation to the next, as Pauline Hillaire accounts in chapter 7, "A Shrinking Land Base, Persecution, and Racism."

The U.S. indigenous population reached its all-time low at the beginning of the twentieth century. Russell Thornton estimates the U.S Native population in the decade 1890 to 1900 had fallen to 250,000 persons. The non-Native U.S. population increased in the century between 1800 and 1900, from about 5 million to over 75 million.[19] Conditions of insufficiency remained emblematic for Indian life until the 1920s, when the Snyder Act (1921) provided congressional funding for Native health, education, and various initiatives. In 1928 the "Meriam Report" (*Report on the Problem of Indian Administration*), published by the Institute for Government Research, documented the failures of the allotment and assimilation policies. A significant date in the era of Indian self-determination is 1934, when Congress passed the Indian Reorganization Act (IRA), also known as the Wheeler-Howard Act, which ended allotment on reservation lands.

John Collier (1884–1968) was commissioner of Indian Affairs when the IRA was passed. Although the IRA was controversial among tribes, most tribes voted to accept it and to proceed with organizing their own tribal governments. The IRA allowed tribes greater independence and control, but often the new governments utilized non-Indian formats and processes, to the loss of ancestral cultural methods and values, as Pauline discusses in chapter 6, "Legal and Land Rights." Joseph de la Cruz, former president of the Quinault Tribal Council and head of the National Tribal Chairs' Association, commented on this problem as contributing to what he called "a contemporary form of colonialism."[20]

In chapter 1 of this book, "Forgotten Genocide," Scälla provides an overview of *Rights Remembered*, including information about how the book came to be and the forms of justice that she hopes this book will support. Chapter 2, "The Building of America," considers the arrival of Columbus, whose accidental landing in the Americas is emblematic of a shift in history, when waves of immigrants began arriving in North America from European and other nations. The arrival of Columbus also symbolizes the instantiation of the Doctrine of Discovery and related ideas of conquest—some of those ideas invoked in the name of God—which endorsed enslavement, subjugation, or domination of Native people and dispossessing them of their lands and property. Chapter 3, "Centuries of Injustice," begins with Pauline's comments on early sources of Indian policy, such as a 1791 speech by President George Washington. The author traces Indian policy through the nineteenth-century events of Indian removal in the eastern United States and the government's initial steps to dispossess Pacific Northwest peoples of their lands.

Chapter 4, "Reservation Creation" accounts the government's first reports about the Coast Salish: reports that were used to make plans for the treaties and reservations in western Washington. These reports are valuable also for the information they contain about Northwest Indian life: both aboriginal and as affected by Euro-Americans. The author explains the mechanism and the injustice of the 1850 Oregon

Land Donation Act, and in her section on the Treaty of Point Elliott she examines some important concepts of Indian law: plenary power and sovereignty. In chapter 5, "After the Treaty," Pauline describes early instances of unfulfilled government promises in the experience of the western Washington Native people. This is the chapter where she has the most to say about introduced diseases and alcohol, both of which she regards as imported forms of debilitation.

Chapter 6, "Legal and Land Rights," marks the start of part 2, "The Twentieth Century and After." In chapter 6, Pauline brings out presumptions of U.S. governmental thinking on Indian policy in the early and mid-twentieth century by detailing the 1927 U.S. Court of Claims case *Duwamish et al. v. U.S.* and the 1951 Indian Claims Commission case *Lummi Tribe v. U.S.* In discussion of these and other cases, the author examines applications of principles important to Indian policy and law, such as the *just compensation clause* in the Fifth Amendment. In chapter 7, "A Shrinking Land Base, Persecution, and Racism," Pauline takes on the topic of discrimination in the domains of (1) policy (as related to land inheritance and probate reform), (2) internalized oppression within a culture, and (3) intercultural racism.

Chapter 8, "Aboriginal Fishermen," is a chapter to which both Pauline and I contributed a lot of effort. Pauline's oral history gives texture to the human experience of fishers and their families and the suffering that they endured in the denial of, and in their stand for, their treaty resource rights of fish and fishing grounds. Pauline roots Pacific Coast Native life in fishing culture and its river- and ocean-based environments, and she invokes environmental principles in this and other chapters. Such principles contribute to a land ethic that can help defend Native lands and natural resources and support sustainability overall. This chapter traces the struggle of Washington treaty-fishing tribes through a century of conflict with state courts, agencies, and non-Native citizens, plus several Supreme Court cases, culminating in the 1974 Federal District Court case *U.S. v. Washington*, better known as "the Boldt Decision." This century of fishing rights events is very informative, from both sociological and legal standpoints, as regards the principles and dynamics of Native rights, not only in the Northwest, but for indigenous people everywhere.

In chapter 9, "Break Through Ahistory," the author contends that elements of the doctrine of conquest that are still functioning must be rejected in order for justice to be attained. She gives examples of organizations, such as the International Council of Thirteen Indigenous Grandmothers and the Episcopal Church, that have publically called for repudiation, by institutions of religion and governance, of these oppressive constructs. Granting the progress that has been made, a moral imperative exists for restoration of conditions for indigenous Americans— Indian, Alaska Native, and Native Hawaiian—and for indigenous peoples worldwide, to have the rights and resources that will permit their flourishing as groups and individuals. In *Rights Remembered*, Pauline Hillaire offers her commentary on American Indian history and the future to encourage reflection, dialogue, and action in the domains of person-to-person, culture-to-culture, and government-to-government relations.

RESTORING AND RESPECTING NATIVE RIGHTS

What kinds of actions can be taken to carry forward the work that Pauline Hillaire calls for in *Rights Remembered*? Rebecca Chamberlain writes in the brief biography of the author in chapter 10: "Pauline goes beyond an historical and critical analysis of the past, as she unflinchingly explores cultural wounds to offer insights into potentials for social change and psychological healing. Pointing out systematic acts of injustice and inequity, she asks herself, and the reader, to take on the challenge of transformation and renewal."

How can the wounds of the past be healed? How can justice for indigenous people best prevail in the sociopolitical and legal domains? How can restorative justice be accomplished? A first question to take up is, "What is it that needs to be healed?" At the level of the individual and the group, Walter Echo-Hawk (Pawnee) provides a list of characteristics of traumatized individuals and populations, such as the transmission of trauma from one generation to the next. Echo-Hawk also lists characteristics of dominant groups that victimize another group, such as having a national narrative grounded in historical distortions that deny national wrongdoing.[21] Pauline's first approach to healing the wounds of history is to encourage truthful examination and dialogue. A main theme of this book is the 1855 Treaty of Point Elliott: the cultural presuppositions underlying it and how its provisions did, and may, play out over time, in connection with principles such as the Supremacy Clause of the U.S. Constitution and interpretations of sovereignty.

In her article "Indian Treaty History: A Subject for Agile Minds," Alexandra Harmon has observed that treaties have a doubled-edged nature.[22] One way of seeing this double-edged blade is to first consider that compromises were made that divided the land and provided for Native nations and for the new United States to coexist as nation-states. In that process, treaties placed limits on the extent of Native sovereignty. The other side of the blade is this: Now that treaties are in place, they occasion serious regard, and a degree of respect, for their capacity to maintain and, where necessary, to restore the rights of Native nations. Pauline Hillaire shows us in this book that "remembering" can operate in the sense of *recovering rights* and also in the sense of the *maintaining respect for rights* that are already being observed.

In Pauline's exhorting Americans—Indian and non-Indian—to exchange ideas and methods, she is exhorting us to transform our means of discovery, our bases of knowledge, and our approaches to problem solving in the direction of more whole and functional forms. She recommends this not only as instrumental for Native rights, but for the sake of environmental sustainability and the cultivation of human culture. In Europe's era of "discovery" and colonization, when popes and monarchs sought to justify their domination of Native peoples—largely for the gains to be had by acquiring Native land bases and natural resources—no less a philosopher than Aristotle was invoked to justify a master-slave relation, as was done in the sixteenth century by Spanish Aristotelian Juan Ginés de Sepulveda, in debates with Spanish Dominican Bartolomé de las Casas, who defended the equality of the Indian soul.[23]

Pauline Hillaire calls us to investigate constructive philosophical influences that occurred between Native and Euro-American thinkers here in North America. Such investigation can extend beyond investigation of the topic that she emphasizes in *Rights Remembered*: the infusion of Iroquois/Haudenosaunee political thought and practice into the formation of early American principles and practices of democratic governance. Native philosophers such as Anne Waters (Seminole) and the late V. F. Cordova (Jicarilla Apache/Hispanic) were leaders in the late twentieth century in investigating Native thought on its own terms and engaging in comparative philosophical research that examines presuppositions and implications of Native and non-Native thought.[24] Scott Pratt is among the U.S. philosophers who have contributed to American Indian philosophy, for example, by investigating possible mutual influences between Iroquois (Haudenosaunee) and early Euro-American thought. A number of studies have examined the possibility of Haudenosaunee influence on the founding of the United States in the sociopolitical sphere; Pratt's inquiry considers possible bidirectional influences in metaphysics and other areas of philosophy as well.[25]

Expanding our methods and perspective can expand our humanity and provide a stronger foundation for problem solving: philosophically and in areas such as policy and law. Pauline calls for greater cooperation among Indian and non-Indian scholars, policy makers, citizens, and others involved in issues of Native justice and well-being. The work of Native Canadian anthropologist Brian Thom exemplifies scholarship that helps sovereign Native nations address philosophical challenges involved in dealing with an overarching government concerning land claims and other matters.[26] Bruce Granville Miller's collection of essays, *Be of Good Mind: Essays on the Coast Salish*, demonstrates collaboration between Native and Non-Native specialists, transdisciplinary approaches, and applicability to the aboriginal rights of Coast Salish peoples—in both Canada and the United States. Miller's earlier work, *The Problem of Justice: Tradition and Law in the Coast Salish World* (with maps by Brian Thom), documents a range of successful social justice and legal initiatives, created and maintained by Coast Salish communities in Washington State and British Columbia. Miller's works, therefore, provide another source of principles and procedures for remembering and restoring Native rights.

Pauline's call for intercultural cooperation is evident at several points in *Rights Remembered*. She makes a case for intercultural cooperation particularly in chapter 9, "Break Through Ahistory." Dale Turner (Teme-Augama Anishnaabe) has written in "Oral Traditions and the Politics of (Mis)Recognition" that "one responsibility of an American Indian intellectual community is to defend the integrity, and legality, of tribal governments in the hostile intellectual community of the dominant culture." He examines the predicament faced by Native people, in Canada and elsewhere, who have been forced to articulate Native metaphysical claims as political arguments. In Turner's view, indigenous ways of understanding the world should remain in Native communities. The twofold task of Native intellectuals, Turner holds, is to explain to the dominant culture why this is so, and to assert and protect their nations' sovereignty. Turner uses the term "Word Warriors" for citizens of indigenous nations who take on this work, and who give attention to how words are used: particularly how words are used to form "cultural landscapes" in the domains of policy and law.[27] Scälla suggests measures of cooperation that preserve the privacy and sanctity of cultural knowledge: "In our tradition, we are welcome to share the celebration-sense of our culture, but not the spiritual-sense. The spiritual-sense of our culture is our own individual and cultural property" (chapter 11, "Earth, Our First Teacher"). Scälla has in her lifetime educated many persons about Lummi and Coast Salish culture. On the face of it, it might appear that her approach is to share about her culture on the premise that if the dominant culture better understood her culture, the causes of justice would be better served. However, this book shows that her view accords more with Turner's: Native Word Warriors must attend to matters of philosophy of governance, policy, and law in the macro culture, while remaining connected with those of their own separate traditions. In her approach, Scälla has demonstrated two features of Pacific Northwest Native culture important for cultural property rights, justice, and intercultural diplomacy. In brief, her work to educate and to share aspects of Lummi and Salish culture manifests the potlatch's spirit of generosity, while at the same time it maintains boundaries of respectful silence concerning the inner dimension of the spiritual societies, knowledge, and practices that are of, and for, the Native community to whom they belong.

Turning now to the indigenous nations of the world, I reiterate the following questions: How can the wounds of the past be healed? How can justice for indigenous people best prevail in the sociopolitical and legal domains? How can restorative justice be accomplished? These questions are addressed by Walter Echo-Hawk in the book *In the Light of Justice: The Rise of Human Rights in Native America and the UN Declaration on the Rights of Indigenous People*. Echo-Hawk served for thirty-five years as a staff attorney for the Native American Rights Fund (NARF) and worked on legislation including the Native American Graves Protection and Repatriation Act (NAGPRA) and federal legislation for Native religious freedom. Echo-Hawk aims to plant seeds of change by explaining the imperatives for, and the functions of, the United Nations Declaration on the Rights of Indigenous Peoples (appendix 2).

At points in history, Echo-Hawk observes, signal events occur that change the course of the future: the "discovery" of America, the founding of the United States on principles of democratic civil freedoms, and *Brown v. Board of Education* (1954), which declared racial segregation unconstitutional. Approval of the Declaration by the member nations of the UN marks such a shift in the course of the future, a shift that can be fully realized only by unified efforts to implement the provisions of the Declaration.[28] *Rights Remembered* contributes to that effort by giving Native evidence, voice, and analysis concerning Native experiences of the injustices of history. *Rights Remembered* sounds a call for reconciliation and the restoration of justice for indigenous peoples. The call for restoration of justice is demanded by—and grounded in— principles of morality, international principles of human rights, and principles of democracy that are strongly connected with the tradition of U.S. democracy.

Human rights have been termed "natural rights" or "rights of [hu] mankind." This idea was understood by the first generation of Euro-American founders of the United States as the body of natural, inalienable rights of all persons, derived from a larger authority and a higher source:

human rights are rights that no just government can deny, and that free and democratic governments are formed to protect. As Alexander Hamilton wrote in the *Federalist Papers*: Each being is endowed with "the sacred rights of mankind" that "can never be erased or obscured by mortal power."[29] One dimension of justice for Native groups and nations is the human rights of each individual; another is the rights of a nation in relation to other nations. Duane Champagne cautions: "Groups such as indigenous peoples, whose values, institutions, traditions, and land claims are not incorporated as part of the act of nation-state creation and consensus, are left with relatively coerced cultural, institutional, and political participation in the national community and state structure."[30] The legitimacy and functionality of democracies depends upon consensus and noncoercion. The history of injustice in U.S. Indian policy, combined with the challenging position of U.S. tribes—as sovereigns over their own affairs, yet existing within and subject to the powers of the United States—requires repair in order that Native Americans are not disenfranchised. The restoration that is needed is not only for Native communities and individuals, but in order that the United States can attain integrity with respect to the First People of this land.

The UN Declaration on the Rights of Indigenous Peoples is an instrument that provides theoretical and practical resources for action to restore and preserve human rights and to perpetuate healing and justice: interpersonal, intercultural, and in the domains of policy and law. Pauline Hillaire expresses pride and confidence in the ideals of the democratic philosophy of governance advanced by the Euro-American founders of the United States, some of whom were influenced by the Iroquois/ Haudenosaunee philosophy of governance. The Declaration, Echo-Hawk writes, utilizes principles of human rights from modern international law, based on precepts fundamental to the best of American democratic principles.[31] The United States has a moral obligation to maintain and defend rational and just policies and law concerning indigenous peoples for three reasons: (1) the obligations of the United States to its Native nations, tribes, and citizens, (2) the benefits of incorporating Native sociopolitical philosophy as one of the dimensions of North American sociopolitical standards and methods, and (3) the responsibility to uphold principles that have established the record of the United States as an internationally respected leader in the protection of human rights.

Following are the essential features of the UN Declaration, as explained by S. James Anaya (Apache-Purepecha), UN special rapporteur on the rights of Indigenous peoples:

> By its very nature, the Declaration on the Rights of Indigenous Peoples is not itself legally binding, but it is nonetheless an extension of the commitment assumed by UN member states, including the United States, to promote and respect human rights under the United Nations charter, customary international law, and various multilateral human rights treaties, including treaties to which the United States is a party. . . . Whatever it's precise legal significance, the Declaration embodies a common understanding about the rights of indigenous peoples on a global scale, upon a foundation of fundamental human rights, including the rights of equality, self-determination, property, and cultural integrity.[32]

As regards what needs to be made whole, well, and functional in the domain of civil liberties for indigenous peoples, we can see from what is encompassed by the Declaration those areas where liberties require restoration or protection: "the Declaration comprehensively covers the full range of property, civil, political, economic, social, cultural, religious, and environmental rights of indigenous peoples. It compiles human rights from the corpus of international law and formulates them into minimum standards for protecting the survival, dignity, and well-being of indigenous peoples. In so doing, the Declaration makes international law accountable to indigenous peoples. It tells us how recognized human rights should be interpreted and applied in the indigenous context, and by defining the content of emerging norms, it speeds their crystallization into norms."[33]

The United States endorsed the Declaration on the Rights of Indigenous Peoples on December 16, 2010, in an address given by President

Barack Obama at a gathering of leaders of indigenous nations and tribes at the White House.[34]

American democratic principles, Echo-Hawk says, "insist on national discourse in the United States on the nature of indigenous justice and rights at this juncture in American history."[35] In order to make amends to Native America, Echo-Hawk says, discourse is the first step.[36] As I watched Pauline write this book and as I helped her complete it, I heard the urgency of her call for national, and personal, conversations on Native rights. *Rights Remembered* is an invitation and an exhortation to such conversations.

Pauline says in chapter 1: "Further research by others on this, my account of the history of my people, is welcome." We have done our best to provide accurate information and to explain ourselves clearly, but inevitably there are errors in this book. So we ask and thank our readers for their patience. We hope that the source citations that we have provided are helpful, because among our goals was to offer context and resources concerning Indian history and policy for readers with a variety of purposes.

Scälla, Pauline Hillaire, dedicated this book to her father, Joseph Hillaire. In the afterword, she speaks of her father, who encouraged her to take on the research and writing of *Rights Remembered*. I close with Scälla's words of prayer for her father's message: *I simply pray that God, the Great Spirit, our Creator, stay with us, guide and guard us, as we bring your message to the world of our friends everywhere.*

A Short Autobiography

Oh, Great Spirit—Let my words come as one of the rightful hosts of this great land. Let not my reach hurt a single soul. We shall welcome forever, like all blessings from You, those who come our way. Our hearts are not asleep this moment; we await your greater plan for us. Oh, hear our prayer for our hopes and dreams for our generations yet to come. Let not their hearts be troubled, for they, too, will believe in You.

I come from the people whose hearts will live forever. We have prayed for that day when all the yesterdays of violence, mistrust, anguish, and desperation will be gone, and the times that You have changed for us will be open to all of us forever.

I have tried, and I have failed. Many have tried, and many have failed. It is as if a stronger god exists, insisting that the new hosts of our nation will forever be cursed, no matter the race, creed, or spiritual need. O Great Spirit, guide us through this future that was foretold by our ancestors. We look to you through despair and hopelessness, grateful for all that You have done to provide our survival today. *á, si?ám', siɬsi?ám', hay sxʷ q'ə—O, Lord, Lord on high, thank you.*

My people survived all the elements of our past. We accept with open hearts the Holy Trinity Above: God the Father, God the Son, and God the Holy Ghost. We do not believe that there is racism, prejudice, or unfairness in the place where They live. Our ancestors lived with the power of the Almighty Creator of All, Mother Earth, and Father Sea.

The Great Spirit provided for all our needs; prayers were offered to All Above. How can anyone lose with these Mighty Powers on our side?

My dear people, I have written this book very well knowing that it was not done to make you feel happy or secure. Truth can sometimes be painful. During my years of writing this book, I have cried, laughed, gotten way angrier than a wet hen, and been filled with hope that perhaps somebody would understand my personal *why*. After all, understanding is within the nature of humankind. If they can change their clothes from time to time, they can also change their minds. As a storyteller, a song keeper, and a cultural historian, I've had a very hard time making my way through this world filled with snobbish pride and prejudice. My elders taught me over and again that the ignorant are very strong.

I have not detailed every date and place of smallpox, measles, flu, and so forth. I have not brought out legends as well I could. I am not an anthropologist that I may bring out reasons why certain types of Indians flatten their heads. I have not brought out the various types of canoes or longhouses that Indians created for themselves, their friends, and their family. I have not mentioned all I know about the mountain passes and how they were decided and created. But, I find each and every detail about these subjects extremely interesting, and each qualifies for books to be written about them.

I am praying for land enough for our younger generations, because the boundaries, in both water and land, were just taken away without fair purchase or compensation. Government officials' minds were made up about us—sometimes before they ever saw us for the first time. Therefore, I quote word for word from government documents to show how government officials looked down on us and how they talked about us behind our backs. They took over our resources and settled properties, after ordering us to clear our homesteads and to make farms, which we did. But then settlers moved onto those cleared lands.

The skills that have been passed down to me from my mother and father—as well as other elders in my life—have saved my life so many times, and for that, I am most grateful. For I do consider that I have had a good life because of them. I've logged, fished the river, and picked strawberries, raspberries, and blackberries every summer before school started. When some tribal members my age quit school, I wanted to quit too, but my mother absolutely refused. So, I kept going and graduated in 1949. After high school, I moved to the Colville Indian Reservation, where I got a job right away. My father arranged a job there for me with Mr. Frank George, tribal operations officer for the Colville Tribe: typing, filing, taking tribal government council minutes, traveling with the council when they needed me to do so. I truly loved that job. But like most young people, I fell in love, got married, and had children. The Colville Tribe would send for me, though, when they needed help, and I would gladly go. Paperwork for per capita payments was difficult to complete in time, and so my help was appreciated. In 1958 we moved back to Lummi and lived in the old mansion (homestead) on Hillaire Road (now called Lake Terrell Way) and Slater Road. Our children were small, and this was a perfect place to survive for a while. My husband got restless to work, and better times were to be had back on the Colville Reservation, so we moved back over there, where he could get a job easily. He operated heavy equipment. Because I needed help with the two children we had by then, my husband chose to follow the fruit (picking apples, pears, peaches, apricots, etc.). We lived in the cabins each orchardist provided for their "pickers." I canned the wonderful fruit and even went out and picked with my husband. We had a great time during those months of the year, even though it meant moving from one place to another at the end of each season. But getting acquainted with other Indians made it a joyful time for me.

The Colville Confederated Tribes hired me again and again throughout those hard years. The last job that I had there paid very well, and our administration created a curriculum equal to that of the trade unions. This went well. By then, I was able to move ahead in jobs: the U.S. Postal Service in Nespelem, Washington, and town clerk for the town of Nespelem. My children were growing up. My husband chose to go and fish at Celilo Falls, so off we went to live in Celilo. I found a part-time job in a restaurant and had the help of a dear friend who ran her own small shop and café. It was through her that I found a babysitter for the part-time job I held in the highway restaurant. That was one of the most interesting times of my life for the sake of the kind of research I was doing. You see, I had never forgotten what my father wanted me to do for our Indian people.

At Celilo, I developed a great friendship with a lady by the name of C. Ives. She lived in Yakima. She invited us to go there because jobs were a lot easier to get in Yakima. So we went, and looking back, she was telling us the truth. There were dams being built on different parts of the river, and it was very easy for my husband to get a job at the Grand Coulee Dam, Chief Joseph Dam, and Azwell. The orchards were always nearby, so we lived good lives there, and our children were allowed to play in the shade of the orchards. It was easy to gather fruits and vegetables there, especially in the Yakima area, the "fruit bowl" of the region.

After our fourth child was born, we got a divorce. And at this point in my life, I was so interested in the rights of the Indian people that I decided to go back to school. My sister, Mary Ellen Hillaire, won my children in court. My research kept me busier by the year. Each library where I did research led me to bigger and better libraries, and my research grew. While in Seattle, I worked first for the Boeing Company in Renton, Washington, then at the University of Washington Hospital in the Health Sciences Personnel Office. It was there that I began to meet even more interesting people: Professor Erna Gunther, Quinault educational administrator Emmett Oliver, and Mary Louise Mahdi, an editor for the Open Court Press in Illinois. Each of them encouraged my research. But alas, I couldn't write. One day I was working in the personnel office and I was doing my best, and along came Professor Gunther, who was an anthropologist at the University of Washington. And she held her purse—she was short and she was stout, and she held her purse right in front of me—and she said, "You're Pauline Hillaire, aren't you?" "Yes, I'm Pauline Hillaire, may I help you?" And so no, she wanted me to write a book. She said, "I know you because your family is so expansive; I know that you have many elders, many doctors in your family." She wanted me to write a book; oh my. There I was, just a secretary, and so write a book? She convinced me that I could write a book. So she organized a sabbatical for me. She organized a sabbatical so that I could spend time doing research and writing my book. But at first, every time I'd try to write, I'd end up with a poem. Professor Gunther told me that every sentence that I wrote in my first try, *Indian Policy: Crime or Reason*, could be an entire volume. But I just couldn't write an entire book. I continued my research by reading books and studying the government documents at Suzzallo Library at UW. And I read books suggested by friends, and books from everywhere that I picked up and found interesting, like *Thoughts on Zen*.

The Lummi Tribe offered me a job, and off I took again. I enjoyed my job there because it involved research into the first files ever created by the Lummi Indian Business Council. And I was thrilled, because my father's name was everywhere in those records, and where there were duplicates, I asked for the duplicates. From 1970 to 1973 I attended almost all of the business council meetings with my cousin, Catherine Cagey Tally. We not only had a good time taking cultural classes together, we had a great time at the tribal government meetings. One of the greatest phases of my research was done in this way. I finished my bachelor's degree through the Evergreen State College at this point. The college permitted the Native American Studies Program students to work home-based, and I graduated in 1973. I never once surrendered my research; I continued to read newspapers, magazines, and books that I found interesting. One day I found myself old and thought I'd better do something with all the research I had gathered over the past forty-three years. And here I am, writing my own biography for it. Way in the back of my mind, I feel a tiny twinge of fear for it, but I quickly lose the feel of that fear, and I just go on.

I am very proud of the fact that I was involved in my sister Mary Ellen's dream for a longhouse at the Evergreen State College after my graduation there. And stemming from the contacts I made there, I became involved in the design of the Smithsonian's National Museum of the American Indian in Washington DC. Both of these experiences cause me to swell with pride, not only for partnerships and far-reaching planning with Indians I met from tribes all over the United States, but for the experience of being in Washington DC, where my grandfather, father, and sister pleaded for the cause of Indian people, especially our tribe, the Lummi Tribe.

Once these life events had passed by, I led a dance group called Children of the Setting Sun, which my grandfather, Frank Hillaire, started in the nineteenth century. My father had led the Setting Sun Dance Group after my grandfather left us. My cousins, Joe Washington and Jack Cagey, led that dance group also, with dancers from their families. My group's members were from high school and college. In addition, I found the necessity of bringing in elders from the community to join us. Sometimes just one would show up, and other times there'd be six or seven elders joining us. Now, this was truly one of the greatest times of my entire life. My father had depended on my good memory a long time ago for learning the songs. And my memory served me well, as it does this moment. My work with the Setting Sun Dance Group lasted for seventeen years, starting at the Northwest Indian College in Bellingham, where I worked in the library. The students were comfortable and happy with the group and learned a lot of our culture from this experience.

In researching the history of the Setting Sun Dance Group, I was able to collect pictures from the years of my grandfather's leadership, my father's, and my own. And it makes such a beautiful history; the pictures alone bring their own kind of reward. I earned the Washington Governor's Heritage Award in 1996, which was a great honor. The auditorium at the Seattle Center was filled, and the audience applauded for the longest time. I didn't expect that, but was honored. Outside the auditorium, an Indian lady from Yakama presented me with a beautiful shawl of Pendleton with white fringe. Oh, so touching. But I thank our Creator for all this recognition, for it was He who helped us survive. I am a full-blood registered Lummi Indian and proud of it.

Prologue

The Abundance That Was the Great Northwest

Before I begin talking about the founding of the United States, Indian policy, and the creation of the treaties and reservations, the following pages tell something of the great abundance of our lands and waters in the Northwest. I tell of these things partly to paint a picture of what was lost to us, but also to show what we still have, and why is it so important that our land rights and our culture be restored and preserved. The first government reports about our area note that our people were rich in foods; it was a fool who could not find food in the bountiful supply. But, the European Americans did not believe in the Great Spirit from Mother Earth and Father Sea. In fact, they thought we were ignorant savages; that was more to their liking and satisfied their goals, as first expressed in papal bulls and the Doctrine of Discovery.

The enormous size of our timber should go down on the great side of our history. A government document of 1858 explains the size of the cedar and fir trees at Squaxin Island. An Indian agent for the Puget Sound District wrote: "To a person who has never been in this country, it is almost impossible to give a correct idea of the immense size of the timber. The fir and the cedar trees grow to the extraordinary height of 250 feet tall and are from four to six feet in diameter. The fir can be felled by boring and burning, but the cedar has to be chopped. After they are upon the ground, it requires a great deal of labor to get rid of them. The land, after it is cleared is of good quality and produces well."[1]

If this were left to Indians, they wouldn't just "get rid of" trees. It takes a great deal of labor to process cedars to make any and all cultural implements and artifacts. The cedar tree is our Tree of Life. It provides so much more than just beautiful scenery. From the roots and inner bark our women make fine cedar baskets, including watertight baskets. From the inner bark women make rope for our fishermen, clothes for all ages and all seasons. From the wood our carvers make so many things, I don't think that I can name them all here, but there are spoons, and boxes for storing various items from kitchen to carving tools. Carvers make masks, totem poles, canoes, and grave markers, as well as items for food storage. From the branches they make clam baskets and other storage items. Houses are made from the wooden planks and logs.[2] Our Tree of Life sustained so many generations of our aboriginal Americans here in the Pacific Northwest. It is so sad that now only a few cedars are growing here and there, and they're going down, down, down in history.

Currently, a burned stump on 1-5 near Arlington, Washington, is made into a monument. A car can drive through the middle of it, leaving plenty of room on either side. Another stump, also burned, remains as a reminder of the "Big Burn" at Lummi. In November 2009 at a construction site across from our Lummi Indian Clinic, we had to stop and wait for a big stump being removed by a gigantic truck. It took up more than one trailer, so a second trailer had to be dragged along behind. It was about the size of the bus coming from the opposite direction, a city transit bus. What a sight. My thought was, why can't we preserve such monuments for posterity here on the Lummi Indian Reservation?

My brother Lewis lived in a stump near his first wife's home before they were married. I was in it visiting him. He had a small stove, homemade chairs and a table. His food and tool supplies were handy, and he kept a pile of chopped wood close to his stove. And he always had a coffee pot ready to make coffee for visitors. Our Creator blessed our people with this Tree of Life, and my prayer is that today's people watch for chances to bring the cedars back for our up and coming generations. My brother had a tin roof on his cedar house. Perhaps it was a handier thing to do at the time; these were hard times for the whole country. But my mother and brothers (I had seven brothers, and we were seven sisters with the same mom and dad) always had a garden. I must brag about those gardens.

One of our gardens was on Gooseberry Point on the hill above the Hale Pass Ferry Landing. We had an orchard inland from the main road, Lummi View Road; cherry trees and apple trees grew there. A big opening to the surrounding forest existed there. The ground was extremely rich. Our potatoes grew to an enormous size; thinking back now, I believe they must have been eleven to twelve inches long and five to six inches around. When we cooked them, we cut them in half twice, making four long pieces, and then chopped them into two-inch sizes to cook. One potato served seven hungry Hillaires, and the Hillaire appetite was good.

Time after time, according to the government documents, particular Indian agents in the Pacific Northwest region, through friendship or admiration, brought out viewpoints commending the Indian people of this area. The same Indian agent who remarked on the size of our cedars, Michael T. Simmons, wrote the following to the superintendent of Indian Affairs for the Washington and Oregon Territories:

> After reading this, I think that you, sir, must agree with me in think-ing that humanity, as well as justice, make it an imperative duty of the Government to adopt some plan by which the Indians can be separated from the whites. Their forbearance has been remarkable. While they had the power of crushing us like worms, they treated us like brothers. We, I think, should return their kindness now that we have the power, and our duty is so plainly pointed out by their deplorable situation. My own impression is that the speediest and best way of settling all these difficulties is the ratification of the treaties. Their agents will then have the means in their hands of supplying all that I think now is wanting to enable them to govern these unhappy creatures, and to lay the groundwork of civilization for their children to improve upon.[3]

Several such statements were made throughout the main timeframe of my research: the decade before and the decade after the Point Elliott Treaty of 1855. And because of my pride in my family, I sense that more could be said about Indian honor and integrity, strength and courage. My father and one of his dear friends, believe it or not, kept several white families in Bellingham alive by bringing them food when they hadn't known what to eat or how to prepare it. Many years went by, and one of the lawyers hired by Lummi Tribe came to a potlatch and told how his family and others nearby were supplied with food. These white settlers didn't know when or how to prepare the foods provided by Mother Earth and Father Sea, until my father and his friend helped them figure this out. Keeping a family from starving is important.

Many of our healing herbs and sources have disappeared. A couple of us went to where there used to be plenty, but no more. And the water in the Hale Passage was so clean and clear; as children riding along with our fishermen, we could see the bottom; but that was in our youth. We're all very old now. Today, you can't see the bottom, even just a few feet from the shore—pollution. My stepfather took all of us for a boat ride around Lummi Island when I was twelve or thirteen. We were entertained by what we saw at the bottom near the shores. Fascinating: turtles, fish, many other sea creatures, too many to name. But now when we ride across to Lummi Island on the ferry, you cannot see the bottom near the shores anymore. It is something I experienced firsthand, then and now, for comparison. Hale Passage, alone, is a wonder for its beauty. When I was very young, from the fourth grade up to graduation, every March or April the entire family that was left at home would watch the Minke Whales (Black Fish) passing east, toward Bellingham Bay from Gooseberry Point. They caught our eye because as they were swimming, they rolled. Because there would be a long lineup of them (perhaps fifteen or more), they looked like they were playing: diving, looking every bit like they were rolling past our home. They don't do that anymore, perhaps because of the sonar, the boat traffic, the fact that the fish are depleting so rapidly, or what. No one speaks of them anymore, but, oh, what a wonder to watch them roll and play as they traveled.

At Gooseberry Point in about 1948, my stepfather called all of us outside; it was nighttime. But he was just happy; he called my mother, and all of us followed her. Outside we saw another wonder of the universe. He pointed to the sky. What a sight. The stars were falling from the sky by the thousands, I'm guessing. It appeared as though they were all coming from the center of the sky above and falling every single direction; what a memory. I consider myself most fortunate.

One of the biggest companies in Bellingham, the Georgia Pacific, was closed down a few years ago because they were charged and found guilty of dumping chemicals into our Bellingham Bay. Mercury was one of the pollutants, and people tell me it is extremely difficult to rid mercury from the bottom of the bay. What can a person do? During World War II, we'd park along the Lummi Shore Road and watch our fishermen catch fish by purse seine. Oh, what fun. Our children did not have a chance to see any of these great and beautiful things. The bay is far less useful today: mercury, oil, and sometimes sewage. From pictures taken from a plane, you can easily see the pollution in the water coming from the several refineries next to the reservation. There's also an aluminum plant nearby, and there are many farms along the length of our river as it runs down from the mountains. What chance do our natural plants have of growing among the pollution seeping from those settlements? But maybe someday we'll have a better source of energy to power our homes with electricity. We do have wind; sometimes the wind blows up to seventy-five miles an hour. I see a few yard decorator windwheels. We need the real kind for our wind, especially that south and west wind. The Lummi Nation did a study in 2011 to look at the pros and cons of wind energy for the reservation. I, for one, am very happy about those people who are thinking of our Mother Earth, like Al Gore; I believe him—global warming is evident in our world today.

When I was in my teens, I fished the river, and boasting as I am, the real truth of the matter is that we caught fifty pounders regularly. But I remember one time, I had to lift a fish that big out of our skiff, up above my head to the fish buyer. Still amazes me. These days, the fish are all small. And I'll never forget the times when my brother Ben would hunt deer on the land where I was raised; he used bow and arrow on everything he hunted. What an amazing country we lived in long ago. Even if I do not go on here, there are other things to tell about: the mountain passes, traditional customs of immense interest, genealogy, our six types of canoes, and our longhouses. But I am satisfied with what I have shared with you with this section, "The Abundance That Was the Great Northwest."

Part 1

The Nineteenth Century and Before

Were you there
when they crucified my people?

Were you there
when they crucified my tribe?

They took everything away, everything
they lived for

Were you there
when they crucified my people?

Were you there
when they crucified my tribe?

They took everything away
Then mocked their nakedness

Were you there
Were you there?

> *Pauline R. Hillaire*
> *Lummi*

CHAPTER 1

Forgotten Genocide

Let's trade places. You be "Indian" and I'll be "white," for the sake of a better understanding of how your mind might work, as compared to how mine has worked all these years, especially where it concerns this, my intense study of America's aboriginal people, my ancestors, from the beginning to now. To make a long story short, I come along to your country, assert my laws of discovery, claim your birthplace as well as the birthplaces of all of your friends and neighbors across this great continent, and take over, using my military along the way. Arriving in the New World are missionaries, merchants, and ships filled with people (many of them sick) escaping the old countries in Europe, governments that were not only cruel but also oppressive of individual, family, and community rights. You did not give up your right to this land. The fight was on.

I threw every type of unfairness against you, pretending all the while that I was an honest, upright citizen of America, the New World. Over five hundred years pass. My progress is celebrated; yours is cut off from the beginning. My laws were written; yours were silently understood by your people. I have written my history; yours is hidden or forbidden. I have been busy changing your homeland, withholding your customs and traditions from you. Your languages and cultures are nearly destroyed. It was expected that you will be another me sooner or later; but will you? Your land is extremely limited after these past five hundred-plus years.

We made solemn agreements: nearly four hundred treaties were ratified.[1] My numbers grew from birth and immigration, while yours declined; yet you survived. But still, you are disgusting in my view: ignorant and savage. Your past has been removed by my version of history. I ridicule your silence and ignorance, wondering why you never learn "citizenry," "civilization," or "gratitude." You do not give me credit for creating "the land of the free and the home of the brave." I expect you to disappear, whether by fading away, or by blending in.

WHY I WROTE THIS BOOK

My father, Joseph Hillaire, on his deathbed, shared extremely valuable information with me about the clash of our two cultures that went on during his youth; he was born in 1894. My father's interest remained focused upon Indian causes throughout his life. He asked me to find certain laws, certain letters, remembering one thing: too many years have gone by, and the government has forgotten our rights that are preserved by what the U.S. Constitution calls the Supreme Law of the Land—the treaty. My father told me to look up our 1855 Treaty of Point Elliott, the Omaha Treaty, the Wheeler-Howard Act, and letters between Washington territorial governor Isaac I. Stevens and President James Buchanan. And my father told me his version of the explorers crossing the Atlantic to North America. It was of great interest to me. I wanted to make this investigation a reality.

I gathered that information, but reading it caused me such sadness, depression, and disappointment in our government. Some of the information that my father shared was what he had gleaned from the office of the Lummi tribal government during the 1920s. Like my father, I had worked for the Lummi Tribe, in the 1970s. Before that, in the mid 1960s, I had thought of a solution. I was working at the University of Washington for the Health Sciences Personnel Office, and I knew my way around the campus. At the university's Suzzallo Library I searched for the government documents section and found it—even the papal bulls. What an amazing phenomenon. White people had saved all this information? The papal bulls gave European explorers authority to take over new lands and to conquer and enslave "savages" in the name of Christian rulers, kings, and queens.[2] The government documents turned out to be a great resource for me concerning Indian history. Historical records, Indian policy books, and books authored by Indian and non-Indian writers (historians, anthropologists, and legal scholars) helped also. Tribal history and family history from our Coast Salish oral tradition provided information from sources that are not often considered part of the "historic record."

I wrote this book with hope for a better future: for greater justice for Indian people in America, and for reconciliation between Indian and non-Indian Americans, based on recognition of the truths of history. Bringing out Indian America's ahistory is important to all American citizens. Therefore, in this book a review of U.S. Indian policy is opened to reason, based primarily on review of government documents mainly from the 1840s and 1850s. Along with our Native oral history, documents in the *U.S. Congressional Serial Set*, in particular, the reports of the commissioners of Indian Affairs, provide the main historical record of U.S. Indian history and policy.[3] These document are not easily accessible to most readers: Therefore, I quote portions of the government reports so that readers may reflect for themselves.

The focus of this book is the time surrounding the Point Elliott Treaty of 1855. The U.S. presidents for those years were the tenth through the fifteenth presidents: John Tyler (1841–45), James F. Polk (1845–49), Zachary Taylor (1849–50), Millard Fillmore (1850–53), Franklin Pierce (1853–57), and James Buchanan (1857–61). In their presidential addresses, they did not say much about the status of Indians. Before this time was the presidency of Andrew Jackson (1829–37), the nation's renowned Indian fighter, who was in charge during "Indian Removal." There were countless others who affected Indian policy and life: Indian agents, superintendents, and commissioners; secretaries of the interior, military leaders, surveying engineers, traders, missionaries from several churches (such as Catholic and Methodist), and employees hired by the government to staff the various offices established for Indian Affairs. Not every individual was ignorant or hostile toward Indians, but damage was done that continues in many forms today. True, the face of the presidency changed, as did all other offices of government, but Indian policy ruled most every area of life for American Indians. Owing to this history, and because of weak communications within and between tribes, individual Indians (like myself) still don't fully know where we stand as Americans.

I had to search out the Pacific Northwest tribes and my tribe, the Lummi, in the long rambling reports, but I appreciated all I could learn about how America dealt with Indians in general. Further research by others on my account of the history of my people is welcome. I quote from the government documents, providing quotations especially about the influx of white people who arrived in our aboriginal homelands of the Northwest, U.S. policies that affected the Pacific Northwest coastal tribes, and quotations that support my main message: that our rights as Indian people must be remembered and restored, by both Indian and non-Indian Americans.

This book looks back to Columbus's arrival, and it looks to the future. The focus of part 1, "The Nineteenth Century and Before," is the time when our treaties were negotiated in the Northwest. Part 2, "The Twentieth Century and After," tells about the experiences of my parents, born in the late the nineteenth century, and my own generation, born in the twentieth century. My generation was the third generation born after our ancestors signed treaties and our Northwest communities were changed forever by U.S. Indian policy, both on and off the reservations. Part 3, "Oral History and Cultural Teachings," contains oral tradition, poetry, and oratory. I speak also about the twenty-first century: how events of history, Indian policy, and the loss of our lands continue to affect today's Indian people, especially our youth, and I speak about possibilities for a better future.

This book is part of my healing experience so far. I wrote this book because I had bottled up all the abuse and dysfunction that was bashed in on me. With my education, convictions from the teachings of my elders, and the logic and common sense I was born with, I pray to the Great Spirit/God that persons beyond just myself will benefit from this effort. May white America understand that Indian people today are born of lineages who survived encounters with their ancestors. Many Jews survived their holocaust, as we have survived our genocide. May we together find that Providence is on our side: European Americans, American Indians, black Americans, and all those who have found comfort in the message of the Statue of Liberty.

If I had been born during the time when white people first colonized the Northwest, I am not certain that I could have survived it. Besides the injustices of Indian policy, non-Indians brought diseases, weapons, and the impudence of prejudice and racism. But I have always fought for my existence, although not against armies. Now I find myself fighting for my existence by writing this book, which I hope someone will read. I am fighting for my family, my tribe, and my culture: for land rights, justice, and to help obliterate the prejudice and racism that is still held against Indian America, by whoever may still hold it. White Americans and immigrants have grown curious about American aboriginal history. What was it like? They did not learn about the Indian perspective when they studied American history in the schools they attended. By researching aspects of Indian America's history, we get a more complete picture of America's history. These are the connections that historians, anthropologists, and writers like myself are trying to bring to life. This first chapter gives an overview of the topics discussed in this book.

INDIAN AMERICA'S AHISTORIC PAST

Now, in contemporary times, the genocide of America's Native peoples and cultures is mostly forgotten. What do we do now? I wrote this book because much of our true Indian history is ahistoric (not recorded or acknowledged), and many of our rights have been forgotten. I believe that when non-Indians come to know us, and come to a more complete and truthful understanding of America's history, that we—Indian and non-Indian—can together restore those forgotten rights; thus the title of this chapter, "Forgotten Genocide," and the title of this book, *Rights Remembered*. This book tells of how Indian rights have been remembered by some of our Native leaders and how our rights must be remembered by today's American leaders and people. Our Indian history may appear to be forgotten, but throughout all these five hundred-plus years, records and remembrances remain, thanks to our Native oral traditions and the Indian value of *talk*. The records and remembrances of our ancestors, who lived before Europeans ever "discovered" us, are still with us.

The phrase "forgotten genocide" may sound to you like my justification for our silence all these years. On December 9, 1948, the United Nations General Assembly adopted the "Convention on the Prevention and Punishment of the Crime of Genocide" (Resolution 260 [III] A).[4] Article 2 states that genocide has the following forms:

(a) Killing members of the group;
(b) Causing serious bodily or mental harm to members of the group;
(c) Deliberately inflicting on the group conditions of life calculated to bring about destruction in whole or in part;
(d) Imposing measures intended to prevent births within the group;[5]
(e) Forcibly transferring children of the group to another group.

Indian America has suffered all these forms of genocide. At the root our thriving as Indian people was damaged by the loss of the lands that supported our livelihood and way of life. Cultural genocide, as well physical genocide, went on from the time of first contact. Cultural genocide and its ongoing effects from earlier history are still suffered by Indian America today. One of the main messages of this book is an invitation for us to interact, to make things right for our growing populations. We cannot turn back the years on the gun violence and infectious diseases of the past. Nor can we do anything about the damage done by the settlers and missionaries of the past. But we can learn from the thinking and the deeds of presidents, Indian commissioners and agents, the military, and the courts. American citizens today are more ready than ever for truth; truth and grace are synonymous.

In her book *A Century of Dishonor: A Sketch of the United States Government's Dealings with Some of the Indian Tribes* (1881) Helen Hunt

Jackson quotes the eighteenth-century Swiss political theorist Emmerich de Vattel on the subject of natural law:

> It is a settled point in natural law that he who has made a promise to any one has conferred upon him a real right to require the thing promised; and, consequently, that the breach of a perfect promise is a violation of another person's right, and as evidently an act of injustice as it would be to rob a man of his property. . . . There would no longer be any security, no longer any commerce between mankind, if they did not think themselves obliged to keep faith with each other, and to perform their promises. . . . Treaties are no better than empty words, if nations do not consider them as respectable engagements, as rules, which are to be inviolably observed by sovereigns, and held sacred throughout the whole earth.[6]

Helen Hunt Jackson grew intensely concerned with the Indian cause during the late nineteenth century. She became a groundbreaker for Indian rights. She was dedicated to policy reform for Indians. Her goal was to encourage the government to right the wrongs that had been committed. Grace Gouvier introduces the 2006 edition of Jackson's book and explains what motivated Jackson's message to U.S. politicians and citizens: "Government Indian policy had become entrenched in patronage and inefficiency, which resulted in graft, fraud, and abuse of Native Americans."[7] By her work, Jackson incited others unto their own best works.

Statements concerning America's Indian policy throughout history are available to us in the government documents at this moment. Therefore, we can interact with them for purposes of examining our Indian history. The truth of Indian America's history deserves recognition. Both aboriginal Americans and Americans who descended from the founders of the United States need to face some weaknesses in ourselves as "first" Americans. Weaknesses have a truthful side. We have nothing to fear about uncovering this ahistory. How else can we right the wrongs?

Please refer to the book *Native Seattle* by Coll Thrush. The author quotes Major J. Thomas Turner, writing in 1914: "Times have changed . . .

there are no more Rocky Mountains . . . no more Indians, no more buf-falo, and the Great Plains have disappeared. Come to think of it, were there ever any, or were [sic] their existence only an iridescent dream?"[8] Edith Sanderson Redfield wrote the following poem:

All, all are gone, the men, tepees
E'en gone the trickling streams, the trees.
Seattle now in pride surveys
Its ports—its buildings—railroads—ways,
Where money comes and money goes;
Whose right supreme? Who cares? Who knows?[9]

Helen Peterson Schmitt, daughter of Karl Peterson and a Makah Indian woman, describes Seattle in the 1930s as a city that hung "No Indians Allowed" signs in their shop windows, leading her to hide her Indian ancestry. At first she identified only with her Swedish side and the lutefisk, glögg, and hambos of her father's people, until years later, when she identified herself as an Indian person.[10] Indian victims' scars from the white man's scorn are still seen on the persons of Indian America today. Many such persons can be seen today, in the doorways around Seattle taverns near Pioneer Square. Even though the Indians are mostly gone from public view, totem poles stand to attract visitors to the city.[11] The poles stand, in a place mostly cleared of its original inhabitants, like exclamation points: proof of Indians' indictment.

The general approach toward Indians by the Europeans who first arrived in the New World was *kill, conquer, and occupy*. The violence slowed down with the creation of the U.S. Constitution and the establishment of American democracy. Indian Affairs documents from the 1840s and 1850s demonstrate for me the general attitude of white America toward Indian America: the celebration of the first group and the degradation of the second. *A History of Indian Policy*, written by S. Lyman Tyler and published by the Bureau of Indian Affairs (1973), says of approaches the U.S. government subsequently used toward Indians: "The refusal of the United States to adequately protect Indians in their rights against non-Indians played an important part in the failure of the *concentration policy* (concentration of Indians in particular areas to clear land for white occupation), *the reservation policy* (relocation of tribes to parcels of land for one or more tribes to inhabit), and *the allotment policy* (division of tribal lands for individual ownership, to break down Indian culture and unity). During each of these three periods, the Congress, time after time, responded to local non-Indian voters to the detriment of the Indians."[12]

The American Indian Policy Review Commission was established by an act of Congress in 1975, partly in response to Indian activism of the 1960s and 1970s. In 1975–77, the commission traveled to various reservations and cities of the United States, collecting information about conditions in the lives of American Indians. The commission's *Final Report* (1977) states, "The policy implementing this relationship [U.S. and Indian] has shifted and changed with changing administrations and passing years without apparent rational design and without a consistent goal to achieve Indian self-sufficiency."[13] A separate dissenting view by Congressman Lloyd Meeds (D-WA), vice-chairman of the Review Commission, made this criticism:

> Unfortunately, the majority report of this commission is the product of one-sided advocacy in favor of American Indian tribes. The interests of the United States, the States and non-Indian citizens, if considered at all, were largely ignored. This was perhaps inevitable, because the enabling legislation which created the American Indian Policy Review Commission (Public Law 93-580, 88 Stat. [1975]) required that five of the eleven Commissioners be American Indians, and that each of the investigating task forces be composed of three persons, a majority of whom were required to be of Indian descent [Public Law 93-580, § 4(a)]. As a result, of the 33 persons appointed to lead the task forces, 31 were Indian.[14]

But "one-sided advocacy" has been practiced consistently by white America in the history of U.S. relations with Indian tribes. Congressman Meeds continues: "With due regard to those who worked on the task forces, the reports were often based on what the members wished the law to be. . . . Despite contemporary litigation, most Americans are justified in believing that 400 years have been sufficient to quiet title to the continent."[15]

Would Congressman Meeds agree that two centuries of treaty abuse is sufficient to quiet U.S. authority over abused treaties? Throughout America's Indian history, approaches to "the Indian problem" have assumed or advocated for the extinction of Indian civilization using treaty abuses, shifting policies, unwarranted military force, and neglect. Would two-plus centuries of such abuse quiet U.S. authority over aboriginal America, especially after Indians gained the right of citizenship in 1924?

Education of Indian children, in order to acculturate them into white society, was carried out in military-style schools, with little or no supervision to constrain or prevent physical and emotional abuse of the Indian students.[16] Our ahistory in this regard was experienced by my mother and my father, both born in 1894. Indian students withstood vile, degrading, or humiliating punishment. Many were too young and innocent to know how to protest and did not yet know how to write. If they could have protested, maybe they could have written to their parents or chief. Some children did write letters, and later, as adults, some provided oral history about boarding school conditions.[17] The government's documents contain reports of abuse of students in Indian schools: an example is the 1931 U.S. Senate report *Survey of Conditions of Indians in the United States*. The interviews in Tacoma begin with the subject of possible abuse of Indian students.[18]

On the Lummi Reservation we not only outgrew the available reserved land with each generation, but the Bureau of Indian Affairs facilitated white settlement on our reservation by means of land policies more beneficial to the non-Indian than to the impoverished Indian. This happened while the BIA was supposed to be protecting our lands, as the law provided. As a result of these white settlements, a large percentage of the residents of the Lummi Reservation are non-tribal-members. The five major white settlements on our reservation have reduced the land meant for our economically struggling people. Non-Indians do not have to pay property taxes to our tribal government, according to law. Civil suits may be brought against white residents of the reservation, but in practice this is almost never done. Crimes are committed in Indian Country all over the United States. In most states, major crimes on reservations are handled by the federal government, and Indian federal cases are almost never solved.

U.S. representatives Patrick J. Kennedy (D-RI) and Dale Kildee (D-MI) issued an important statement in 1997:

> In 1832, Supreme Court Chief Justice John Marshall held in the case of *Worcester v. Georgia*, that "Indian nations had always been considered as distinct independent political communities, retaining their original natural rights, as the undisputed possessors of their soil." Marshall's decision found a basis in Article I Section 8 of the Constitution, which gave Congress the power to "regulate commerce with foreign Nations, and among the several States, and with Indian Tribes." Congress has also passed legislation stating that "the utmost good faith shall always be observed towards the Indians; their land and property shall never be taken away from them without their consent; and their property, rights, and liberty, shall never be invaded or disturbed."
>
> Indian Country is not asking for our popular consent, but rather for Congress and the courts to uphold what is theirs by right under the Constitution. Anything less is not just unfair to our nation's first Americans, but also undermines the principles that guide our nation.[19]

Many publications have spoken for this right, and given the number of readers who agree, there is enough support for American Indians to stand up and reclaim their rights: not just as First Americans (after all, some of you can be called First Americans, too) but also as America's aboriginal people, who were well established on this continent, with silent agreements and oral traditions handed down from one generation to the next, for thousands of years.

When we add this to the evidence such as we find in the *American Indian Policy Review Commission, Final Report*, there is enough support already written, and perhaps silently supported by readers of such publications and their friends. Just counting my relatives within the Point

Elliott Treaty tribes, there are five hundred living people, plus their friends of all races, who agree with us. This is not a guessing game for me. The facts in this book, the support of my friends and relatives, and, hopefully, the support of my readers may help remind the citizens and leaders of the United States that it has forgotten its obligations to its aboriginal people.

BUILDING ON THE SOLID GROUND OF TRUTH

Please understand that I do not intend to hurt anyone's feelings, which often occurs in conversations about America's aboriginal people. I strongly believe that God created our diversity in the world's multiple cultures. How can we argue with Him? Additionally, no one today can say that they came across the Atlantic with Columbus; therefore, no guilty feelings, please. What I write here regarding the treatment of America's aboriginal people must be put on the scales of justice, for all citizens to judge whether we have built our nation in the strongest way. Our government must have the soundest foundation possible, in order to have integrity and vitality for the future.

Columbus was, in fact, lost, on his first trip to this New World. He thought he had landed in the East Indies; therefore he called us "Indians," and that has stuck through the ages.[20] We were villages and tribes with our own forms of government and yearly cycles of sustenance, and well grounded on this land we called Mother Earth. In fact, because we were so well grounded on the face of Mother Earth, and because we were too many to simply slaughter, we survived together. Given that the U.S. Constitution received inspiration from the Iroquois Confederacy, why not acknowledge the Iroquois people who shared their ideas about governance? Let's get the best of both worlds of Indian and non-Indian America into our history books in all public schools. So far, much that is good and true about aboriginal American tribes remains ahistoric, while stereotypes and omissions of fact still exist in our history books, textbooks, and the politics of the press, and these are widely accepted by the public and in school curricula. We have heard the romanticism about the "Noble Indian" and the myth of the "Vanishing Race." It is time to change all this, to reflect our reality as Indian people in America today. The Bible teaches us to build our homes on solid ground. The same should go for building our house of government. The strength of truth cannot help but create courage for every generation of American citizens. Circulating lies about aboriginal Americans doesn't cut it for any of the peoples of the world. Looking down on us is an insult to them too.

In our ongoing ahistoric position as Native people, parts of our valuable history are omitted. As an example, I must share a little episode with you. Around 1860, a ship landed on Orcas Island (map 2) near Cow Point. The ship had about three hundred Hawaiian people on it. These Hawaiian people were brought to Lummi Country to dive for oysters, to see if there were pearls in them. They never found pearls, nor did they return to the Hawaiian Islands. They gradually intermingled with the aboriginal people of Lummi Country and surrounding regions. Their descendants have been here ever since; many of them became part of our family, community, and tribes, and we are proud of that heritage. They accepted us, and because it is the First Law of our culture, we accepted them. The evidence for this is threefold. My father recounted it during my genealogical studies with him in 1945, and a Lummi elder, Johnny Solomon, told me this same story during when I was leading the Lummi Setting Sun Dance Group in the 1990s. There are also books about it, which mention ancestors of my own family.[21] My paternal grandmother, Agnes, wife of Frank Hillaire (Haeteluk), had some Polynesian blood. Hawaiians in their own homeland experienced much of what Indian America experienced: new diseases, missionary activity that aimed to destroy Native culture, settlers seeking to profit from Native land and resources, and government policies made to serve those interests, backed at points by a martial approach.

By 1924, all Indians were eligible for U.S. citizenship.[22] After our Indian soldiers fought shoulder to shoulder with other Americans in World War I, Indian veterans had become eligible for U.S. citizenship in 1919.[23] Not all Indians who were eligible for citizenship accepted this offer from the government. Some had received U.S. citizenship earlier, in the late nineteenth century, by accepting a land allotment.[24] The granting of citizenship might sound like an acknowledgment of Indian rights, but at that time in the government's thinking, it was partly just another step in trying to absorb Indians into U.S. culture.

The United States began regulating the sale of liquor to Indians in 1832. Laws were amended over time, especially after the passage of the land allotment act (the Dawes or General Allotment Act, 1887). The government still prohibited Indians from buying liquor, even those who were U.S. citizens on the basis of their holding land allotments.[25] In 1919 the Eighteenth Amendment was passed, and Prohibition made it illegal for all Americans to manufacture, buy, or sell alcohol. Many Indians had been buying bootlegged alcohol up until that time anyway. When Prohibition was repealed by the Twenty-First Amendment in 1933, the Indian prohibition law stayed in force. During World War II, about twenty-five thousand Indian men, and women too, again joined with other Americans to serve in the U.S. military.[26] Prohibition of alcohol use by Indians was not repealed until 1953. One factor that helped Congress see the discrimination that this involved was their recognition of the rights of Indian veterans.[27]

Even though our Indian men and women joined all other Americans in war, this did not mean we were actually "equal." There were still racial barriers in America's "civilization." Indians did not ask for help from our U.S. government when Mexicans took away our jobs harvesting berries west of the Cascade Mountains and apples east of the Cascades. The Blackfeet did not object when Chinese men took over their jobs on railroad construction. No one complained; we just accepted these takeovers in silence. Jobs were worth the struggle, but it shouldn't have been such a struggle. The racial barrier still limits us; a main reason is inadequate education. In the boarding school era, Indian youth were trained for low-skilled jobs, and many young women were trained for service as maids to white families. Inadequate education still restricts a lot of Indian people to lower-paying jobs. But this is changing. Education is one of our values, too, as well as being one of white America's greatest values—along with capitalism, imperialism, power, and wealth. It has always been that way with the two-edged sword of Americanism.

A VIOLENT HISTORY IN A NEW LAND

Looking at our nation's past, we see a violent picture! Violence was a natural part of life for the colonizers of America. Habits are easily built and carried forward to the next generation, by living example. That is how habits were built via the Indian oral tradition. America's violent ways have continued forward from the centuries of violence in Europe. In early history there was violence among the Huns, Romans, Saxons, Anglo-Saxons, Celts, Goths, Franks, and Vikings. The Roman Empire persecuted Christians. During the Crusades there was conflict between Christians and Muslims. In Asia there was Genghis Khan, followed by Timur (Tamerlane) and their Mongolian Empire, which spread through Asia into Eastern Europe. All this took place by the thirteenth century. Columbus and other navigators—then colonialism—soon followed.

Between 1852 and 1893, the United States advanced on Argentina, Nicaragua, Uruguay, Japan, China, Angola, and Portuguese West Africa. All of these advances by our military were to "protect our business interests," according to U.S. officials.[28] Even though these military advancements have been to the advantage of U.S. global interests, the method becomes a role model for our nation's youth: Be aggressive! We are encouraged to feel patriotic when we hear of such violence. After all, it could mean advancement for our people somehow.

A few European explorers, such as Leif Erikson, settled in North America (perhaps in Newfoundland, Canada) about five hundred years before Columbus. My ancestors occupied our Native homeland in the Northwest Coast around ten thousand years before that. Europeans started arriving in large numbers after the arrival of Columbus, only five hundred years ago. While my ancestors were happily living off the land, the newcomers from Europe were trying desperately to escape violence and oppression (political, economic, and religious) in their old countries. Our lives at that time were very different. The immigrants came from Europe, which was in the Mechanical Age of factories and steel weapons, while American Indian cultures were still rooted in the Stone Age. In Euro-America's desperate attempt to relocate away from the cruelty of the old countries, it used approaches of the old countries: force and violence. Euro-Americans slowly changed from their principles of *kill, conquer, and occupy.* They adopted democratic ideas of the Iroquois and developed other good ideas of governance. But at the same time, they continued to use the force that was familiar to them. Over time, it became more and more comfortable for them to use force against America's aboriginal people.

At the time of our first encounters the land provided for us—for our every need. As our ancestors watched these white strangers, every move must have been phenomenal to them. Listening to our elders' speeches from long ago, and even today, shows that almost every time you hear Indian America's inner thoughts on white America, you can hear the surprise, and even shock, about what the white Americans "were doing next." It was as if Indian America were watching a movie. As conditions changed, Indian people continued to look to see where they would fit in, or not fit in. And if Indians were not going to fit in, then where would they go? Would they truly vanish; would they all end up dead? There was no other place for them to go, the way that white America escaped their abusive governments of Europe.

White America's struggle for freedom from their old countries' oppressions did not succeed in taking everything from Indian America. We still carry this in our souls and spirits:

There is Someone Greater than us,
    for this is where He's been.
There is someone greater than us;
    for this (the Earth) is what He's given us.

This is a cultural and family prayer handed down to me.

Indian America found where they could be helpful to some white Americans and not others. They learned that some white Americans were helpful to Indians. Looking at it this way makes me feel more understanding about the entire ahistory of Indian America since 1492. Slaughter, yes, genocide, yes; but most importantly, survival. Official American history tells very little about the good things that Indian America did—such as contributing to America's medical knowledge of herbs. Nor does American history fully acknowledge the irony of our friendship. But these facts are part of the story of America's progress.

At first, we did not know of each other, Indian America and white America. Then opposing views clashed, leading to devastating cultural conflicts. God helped us survive that. But power remained on the dominating side of white America. The weapons and the policies won out. We, the descendants of the Indian people who survived, see that the great scales of justice still need to be balanced for Indian America. Our land was dangerously diminished, our treaties only partially paid, and their terms violated. Our tribal governments deserve respect and joint effort with the U.S. government. Land has always taken priority in America, and now the management of our affairs is under the Bureau of Indian Affairs, itself under the Department of Interior. At least we are placed equal with land as part of America. Our numbers are minuscule in comparison to the total U.S. population,[29] but we are an important part of the United States. Aren't you tired of the old ways of violence, coercion, and neglect? We are tired of our forgotten genocide. But all is not lost, and much is hanging in the balance.

PREJUDICE AND POVERTY

It was impossible to wipe our people out on the scale that Germany did the Jews. At first we were America's necessary evil: too many to slaughter and too necessary to keep for guidance about this land and how to locate and utilize its resources. This fact is sometimes included in today's books authored by scholars. For example, aboriginal fishermen's knowledge was useful to the non-Indian commercial fishing canning industry as it got established in the Northwest, as shown by anthropologist Daniel Boxberger.[30] Intermarriages between white and American Indians took place, although cultural and legal prohibitions existed at times, as it has been with marriages between whites and other races. Some Indian/white marriages were by choice. In others, white men married Indian women as another way to gain Indian land.

Our poverty began with land loss. Unlike non-Indian America, with land assured for its children, grandchildren, and great-grandchildren, such is not the case for Indian America. The treaties signed between the U.S. government and the many tribes established vast areas for the new nation. Some people may think that our land loss ended when treaty making ended, but much more land was lost by U.S. policies that followed. This book tells about just one region in the Pacific Northwest, but similar suffering, and worse, occurred across the nation. About two-thirds of reservation land across the United States was lost through the Dawes Allotment Act of 1887. Currently there is land on our Lummi reservation occupied by non-Indian people who oppose Indians and the old Indian way of life. There are U.S. citizens, some of whom live on our reservations, who would like to see our treaties abrogated and our sovereignty destroyed.[31]

In early history Native people received no information from the government concerning the value of acreage. In recent history many Indian people have not understood the value of grant dollars in relation to their tribe's total membership. Today it often happens that financial assets are not adequately spread among a tribe's total membership. Our youth suffer the most from this, and they are helplessly caught in white America's education policies. American Indians have slowly tackled this problem by trying to make Native youths' education relevant to their cultures and communities, looking to the future as well as to the past. Many educators, Indian and non-Indian, are doing our utmost to conquer the crippling effects of white America's education policies on the nation's Indian youth. In many cases our youth are trained to work outside our tribe, and they do just that for the rest of their lives, while many of them stall, not wanting to leave their homeland, where opportunities are few. Some try to commute to outside jobs, which is difficult. Others fall into drug and alcohol addiction and poverty of body and spirit.

Teaching the whole child came into play within our tribal school systems, but it may have come too late for those who had fallen into addiction. Whole families fall into those traps, even if just one person is totally addicted. And poverty rambles on timelessly. Just a generation ago, our culture taught the whole child. It was the three Rs in school, and culture was taught at home and in the community. But in the early part of white-Indian history, much of our culture at home was barred from us: our clothing, our language, our ceremonies and songs.

In the Northwest our potlatch gatherings and ceremonies were banned; people were not allowed to participate in any of these basic cultural ways. In 1882 Secretary of the Interior Henry M. Teller wrote a letter to the commissioner of Indian Affairs instructing him that Indian agents must stop Indians from "heathenish practices" such as ceremonies, dances, and feasts. Teller argued that Indian gatherings were "intended to stimulate the warlike passions of the young warriors of the tribes" and were occasions for the people to affirm young men's boasting of "falsehood, deceit, theft, murder, and rape." A Court of Indian Offences was established at each Indian agency to judge wrongdoing. Such tribunals were generally formed of the agency's three highest-ranking Indian police officers.[32] In Canada the potlatch—and practices such as spirit dancing—were prohibited by law from 1885 to 1951.[33] The banning of ceremonial gatherings created total misery. The deprivation of our spiritual rights also damaged family structures. Thankfully, there were those who remembered and carried on the knowledge, facing threat of penalty and sometimes imprisonment. Preservation of our ancestral traditions is an important way that our ancestors have remembered our rights throughout history. But, tribes and individuals today still struggle with ongoing problems that resulted from these restrictions on our spiritual life.

Our Indian nations, although recognized as sovereign nations, are also considered domestic, dependent nations. Economically, they are dependent to varying degrees on county, state, and federal government for resources such as education, housing, and infrastructure. It is my belief that circumstances will improve in future generations. This is among the greatest of my dreams for my family, my people. We were finally granted citizenship in our own land, and eventually the law permitted us to drink alcohol alongside the rest of America. But my people would like to see intercession of the Great Spirit, God, to bring us good lives such as we deserve after centuries of injustice in our own country. Let the great scales of justice become balanced for us. This does not mean that we will give up our efforts; U.S. Indian policy must restore conditions for justice, and we will do our part.

Now in my eighties, I can truly say I have watched my children grow up in a world of racism, prejudice, and poverty. It has made me feel helpless, as I was in the same position. I dread watching my grandchildren struggle with racism, prejudice, and poverty. May the great scales of justice be balanced before my great-grandchildren, as beautiful as they are, are forced into a world of racism, prejudice, and poverty. As hard as I try to prevent this, I know I am helpless, no matter how I approach the definitions and actions of racism, prejudice, and poverty.

Like some of my ancestors, I share, share, and share my knowledge of Indian cultural and village customs when I am invited to do so. What have I shared? Legends, songs, history, genealogy, poetry, friendship, ideas for the enhancement of our dying earth—our dying rivers. My work has included leading our Lummi Setting Sun Dance Group, my teaching of legends and songs, and sharing the slide presentation "A Century of Coast Salish Life at Lummi."[34] Against the objections of some Indian people, I share—not just with my family and community, but with non-Indian America—as much as I can possibly share.[35] All my valuable sharing has been at minimal cost to the public. We cannot share it all until we are almost too old to share at all.

White America has also shared with me. I have had some outstanding physicians who have taken care of my medical needs. Non-Indian America has shared with me many individuals who have become great, kind friends to me and to my family. I just do not give up, and I advise our younger generations to never give up on the good efforts they will come to know. The Earth is our first teacher, after all. We try during our time, and we pray never to lose our common sense or logic. I see a good future of mutual understanding between Indian and non-Indian

Americans. And my praises become more abundant that our Earth and our rivers will live. They provide a foundation for our lives, and I pray that they will be there for each new generation.

You might ask, "In what situations in my lifetime have I suffered through racism, prejudice, and poverty?" We know that our Indian ancestors, for the most part, did not survive racism, prejudice, and poverty. But at this point in history, I have accepted that "It's my turn now." In our area of the Northwest, Indian students were permitted to enter public school after World War II. I went to public school at that time, and for the first few months I noticed that the teacher would not collect our papers as she did for white students. So, I took it upon myself to gather each of the Indian students' papers and walk them up to the teacher's desk. Finally that treatment stopped, and she collected our papers at the same time that she collected her white students' papers. See chapter 7 on persecution and racism, and read the sources that are listed in my bibliography. These sources spell out the imbalances of justice for each generation of Indians in America. For contemporary accounts, see *Racism in Indian Country* by Dean Chavers; it covers racism in health care, natural resources, and many other areas.

THE INDIAN VALUE SYSTEM

How do white and Indian cultures differ? Compare our value systems, if you are clear on either one. As for myself, I see the value system of the United States as being based on the nation's view of progress: the use of money, the use of power, and the use of people, without much consideration for the dignity of the individual. Indian America's value system depends on the environment and a strong relationship of the person with land, work, exchange, and other. We depend upon the land. Our relationship to land is unique as compared to most cultures in America.

The Iraq War showed us something about ways of knowing and valuing. No matter how it started—whether it was off target for one cause or on target for another, off target for 9/11, or on target for Saddam Hussein—we are left with the questions of which target was on our table at a specific time, and which target was most urgent? That's up to you; but if you are open to suggestions from Indian America, it would not hurt (but it's probably impossible) to change the United States' accepted value system from its focus on materialism and power. Is it ethical to confuse one value (retaliation for 9/11) with another (a surprise attack on an old problem of dictatorship) to ultimately become off target? In the timeless value system of American Indians—relationship to land, work, exchange, and other—the Indian watches: observing and learning—then interacting—which is more like a law of nature. In this way, jumping to conclusions is not an option: analysis promotes a more careful advance. It gives a person more time to evaluate the advantages against the disadvantages. Today, after the fact of 9/11, it's over, and the government is on to the next problem.

When we build a relationship with land, our involvement is endless learning. With work, there is ever-advancing interaction, but built on a relationship with the living land. In building relationships through exchange, we expand our family and social life on the principles learned from elders: our living example. In building a relationship with other, we follow the ceremonial commands of our culture: ceremonies, such as potlatch, naming, baptizing, first salmon ceremony, berry picking, marriage, and so on—creating a relationship with other by having respect and ultimately by using the Golden Rule, or respect as taught by the living example of Mother Earth. The "unknown" in the old Indian American culture was an ever-advancing learning through legends, observation, and the discipline of minding one's own business. Imaginations wander, curiosity is aroused; experiences wander ever so slowly upon the target. This characterizes the American Indian relationship with the unknown.

American Indian games of competition are used for entertainment and for the passage of time during long seasons. *Slahál*, in particular—the game also called the Bone Game—is a game in which we sing songs, where the value of "exchange" comes alive. Trading is one name for exchange; gift giving is another. This game can become more and more exciting, even addicting, as we see in the legend about the fish called the Sucker and the Eel. To make a long legend short, two creatures played *slahál.* On and on the game progressed. The sucker was the winner each time, and the eel the loser. Upon losing everything, the eel (even though he had nothing left of his earthly possessions) challenged the sucker, who had bones at the time, and declared loud and clear that he would go to the mountains and get "magic power" to win everything back. The sucker agreed and proceeded to wait. When the eel returned, the game began, and went on and on. After days and nights of gambling, the eel lost again. That's why today the eel has no bones and the sucker has too many: the eel had bet the sucker all his bones for this last game. Who was jumping to conclusions before his time? Games and spiritual ceremonies are filled with music. I think there's a song for just about everything in the Indian world: pulling canoes, picking berries, welcoming special persons and special events, farewell parties, and so on.

From what I have observed of America's value system, values are expressed in mottos, music, boasting, commercial advertisements, and personal expressions of style, with egotistical features often displayed in plain view. No single museum could contain samples of all the artifacts of American culture that are now being produced in the United States. Each piece would tell a story of a vast materialistic culture.

JUSTICE SHOULD NOT TAKE THIS LONG

Legal concepts such as the "Doctrine of Discovery" and "plenary power" have us trapped in the jaws of white America. We must unshackle our way of life, by way of good policy. We have been managed by the BIA in such ways that it was not possible to pursue happiness like other Americans. We are last on the list, from our place in the records of history, to the seizure of our property. We need land and resources enough for our children and grandchildren that we may build homes, develop our tribal governments, care for our weak and helpless, and provide for our future generations.

From the beginning of human habitation here in the northern Puget Sound area, until we signed a treaty in 1855, our Point Elliott Treaty tribes owned a tremendous amount of land. In lawsuits against the United States, our tribes were told that the government had overpaid us for our land, because of the services that had been provided by the Bureau of Indian Affairs. The government did not pay fairly for our land, or for the vast territory that the United States claims for all their future non-Indian generations. The United States did not explain just how much per hour, paid to how many non-Indian workers, those "services" were worth, in order for the U.S. government to have paid for such a vast territory. How can any number of hours of BIA services, and the few goods that were provided in payment, equal the value of our vast homelands in the Northwest?

Indian America's land bases have been squeezed with a slip-sliding approach to policy and law. In 1855, when the Treaty of Point Elliott was signed, there was not even enough land provided for the generations living at that time: the treaty signers and their families. The government expected that we would die out or mix in with white society. But now we have new generations without lands. The Dawes Severalty Act (General Allotment Act) of 1887 caused the tribes of the United States to lose at least 65 percent of the lands that they had reserved by treaty. An 1881 government report, *Codification of Laws on Survey and Disposition of Public Land*, indicates that the 149 Indian reservations in the United States contained 143,525,960 acres, "two thirds of the area of which will eventually be restored to the public domain for sale and disposition, after purchase of occupancy title from Indians."[36] Thus, the United States violated—without remorse—the terms of our treaties.

Allotments began at Lummi three years before the Dawes Act went into effect.[37] Provision for allotment was written into the Pacific Northwest treaties. One of the provisions of Article 7 in the Treaty of Point Elliott is that the U.S. president may cause the reserved lands "to be surveyed into lots, and assign the same to . . . individuals or families." Much of our land was lost, and now 23 percent of the Lummi Reservation is owned by non-Indians, according to the 2008 Lummi Nation Atlas.[38]

What about us, the generations born after the treaty? We who have been kept at the lowest-paying jobs? Myself, I've had sixty years of work. In my place, wouldn't you say the same thing? I am tired of all the oppression, neglect of individual human rights, and inhumane policies that keep American Indian individuals poverty-stricken. American Indian land bases were nicknamed "government created ghettos." "Reservations" were the "garbage cans," and the BIA was the trashcan lid. But with my elders' teachings, I always rose above my problems, gained footing again, and continued my battle for our future generations.

The International Labour Organization's "Convention 169 on the Rights of Indigenous and Tribal Peoples" is the only internationally binding convention that applies specifically to indigenous peoples. Fewer than twenty nations have ratified it, and the United States is not one of them.[39] Consider the nation's refusal to ratify this, and most other international agreements regarding indigenous rights.

Plenary power—the nearly absolute legislative authority of Congress—has limited Indian America's claims to justice. Add to this the racism and prejudice of today's American businesses and people. Wouldn't you be tired of all this, too? Maybe they just forgot; maybe they are buried in all the politics of the world they are trying to claim. I learned this at the time of the Longest Walk in 1978, a five-month walk across the country from California to the nation's capital made by people of many tribes, who made that walk to symbolize the forced marches of Native peoples from their lands and to convey messages to the nation's government and citizens about our treaty rights and human rights.[40] In 2008 the Longest Walk II was joined by Indian people from across America who again walked to Washington DC. They made sensible claims for justice from the U.S. government. My Lummi Longhouse elders participated in the Longest Walk I in 1978. That's the year I wrote the monograph *Indian Policy: Crime or Reason?*[41] As regards the reputation that this nation wants the world and its own people to see, justice should not take this long. It has been more than two centuries since treaty obligations were incurred. Government, we have been knocking at your door long enough; it is time for you to respond.

The "American Declaration of the Rights and Duties of Man" was the world's first international human rights instrument. It was adopted at a conference held in Columbia in 1948, where American nation-states established the Organization of American States (OAS), of which the

United States is a member. If you read the "American Declaration of the Rights and Duties of Man," which the United States ratified by virtue of belonging to the OAS, how much do you think its provisions actually apply for Indian America?[42] My tribe, the Lummi Tribe, was refused its land-claims against the United States, claims pleading for justice well deserved. I have seen many claims of this type, which were refused to aboriginal Americans.

In our inland Pacific Northwest, a citizens' group in the Nez Perce Country of Idaho offered bounty hunter awards for Indian scalps at the following rates: for males, $100; for females, $50; and $25 for "anything in the shape of an Indian under ten years of age."[43] This occurred in 1866, just twenty-eight years before my parents were born. It is understandable why my mother, when someone came to the door, answered it without us kids around, so she could learn the purpose of the visitor. The desecrated bodies of Indian people, especially the strongest leaders, were sometimes displayed by Anglo-Europeans, as a show of strength and intimidation. The Wampanoag chief Metacom (also known as Pometacom or Metacomet, and called King Philip by the British) was decapitated in 1676 at the end of King Philip's War. New England colonists placed his head on a stake at Fort Plymouth, where it remained for over twenty years. Here in the Northwest the Yakama leader Peo-peo-mox-mox was shot by members of the Oregon militia, and his scalp and ears were sent back to his home community as a violent sign of intimidation.[44]

Liquor was widely used as a means to weaken Indian people and communities. Benjamin Franklin states in his autobiography: "if it be the Design of Providence to extirpate these Savages, in order to make room for the Cultivators of the Earth, it seems not improbable that Rum may be the appointed Means. It has already annihilated all the Tribes who formerly inhabited the Sea-coast."[45] Episodes of slaughter by the U.S. War Department were visited upon aboriginal Americans including the Delaware, Cheyenne, Nez Perce, Sioux, Ponca, Winnebago, and Cherokee.[46] For many Indians and their friends the Hawaiians, disease was a significant means of destruction. According to Russell Thornton, the diseases brought to America by Europeans were "smallpox, measles, bubonic plague, cholera, typhoid, pleurisy, scarlet fever, diphtheria, mumps, whooping cough, colds, the venereal diseases gonorrhea and cancroid, pneumonia and some unusual influenza and respiratory diseases, quite probably typhus and venereal syphilis, and only remotely possibly, tuberculosis." Smallpox was responsible for the most deaths.[47] The proof of Indian deaths by epidemic disease is evident in government census reports. I have been called to task on this issue several times; my research was tested again and again, but it was right. The census records are stored at the National Archives in Seattle, on Sand Point Way. Today, people just looking at us probably think we are okay. Maybe they even think we are lucky to be Indian American—that is, if they can tell us apart from all the other people of color in America.

In the 1950s the Lummi tribe filed a suit against the United States, and Indians of Lummi testified before the Indian Claims Commission that Lummi territory had extended for miles in all directions around the reservation before the treaty was signed.[48] Lummi homelands went as far north as the Canadian border. They included all of Lummi Island, all of Orcas, Waldron, and Shaw Island, the western half of San Juan Island and the northwestern half of Lopez Island. The territory extended east to the northwestern end of Lake Whatcom (see map 2). The Lummi have always thought that the treaty made an unfair settlement for all the valuable land and water rights they had once owned. Our language and most of our culture were removed from us, with the government's hope that we would become mainstream Indian/white American citizens: farmers of pigs, cows, horses, sheep—but none of these was native to our homeland.

In 1974 federal judge George Boldt ruled that our fishing tribes were entitled by treaty to 50 percent of harvestable fish and shellfish.[49] According to the law, we now share fishing "in common" with non-Indian fisherman, but we do not have much in common in methods of fishing or places of fishing. Today there are hardly any fish to be caught, and they are so depleted that some types are at risk of becoming endangered species. This is not the fault of Indian America; the entire Indian American population equals less than two percent of the general population.

No one professes to know our complete history, and if I can pick out some good times from it, certainly others can. But who wants to talk of a cheating government? Who wants to talk of military-like schools for our parents? Who wants to talk of how the justice system of their great America treated the aboriginals of our land and how it treats us today? Or how their land increased, while ours was decreased, legally but unjustly? Who wants to talk about how worried I am for space for my beautiful grandchildren and great-grandchildren, for space to build comfortable homes, and to enjoy at least half of what we did when we were their age? Sure, our "reservation" was enough for one generation. We were either to become extinct, or to blend in with the rest of America. But no; few people want to talk about those things, even if those things are as real as your own life is right now.

Friend, let's have a moment of silence and pray for my future generations, that they will have homes: fixed, settled and permanent; comfort, even happiness—that they may achieve their dreams. They are beautiful people. If they'd had the opportunities that European Americans had during treaty-making days, who knows where America's indigenous tribes would be today? We may always wonder.

Even though we got past the dynamic of *kill, conquer, and occupy*, nothing changed very much as long as the United States Department of War ruled over us as the weaker population. We acknowledged your forces of gunpowder and germ warfare. We made treaties with the United States, and nearly four hundred of them were ratified and are binding.[50] But still we wait for them to be completely honored. True, since our treaties were enacted, we have experienced some good. But we remain in the hope that the nation's young government might mature, and that aboriginal America will receive the justice it is due. It has been a long time.

CHAPTER 2

The Building of America

Columbus, everyone knows, set the stage for the "discovery" of American Indian homelands in the fifteenth century. Europe wanted better access to trade and power in Asia. Columbus was one of few navigators willing to sail in search of a shorter route to the East Indies. Not everyone at that time believed that the earth was round, but Columbus accepted the evidence. However, he underestimated the size of the globe and thought that Europe and India were on opposite shores of the Atlantic Ocean. So when he made it across the Atlantic, he had arrived in the Americas, not the East Indies. He did not expect to meet us American "Indians" and to find us so strongly bonded to the land.

COLUMBUS AND THE DOCTRINE OF DISCOVERY

Queen Isabella and King Ferdinand of Spain furnished the ships and made Columbus's voyages possible. Papal bulls (directives from Catholic popes) provided the authority of the "Doctrine of Discovery," which empowered explorers from Europe's Christian nations to take possession of the world's lands not held by Christian rulers and to subjugate non-Christians.[1] Such an approach cannot be said of the way taught by Jesus. But understanding our Indian ahistory requires understanding something about the political side of Christianity during Europe's "Age of Discovery" (the fifteenth to seventeenth centuries). The Doctrine of Discovery justified an ongoing process of destruction for indigenous

Americans: destruction of our freedoms, our homelands, lives, liveli-hood, and ways of life. Pope Nicholas V issued the papal bull *Dum Diversas* in 1452. It authorized King Alphonso V of Portugal to reduce "Saracens (Muslims) and pagans and other unbelievers" to perpetual slavery. Pope Nicholas V also wrote the bull called *Romanus Pontifex* (1455), which authorized the enslaving of non-Christian peoples and the taking of their lands. *Romanus Pontifex* is less aggressive than *Dum Diversas* (which carries the tone of the Crusades). *Romanus Pontifex* is also more paternalistic. *Romanus Pontifix* begins as follows:

> The Roman pontiff, successor of the key-bearer of the heavenly kingdom and vicar ["representative"] of Jesus Christ, contemplat-ing with a father's mind all the several climes of the world and the characteristics of all the nations dwelling in them and seeking and desiring the salvation of all, wholesomely ordains and disposes upon careful deliberation those things which he sees will be agreeable to the Divine Majesty and by which he may bring the sheep entrusted to him by God into the single divine fold, and may acquire for them the reward of eternal felicity, and pardon for their souls.[2]

From that point on, *Romanus Pontifix* continues with the same type of message as *Dum Diversas*, authorizing invasion, capture, subjugation, and taking possession of indigenous people's property and goods. The first papal bull in behalf of Spain was *Inter caetera divinai* (1493). When Columbus set sail, the arrangement was that he would take possession of any lands he "discovered" that were not under dominion of any Christian rulers. After Columbus's return, Pope Alexander VI issued *Inter caetera divinai*, which claimed Spain's right to any lands that had already been "discovered" by Columbus or that would be "discovered" by Spain in the future.[3]

It was not until sometime after landing in the Bahamas, at a place he named San Salvador, that Columbus realized he was not in the East Indies. This was when we Native people of the Americas were named "Indios." He attempted to bring twenty-some "Indians" back to Spain, but most of them died on the journey. The ones who survived were paraded through the streets of Seville and Barcelona to gain support for Columbus's expeditions. On his second trip in 1493, Columbus sent American Natives back to Europe to be sold as slaves.[4] It was not until 1502 that he set foot on the mainland of the continent, in South America. After a total of four voyages to the "New World," Columbus returned home without much ado. He died the death of a humble man in 1506, without a fraction of the recognition he has had since then.

PRECOLONIAL AMERICA

Besides Columbus, there were other expeditions to North America, led by Leif Erickson, Magellan, Balboa, Lafayette, and others. The first colonists in the New World were the Spanish, who founded settlements in present-day New Mexico and Florida in the sixteenth century. In the seventeenth century the British started their colonies. There was the colony at Jamestown, Virginia, that of the Pilgrims at Plymouth, and there were others, along with groups and individuals from the Netherlands and other European countries. Navigators started exploring the Northwest Coast in the sixteenth century: Spain, England, and later the United States competed in claims to ownership (see appendix 3). On the east side of North America, where colonialism got its start in the new America, colonists soon began enslaving African people in order build up their own wealth; slavery continued until it was abolished in 1865 by the Thirteenth Amendment to the Constitution. Europeans continued to arrive in America in search of freedom from multiple forms of oppression in the old countries: religious, political, social, and economic. When mass production began in Europe in the eighteenth century, the gates closed on countless workers, precipitating expeditions for new opportunities. As machines were invented to assist with farming, landowning farmers discharged workers who could no longer serve their purposes. Many of these workers were encouraged to leave the Old Country, as were prisoners. Some of these individuals manned the voyagers' ships to North America. European nations were solidly established with money and the many uses of metal. This gave them more confidence as they explored for new land. Among wealthy

European families, it was often the younger sons who immigrated to America, because in those cultures it was usually the firstborn son who inherited the family estate. Therefore, many of the younger brothers set out to make their fortune. The race was on.

Ships arrived in the New World loaded with people from various European countries. Our American Indian ancestors had to contend with these newcomers and accept the presence of fortune seekers and military men from various countries. Among the hard-working newcomers were unprincipled, unscrupulous men and women, watching for a chance to surreptitiously rip off their new fellow citizens. Many persons arrived before the Statue of Liberty was erected, with her message of freedom.

In the beginning, the founders of the United States were competing for land while they were trying to establish a new economy and government. Great Britain, France, and Spain all held land and control of particular regions, at least in the early years. Indians, whose homeland all this land was, stood in the way. Some who were not slaughtered interacted with the newly arrived Europeans. This is how the Confederacy of the Five Nations came into the picture of early America, with the Haudenosaunee or Iroquois people of the Northeast introducing their form of government. Haudenosaunee means "People of the Longhouse." It was well known to the first Europeans in America that the Iroquois form of democratic government and confederacy had strength. In 1744 Canasatego of the Onondaga, a speaker for the Iroquois League, relayed in a council for the Treaty of Lancaster how the Indian government was so successful.[5] The Iroquois Confederacy was made up of the Mohawk, Onondaga, Seneca, Cayuga, and Oneida Nations, and in the eighteenth century the Tuscarora joined them. Benjamin Franklin published the report on the council where Canasatego spoke. This is one of the ways that Franklin and other revolutionary leaders learned about Iroquois governance. Franklin asked, in essence: "If the Five Nations' form of confederacy works for the Indians, why couldn't it work for our thirteen colonies?"

The British eventually recognized America's independence. The Peace of Paris Treaty, signed in 1783 by Great Britain and representatives of the United States, ended the Revolutionary War and showed Britain's acceptance of the independence of the thirteen colonies. The document failed to mention indigenous Americans. Britain gave up its land claims, but no arrangements were worked out concerning Indian lands formerly held by the British. Britain's Indian allies now had to deal with the Americans, who regarded their new lands as American acquisitions, without recognizing that the lands were Indian homelands.

Debate over the U.S. Constitution culminated after several years of discussion, and the Constitution was signed in 1787. The Constitution contains some foundational points about Indian rights: that the treaty is the supreme law of the land, and that Congress has the sole power to regulate commerce "with foreign Nations, and among the several States, and with the Indian Tribes" (Article 1, Section 8, Clause 3). The Commerce Clause, as it is called, is the part of the Constitution that acknowledges the sovereignty of Indian tribes, regarding them on the same basis as states and foreign nations, with which only the federal government has the power to transact.

The neglect of Indian America in America's early formation was one step, I believe, in the failure to establish a strong relationship between the U.S. government and the tribes, when the United States first started to gain independence and power. All three times that Britain and the United States negotiated treaties — after the Revolutionary War, in the post–Revolutionary War's Jay Treaty, and after the War of 1812 — the British proposed a neutral Indian country between the United States and Canada. But in the end, land remained only for Canada and the United States.[6] American Indians experienced the settlers expanding into their villages and homesites. So much was happening all at once. It was easy for Anglo-Europeans to turn the old wheel of violence on the newly discovered continent. The documents of the U.S. House and Senate reveal the government's attitudes and policies toward Indians, as white America grew and stretched west.

PRINCIPLES BEHIND NATIVE RIGHTS

Having read Helen Hunt Jackson's book *A Century of Dishonor*, I applaud her efforts to awaken America to the injustices it committed against our aboriginal people. At the same time, I applaud the best results of American democracy and our founding documents, the Declaration of Independence, the U.S. Constitution, the maps created by the explorers, and their persistence at all cost. In the beginning the leaders of the new America gathered to transcend the oppression and violence of the governments of Europe. This was a group of men, growing in number, who were intelligent and wise. The forefathers of America took up the challenge of creating a new nation in the New World. Some of them ended up serving as presidents of the new nation. Considering the time it took to create a new nation, one could not say now, in retrospect, that it could have gone any faster than it did. Changing one's mind can take a long time, and changing from one culture to another can take much longer. It must have looked like a losing battle to white America that it could obtain a new world. Indians, in response to their "discovery," also had to adjust from their own deeply rooted cultures to a new system of governance, knowing that it couldn't be honorable, just, or fair. They suffered greatly at the hands of their "discoverers." Looking back, can we figure out the ingredients, so to speak? Can we figure out the dynamics involved in creating this new world?

Helen Hunt Jackson spells it out with compassion for America's aboriginal people. We can say, looking back on our real history, that it was a truly awful picture of violence here in this new world, and confusing, too. But not everyone was caught up in the violence and confusion. Helen Hunt Jackson is an example of compassion, on one hand, and intelligence and common sense, on the other. In reading her book, I found that she could easily be my sister. She researched official U.S. government reports, especially from the War Department, and I researched U.S. congressional documents concerning Indian affairs. Like Helen Hunt Jackson, I was astounded by America's Indian ahistory and horrified by America's history. In 1879 Jackson organized, along with Senator Henry Dawes (R-MA), the Boston Indian Citizenship Association. In the late nineteenth century there were several "Friends of the Indian" groups, formed of white persons who wanted to protect Indian rights. Most of these reformers were liberals who wanted to help Indian people, but they saw Indians' assimilation to white culture as the right road. Reformers convened semi-annually at Lake Mohonk, near New Paltz in upstate New York. Many federal Indian policies, including allotment of tribal lands, began as discussions at the Mohonk conferences. Jackson's focus was on Indian land rights, rather than on the acculturation of Indians. She passed away two years before Congress approved the Dawes Act, and reservations were divided into parcels held by individuals, so her thoughts on allotment are not clear.[7]

Benjamin Franklin's words are embossed upon the red cover of her book: "Look upon your hands! They are stained with the blood of your relations." Franklin's words foretell the story that unfolds in *A Century of Dishonor*, which chronicles abuses by the U.S. government of Native people and treaties. Jackson sought to galvanize the American people and their leaders against further abuses of Native people. So strong were her beliefs that when the book was published in January 1881, she sent, at her own expense, a copy to each member of the U.S. Congress, urging them to read it and act to restore the United States' honor. This was like my journey, in my plight to eke out justice and land for the descendant generations of our treaty signers of 1855. My first publication was a pamphlet titled *Indian Policy: Crime or Reason?* published by the *Omak (WA) Chronicle*, in conjunction with the Long Walk in 1978. I was shouting across the land to Congress to stop—stop violating our sacred treaty rights!

Helen Hunt Jackson's efforts for justice for Indians began in 1879, when she attended a lecture by Ponca chief Standing Bear and heard his story of forced removal to Indian Territory (present-day Oklahoma). It must have been a convincing lecture. For years, you see, she researched her book with a very strong drive for justice. Statesmen, politicians, and philosophers stepped up to the plate at her challenge. She quotes Timothy Walker, who made this summary of Indian land rights in his 1846 work, *Introduction to American Law*: "The American doctrine on the subject of Indian title is briefly this: The Indians have no fee in the lands they occupy. The fee is in the Government. They cannot, of course, aliene them [alienate their lands] either to nations or individuals, the exclusive right of pre-emption being in the Government. Yet they have a qualified right of occupancy, which can only be extinguished by treaty, and upon fair compensation, until which they are entitled to be protected in their possession."[8]

A "qualified" right of occupancy is all that aboriginals had. Jackson cites *Abbott's Digest* and proclaims: "The right of occupancy had been recognized in countless ways, among others by many decisions of courts and opinions of attorney generals." She continues: "It being thus established that the Indian's 'right of occupancy' in his lands was a right recognized by all the Great Powers discovering this continent, and accepted by them as a right necessary to be extinguished either by purchase or conquest, and that the United States, as a nation, has also from the beginning recognized, accepted, and acted upon this theory, it is next in order to inquire whether the United States has dealt honorably or dishonorably by the Indians in this matter of their recognized 'right of occupancy.'"[9]

Jackson wrote the following in 1881, concerning the lack of response to the many tribes' efforts and the efforts of Indian historians and authors, and her words still apply today: "It is necessary, therefore, in charging a government or nation with dishonorable conduct to show that its moral standard ought in nowise to differ from the moral standard of an individual; that what is cowardly, cruel, base in a man is cowardly, cruel, base in a government or nation. To do this, it is only needful to look into the history of the accepted 'Law of Nations' from the days of the Emperor Justinian until now."[10]

Vattel explained the "necessary law of nations," which is part of the basis of Indian land rights, in terms of "the application of the law of nature to nations." He says of the law of nations: "It is necessary, because nations are absolutely bound to observe it. This law contains the precepts prescribed by the law of nature to States, on whom that law is not less obligatory than on individuals; since States are composed of men, their resolutions are taken by men, and the law of nations is binding on all men, under whatever relation they act. This is the law which Grotius, and those who follow him, call the Internal Law of Nations, on account of its being obligatory on nations in the point of conscience."[11]

Jackson sums up centuries of agreement about the moral principles at the foundation of Native land rights: "Hundreds of pages are full of apparently learned discriminations between the parts of that law which are based on the law of nature, and the parts which are based on the consent and usage of nations. But the two cannot be separated. No amount of legality of phrase can do away with the inalienable truth underlying it. Wheaton and President Woolsey today say, in effect, the same thing which Grotius said in 1615, and Vattel in 1758."[12]

In the beginning, contact with Euro-Americans was a constant nightmare of disbelief for Indian America. Indians across the continent were living on this land before "discovery," within the perfect order of nature. They lived in relation to Mother Earth and acknowledged this as a blessing. So, if Indians lived within the perfect order of nature, and if philosophers of the past and present agree about the moral principles behind Native rights, how do we reconcile these facts with a government's abuse of its own citizens (all Indians have been eligible for U.S. citizenship since 1924) and a government's abuse of its aboriginal residents, who were here thousands of years before the earliest explorer?

Please see in *A Century of Dishonor* Jackson's account of an event that occurred in the history of the Indians of the great Pacific Northwest. The story goes that there were four Indian men at a ferry landing upon the Coquille River. Indians normally hunted ducks in that area. One morning, a white man heard a bullet whiz by him. Vengeance was presumed justified; he gathered up the four Indian hunters, then he marched them a long distance as he gathered up more white men. Early the next morning, he led the group to the nearby Indian encampment, where the white men shot every Indian in sight. The chiefs gathered their people to hear the military report of this barbarous act. The military asked the surviving Indian duck hunters their side of the story. An old Indian man said they hadn't done much of anything: there were some ducks there, and they had shot a few for their next meal. None of the white men on a nearby ferry crew had been injured. The military man asked the Indians to turn in their guns. There at the encampment, the military gathered five guns and pistols, two of which were unserviceable. The

Indians were innocent, but a slaughter of retaliation was made against them, and the only thing they could do was to put it behind them. The Indians vowed they would remain peaceful.[13] Justice was not served between white and Indian. You answer the question as to whether or not justice was served for the white men.

In *A Century of Dishonor* history is documented by U.S. military men on the frontier. The book contains a section of over thirty pages attesting to massacres committed by white America upon Indian America.[14] Not many Americans would want to own up to that. These reports are quotations from U.S. military men. This is frightening. However, I believe that today most white Americans' hearts are in the right place when it comes to fairness. President Obama hopes for change: that the wealthiest people can benefit from opening their minds to the poverty-stricken people in our country and around the world. Consideration, diplomacy, and hospitality from both sides could greatly benefit all. But this might remain a dream, unless we act.

OFFICIAL VIOLENCE

For such a young nation, America has participated in many wars: the Revolutionary War, War of 1812, Mexican-American War, Civil War, Spanish-American War, World War I, World War II, Korean War, Vietnam War, Gulf War, Iraq War, and War in Afghanistan. With all this international conflict, relationships with the Indian nations that exist within U.S. borders have not been a big priority for the U.S. government. In addition to wars conducted to defend American land, lives, and principles, violence has been committed by the United States upon many nations because of the desire for expansion and foreign markets:

   1852–53: Argentina—Marines were landed and maintained in Buenos Aires to protect American interests there during a revolution.

   1853: Nicaragua—Military power was used to protect American lives and interests during a political disturbance.

   1853–54: Japan—Warships are used in the Perry Expedition to force Japan to open its ports to the United States.

1853–54: Ryuku and Bonin Islands—Commander Perry made a naval demonstration there, landing marines twice, securing a coaling concession from the ruler of Naha on Okinawa and on Bonin to secure facilities for commerce.

1854: Nicaragua, San Juan del Norte—Grey Town was destroyed to avenge an insult to the American minister to Nicaragua.

1855: Uruguay—U.S. and European naval forces landed to protect American interests in an attempted revolution in Montevideo.

1859: China—Military intervention to protect American interests in Shanghai.

1874: Hawaii—Military intervention to protect American lives and property, but actually to promote a provisional American government under Sanford Dole (whose family founded the Hawaiian Pineapple Company).

1894: Nicaragua—Military intervention to protect American interests at Bluefields, following a revolution.[15]

"To protect American interests" became an oft-used phrase. The events listed above cover the time period of 1852 to 1893—only four decades. Violence has been a model for the U.S. approach to Indian nations and nations overseas, especially small countries occupied by people of color.

As the Spanish American War began in 1898, a *Washington Post* editor wrote: "A new consciousness seems to have come upon us—the consciousness of strength—and with it a new appetite, the yearning to show our strength. . . . Ambition, interest, land hunger, pride, and mere joy of fighting, whatever it may be, we are animated by a new sensation. We are face to face with a strange destiny. The taste of Empire is in the mouth of the people even as the taste of blood in the jungle."[16] In the late 1890s Teddy Roosevelt said, "No triumph of peace is quite so great as the supreme triumph of war."[17] A British witness to war in the Philippines stated, "This is not war, it is simply massacre and murderous butchery."[18] Considering all the war and military action that America has conducted, how can we count the cost of these actions? Violence is self-defeating: how can we stop violence with violence? Our youth are watching, listening, and learning. If we say we are a moral nation, we must walk our talk. Isn't that a universal teaching? Are we properly demonstrating to our youth about what is best—whether peace or violence?

Great things have happened in the building of America. Gigantic parks were left to nature, ideas gave birth to invaluable inventions, and medicine has advanced. The average life span is not forty-five years of age anymore; it's more like seventy-five years these days. People like you and I are breaking through the barrier of extreme violence. What role our government should take today is the question everybody is asking. We all hear the answers, including the need for governmental transparency, accountability, and trust. Outward corruption may come to the end of its trail, but does it still operate in smaller ways—sneakier ways? Some countries have changed from communism and dictatorship to better forms of government. Some people, among them our own neighbors, have quit crime (even organized crime) to make better lives for themselves and their loved ones.

U.S. Indian policies have improved, along with the attitudes of citizens toward American Indians. Today, we can speak our Indian languages, sing our cultural songs, dance our cultural dances, and hold our traditional ceremonies. Not long ago, these were banned from our reach to teach our youth. We are grateful for this remembrance of our rights by the government, made possible by our ancestors, who remembered our traditions. No more will we hear words like those of Sir Jeffrey Amherst, commander in chief of British forces in North America: "Could it not be contrived to send the smallpox among the disaffected tribes of Indians? We must on this occasion use every stratagem in our power to reduce them." Amherst was writing to a frontier officer, Colonel Henry Bouquet, who replied that he would try to follow the British general's advice and added that he would even like to hunt "the vermin" [Indians] with dogs. Sir Amherst wrote him again: "You will do well to try to inoculate the Indians by means of blankets, as well as to try every other method that can serve to extirpate this execrable race. I should be very glad your scheme for hunting them down by dogs could take effect; but, England is at too great a distance to think of that at present."[19]

Dare we discuss how the wealthiest people in America got wealthy? Or how the most poverty-stricken people got so poverty-stricken? Underneath, there is a silent war between the rich and the poor of America, carried on through policies and social customs. Even some churches don't seem quite sure that the souls of "the least of these" have actually been saved. As a descendant of an aboriginal American tribe, I keenly sense the tragedies of my people, while at the same time, a humorous note strikes. Some Indian people are where their conquerors would like to be, living peaceful, happy, productive lives, while wealthier white America hunts without mercy for that same peace.

Since the founding of the United States, consistent efforts have been made to place the nation on a path to peace and prosperity. Yet the country has been plagued with problems at home and abroad; American history is often taught as if it were a series of wars. The lineup of U.S. presidents shows many styles of leadership; a few presidents were great, while others left trouble as they left office. The country has undergone cycles of economic crisis, and even recently the nation's whole economy was on the edge of disaster. But thanks in part to the Iroquois sharing their concept of the Great Peace Confederacy, the United States overcame the approach of *kill, conquer, and occupy*, and democracy has led the way, as though from darkness into brilliant light. However, our nation's practice of democracy has also been plagued by shadows of despair: the despair of poverty-stricken people divided from the extremely wealthy. The division between the very poor and the wealthiest citizens has been solidified: in day-to-day life and in laws and policies that perpetuate the divide. The rich rule, in spite of democratic governance. This is no surprise to most of us.

Today our economy cannot live without the reality of war in various parts of the globe. We need to "lift the sky" for American politics around the world, so that other countries have a good example of what is going on in the United States. The ideals of democracy are good, but Americanized politics remains a step behind. Self-interest keeps it falling short of the political principles established by the nation's founders. This reminds me of a story from when I was in college. I was taking a psychology class. My friend was in a different psychology class. We studied the precepts of the same story. It was a story of an African American woman who was oppressed by almost everyone with whom she was in contact. However, she didn't give up. She grew beyond the tempest of prejudice, racism, and others' presumed superiority. Through her training, education, and maturity she became a leader in her region. Now she sees, she's in a place where she could become the oppressor, instead of the oppressed. But as a woman, a giver of life, she used her decisiveness to increase the chances of life for her people.

Oppressors in the Old Countries treated Europeans badly, and white America kept turning the old wheel of violence and subjugation upon the aboriginal tribes of America. The book *Indian Oratory: Famous Speeches by Noted Indian Chieftains* contains shining examples of Indian oratory from across this continent.[20] The speeches of my father, Joe Hillaire, sound similar to Indian oratory of earlier speakers. Listen to Indian speakers of today address their people: Vine Deloria Jr., Oren Lyons, Dennis Banks, or your local tribal chair. All convey the same message: "Wise up; we're still here. Let's make the most of what we have left."

TECUMSEH'S VISION OF AN INDIAN CONFEDERACY

Chief Tecumseh of the Shawnee was a vibrant person. His love was not just for land; it was for his people. His mature vision came at just the right time in history to intelligently observe white America and Indian America: to see the interactions and to understand the reasons behind each group's actions, interactions, and ultra-actions, between and among themselves. Tecumseh was also a warrior. Controlling his own behavior, he saw answers for the confusions between white America and red America. My mother taught us Tecumseh's self-control behavior. She told us: "If you have self-control, you can go anywhere." And by that time, we knew that it was a big world.

The following legend grew from my mother's instruction, in connection with a book on the subject of Tecumseh.[21] Tecumseh traveled determinedly from tribe to tribe, up and down the Mississippi and Missouri Rivers. He brought together leaders and warriors at their own sites, up and down these major rivers. His message began with a small flame in his heart for the safety of the children, the safety of the elders, and the possibility of the tribes remaining in the land where each was born and lived. At these council meetings, he made sure they served "Black Drink." This tea, brewed from the dried leaves of the yaupon holly (*Ilex vomitoria*) was partaken of by Southeastern Indians in social gatherings, and it was used as physical and spiritual medicine.[22] In Tecumseh's conferences, Black Drink enhanced the thought process of the participants.

Tecumseh proclaimed to each tribe, in flowing oratory, the need for all tribes to unite in one cause, and that was to keep their homelands. His aim was to form a confederacy of all the tribes of the Ohio Valley, up and down the Mississippi and Missouri Rivers. He worked along with his brother, the spiritual leader Tenskwatawa, to bring Indian people together.[23] He acted in unity with the warriors, who knew the land; the warriors, who had wisdom with all their might; the warriors, who could read the behavior of the lost and find white soldiers who didn't know their way around that world. As he gathered the warriors here, there, and everywhere, without knowing it, Tecumseh helped make the Black Drink popular among tribes in that large region. Today, my relatives and I exclaim, "Let's go for a Black Water ceremony," and we have coffee and talk. But we grow weary of coffee, as Tecumseh and his followers must have grown weary of Black Drink. The idea is still there: to stop overpopulation and the ruination of Mother Earth. She is still sacred to us.

As time went on, methods of violence—and our methods of surviving it—cycled. The government records tell the story. So also, words that stem from the deepest roots of truth continued to be spoken and written. In 2001 historian Howard Zinn wrote, "There is no flag large enough to cover the shame of killing innocent people for a purpose which is unattainable."[24] And so we must believe that our time has come. Dare we must to trust the wise people of our country and to find in our history those truths that must be analyzed, at least into graceful comments.

The time of the first contact between Indians and Europeans was not that long ago, and since then we have lived through many stages of American Indian history. The violence of injustice against Indian America has taken different forms, but it has not ended. And so we must find a way forward as Americans on common ground. U.S. Indian policy is still not free of the oppressive ideas contained in the papal bulls. It is time to reject the Doctrine of Discovery. Together we stand; together we soar.

CHAPTER 3

Centuries of Injustice

In the changing circumstances of the new United States, the government tried various policies to deal with the "Indian Problem." The stage was being set for a clash of cultures across the nation, which eventually reached the tribes of the Pacific Northwest. The main players were the settlers (some of whom were paid in land to help establish the new nation's coast-to-coast ownership), traders, government officials, Indian agents, military forces, and missionaries. The other players were the Native people of the Pacific Northwest Coast, of whom there were many, because of the land's bountiful resources, and because at first, they were not yet decimated by disease and the loss of lands, waters, and resources.

The U.S. government grouped the many Native communities in western Washington into a smaller number of "tribes," to simplify their dealings with Indians in both the treaties and in the administrative burdens that followed. As I said in my book *A Totem Pole History*, we identified ourselves by our house: "They don't say 'clan,' they don't say 'tribe,' they don't say 'I come from Bellingham.' They say, 'I come from the house of Haeteluk'"[1] One or more extended family houses was a named community or village, each with its own leaders. Villages were connected by family relationships, culture, and economy. But the idea of large "tribes" in western Washington, with many villages under one leader, was an idea invented by U.S. policy makers for their own convenience.

Government officials and scholars sometime called villages "bands." "Band" could also refer to a small group that lived apart from larger communities.[2]

Indian policy existed even before the United States formally established its new government. One of the most important documents of U.S. Indian policy is the Northwest Ordinance of 1787. In those days, the "Northwest" was not the Pacific Northwest, but the area northwest of the Ohio River, which was the far northwest region of the new America. The document states the following: "The utmost good faith shall always be observed towards the Indians; their lands and properties shall never be taken from them *without their consent* [emphasis added]; and in their property, rights and liberty, they never shall be invaded or disturbed, unless in *just and lawful wars* authorized by Congress [emphasis added]; but laws found in justice and humanity shall from time to time be made, for preventing wrongs being done to them, and for preserving peace and friendship with them."[3] But notice the loopholes, especially when it comes to not taking Indian lands without Indian "consent" or "just and lawful wars." The language of the Northwest Ordinance is carefully written and flatters white America falsely. Loopholes like this were, and still are, used to defray Indian land claims against the United States. One of the lessons for us is that attention to language is also important when making land claims against the federal government.

George Washington was a major influence on the future of U.S. Indian policy. He spelled out an approach that set a course for the future, whether he thought of it himself or was mainly expressing ideas of the leaders of his time. In a speech to Congress in 1791, two years after his election as the first U.S. president, he said of Indians:

> It is to be sincerely desired that all need of coercion in future may cease; and that an intimate intercourse may succeed, calculated to advance the happiness of the Indians, and to attach them firmly to

the United States. In order to do this it seems necessary — that they should experience the benefits of an impartial dispensation of justice; that the mode of alienating their lands, the main source of discontent and war, should be so defined and regulated as to obviate imposition and, as far as may be practicable, controversy concerning the reality and extent of the alien nations which are made; that commerce with them should be promoted under regulations tending to secure an equitable deportment towards them, and such rational experiments should be made, for imparting to them the blessings of civilization as may, from time to time, suit their condition; that the Executive of the United States should be enabled to employ the means to which the Indians have been long accustomed for uniting their immediate interests with the preservation of peace; and that efficacious provision should be made for inflicting adequate penalties upon all those who, by violating their rights, shall infringe the treaties, and endanger the peace of the union. The system corresponding with the mild principles of religion and philanthropy, towards an unenlightened race of man, his happiness materially depends on the conduct of United States, would be as honorable to the national character as conformable to the dictates of sound policy.[4]

In this portion of Washington's speech we see themes that continue to play out in the history of U.S. Indian policy. His speech sounds noble but contains the following presumptions: (1) Indians are uncivilized, and (2) Indian policy should keep the peace, which is hard to keep when one's nation is usurping other nations' lands and freedoms. Washington did, however, express the belief that treaties with Indian nations, like the United States' treaties with European nations, deserve to be ratified by the U.S. government in order to be considered binding, and that precedent has continued.[5]

Dealings concerning Indians were first conducted under the U.S. Department of War. The *Checklist of United States Public Documents, 1789–1909*, gives this summary of the government agencies responsible for Indian policy:

The earliest ordinances for regulating intercourse with the Indians antedate [predate] the establishment of the Federal Government. The Act establishing the Department of War, August 7, 1789, assigned the supervision of the Indian Affairs to that department, and from the beginning there were, in the parts of the country occupied by Indians, officials who exercised, sometimes in connection with another office, the duties of a "superintendent of Indian Affairs." Acts with various provisions for regulating trade with the Indians were passed on March 3, 1793, April 18, 1796, March 30, 1802 and subsequent dates. The office in Washington seems to have had its beginning in the appointment, under Act of April 21, 1806 (Statute L, V. 2, p. 402), of a "superintendent of Indian trade, whose duty it shall be to purchase and take charge of all goods intended for trade with the Indians. This office was abolished by act of May 6, 1822. The Office of Indian Affairs was established March, 1824, and placed on its present footing by Act approved July 9, 1832 (Stat. L, v. 4, p. 564) which made provision for the appointment of a "commissioner of Indian affairs, who shall, under the direction of the Secretary of War . . . have the direction and management of all Indian affairs, and all matters arising out of Indian relations. On the organization of the Department of the Interior by act of March 3, 1849 (Stat. L. v. 9, p. 395), this office was made one of the bureaus of said department, with which it has since been connected.[6]

The first four commissioners of Indian Affairs, from 1832 to 1845 (under Presidents Jackson and Van Buren) reported to the U.S. secretary of war. Beginning with President Polk, they reported to the secretary of the interior.[7] Indian policy varied under the many different U.S. administrations, and attitudes toward Indians could override policy. Felix S. Cohen writes in his 1942 *Handbook of Federal Indian Law* that the commissioners of Indian Affairs "have set forth in the Commissioners' *Annual Reports*, and in unofficial writings, their views on "the Indian question," and that these expressions are in many ways the most useful guides to the variations of Government Indian policy."[8] Of the thirty-three commissioners during the first hundred years of official U.S./Indian relations, only two, George W. Manypenny (1853–57) and John Collier (1933–45), seemed to commend Indian culture and survival.

John Collier was appointed commissioner of Indian Affairs during the presidency of Franklin D. Roosevelt. Collier's reforms were a dramatic change from earlier policies of suppression and removal. Collier admired the aboriginal value system, which he said was essential to the preservation of Indian life and added to the strength of American culture as a whole. It was under Collier that the Wheeler-Howard Act or Indian Reorganization Act (IRA) was passed in 1934. The Wheeler-Howard Act rejected the failed policies that tried to assimilate Indians into white society; it turned in the direction of restoring Indian America's tribal self-determination, albeit in a limited way. Collier accomplished a great deal, but he was not able to succeed with all the reforms that were needed.

Back in 1832 the first Indian commissioner, Elbert Herring, had written: "tribes numerous and powerful have disappeared from among us in a ratio of decrease, ominous to the existence of those that still remain, unless counteracted by the substitution of some principle sufficiently potent to check the tendencies to decay and dissolution. This salutary principle exists in the system of removal; of change of residence; of settlement in territories exclusively their own, and under the protection of the United States; connected with the benign influences of education and instruction in agriculture and the several mechanic arts, whereby social is distinguished from savage life."[9]

In Herring's 1832 report, he commended the policy of removing Indians to west of the Mississippi, to clear the eastern United States for white settlement: "In the consummation of this grand and sacred object rests the sole chance of averting Indian annihilation. Founded in pure and disinterested motives, may it meet the approval of heaven, by complete attainment of its beneficent ends!"[10] If this was not a grievous comment, then it was tough love. For Indians, removal was ultimately cruel. However, appearing also in Herring's 1832 report is "the first mention of vaccination as a health measure for the benefit of the Indians, and the employment of physicians by the Bureau."[11] This was not his only effort to benefit the Indians; he recommended "something, however simple, in the shape of a code of laws, suited to their wants . . . devised and submitted for their adoption, to obviate the inconveniences, and secure the benefits incident thereto, in the relations that are springing up under the fostering care of the Government."[12] Herring also supported President Jackson's practice of using of military force for Indian removal.[13]

I can understand the confusion felt by Indians long ago. Somehow, the United States seemed to recognize the right of Indian nations as sovereign nations with property rights, while at the same time, it assumed its own right to extinguish Indian title to land and had a low opinion of Indian people:

> As impatience of regular labor, exhibited in unsteadiness of application, is the radical defect of the Indian character, it is but a dictate of common sense to address ourselves first and mainly to its correction. This effected, a foundation is laid upon which our best hopes for the reclamation of the savage may be safely built. Without it, no matter to what extent we may educate a few individuals of a tribe, lasting good is rarely produced. The merely book-taught Indian, if the radical failing be unreformed, is almost certain to resume, at length, the barbarism of his original condition, deriving no other advantages from his acquirements than a more refined cunning, and a greater ability to concoct and perpetrate schemes of mischief and violence.[14]

Just when and how we were labeled "savages," "depraved," and "lazy," and so on, I do not know, but some Indian Affairs officials had a good word to say about us. Some of them praised the land, our Mother Earth, and I am grateful for that. The historical records of U.S. Indian policy contain debates among U.S. officials about the merits of amelioration, bold shows of military power, and various efforts to "civilize" Indian people. Within these debates, the Indians' right of occupancy was their only stronghold, a right that even some European political thinkers were motivated to uphold.[15]

It was not only the violence of ideology and policy that Indians faced; citizens too, could be violent: Indian commissioner George W. Manypenny wrote, "In the din and strife between the anti-slavery and pro-slavery parties with reference to the condition of the African race there, and in which the rights of the red man have been completely overlooked and disregarded, the good conduct and patient submission of the latter contrasts favorably with the disorderly and lawless conduct of many of their white brethren, who, while they have quarreled about the African, have united upon the soil of Kansas in wrongdoing toward the Indian."[16]

Manypenny believed that Indians needed their own fixed and permanent habitations:

> Without a fixed, permanent, and settled home, in my opinion, all efforts to domesticate and civilize the aboriginal race will, hereafter, be as they have heretofore, prove of but little benefit or advantage. Many think that, with all the efforts and means that may be put into requisition, the extinction of the race cannot be prevented, that it must decay and waste away; and this view is strengthened by the experience of the past. But if this be so, it does not discharge the government of the United States and its citizens from the performance of their duty; and every effort is demanded by humanity to avert a calamity of this kind. Many of the Indians are impressed with the idea that they belong to a race that shall become extinct, and the opinion produces such gloom, despondency, and even despair, as to wither their energy and destroy their aspirations.[17]

Manypenny wrote these remarks in a report in 1855—twenty-five years after the Indian Removal had started more upheaval for tribes across America.

INDIAN REMOVAL

The Indian Removal Act of 1830 authorized the federal government to negotiate with tribes for removal from their lands, forcing westward many Native people whose homelands were in the eastern United States, so that white Americans could have the eastern lands.[18] Making treaties would enable the U.S. government to claim, at least theoretically, that tribes had agreed to move, paving the way for removal. President James Monroe allowed for removal of Indians in his 1824 Message to Congress, and a decade later, Andrew Jackson was the president in charge of removal.

Look at a map of the present-day reservation lands in the United States and notice how little Indian land remains east of the Mississippi and Missouri Rivers.[19] Starting in 1830, the U.S. Congress ordered removal of Indian tribes from the eastern United States to lands west of the Mississippi and Missouri Rivers.[20] Among the events that followed was the Cherokee Trail of Tears in 1938–39.[21] This was not the only removal that occurred; the Long Walk of the Navajo, for instance, took place in the 1860s.[22]

By the middle of the nineteenth century, the westward surge of white America grew even more expansive: white America also wanted the western lands. In 1841 John Canfield Spencer, the secretary of war under President John Tyler, wrote in his report: "The policy of removing the Indians from their Native homes, to make room for the white man, and of collecting them in large bodies on our western frontier, is not now debatable."[23] The government documents show that the next U.S. policy strategy was to force Indians in western America out of their homelands, too. Fewer than twenty years after Congress passed the Indian Removal Act of 1830, which was supposed to leave the western lands for Indians, the government was at work to take Indian lands in the Pacific Northwest.

DISPOSSESSION REACHES THE NORTHWEST

In 1850 the acting commissioner of the Department of the Interior, A. S. Loughery, wrote to three new Indian commissioners of their appointment "to negotiate treaties with the several Indian tribes in the Territory of Oregon for the extinguishment of their claims to lands lying west of the Cascade Mountains, under the act of 5th June last."[24] This vast region was, and still is, the ancestral homeland of many Pacific Northwest tribes and bands.

The tract of country lying west of the Cascade Mountains, extending to the Pacific Ocean, reaches from 42° to 49°, and has considerable width. It is inhabited by numerous tribes of Indians, many of them small in numbers, and others comprising two, three, and four hundred warriors; some at the extreme south and others at the extreme north. There are some ten or twelve of them. Our knowledge on that subject is not very accurate. It rests mainly on the observation of those who have resided there temporarily, some of them for two or three years. The locality of these is not well known.[25]

In 1850 E. A. Starling, Indian agent for District of Puget Sound, wrote the following in his first report to the superintendent of Indian Affairs: "Shortly after my arrival [at Steilacoom], although the rainy season had commenced, the Indians came by tribes to see me, being impelled thereto seemingly by curiosity and an expectation of receiving presents; and all extremely desirous to learn the intentions of the government in regard to purchasing their lands."[26]

My father, Joe Hillaire, taught me that the many tribes and villages had runners, who carried news of the progressions of the whites. Potlatches had been our custom since long ago. The giving of gifts, therefore, was greatly expected. Any news of land purchases was important for Indians to hear about. Time passed, and the influx of settlers continued. With conflict over Indian lands that were being inhabited by the new settlers, anxiety on the part of the tribes, and impatience on the part of white America, tensions ran high. The federal government wanted to clear coastal Washington of Indian people and move them to the plateau region, east of the Cascade Mountains. In his letter stating the government's aim to extinguish Indian title to lands on the ocean side of the Cascades, Indian commissioner Loughery speaks of the white settlers' frustration to gain possession of lands: "The inhabitants complain that they have been there for several years and have been obliged to make settlements, improvements, etc., and not one of them can claim a perfect title to any portion of the soil they occupy. It is indispensable that this question be settled in some form or other."[27]

Efforts to remove Washington's coastal people to the other side of the mountains failed (see chapter 8, "Aboriginal Fishermen"). This removal attempt, aimed at Coast Salish fishing tribes, took place in 1850, five years before the signing of our treaty! The government intended to take over all Indian coastal lands for white industry and occupancy: "The object of the government is to extinguish the title of the Indians to all the lands lying west of the Cascade mountains, and, if possible, to provide for the removal of the whole from the west to the east of the mountains; but should you fail in inducing the whole to remove, you will then induce as many as you can procure acquisitions of territory from; but no effort should be untried to procure the removal of the whole, thereby leaving the country free for settlement by the whites."[28]

Indian commissioner Loughery's 1850 report represents the thinking of U.S. officials on the subject of how they could justify paying the lowest possible price:

> It is presumed the lands to be ceded will not be found to be of any very great value, and in many cases it is presumed the consideration will be merely nominal; but in others, where the land is of more value, of course a greater sum will be allowed. The maximum price given for Indian land has been ten cents per acre, but this has been for small quantities of great value from their contiguity to the States; and, it is merely mentioned to show that some important consideration has always been involved when so large a price has been given.[29]

This paragraph of small print ends with the following remark, which outlines the practice that Indians should be "paid" for their ceded lands, not in money, but in goods and services: "it is extremely desirable that the whole annuity be absorbed, by treaty stipulation, in objects beneficial to the Indians, and that no part of it shall be paid to them in money. The objects provided for should be agricultural assistance, employment of blacksmiths and mechanics, farmers to teach them how to cultivate the soil, physicians, and above all, ample provisions for purposes of education. After providing for the objects, if any portion of the money remain, it should be stipulated that it be paid in goods to be delivered to them in their own country."[30]

Such an unjust transaction would not be acceptable today, especially for the beautiful Pacific Northwest region. The government's equivocation on "payment"—calling inadequate services and inferior goods "payment" for our land—is part of our ahistory. Many Americans recognize that Indians were cheated but are unaware of the means and the extent, and how this still affects modern Indian life. For Indian America, U.S. commitments not honored still reverberate. Dare we correct the ahistorical status of Indian America to give Indians credit where credit is due, and open the door to total pride for white America, not just partial pride? Can we straighten out the twists in the way that this history is remembered?

At times, the U.S. government assured protection for American Indians and white settlers in the same areas, with the aims of protecting borders and minimizing conflict between the two groups. As the centuries moved on, it is plain to see that some of the individuals who worked between the U.S. government and Indians tried as best they could, under difficult conditions, to carve out a life and culture for both Euro-Americans and Indians. It has not been said enough that Indians, as products of their environment, were contented people whose every need was met by their landscape: for food, shelter, trade, ceremonies, and so on. Indians of the great Pacific Northwest already had permanent homes and all the accommodations of a civilized world in the perfect order of nature, which had worked for centuries. Theirs was a complete economy, encompassing all facets of their lives as individuals, families, and communities. It is this complete culture and economy that made their Indian civilization.

But for the most part, white America saw white civilization as the only real civilization. It is no wonder that white America was so opposed to the diversity of the two cultures. One was solidly grounded in the natural environment and in principles that were unwritten, but understood. The other was caught in the confusion of creating new economic and governmental systems for two civilizations (one of them not its own), with its own government under construction, while adapting from an old world to a new one. Building a single government that incorporated our two very different cultures would have been extremely difficult in this country's old days.

NEW ARRIVALS IN THE NORTHWEST

Imagine the rapid whiskey trade in the Pacific Northwest and its newness to Indian America, the discovery of gold along the Fraser River, ever new immigrating settlers, buildings going up, canneries—the excitement of it all—traders, settlers, gold miners, Indians, military officers and accompanying soldiers. Before the Oregon Treaty was signed in 1846, the United States and Great Britain were vying for land, with slogans like "54-40 or fight," referring to the northern boundary of the Oregon Country. U.S. officials commanded agents prevent the British Hudson's Bay Company from setting up any more forts or trading posts and to stop U.S. Indians from trading on the Canadian side. A publication of the Whatcom Museum in Bellingham estimates that during 1858, the year of the Fraser River gold rush, the non-Indian population of Whatcom County, where the Lummi Reservation is located, went from fewer than one hundred to nearly ten thousand.[31] With this picture in mind, it is easier to understand the complexities, as well as the different goals, of the various kinds of people involved in this span of history. It gives one an idea of what was really happening at this time in the Northwest: a "duke's mixture" of people and varieties of confusion about America's aboriginal people, who were probably as good as other aboriginal people in the world, maybe better than many other "civilized" people. My heart breaks for them as I read of their real experiences with the U.S. government, of which they initially knew nothing.

Liquor was just one of the white man's weapons. In his 1842 report as the secretary of war, John C. Spencer wrote that the circulars and instructions given to Indian agents, superintendents, and military commanders did little good against distribution of "ardent spirits" to Indians:

"The cupidity of the white man, boasting of his superior civilization, stimulates his craft in devising the means of evading the laws, and still further brutalizing his ignorant, weak, and yielding red brother."[32]

The Indian Affairs reports tell how depositories for liquor were erected in Indian country, where the government had not yet devised laws regulating liquor distribution. Page after page of Indian commissioners' reports nearly wear out the words about alcohol and "depraved Indians," owing to the introduction of alcohol by the British and the Americans. Liquor was often watered down—sometimes mixed with peppers to make it taste stronger ("firewater")—and liquor was mixed with who-knows-what other dangerous fluids, so that traders could make even more profit, while taking advantage of inebriated Indians. Exactly whose fault is it that these Indians were "depraved" and miserable? Aren't all alcoholics in this same predicament? But who brought alcohol onto this continent? Aren't they also depraved and miserable? Can't we together conquer the enemy of alcohol abuse?

INDIAN POLICY: CRIME OR REASON?

If we review American history with open eyes, we see a variety of forms of genocide against Indian America: over five hundred years of destruction and annihilation. Some justifications defend the progress of the new American civilization. But are we any better off now than what the old European countries suffered before explorations across the Atlantic? I fear counting the lives lost through the wars we've been through, plus lives lost due to new diseases, AIDS, cancer, and just plain poverty, which afflicts cultures throughout the United States. The only Americans free of having racism and classism burden the depth of their life force are those who possess wealth and power: the descendants of the White Fathers, those who gained their wealth in our aboriginal peoples' loss of life, freedom, and the resources of our homelands.

Joel Palmer, superintendent of Indian Affairs for the Oregon Territory, reported the following in 1854 about his visit to several bands of Umpquas, a tribe of present-day Oregon:

They said, truly, that they were once numerous and powerful but now few and weak; that they had always been friendly to the whites, and desired them to occupy their lands; that they wanted but a small spot in which they might live in quiet. Many of their number they said had been killed by the whites, in retaliation for wrongs committed by Indians of other tribes, but that they had never offered violence in return. That they should receive the means of subsistence for the few years that they will exist, they claim to be but just, in return for lands once yielding them abundant supplies. A few presents were made them, and sub-agent Martin instructed (A) to secure them small tracts of land, on which I learn they are now cultivating potatoes, corn, peas, and other vegetables, giving promise that under the wise and fostering government they may become a domestic and agricultural people.[33]

In the extensive reports explaining why these Indians were so destitute, it was made clear that they were refused guns and ammunition for hunting, and their root crops were destroyed by settlers' occupation of their land and by unusually severe winters. Other conditions destroyed their courage. These explanations appear in a government agent's report of 1854, the year of our Point Elliott treaty negotiations. A report by Commissioner Manypenny, written just a year after the signing of the Treaty of Point Elliott, conveys this message to Congress: "It cannot be disguised that a portion of the white population of the Pacific Territories entertain feelings deeply hostile to the Indian tribes of that region, and are anxious for the extermination of the race."[34] So, in my uncovering the ahistory of Indian America you must understand why I go through tears, laughter, astonishment, and hope for a better road for all of us.

In the twentieth century our main claims would be for our lands and fishing rights. Back in the mid-nineteenth century, Manypenny reported on how the rage for land speculation affected Native rights:

The existing laws for the protection of the persons and property of the Indian wards of the government are sadly defective. New and more stringent statutes are required. . . . The rage for speculation and the wonderful desire to obtain choice lands, which seems to possess so many of those [settlers] who go into our new territories, causes them to lose sight of and entirely overlook the rights of the aboriginal inhabitants. The most dishonorable expedients have, in many cases, been made use of to dispossess the Indian; demoralizing means employed to obtain his property; and, for the want of adequate laws, the department is now often perplexed and embarrassed, because of inability to afford prompt relief and apply the remedy in cases obviously requiring them.[35]

Commissioner Manypenny also wrote: "To preserve their property and to give them the blessings of education and Christianity is indispensable to their continuing 'long in the land' which God gave to their fathers and to them, I sincerely hope that our government will have the aid of all its good citizens to faithfully executing its high trust and discharging its obligations to the remnants of the Indian tribes now left to its oversight and guardianship, so that they shall be intelligently and generously protected and cared for in all that makes life useful and happy."[36] What a statement. And what a name: "Manypenny."

Look at how our original treaty membership is growing. It's a miracle! Not only did we survive, but we are growing in greater numbers with every generation.[37] My extended family is expanding in each generation from me to my children, grandchildren, and great-grandchildren. My great-great-grandfathers were among the leaders who signed the Treaty of 1855, and they received allotments via the Dawes Allotment Act. There was nothing for the rest of us; five, six, and more generations are out in the cold. If it weren't for the HUD Home Program, first introduced to Lummi in the early 1970s, I would have nothing at all. I am left out of my parents' land because of the de facto termination tactics of the Bureau of Indian Affairs: hidden and unfair policies regarding inheritance. I am left out of fishing because I am too old. My family consequently loses out too. So, why shouldn't I worry? They are just as worthy and beautiful as any other people I've seen in all my years.

Indians remain disadvantaged when it comes to the economy. In the

Northwest, we have and sell salmon, but that resource has been depleting for a century. We cannot "gather" from the wild environment as we used to do a century or more ago. Our neighbors, "white people," do not allow us to gather from the forest (where there are now only a few trees anyway). But we need cedar, spruce, oak, and alder, and we need to pick berries and gather barks and herbs—all the cultural things normally done in our locale. "Trade" is out of the question until the tribe sets up a "trading post" near the freeway, where we can sell our cottage-type products. This would give us a chance, but it will not make us wealthy.

I refuse to overlook our progress as a tribe. I give our tribal leaders credit where credit is due; they are slowly getting to where they can make changes. They have succeeded with many projects such as repatriation and tax reforms; they have provided an economic base, developed a school for our Lummi youth, provided for elders' needs with the Little Bear Creek Assisted Living center, and established a transit facility, a mini-mart gas station, a small grocery store, a casino, and a hotel. They continue a program at our reservation-based college, Northwest Indian College, in "Indianpreneurship" that prepares graduates for small business operation and encourages artisans in their respective fields of art. The roads have light fixtures, just like downtown. Sidewalks are being constructed. New homes and new trailers are being provided for those in need of homes. But more space is needed upon which to build homes, for thousands more persons. We pray that we will never repeat the days of great deprivation that we knew in earlier history. It may not have been done on purpose, but it occurred, through delays due to the distance between Washington DC and the Pacific Northwest, because of poor planning and miscommunication, because of greed and a sense of entitlement, and because of abhorrence for, or just disregard of, Indian people.

Indian Policy: Crime (not rhyme) or Reason? The answer can only be crime. But how many dare to look into the records and the unwritten history of the United States? For a country like America, stopping large-scale violence would require restructuring our nation in a new direction, away from the destruction inherited from—and displayed by—the "great powers" of the world. Our roads, our bridges, our buildings, our dams, our minds: we must ready ourselves for efforts other than the destruction of our neighboring nations.

Discovering America was not an act of heroism. It was partly an act of desperation for white America to come from the Old Countries of Europe. And the shock to Indian America seems unending. Meanwhile, back in the wilderness, our great white forefathers were making themselves rich, in accord with principles introduced by the Doctrine of Discovery and the papal bulls, the latter of which authorized subjugation of "heathens." And this is what they judged Indians to be, despite our belief in the Great Spirit, Mother Earth, and the Creator. Today, discrimination occurs in forms such as low wages and underemployment of Indian people, who are often either undereducated or overeducated for the jobs for which they apply. Our dream of a higher goal is aborted at that point. And as laid-back as we are, many have simply accepted this bleak fate.

It's easy to forget the Indian civilizations. However, they were so firmly established in their unique forms of government derived from their tribal unions, family, community, arts, music, and ceremony. They were aesthetically and spiritually organized according to the laws of nature in their traditional territories, such that one cannot imagine their thriving best anywhere except in their own homelands. Displacement is a first step in cultural genocide.

From the very beginning of U.S. Indian policy, continuing through the present day's neglect of Indian American rights, and with the immigration of new populations from many countries around the world, it is easy to see which group is dominant in American society. This book calls for renewed attention to Indian America: from the U.S. president, Congress, Indian Affairs officials, and American citizens. My message? Well, first of all, do you think that the issues brought forward from the records of U.S. history are loud and clear enough? A first step is better understanding America's Indian history and the continuing effects of that history for American Indian people today.

CHAPTER 4

Reservation Creation

This Constitution, and the laws of the United States which shall be made in pursuance thereof; and all Treaties made, or which shall be made, under the Authority of the United States, shall be the Supreme Law of the Land.
—U.S. Constitution, Article 6, Sect. 2

I wish to exclude the Man of 1492 in this chapter; he has been covered in a previous chapter anyway. But he cannot be completely overlooked, for this book suggests that Indian America's history has been forgotten, or put aside. However, treaties that were made across the entire United States cannot be discarded so easily. Nearly four hundred ratified treaties with tribes are currently recognized by the U.S. Department of State.[1] For present purposes, there were three kinds of treaties: (1) peace and friendship treaties, (2) treaties of acquisition, whereby acquisition of land was accomplished by minimal cost or colonization, and (3) treaties accomplished by promises that if a tribe were "removed," other land would be provided for that "removed" tribe, in whole or part. The Treaty of Point Elliott, to which the Lummi and other northern Puget Sound tribes are party, was a treaty of acquisition. It is also a peace treaty, in which the tribes promised to be friendly to U.S. citizens, make no depredations on them, and avoid war with other tribes, except in self-defense.

HOW THE NORTHWEST WAS LOST

Now we take up our early history of how the United States obtained the Indian lands of the Northwest. The secretary of war wrote the following in a letter dated August 31, 1848: "The President of the United

States has judged proper that the United States be divided into two military geographical divisions; and that each division be subdivided into military departments."[2]

Along with the two divisions, Eastern and Western, the U.S. government created the Third or Pacific Division. The Pacific Division had two departments: No. 10, the Territory of California, and No. 11, the Territory of Oregon.[3] The Oregon Territory stretched from the Rocky Mountains to the Pacific Ocean; the Oregon Territory covered all the land north of California to the 49th parallel (the northern border of present-day Washington State), where the United States and Britain had drawn the line in the 1846 Treaty of Oregon (map 3). The Oregon Territory was assigned a regiment of mounted riflemen (sixty-four men to a regiment) and two companies of the Fourth Artillery. The task of the military in the California and Oregon Territories was to "establish posts and garrisons within their respective commands."[4]

At that time in history it took several months to travel from the East Coast of North America to the West Coast. Today this transit takes but a few hours by air; however, before the railroads it was a hard journey overland on the Oregon Trail or by sea. Hazard Stevens's biography of his father, Isaac I. Stevens (1818–62), Washington Territory's first governor and superintendent of Indian Affairs, contains an account of the family's journey from Massachusetts to Washington Territory via Panama. They left by ship in late September and reached Olympia in December, after a difficult journey, during which Mrs. Stevens and their young daughter became ill with Panama fever.[5]

President James Polk, in his 1848 address to Congress, said the following about early U.S. failures of diplomacy with the Pacific Northwest tribes:

It is the policy of humanity, and one which has always been pursued by the United States, to cultivate the good will of the aboriginal tribes of this continent, and to restrain them from making war, and indulging in excesses, by mild means, rather than by force. That this could have been done with the tribes in Oregon, had that Territory been brought under the government of our laws at any earlier period, and had suitable measures been adopted by Congress, such as now exist in our intercourse with the other Indian tribes within our limits, cannot be doubted. Indeed, the immediate and only cause of the existing hostility of the Indians of Oregon is represented to have been, the long delay of the United States in making to them some trifling compensation, in such articles as they wanted, for the country now occupied by our emigrants, which the Indians claimed and over which they formerly roamed [*author's note*: inhabited].

This compensation was promised these Indians by the temporary government established in Oregon, but its fulfillment had been postponed for around two years whilst those who made the promise had been anxiously waiting for Congress to establish a territorial government over the country. . . . A few thousand dollars in suitable presents, as a compensation for the country which had been taken possession of by our citizens, would have satisfied the Indians, and have prevented the war.[6]

A few thousand dollars in "suitable presents"! An 1841 report of the secretary of war shows that the U.S. government intended to occupy and possess Pacific Northwest Indian homelands, using military force against the Indians as necessary, well before the treaties were enacted: "it is indispensable that a chain of posts should be established, extending from the Council Bluffs [Iowa] to the mouth of the Columbia River [at the Pacific Ocean on the border of present-day Oregon and Washington], so as to command the avenues by the which the Indians pass from the north to the south; and the same time maintain a communication with the territories belonging to us in the Pacific."[7] The treaties in northwest Washington Territory were signed in 1854 and 1855, so this quotation from Secretary of War John C. Spencer shows that the United States had presumed its power and ownership at least thirteen years before that.

From long before the first meeting to negotiate our Treaty of 1855, the white government has been dishonorable. We must break through those ears of stone, and if we come from the Stone Age, can we or can we not do that? Many Indian leaders and authors have answered *yes* to this question. But Indians' calls for justice and land rights have not been understood or accepted, given that we have not received an adequate response the U.S. Congress, or from any president, to alleviate the pains for land of the U.S. tribes, who from the beginning have been treated dishonorably or, at best, ambivalently.

If only the silent occupancy of Indian people could have been recognized. If only, as in our historic oral tradition, Indians could now describe the lands they occupied for sustenance, and the government accepted this. Based on information provided by Lummi elders born in the nineteenth century, my father, Joe Hillaire (1894–1967), made the map, showing Lummi boundaries and village sites, that was submitted as evidence in the 1927 U.S. Court of Claims case *Duwamish Tribe of Indians et al. v. U.S.* The court rejected the map because it was not "ancient," "official," or "made by surveyors."[8] While the details of Indian policy changed according to changes in leadership among the great white fathers, some things have not changed for Indian America. Reforming Indian policy requires overcoming the thinking behind the Doctrine of Discovery, which still has influence today. And to do that, we must remember our own rights and communicate to government leaders the basis of those rights.

GOVERNMENT REPORTS ABOUT THE COAST SALISH

Traveling agents of the government were assigned to investigate the tribes: each tribe's habitat, habits, resources, and whether or not they were "warlike." If the tribe was warlike, the government officials were to present them with gifts and to submit annual reports on the situation. If the tribe were friendly, the officials were to make treaties with them. Although this sounds as if it were a smooth operation, it wasn't. Someday one of my descendants will look into the government documents and read the small print to find out just how America thought about us.

In 1849 Joseph Lane, superintendent of Indian Affairs and governor of the Oregon Territory, wrote a report indicating the intentions of the U.S. government to place Indian people on lands separate from non-Indians:

"Surrounded as many of the tribes and bands now are by the whites, whose arts of civilization, by destroying the resources of the Indians, doom them to poverty, want, and crime, the extinguishment of their title by purchase, and the locating them in a district removed from the settlements, is a measure of the most vital importance to them. Indeed the cause of humanity calls loudly for their removal from causes and influences so fatal to their existence. This measure is one of equal interest to our own people."[9]

Reservation creation would require the U.S. government to take a number of counts of Indian residents of the region, and to become familiar with their characteristics. In the "Tribal Member Census of 1841" by Captain Charles Wilkes (a U.S. naval captain exploring the Northwest as part of the U.S. Exploring Expedition, 1838–42), the estimated population between Olympia and Nu-wau-kum River was 2,689. For Lummi, including the Lummi River and Peninsula, Wilkes estimated 450 persons, plus 300 at Birch Bay.[10] According to W. F. Tolmie's "Census of Various Indian Tribes Living on or near Puget's Sound" in the autumn of 1844, for the Lummi (Nooh-lum-mi), there were 65 Men, 57 Women, 52 Boys, 47 Girls, 23 Slaves. Total: 244. Tolmie also counted sixty canoes and fifteen guns.[11]

For Indian Affairs purposes, the Oregon Territory was divided into two sections: North of the Columbia River (present-day Washington) was assigned to Indian agent J. Quinn Thornton and south of the Columbia River (present-day Oregon) to Indian agent Robert Newell. Mr. Thornton called upon thirty tribes and bands north of the river; and Mr. Newell called upon thirty-five, reporting specific details about them. Their reports show that the total number of tribes and bands (sixty-five) was reduced due to land loss, consolidation on multitribal reservations, and sickness.[12]

The Lummi Tribe was spelled the "Nooklulumu" and "Nook-lumi" Tribe, and it was said to number 220 persons. We were called warlike and the disposition to whites was unknown; the Lummi lived by hunting and fishing.[13] Back in 1850 there were many more tribes and bands than there are now. Governor Lane referred to sixty-five that year. The government documents show the history of treaties, land cessions, changing Indian policies, and one tribe or band after another dropping away. They were congregated on reservations with other tribes and bands, traveled to Canada to settle, or were wiped out by disease, smallpox being the most devastating. Only twenty-nine federally recognized tribes remain in the state of Washington today, and most of these tribes do not have their own reservations (map 7).

In 1850 Indian agent E. A. Starling wrote: "it is seldom, if ever the whole tribe is found together. I have asked the chiefs of all the tribes I have seen to find out the number of men, women, and children, and let me know their exact numbers." Counting tribal populations frustrated the Indian agents, and they continued to complain. Starling made a rough map in his memory, for he had no supplies to make one of paper. He estimated that there were 6,320 Indians in and around the Puget Sound region: "I will give the names and location of the tribes on the east side of the sound first: commencing at Budd's inlet, the extreme south of the sound, and going north of the 49th degree of latitude, or Point Roberts, immediately below the mouth of Frazier's [Fraser] river . . . I will then commence at Cape Flattery, on the straits of Fuca, and give the names and location of the tribes inhabiting the west side of the sound to Budd's inlet. The tribes who do not frequent the sound, I will give lastly."[14]

Starling's spelling of the tribes' names makes his report and chart difficult to read. But judging from the description of locations of tribes on his chart, for the "Ne-u-tub-vig," located at the extreme north end of Whitney's [Whidbey] Island and the country between the Skagit River and Bellingham Bay, near today's Lummi Reservation, Starling lists their number as four hundred. This may include Skagit, Samish, and Lummi.

> The Ne-u-lub-vig and Misonks speak the same language, as also I am informed, the Cow-e-na-chino and Noot-hum-mic. None of these four tribes, with an occasional exception of the Ne-u-lub-vigs, ever come into the American settlements. They go to Vancouver's Island to trade . . . The character of all these Indians is similar as a general

thing. They all depend upon fish, berries, and roots for their main subsistence, and all possess a desire to copy after the whites. The pride they take in dressing in cloth, and of being taught to have dropped their savageness, and to have approached, however distantly, to the manners and likeness of the whites, forms a most marked difference between them and the Indians formerly inhabiting the eastern part of the United States.[15]

An 1850 report by Indian commissioner Luke Lea to the superintendent of Indian Affairs spells out the belief that the two alternatives for Indians were acculturation or extinction:

The rapid increase of our population, its onward march from the Missouri frontier westward, and from the Pacific east, steadily lessening and closing up the intervening space, renders it certain that there remains to the red man but one alternative: early civilization, or gradual extinction . . . If this can be attained; if they can be taught to subsist, not by the chase merely [*author's note*: the Indians of the Pacific Northwest did not live by the "chase"]—a resource which must soon be exhausted—but by the rearing of flocks and herds, and by field cultivation, we may hope that the little remnant of this ill-fated race will not utterly perish from the earth, but have a permanent resting place and home on some part of our broad domain, once the land of their fathers.[16]

Three years later, in 1853, Indian commissioner George Manypenny sent a list to Washington territorial governor Isaac Stevens, with specific instructions for collecting more information on the Washington tribes, about which the government still knew very little.[17] Isaac I. Stevens, Washington State's first territorial governor and superintendent of Indian Affairs from 1853 to 1857, reported the following to Congress about our area: "The tribes living upon the eastern shore possess also territory upon the islands, and their usual custom is to resort to them at the end of the salmon season; that is, about the middle of November. It is there that they find the greatest supply of shellfish, which form a large part of their winter stock, and which they dry for both their own use and for sale to those of the interior. The summer and fall they spend on the main, where they get fish and put in their potatoes."[18]

Governor Stevens's estimate of tribal populations in January 1854, a year before the Point Elliott Treaty was signed, gives the following counts: Duwamish, 162, and together under Duwamish: Sa-ma-mish and S'ke-tehl-mish (at Duwamish Lake), 101; Smel-ka-mish, 8; Skoke-dh-mish, 50; St-ka-mish, 30. The number of Duwamish, plus subgroups at the White, Green, and Main White Rivers equals 351. Stevens estimated that there were 300 Skagits, plus 300 more persons under the Skagit heading, in the groups N'qua-cha-mish, Sma-leh-hu, Mis-kai-whu, and Sa-ku-me-hu living along the Skagit River and its branches. An additional 300 persons are listed under Skagit at the north end of "Whitby's" (Whidbey) Island and the "Sinamish" River, in the groups Squi-na-mish, Swo-da-mish, Sin-a-ah-mish; Samish, 150; Nooksack, 450; Lummi, 450; Shim-i-ah-moo, 250.[19]

As regards the current tribes that are parties to the Point Elliott Treaty, such as the Lummi, Nooksack, Upper Skagit, and Swinomish, there were approximately 2,450 persons, according to Stevens's estimates. The area that Stevens describes includes the San Juan Islands and the territory of the Skalakhan (Sq'eláxen) Tribe. His count seemed to have missed the Skalakhan, whose descendants are now part of the Nooksack and Lummi tribes. A few decades later, one of the government's goals was to consolidate the Skalakhan and other island tribes onto the Lummi Reservation. In earlier history, the Skalakhan lived on the islands in our area, but at the time that the government was starting to count Indians, the Skalakhan lived near the Nooksack River in an area around Lake Terrell, near the town we now call Ferndale, where a ferry was operated by Lummi Indians. The Skalakhan were eventually ordered to move to the Lummi area, next to the Lummi village at Fish Point.

George Gibbs, a lawyer, surveyor, and ethnologist who took field notes on Northwest Coast tribes and languages and who was a leader in the writing and negotiation of treaties, reported the following in 1855: "The Lummi, living on a river emptying into the northern part of

Bellingham bay and on the peninsula, are variously estimated at from four to five hundred. Their chief is Sáhhopkan; in general habits they resemble the Clallams. Above the Lummi, on the main fork of the river, which is said to rise in and carry off the water from Mount Baker, is still another considerable tribe called the Nooksahk. They seem to be allied with the Lummi and the Skagit, and . . . speak a mixed language. They are supposed to be about equal in number to the Lummi."[20]

George Gibbs's report mentions two Coast Salish tribes that today live in British Columbia: the Semiahmoo on the mainland and the Cowichan, who are mostly on Vancouver Island. "The Shimiahmoo inhabit the coast towards Frazer River; nothing seems to be known of them whatever. They are probably the most northern tribe on the American side of the line, the Kowailchew lying principally, if not altogether, in British territory."[21] This geographical area was a fishing site for the surrounding tribes, a shellfish-gathering area, kind of an Olympics arena for various Indian sports, a place for canoe racing, curing salmon, and storytelling, a playground for children, and a picnic area "in common" for nearby tribes. At least it was until the white fisheries built traps in front of the Indian reef netting areas. Gibbs gives the following information about the rapid decline of the number of Coast Salish people: "Upon the estimates above stated, the whole number of all the Indians south of Puget's Sound, and between the Cascades and the coast, would amount to about eight hundred and fifty, in place of three thousand, the estimate of Captain Wilkes in 1841—a diminution of –% per annum."[22]

The original document has a dash preceding the percent symbol, with no numeric percentage provided. Captain Wilkes's 1841 population estimate was actually 3,779, not "three thousand." Based on these population estimates of 3,779 being reduced to 850 persons, the deaths over the fifteen-year period would have been about 76 percent, equivalent to 5 percent per year. Regarding the disease and alcohol that was destroying the people, Gibbs wrote:

Scattered as most of them are in small bands at distances apart it hardly seems worthwhile to make arrangements looking forward to permanence or involving great expense . . . They are all intemperate, and can get liquor whenever they choose. They are, besides, diseased beyond remedy, syphilis being with them both hereditary as well as acquired. The speedy extinction of the race seems rather to be hoped for than regretted, and they look forward to it themselves with a sort of indifference. The duty of the government, however, is not affected by their vices, for these they owe, in a great measure, to our own citizens.

Gibbs ponders the future of the several tribes and bands he has reported on:

No essential advantage would, it is feared, be obtained by removing them to any one location, for they would not long remain away from their old haunts, and probably the assignment of a few acres of ground for their villages and cemeteries, and the right of fishing at customary points, would effect all that could be done. Still, if they should manifest such a wish, the experiment might be tried of settling each tribe in one village at some place not yet occupied, and constituting a reserve. This, except during the salmon season, might remove them somewhat further from temptation.[23]

Gibbs's words above are from a report submitted to Congress in 1855, the year that our Point Elliott Treaty was signed.

INDIAN/WHITE RELATIONS

Both Great Britain and America found great trade opportunities with Indians in furs, fish, and other items. The government gave orders about preserving American interests. Indian commissioner Luke Lea wrote to the secretary of the interior of efforts to "embrace every opportunity to impress on the Indians that it is the American government, and not the British, that confers upon them these benefits. The Indian should also be prevented from crossing the line into the British possessions."

Notice was provided in Lea's letter that two Indian agents were appointed to his post, one for east of the mountains and one for west of the mountains. The letter continues with a statement about not pay-ing Indians: "In this connexion, it is proper to mention that it is the policy of the government, as far as possible, to avoid the payment of money, by way of presents or otherwise, to Indians; they are wasteful and improvident, and but rarely expend money for any useful object; they should receive nothing but what will tend to their happiness and comfort."[24]

Since the land had provided for every need of the Indians, what really did they need, other than money for the land that continued to be overtaken? Indians needed money to buy supplies from the trading posts in the United States or Canada, mainly because they were losing the use of the lands that had always provided their entire livelihood. The rest of the report lists the various kinds of missionaries that arrived throughout the region and a budget disclosure of $20,000 for build-ings and salaries for agents, including $8,000 for Indian Affairs to pay for interpreters, presents, provisions to Indians visiting the agencies, contingent expenses, travel to Indian Country on business, rent, fuel, stationery, and the collecting of statistical information.[25]

Indian agents' instructions were very clear, and while practice didn't always match principle, they were instructed to follow polices to the letter and not to overstep their bounds. Commissioner Manypenny con-tinues: "Should you deem it advisable to negotiate treaties of peace and friendship with any of the tribes you may chance to meet under such circumstances, you will consider yourself authorized to do so; but you will be careful to make no promises of presents or provisions to them beyond what it may be in your power to fulfill at the time of such negotiation."[26]

Regarding the land in our Pacific Northwest region, the U.S. officials found that "the ruggedness of the country and the dense forests which cover it" made it extremely difficult to bring about the consummation of trade agreements and "regulation on wreckages" (government officials had difficulty with the wreckage of sailing vessels, which they thought was caused by Indians).[27] These problems were cited as just cause for commissioners to request more funds for travel in this brushy, thickly wooded region. Because the rugged terrain made it difficult for foot soldiers, they also cited the rough terrain to justify use of ship-mounted guns to fire upon Indian villages. Indian commissioner Lea's letter to the secretary of the interior in 1852 starts with this concern: "The opinion is extensively entertained that our whole course of conduct towards the red men of this country has been marked by injustice and inhumanity."[28] Indians were subject to the white justice system, whether just or not, and the death penalty could be enforced: "As an additional section, it is recommended that in all cases where the military forces of the United States shall be employed against Indians, and shall take as prisoners or enforce the delivery of persons accused of any crime, it shall be competent for them to try by court-martial and inflict such punishment as the case may warrant, even to that of death."[29]

A word here about how the killing of a settler at Fort Steilacoom was handled by the U.S. government in 1849: This was one of the first events that occurred in the Puget Sound area when white people first started to settle here, and it was a harsh beginning for Indian/non-Indian relations. A Mr. Leander Wallace was killed, and the immediate assumption was that there were six guilty Indians. Dispatches of correspondence flew, the last of which was a message from the superintendent of Indian Affairs calling for a trial and for attaching Lewis County to the First Judicial District, since Lewis County was still too new for a trial to be held there otherwise. The letter authorized payment to those involved with the trial.[30] Governor Lane offered a reward of eighty blankets to Snoqualmie tribal members who would turn in those six Indians to Captain Hill. The death had occurred on or about May 17, 1849. Snoqualmie Indians were rewarded with eighty blankets for turning in six of their members. The six men were tried on or about October 22, 1849. They were tried by Court Martial of the Department of War. Governor Lane states in a letter: "I am clearly of opinion that the trial and punishment of the Indians, in the presence of their tribe and other tribes and bands bordering the sound, was the true policy; and has, no doubt, made an impression upon their minds sufficient to deter them from similar offences."[31]

Lane thought that it was bad policy to do anything other than assign severe punishment, on the assumption that Indians might commit a crime again, or turn in their slaves, or accept rewards for turning in innocent fellow tribesmen. Such results could undercut the government's ability to handle offenses. It was all over for two of the accused Indians, who were hanged on the day of their trial.

Law and policy was unjust to Indians in other ways too, even to the extent of authorizing that Indian children could be taken from their homes: "Binding a child" meant taking a child from Indian parents and placing him or her with "a citizen of good standing" for an education of sorts, intending to "civilize" the young person:

> I would therefore recommend that the superintendent of Indian Affairs, or any full agent, under such general regulations as the superintendent may direct, be authorized, with the consent of the parents or next relations, to bind any Indian child as an apprentice to a citizen of good character and standing, on such terms and for such time as may be agreed upon, not, however, to extend beyond the period when the apprentice shall reach the age of twenty-one years; the contract subject to be terminated by the superintendent or agent; should he be satisfied of personal ill-treatment, immoral use, or an intention to leave the Territory. As the practical details of such a system can hardly be perfected in advance, and as abuses might arise which would require an earlier action than could be procured from Congress, it is suggested that the superintendent be vested with entire powers, subject only to the revision of the department.[32]

In later history, the United States developed Indian boarding schools to "civilize" Indians by attempting to reprogram entire generations. Whether it was boarding schools or "binding" of children, the intent was to destroy Indian culture, and many kinds of abuse were carried out, by policy and by individuals.

ECONOMIC RELATIONS

Clear across the continent, Indian tribes had resources and trade items for their visitors and now for the growing economy. The earth provided each tribe with a wealth of different resources for use and trade. Rice, corn, potatoes, fish, furs and other animal products, wheat, timber, oil, gold, uranium, ores, molybdenum (a metal hardener), coal, herbs for medicine, water, arts, crafts, and other items. In our area, after Europeans arrived in Canada, we started growing potatoes for ourselves, and as more Europeans arrived, they depended more on us for potatoes. Our Indian resources provided material for a booming trade industry for young America. At first, there were battles going on between American and Canadian officials, U.S. government agents, traders, and Indians; we often had to deal with more than one "middleman."

Don't forget, the middleman also had to be paid. Red tape is prevalent in Indian Country, and we are not a squeaky wheel type of people. Our ancient Northwest Coast civilization had payment plans, but they were always called "thank you" plans and made at potlatches before witnesses, who bore the news of these plans to their individual tribal organizations. Americans, before and during the Great Depression, had this form of payment or thank you. Doctors were paid in unorthodox ways, either by favors or gifts. Although this meant hard times, it ultimately meant much simpler lives. Later the middlemen for Indians included employees of the Bureau of Indian Affairs. True, there are very dedicated BIA employees, but history shows this office as having had some of the worst kind of middlemen.

In the *Handbook of Federal Indian Law*, Felix S. Cohen states: "Trade was one of the inevitable activities that arose from contact between Indians and whites, two distinct races, engaged in unlike activities and possessed of different types of goods."[33] This account negates any claims that Indians were lazy. Cohen's discussion of Indian trade also proves beyond doubt that the U.S. government made efforts to thwart the avarice of unprincipled white men to cheat Indians out of all they could, because the Indians were novices. And the land held plenty. Manypenny wrote to the secretary of the interior in 1853: "The present license system by which, under the Intercourse Act, trade is regulated among Indian tribes, is defective; and, as administered for many years, it has become an evil of magnitude. The whole trade of the Indian tribes is thrown into a few hands—a monopoly is built up, and an interest fostered, which from the very nature of things becomes formidable, and is liable to be wielded against the views and wishes of the government, and the true interest of the Indians."[34]

An important topic in the *Handbook of Federal Indian Law* is tribal income from tribal resources, and believe me, the U.S. government has been resourceful when it comes to the valuable materials contained in Indian lands.[35] The principal source of tribal income has been the sale of tribal resources, chiefly land, timber, minerals, and water power. For more than a century, the power to sell such resources on Indian land was in the hands of the United States, rather than the tribes. Therefore, most of the tribal income received prior to 1891, when the first general leasing law was enacted, was paid to the tribes by the United States. Citizens' failure to appreciate the basis of such payments helped create a popular misconception that payments made by the United States to Indians were matters of charity.

Besides the fact the tribes were selling valuable resources, Indians were expected to provide labor in exchange for government supplies. Able-bodied Indian men who received supplies pursuant to appropriation acts were to perform useful labor "for the benefit of themselves or of the tribe, at a reasonable rate, to be fixed by the agent in charge, and to an amount equal in value to the supplies to be delivered."[36] As Cohen points out, "The popular outcry that would have followed the application of a similar rule to white holders of government bonds or pensions may well be imagined."[37] The history of Indian/U.S. economic relations contains many acts and statutes, as well as instructions from Indian commissioners, secretaries of the interior, and U.S. presidents, offering their solutions into the mix. Much has been made of payments to Indians and tribes; however, it can eventually be boiled down with common sense and logic.

The issue of payment to the tribes is a subject of the Trade and Intercourse Act of June 30, 1834 (Public Law No. 23-161). The act contains general provisions for payment of Indian annuities and the distribution of goods. It is important to note that the act authorizes payment in money.[38] In cases where money was promised, but "payment" was only in "goods" or "services," this act was not being observed.

THE OREGON LAND DONATION ACT
(DONATION LAND CLAIM ACT, 1850)

Events on the first shore of discovery, the Atlantic, set the stage for the story that continued on the opposite shore, the Pacific. The attitude of the conquerors changed in their sweep from east to west. However, violence played upon their minds in other ways. They acted so as to suggest a diminished value of the land and to portray Indians' unfamiliarity with white ways as barbarism.

White settlers were paid in land to emigrate westward by means of the 1850 Oregon Land Donation Act.[39] The new settlements would add to the land base and power of the young United States. During this time, according to my father's oral tradition history, the Indian tribes had "runners" who ran from village to village, carrying news about the arriving whites. Because the tribes were located on or near the seacoast, there was no thought of moving locales; they stayed. Indian children and women carried gifts of food to greet the new arrivals, especially the ones on ships. Fresh sprouts and berries as well as dried meat and fish were plentiful. Chiefs, such as Kitsap and Seattle, welcomed them with oratory. The land spoke for itself.

The Oregon Land Donation Act gave non-Indian male settlers, eighteen and older, 320 acres each, and if married, 320 additional acres (a total of 640 acres or one square mile). To get a patent (certificate of ownership), the settlers had to live on that land for four years. This law was extended to December 1, 1853, and again to December 1, 1855. An amendment approved on February 14, 1853 (910 Stat. 158), allowed settlers to acquire the land by a combination of purchase and only two years occupancy.

The Oregon Land Donation Act has been described as a banquet where guests were encouraged to swallow more than they could digest. Some of these settlers complained that their neighbors were too far away for them to visit one another. The story goes that some white settlers were afraid to leave their homes and be at the mercy of the wily Indians for as long as it took them to get to a store and back. If only we, the people who had inhabited that land for thousands of years, could have enjoyed amounts of land as generous of those of the Land Act in our arrangements with the U.S. government, but we could not. We could not enjoy what the white people were allowed to enjoy in our homeland. I can visualize the Indian people's puzzled natures, because if the whites were not friends, they must be enemies. Their whiskey, Bibles, gun powder, rape, friendship, marriage, destruction of our homeland; all this must have puzzled Native people greatly, plus the many unkept promises!

Before Oregon became a territory (1848), the region needed a provisional government. In 1843 residents adopted a code of laws for the administration of that government. This code of laws, called Oregon's Organic Act, incorporated the first four articles of the Northwest Ordinance 1787 as its preamble.[40] Thus, the Organic Act recognized aboriginal land title in the Oregon Territory by affirming the principle of the Northwest Ordinance that "the utmost good faith shall always be observed toward the Indian; their lands and properties shall never be taken from them without their consent." However, the Oregon Land Donation Act was actually in conflict with this principle, because it allowed non-Indians to stake a claim to land, even if Indians lived on it. The act made land available to non-Indian Americans starting in 1850—against both federal and territorial principles of Native land rights and before our treaties were signed—before any Indian land was ceded to the United States!

In the Point Elliott Treaty tribes' U.S. Court of Claims case that began in 1927, the court found that of the area claimed by the Lummi to have been their lands before the Treaty of Point Elliott—249,800 acres (map 2)—the amount of Lummi land lost to settlers by the Land Donation Act was 2,406 acres lost before the signing of the treaty and 926 more acres lost between its signing and ratification (3,332 total acres). However, the Court of Claims determined that it had no jurisdiction concerning the Oregon Land Donation Act because it had been an act of Congress.[41] In 1946 Congress approved the Indian Claims Commission Act in order to permit tribes to use the U.S. Court of Claims to seek redress for broken treaties and to receive compensation for lost lands. When the Lummi Tribe filed an action in 1951, the Indian Claims Commission (ICC) also said that it could do nothing to help the Point Elliott tribes regarding redress of the wrongs the resulted from the Oregon Land Donation Act.[42]

Some arrangements for land holdings around the time of the Oregon Land Donation Act involved personal connections between Natives and settlers:

> In the 1850s, for example, Saneewa, a Snoqualmie headman from an important indigenous town at the foot of the Cascades, came every autumn with his family, his ponies and his dogs to camp in Arthur Denny's pasture. Like Seeathl [Chief Seattle], Saneewa saw Denny, arguably the most powerful man in town, as a strategic ally, but the relationship was mutually beneficial. As the leader of a community located at the western entrance to the lowest pass across the central Cascades, which Denny coveted for a wagon road, Saneewa provided crucial information about the route through the mountains. A few years later, Denny would be among the surveyors to map what they called the Snoqualmie Pass. And as for Saneewa, he and his people were able to remain in the valley where they had always lived, rather than removing to reservations in part because of the relationships they built with Seattle "headmen" like Denny.[43]

Naturally, conflict arose between the settlers and Indians in Oregon and Washington Territories. As Manypenny stated: "the superintendents in those Territories [were] instructed to proceed as early as practicable with the negotiations . . . Indeed the usual order of things has been to some extent reversed, the department having had to invoke the aid of the military for the protection of the weak and helpless Indians from the persecutions and cruelties of the whites."[44] The government documents also contain references to Indians causing depredations upon white settlers. Regardless of the situations that led up to these depredations, after the treaties the payment for any such depredations by individuals could be taken out of a whole tribe's annuities: the annual payments of funds, goods, or services paid by the government to a tribe for ceded land.[45]

THE TREATY OF POINT ELLIOTT, 1855: RATIFIED TREATY NO. 283

The 1855 Point Elliott Treaty between the United States and other northern Puget Sound tribes, including my tribe, the Lummi Tribe, acts as a compact or agreement between the United States and each of these tribes, establishing a government-to-government relationship. The Point Elliott Treaty council was held at Mukilteo (Point Elliott) on a shore about twenty-five miles north of present-day Seattle. The boundaries of the entire tract ceded by the Point Elliott Treaty are spelled out in Article 1 of the treaty (12 Stat. 927). The area ceded by the treaty is approximately 589,013 acres (9,123 square miles), according to available data (see map 6). The original number of acres to be reserved by Point Elliott Treaty tribes, according to findings in the U.S. Court of Claims case *Duwamish et al v. U.S.*, was 44,192 acres, which is approximately 69 square miles. After enlargements and subtractions, the current acreage of the four original Point Elliott Treaty reservations is approximately 49,786 acres (approximately 78 square miles).[46] Thus, more than 99 percent of the aboriginal land was ceded to the United States by the treaty.

The Treaty of Point Elliott was signed by tribal leaders and government officials on January 22, 1855. Eighty-two Indian leaders signed it, representing twenty-two named Coast Salish tribes and bands, "and other allied and subordinate tribes and bands of Indians." The treaty led to the establishment of four reservations along Puget Sound: Lummi, Swinomish, Tulalip, and Suquamish/Port Madison (map 6). The treaty does not specify which tribes and bands would share which reservations. Nor does the treaty specify the boundaries for the reservations; their general locations are listed, to be surveyed later.

The Treaty of Point Elliott lists five reservations; however, as explained by Washington Indian superintendent R. H. Milroy in an 1873 report, owing to the government's ignorance of local geography, the treaty's description of the five land areas is written such that the Tulalip

Reservation overlapped one of them; so at first there were only four reservations under the Treaty of Point Eliott.[47] In 1874 a fifth reservation, the Muckleshoot, was added by Executive Order of President Ulysses S. Grant (map 7). The initial number of square miles reserved for the Point Elliott tribes (initially 69 square miles total for the four reservations) was not even enough for those living at that time, whose numbers had already been reduced by disease and loss of livelihood. The expectation was that our numbers would continue to decline, not to recover, as they have.

The Lummi Tribe is one of eleven present-day Point Elliott Treaty tribes. The Lummi Tribe's population has recovered from about four hundred persons at the time of the treaty to more than four thousand. About a century after the treaty, in 1944, Lummi Day School principal Victor Jones spoke at hearings held by the U.S. House of Representatives' Committee on Indians Affairs, in order to Investigate Indian Affairs: "We have more than one hundred young men of this reservation who are now family heads without land or the possibility of obtaining land on the reservation. . . . The Government should assist this tribe in securing suitable home sites on or adjacent to the reservation for these young people. . . . Such additional purchases should be made by the Government in lieu of lands alienated from original reservations by federal action or federal neglect."[48] That was at least one of the days when rights were heard and possible solutions were presented by Mr. Jones, and by other Lummi leaders, for consideration by members of the U.S. Congress.

The first treaty that was ratified by the U.S. Congress between the United States and an aboriginal tribe was the treaty with the Lenape or Delaware Indians in 1778. The Lenape were then displaced from their homelands, which would become Pennsylvania, New Jersey, Delaware, and southern New York. The Lenape moved westward to Oklahoma and other regions; some even went to Canada. The 1778 Treaty with the Delaware is the one that usually gets named as the first American Indian treaty. However, before that, there were seven treaties made by American colonists backed by British officials, prior to the United States becoming a nation. These treaties were made in the Northeast between 1722 and 1768. These are not treaties that are generally considered binding on the United States.[49] The final treaty that the U.S. government made with an Indian tribe was with the Nez Perce; it was signed in 1868. In the late nineteenth century the United States quit making treaties with tribes, and the trend of Indian policy was to try to turn away from recognizing the political independence of tribes.

In the 1905 Supreme Court case *Lone Wolf v. Hitchcock* (187 U.S. 553 [1903]), Kiowa Chief Lone Wolf took his people's case to the Supreme Court over their claim that their unalloted lands were being sold off without genuine approval of the tribe, as stipulated by treaty.[50] The court asserted the principle of the "plenary power" of Congress, as if "plenary" meant that Congress had absolute power over tribes, and that the government could therefore disregard treaty rights. Plenary power is an important concept to understand for treaty rights and other issues in Indian law and policy. The word *plenary* means "full" or "complete," but plenary power properly concerns the powers of Congress in areas where *only* Congress has power. Wilkins and Lomawaima's book *Uneven Ground: American Indian Sovereignty and Federal Law* explains the meanings and misuses of "plenary power" and other legal doctrines that are essential to understand in order to defend sovereignty.[51] After the Lone Wolf decision, according to Indian affairs historian Francis Paul Prucha, "the idea of requiring Indian consent for the disposition of their land was largely discarded in regard to statutes as well as to agreements, and Congress unilaterally provided for the sale of surplus lands remaining after allotments had been completed."[52]

Dare anyone say we haven't yet learned from American Indian history, after a century and a half of treaty making? Another way that treaties were violated was the government's turning a blind eye to white presence on reservations, which allowed slow takeovers by white settlement and businesses. Such passive methods of injustice don't involve much effort or remorse; this is a pattern we must continue to learn from. Treaties are documents in evidence of a trust relationship that applies both on and off reservations. Trust responsibility requires the fulfillment of treaty promises. The trust relationship entails rights and responsibilities for the parties agreeing to a treaty, the supreme law of the land, according to the U.S. Constitution. Although treaties weakened aboriginal communities in many ways, they helped the cause of the government-to-government relationship between tribes and the U.S. government.

One of the great speeches of history is Chief Seattle's speech, believed to have been made on January 12, 1854, a year before the signing of the Point Elliott Treaty.[53] He stated, in part: "We will ponder your proposition, and when we have decided we will tell you. But should we accept it, I here and now make this first condition: That we will not be denied the privilege, without molestation, of visiting at will the graves of our ancestors and friends. Every part of this country is sacred to my people. Every hillside, every valley, every plain and grove has been hallowed by some fond memory or sad experience of my tribe."[54]

To Chief Seattle I say: We can only dream of what we might do to follow in your great footsteps. Our prayers are for you, for the white people who were in your presence, and for all of us who have survived your forgotten genocide. Together we lift up our hands to honor you. You were placed to speak for your people as they faced the onrush of a sightless new population. Thank you for taking a strong hold, and with the treaty, preserving our right to fish. We hear the sacred call. And like you, 'til the end of our days, we dedicate our lives to the spiritual betterment of our world, that not all will have died in vain, and that Mother Earth will hear our reply: "Yes, we will do our best!"

In 1853 Isaac I. Stevens (1818–62) was appointed governor and superintendent of Indian Affairs for Washington Territory. He was responsible for acquiring Indian land for the U.S. government, and he was also the initial surveyor for the new railroad lines to the Pacific Northwest (map 8). Stevens negotiated ten Pacific Northwest treaties in 1854-56: five of them in western Washington (map 6). Stevens had been in the territory only a year at the time of the first treaty councils, so he could not have known much about the Indian way of life. The report of the Point Elliott Treaty proceedings, handwritten by George Gibbs, states that 2,300 Indians gathered at the treaty council at Mukilteo or Point Elliott, "and sticks were returned for 700 absentees, chiefly old men, women and children" (to indicate the number who dwelled in various villages). The larger tribes' leaders, who spoke at the council, were seated in front: Seattle (Duwamish and Suquamish), Patkanim (Snoqualmie), Goliah (Skagit), and Chow-its-hoot/Chowitsut (Lummi). Leaders of the other tribes, bands, and houses were seated behind them, and the people were seated in the groups to which they belonged. The Coast Salish did not have "chiefs" over large areas. Each village and area had several leaders that the people chose. The idea of "chiefs" was something that the government created in order to transact with "tribes" in our area.

The treaty council notes made by Gibbs include the speech made by Colonel Michael T. Simmons in Chinook Jargon (fig. 6). Speeches were given by white representatives and by Native leaders. Interpreters repeated the speeches, using Tsinuk Wawa (Chinook Jargon), English, and various Native dialects. The treaty negotiations would have been very difficult, even in the best of circumstances. Tsinuk Wawa, used for negotiating the Puget Sound treaties, is a trade language created by white and Indian people, using vocabulary from the Chinook language (a U.S. Pacific coast language in the Penutian family), the Nuu-chah-nulth language (a Wakashan language of Vancouver Island), Canadian French, and English. The leaders and the people attending the treaty council were from a large area and spoke different dialects—some similar and some very different—so there was not even a common language among the Indians. Sometimes a speech would be translated not just from one language to a second, but from the second language to a third. The language that was used was different from any Indian dialect and different from the English spoken by the white Americans. If today we tried to create a treaty again, with the English language that we both know, it would be easier. But I do not think that we could easily carry out such an important land transaction for as many Indians who need land now. This is truly not a joke. We would find out just how much we know about each other even today.

Stevens's speeches at the Washington Territory treaty council have a paternalistic tone. In transacting the first treaty, at Medicine Creek in the southern Puget Sound area, he spoke of the U.S. president as the great white father and of the father's concern for his children. In the Point Elliott Treaty negotiations, Stevens spoke of himself as a caring father. At the conclusion of the treaty negotiations Chief Seattle presented Governor Stevens with a white flag, saying that it should always "be clean and never stained with blood."[55]

As our ancestors came to experience the consequences of the treaty negotiations, they uncovered the hidden intentions of the treaty negotiators, government officials, and military companies, as well as the one whom they knew as the great white father. Today treaties have enormous implications for those who study them, but, just reading them is not that painful. Treaties became devices for weakening the independence of tribal governments, which ideally are based on the guardianship and guidance of nature and oral tradition. For example, at the time of the Point Elliott Treaty the Lummi Tribe was led by more than one chief and by means of traditional ceremonies and cultural practices. Reservation creation was difficult at best. Look at today's politics (not of Indian origin). There is too much greed, and greed does not reflect real need. But greed might always play an important role in America's way of sharing.

When one reads the reports on Indian affairs, it is easy to hear the despair of the Indians and the groaning tone of the officials explaining these Indian matters to Congress. The government continued to make treaties with Indian tribes without the presence of impartial overseers. The only observers of treaty negotiations were the interpreters, and perhaps some Indians with whom the whites had special relationships. It could not have been possible for Indian leaders to have a clear picture of the arrangements the whites were presenting. The treaty spells out that the Point Elliott tribes would be compensated for their land by a particular sum "applied to the use and benefit of said Indians, under the direction of the President of the United States" (Article 6) and by educational, medical, and agricultural training and other services (Article 14). Consider Commissioner Manypenny's earlier recommendations for the distribution of items to Indians, in place of payment for valuable land ceded to the government:

> Whatever may be the extent of consideration allowed for lands hereafter ceded to the government by an undomesticated tribe, it should consist chiefly of goods, subsistence, agricultural implements and assistance, stock animals, and the means of mental, moral, and industrial education and training [*author's note*: taking the place of centuries of subsistence by gathering from land, sea, and sky]. Let this principle be adopted with all the tribes, wherever located, to whom we have not set the pernicious precedent of payments in money, and thus freed from the injurious effects of money annuities, they will present a more favorable field for the efforts of the philanthropist and Christian.[56]

This kind of thinking was at the root of our being declared "incompetent" to receive money as payment for ceded lands. Such statements set a precedent unworthy of the property ceded to the government in the Pacific Northwest or anywhere else in America. No such principle was included in the Treaty of Point Elliott negotiations. The Lummi Tribe's first magazine, the *Squol-quol*, published the minutes of the negotiations that took place before the signing of the treaty. Not one speech made by the chiefs and headmen of the tribes mentioned such a strange negotiation; they understood that they would receive money for the land ceded to the government.[57] Furthermore, the treaty indicates the number of dollars that the tribes would receive for the ceded land (fig. 7).

The great waters of Puget Sound were never even considered as an actual purchase. Strange? No. Consider this remark from *The History of Lummi Fishing Rights* by Ann Nugent: "Water resources were of no significance to the non-Indians. . . . It was clearly evident that the authorities who recorded evidences regarding the negotiations of the treaty wanted the Indians to continue in their fishing."[58] Yet, the state of Washington has dug their heels in the sand ever since, wanting complete rule over the "in common" places of our country. But according to the treaty, we did not cede the waters. This is an important point as regards our fishing rights. In 1934 when the U.S. Court of Claims denied the Duwamish, Lummi and other tribes their petition against the U.S. government for treaty violations and the unjust taking of Indian lands, one of the reasons given was that Indians had not surveyed the lands that they claimed—lands that they had "exclusively possessed, owned, and held immemorially" as our claimed lands were described in *Lummi Tribe v. U.S.* It was not because of negligence that the Indian tribes did not survey their lands; it was negligence of the United States to make such a criticism, since at that time Indians were not knowledgeable of the white culture's surveying procedures. Apart from the mistakes that we know were made, I do not think we can say for certain that government surveyors measured and marked all Indian lands fairly and accurately. Indians had, and still have, other ways of identifying our Indian territory, and now we also have our own surveyors.

A quotation from a document titled "Indian Policy" by Washington superintendent of Indian Affairs Isaac Stevens spells out a suggested plan for "paternal care by the government" and shows why our relationship grew at such a slow pace: "If a measure could be adopted which would give permanency to the relation of master and servant, and at the same time protect the rights of the latter, the value of Indian labor would be greatly raised. The employment of Indians as farm-servants would be especially useful to them, as at the expiration of their term of service they would carry back with them a sufficient knowledge of agriculture to improve their condition at home." Governor Stevens's report to Congress concludes with his estimates of the populations remaining in the Northwest Indian tribes: east of the Cascades, 6,500; west of the Cascades, 7,559. In this report, dated 1854, the Lummi tribal membership numbered only 450.[59]

In reviewing the government documents, I find many judgments against the Indian as all manner of savage (and servant to master, in the passage above) and the white man often referred to as unprincipled, unscrupulous, and predatory upon the Indian and his annuities. We did not have our best foot forward, did we? Our ancestors' unfamiliarity with white measures of money and acreage went to the benefit of white America. Our tribe did not receive money, just annuity goods and services, as payment for ceded land. Meanwhile, we waited in a sinful manner, because our thoughts grew against the government for not treating us right. Since we could not gather, hunt, and fish for subsistence as our ancestors had for thousands of years, we were pushed into the "money" field, but without the benefit of education for it. Indian commissioner George Manypenny wrote a century and a half ago: "I do not see how the obligations of the government to its Indian wards can be fully met and faithfully discharged without the aid of penal statutes to protect them from the evils referred to; and under a full conviction of the necessity that exists, and a deep sense of duty, I recommend that the subject be brought to the attention of Congress."[60]

Manypenny made commendable remarks in 1852 about the government's good faith in the Indian: "He will then be placed in a position where the efforts of the government and the benevolent, unembarrassed by opposing forces and influences, would be left to adopt and prosecute the means most efficient for the elevation of his intellectual and physical powers, the culture of the better feelings and sympathies of his nature, and the development of his capacity to improve in the arts and sciences."[61]

Today I believe that some people have good opinions of us as Indian America, and some of us have high opinions of white America. Perhaps some among our current generations of Indian and non-Indian Americans are just as innocent and nonjudgmental as Indian America was at first. I prefer to believe in the status of real maturity in all cultures.

Treaties are of great importance for tribes because they document rights that we retain as sovereign nations. Treaties can also document rights that are granted. It is easy to misunderstand, and to think in terms of treaties as *giving* rights to Indians, when the treaty is *reserving* rights that we already had. It's similar with reservations. It is not that the U.S. government is reserving some of its land for Indians. No, the reservations are lands that we reserve of the larger lands that we possessed from time immemorial, whether near or far from our original homelands. A nation that could participate in a treaty is a nation that was already maintaining its own rights. In order for American Indian rights to be remembered, U.S. and Indian governments and people need to understand the treaty commitments that they have agreed to uphold. As Indian people, we must provide for our current and future generations, and the United States must observe our rights and honor its treaty obligations. These concern land, yes, but other matters, too. And if a sufficient measure of our lost lands were restored, we could not measure the happiness.

CHAPTER 5

After the Treaty

What happened after the Treaty of Point Elliott was signed? After the treaty, Indian people were uprooted from the lands that had sustained them physically and spiritually. The members of all the tribes and bands represented by the treaty (twenty-two named tribes and bands, plus "other allied and subordinate tribes and bands") were supposed to share four small "reserved" areas. For several of the reservations, the boundaries were not clearly established until 1873, eighteen years after the signing of the treaty. The treaty stated that members of the tribes and bands were to settle on the reserved areas within one year of the ratification, and that "In the meantime it shall be lawful for them to reside upon any land not in the actual claim and occupation of citizens of the United States" (Treaty of Point Elliott, Article 4). Some displaced Indians resorted to temporary shelters, withstanding coastal rains and weather of all seasons. Providers for families tried to carry on with fishing, hunting, and gathering in a shrinking environment. Indians carried on as best they could, among new settlers who had felt free to establish homesteads wherever they chose—and some of these homesteaders were hostile. Only some Indian people went to live on reserved lands, which were too small for food economies based on gathering from the lands and waters, and which had few opportunities for employment.

The two smaller reservations, Swinomish and Port Madison/Suquamish, were, at first, each two square miles in size (1,280 acres each). The largest reservation, Tulalip, was chosen by the government to be the Indian agency, supposedly to have educational and medical services for all Point Elliott Treaty tribes. Tulalip was to have thirty-six square miles of land (23,040 acres). The Tulalip Reservation is shaped like a triangle with one side along the coast, but imagine an area six by six miles in size. The area reserved for Lummi was an island, called Chahchoosen, surrounded by the ocean on the south and rivers on the north (map 9). Its size is not specified in the Treaty (appendix 1, Article 2).

Some tribes were assigned to reservations outside their own homelands, and the people didn't go there, such as the Samish, who were expected to relocate to Lummi. Some groups tried to relocate but ended up going back home, like the Duwamish, assigned to an area inhabited by Suquamish people. Such tribes usually ended up without reservation lands, and of those that survived, some now have federal recognition, and some don't (map 7).

For many Indians, it was a silent time for contemplation as to whether the treaty's promises of reservation land and payments for ceded land would be forgotten. For many whites, it was an anxious time of waiting to learn whether Congress would act quickly enough to secure all that had been invested in the Puget Sound area. There was not room amid this crowd for peace, happiness or comfort, just the tension of waiting.

WAITING

After the treaty, the Indian people felt beaten. No payment came for the land that the white people just took away. It was a couple of years after the treaty that annuities were paid, and there were far more Indian people than the governments had anticipated to be "paid" for the vast lost lands. The annuities were goods that were worth very little. It was not clear where the Indians' new homelands were, their resources were disappearing, their culture and languages were on the road to destruction, there was prejudice and racism against them, and their leaders were becoming old and sick. The "promises" made to them by Governor Isaac I. Stevens had not been kept. Chief Seattle, Lummi Chief

Chowitsut, and the other leaders had so much piled against them; the odds must have seemed like a million to one.

During the time before the treaty was ratified, Indian agent Simmons spoke of a report from Indian agent Fitzhugh concerning the Lummi and Samish (author's notes are in brackets):

> I was sorry to learn from Agent Fitzhugh that his Indians were perishing rapidly. The discovery of gold on Fraser and Thompson rivers has caused an immense concourse of people to gather at this station, it being the starting point to the mines. The Indians have sold all their canoes [that they could have used for their survival], being tempted by the large prices and are now destitute of the means of fishing. The money they have received has been worse than nothing [they did not understand the value of dollars]; it has been the means of their getting quantities of rum. The strangers at this place, if they know the law, do not respect it, and so many of them being there make the efforts of the two men who are interested in the Indians of little avail; consequently they get liquor as easily as a whiteman can.[1]

Destitute Indians, selling fish and furs, went to Victoria and other cities to secure supplies while they awaited payment from the U.S. government, having ceded nearly all of the vast Pacific Northwest. Many events, good and bad, took place between Indian America and white America. In reading the government documents, so often one will read and cry, read and laugh, read and learn, read and think. Agent Simmons, after hearing from agent Fitzhugh of many Indian deaths in the Bellingham Bay Agency, wrote to special agent Smith:

> After reading this, I think that you, sir, must agree with me in thinking that humanity as well as justice, makes it an imperative duty of Government to adopt some plan in which the Indians can be separated from the whites. Their forbearance has been remarkable. While they had the power of crushing us like worms, they treated us like brothers. We, I think should return their kindness now that we have the power, and our duty is so plainly pointed out by their deplorable

situation. My own impression is that the speediest and best way of settling all these difficulties is the ratification of the treaties made.[2]

Regardless of treaty promises, the government did not have sufficient funds to hire enough physicians, nor were there many physicians available in the United States in those years, to fulfill the promise of medical care for tribal members. J. W. Nesmith, Isaac Steven's successor as superintendent for Indian Affairs for the Oregon and Washington Territories, wrote: "The meager appropriations for physicians and mechanics as well as teachers, under the provisions of the treaties, have always been too small to procure the specified services within this superintendency."[3] This was in 1858, three years after the treaty was signed. That same year, special Indian agent Fitzhugh of the Bellingham Bay Agency wrote:

The Indians under my superintendency are Lummi, Neuk-sack [Nooksack] and Samish tribes, numbering in all, some fifteen hundred, men, women, and children included. Since the last census was taken, the increase of these tribes has been very slight. During the last winter a number of them have died from exposure and old venereal. Their condition at this time is anything but satisfactory. Since the discovery of gold in this part of the country [Fraser and Thompson River areas], the white population has increased most rapidly, and all my care and labor have been null and void in trying to prevent the whites from selling whiskey to them . . . In two years time, unless the treaties are confirmed, and these Indians placed on a reservation, the government will have no use for an agent here. There will not be an Indian left to tell the tale that they had ever existed . . . According to your order, I went up in their country and pacified them by paying to the chiefs and the headmen, some $300 in goods, which you had placed in my charge to be divided among the three tribes. This satisfied them for the time."[4]

The Indians, although still in their familiar home territory, were greatly limited by government policies requiring them to stay in one place, as opposed to harvesting over an entire region. Alcohol played a role in Indians' idleness and in their times of anguish in waiting. The U.S. government carried on with utilizing the land and protecting settlers, traders, churches, and, lastly, Indians.

The historic record shows that the Indian agents of that day at times made it possible for the Indians to be heard. In 1858 Indian agent Michael T. Simmons visited Chief Seattle and other Indian leaders and several hundred of their people at the Fort Kitsap (Suquamish/Port Madison) Reservation. His report says he told the Indians that "I had brought them a few presents from their Great Father in Washington; that is a sure evidence that he had not forgotten them; that they must not be down-hearted because the treaties had not been concluded . . . and . . . I signified that I was ready to hear anything they had to say." Chief Seattle's posttreaty speech of 1858 is quoted in agent Simmons's report, along with the speeches of other Coast Salish leaders:

Seattle, a venerable old chief and fast friend to the whites, arose and spoke as follows: "I want you to understand what I say—I do not drink rum; neither does Noweches (another chief), and we constantly advise our people not to do so. I am not a bad man. I am, and always have been, a friend to the whites. I listen to what Mr. Paige says to me, and I do not steal, nor do I or any of my people kill the Whites. Oh, Mr. Simmons, why don't our papers come back to us? You always say you hope they will soon come, but they do not. I fear we are forgotten, or that we are to be cheated out of our land. I have been very poor and hungry all winter, and am very sick now. In a little while I will die. I should like to be paid for my land before I die. Many of my people died due to a cold, scarce winter, without getting their pay. When I die my people will be very poor. They will have no property, no chief, no one to talk for them. You must help them, Mr. Simmons, when I am gone. We are ashamed when we think that the Puyallup got their papers. They fought against the whites, while we, who have never been angry with them, get nothing. When do we get our pay? We want it in money. This governor (McMullen) told us if any bad white men worried us to tell him, and that he would punish them. Whenever I tell the bad white men this they say, "God damn the old fool, he is *cultus*" [an expressive Chinook Jargon word meaning "worthless," "waste"]. The Indians are not so bad; it is the mean white people who are bad to us. If any person writes that we do not want our papers back, they lie. Oh, Mr. Simmons, you see that I am very sick. I want you to go quickly and tell the President what I say. I have done."[5]

Put yourself in Chief Seattle's place. How would you feel? What would you do? You would feel helpless and probably die, too, under your American flag, as he did. It makes me feel sad when I quote him from the government documents, but my strength lies in the fact that the proof is there and cannot be changed or taken away.

Hetley Kanim, a subchief of Snoqualmie, complained that the Puyallup (party to the Treaty of Medicine Creek) got their annuity paid, even though they had fought the whites, while his tribe had not. Kanim made a great speech to Indian agent Simmons, saying: "If you whites pay the Indians that fight you, it must be good to fight." Hiram, a Skokomish, then spoke: "You know what we are, Mr. Simmons. You were the first American we ever knew, and our children remember you as long as they remember anything. I was a boy when I first knew you. You know we do not want to drink liquor, but we cannot help it when the bad 'Bostons' bring it to us."[6]

I completely understand the hungry, weary, sick Indians having to continue waiting for the presents promised them instead of money. And alcohol to a hungry person is "satisfying hunger." Bonaparte, a Snohomish chief, then spoke: "What I have got to say is not of much consequence. My children have all been killed by rum (a fact) and I am very poor. I believe what Mr. Simmons tells us about our treaty, but most of the Indians think he lies; my heart is not asleep. I have known Mr. Simmons a long time, and he never lied to me, and I think he will tell the Great White Father how much we want our pay. I have done."[7]

Other chiefs and headmen also spoke and hopefully were heard at that time, or will be heard now. As a result of this exchange between the Coast Salish leaders and government representatives, Simmons's report says: "The goods for these people, as well as those at Fort Kip-Sap [Kitsap], were turned over to the local agents, with instructions to distribute them to the aged and destitute."[8] Why just the aged and destitute? Why didn't the U.S. government distribute goods to *all* the Indian people who were left waiting after the treaty?

Today, as I read the reports to Congress from the time after the treaty, I cannot help but visualize the demeanors of both white Americans and American Indians. Without today's technology of airplanes, cars, phones, email and so on, the people of the nineteenth century had great disadvantages in carrying out treaty arrangements (the first telegraph message was not sent across the country from Washington State until 1864: it was a message from Governor Pickering to President Lincoln). Indian people needed solutions, yes; but that was not all they had to contend with: illness, death, hunger, pain in waiting, waiting for what was promised in good faith, and facing death before promises were realized.

DISEASE AND ALCOHOL

I have not yet said much of the circumstances surrounding smallpox, or other diseases brought among the Indians.[9] "Captains Lewis and Clark conjectured from the relations of the Indians, and the apparent age of individuals marked with it, that it [smallpox] had prevailed about thirty years before their arrival [1805]. It also spread with great virulence in 1843."[10] Thanks to the government documents, I found reports by several commissioners of Indian Affairs that smallpox epidemics occurred in Washington around the time of our Point Elliott Treaty of 1855 and other Washington treaties. There were epidemics in 1853, 1854, 1855, 1856, 1860, 1869, and 1872.[11] Could these have been spread on purpose? My oldest sister, Molly, told me the following about our maternal grandfather, Harry Price (Petoie), born around 1832. When the sickness went all around the Lummi Reservation, he dug his own grave and sat inside it, just waiting to be taken by the smallpox. Molly was born August 8, 1913. Grandfather Harry Price raised Molly. He had an allotment located at the mouth of the present Nooksack River. His allotment was cut in half when the course of that river was changed by a logjam.

Smallpox devastation is recounted in Washington Territory in an 1854 *Report of the Commissioner of Indian Affairs*. George Gibbs's report speaks of the death that spread from the territory of the Cowlitz and Chehalis in southwest Washington up the coast to the Makah people at the north point of the Olympic peninsula:

At present but few Indians remain here, the smallpox having nearly finished its work during the past year. In the winter and spring it spread with great virulence along the coast as far north as Cape Flattery. Some lodges upon the southern peninsula of Shoalwater Bay were left without a survivor; and the dead were found by the whites lying wrapped in their blankets as if asleep . . . The Willowpahs . . . may be considered as extinct, a few women only remaining, and those intermarried with the Chinooks and Chihalis.

The Makahs, or Classets, inhabit the coast in the neighborhood of Cape Flattery. This tribe, which has been the most formidable to navigators of any in the American Territories on the Pacific, numbered, it is believed, until very recently, five hundred fifty . . . During the last year [1854] the smallpox found its way to their region, and it is reported reduced them to one hundred fifty, their famous chief, Flattery Jack, being among the number who died.[12]

It was said in the report quoted above that Lummi is a branch of the Clallam, but this is the first I heard of that; that we are a distant branch of the Klallam. Smallpox is mentioned so often in the government documents that it frightens me even this minute. There were doctors for the settlers and the army, but not for the Indians. Smallpox afflicted the Yakama and Klickitats, who sought their own ways of healing: A blind old woman of the Spokane tribe knew of an herb, a species of iris that acted as a violent emetic. And it worked only after the smallpox near wiped out her village, but the sickness was stayed. The Kam-ai-ya-kan (or Kamaiakin: a Yakama band) the blind woman said, would have some. She described the plant to her daughter, who found some on the trail between their village and the village of Chief Kamiakin.[13] I once knew a family of Kamiakins who lived in Nespelem,

Washington, and they always had the most wonderful Root Feasts in the spring of the year.

Lewis and Clark estimated Indian tribal numbers at 3,240 along the Yakama and Klickitat Rivers. These tribal areas showed signs of mounds, resembling our root houses. These root houses may have provided these Plateau people protection from summer heat, as well as protection for their stored food in winter. Some of these root houses may have been erected by Skloom, brother of Chief Kamiakin; both of them were signers of the 1855 Treaty with the Yakima. The government documents tell such wonderful stories of the Indians in that area: Yakama, Klickitat, and Spokane. Signs of earthworks interest me, since I lived in that area for some time with my former husband, the late Ed Covington of the Moses Band, Colville Confederated Tribes, in Nespelem, Washington.

Alcohol—the government documents often refer to drunken Indians across the United States. At one point I asked, "Well, who brought the alcohol to this continent?" White America has had access to alcohol for many generations. Indians did not. White America had access to spices unknown to Indian America, spices that counteract alcohol. For example, the Spaniards had, and to this day have, much knowledge about spices. And, believe it or not, spices help build—not immunity—but resistance to the drunken state that comes from drinking alcohol. For countless generations, people in countries that consume alcohol to great measure either drank it slowly or only at specific times of the day, and those generations built up their resistance to drunkenness. Also, they used alcohol as part of their meals, and the food, once filling their stomachs, caused a full feeling whereby no more alcohol was wanted. This did not happen for Indians. They were like children with a new and dangerous toy. If they were hungry, drinking alcohol was a way to fill their empty stomachs. And if their emotions were down (and there was plenty during those years to make them feel "down"), alcohol lifted their spirits temporarily, only to let them farther down into depression or sadness. It gave them false courage to continue life, without having to think seriously about their survival. The newness of alcohol in their systems may have seemed to help some Indians to survive a bit longer.

My paternal grandfather's wife stoutly put her foot down about alcohol, and thereby my grandfather kept busy with planting his orchard, wheat, and garden. He busied himself passing on the cultural teachings of his father, Salaphalano, the Priest (of the longhouse tradition) to which all three of them belonged for their entire lives. Just like non-Natives saying "thank you" to Indians for cigarette tobacco, Indians say "thank you" for alcohol. Both are killers though.

Here is a story I told to the dancers in our Setting Sun Dance Group. I needed the dance group members to understand why they were wearing velvet, a material not available to our ancient ancestors. Our more recent ancestors wore velvet, and also silk and cotton, because of these particular events of history. When traders arrived in the Northwest, they did as they had done clear across the United States and offered to pay the Indians with rum for their fish and furs. But the Indians in this locality kept refusing the "payment" of rum. They would push the rum back to the traders. The traders complained to their superiors. Time and again, these traders were told to add water, molasses, sugar, or juice to the rum in order to improve its taste. They presented it to the Indians each time, but the Indians continued to push the rum away. Soon, the traders ran out of ideas for making a better-tasting rum for these Indians. Then the traders offered to give the Indians something else. This is how we ended up with velvet, silk, and cotton for our new regalia. Once the Indians started trading, never again did they push that rum away. But today Indians, as well as descendants of those traders, go overboard for alcoholic beverages. Now they call the mixes "cocktails." I tell this story to my family and other community members who dare to listen. At one time Indians of the Northwest did not like alcohol. My guess is that there was so much good food readily available to them, and these foods tasted so good, that rum was far off key for their good taste. Not so today. If only we could turn back that clock.

THE POINT ELLIOTT TREATY TRIBES

To look at the treaty-making approach of Isaac Stevens, we have to refer back to the thinking of George W. Manypenny. Manypenny was the commissioner of Indian Affairs in Washington DC from 1853 to 1857, during which time Stevens negotiated treaties in Washington Territory. Manypenny advocated a reservation policy. He thought that Indians should have their own lands—but not remain separated from the rest of American society—in order that they would be influenced by, and integrate into, American society. He believed that Indians should own individual parcels of land, and so the provision to make future allotments of individual parcels was written into the nine treaties that Manypenny negotiated with tribes west of the Missouri River in 1854. According to the sixth article of Manypenny's 1854 Treaty with the Omaha, the U.S. president could order land surveys and allot a quarter-section (160 acres) to an Indian family and allot small tracts to individuals. Isaac Stevens used the Manypenny treaties as a model, and this provision is included also in the Point Elliott Treaty (Article 7), with reference to the Omaha Treaty. Manypenny's approach, carried forward by Stevens in the Washington Territory treaties, grew out of the Indian policy of the early republic, exemplified by Thomas Jefferson's view that Indians would abandon hunting, fishing and gathering and would cultivate farms and the "American" virtue of individualism.[14]

As detailed in chapter 4, total area ceded by the tribes in the Treaty of Point Elliott was almost 6 million acres (approximately 9,000 square miles). The final acreage reserved for the Point Elliott tribes (after enlargements, subtractions, and adjustments) is about 50,000 acres (approximately 78 square miles): slightly less than 1 percent of the ceded area.[15] The treaty indicates that the Tulalip Reservation would have 36 sections, equivalent to 36 square miles (one section equals one square mile; thirty-six sections equal one township). Tulalip, the largest reservation, was designated as the central agency for the Puget Sound tribes, where services and a school were to be located—a residential "agricultural and industrial school" for children from all the Point Elliott tribes. The treaty indicates that the government thought that it could eventually settle all Indian communities who were party to the Treaty of Point Elliott on this small reservation (or elsewhere) at the discretion of the U.S. president (Treaty of Point Elliott, Article 7).

In 1873, eighteen years after the signing of the treaty, surveys were completed, and President Ulysses S. Grant gave executive orders specifying the boundaries of the Lummi, Tulalip, and Swinomish Reservations.[16] Earlier, in 1864, the Suquamish/Port Madison Reservation had been enlarged by executive order. Its final acreage was 7,284 acres (approximately 11.4 square miles).[17] Indian agent M. T. Simmons had visited some of the tribes around the time of the Point Elliott Treaty. He reported that the Suquamish Reservation should "have its line changed as to take in some productive land and an excellent salmon stream."[18] I don't know how much this type of report generally helped, but it seemed that this one did. After various adjustments, the total land reserved in the original four Point Elliott Treaty reservations increased by about 9 square miles: from 69 to 78 square miles. The two largest reservations are Tulalip, with approximately 35 square miles, and Lummi, with about 19.5 square miles, plus tidelands.

The Treaty of Point Elliott (Article 2) identifies the Lummi Reservation as an island, Chah-choo-sen, "situated in the Lummi River at the point of separation of the mouths emptying respectively into Bellingham Bay and the Gulf of Georgia." When the reservation boundaries were surveyed prior to Grant's 1873 order, the island of Chah-choo-sen measured 11,211 acres (17.5 square miles). The United States excluded 820 acres from Lummi's land base and added 2,170 acres (map 9). President Grant's 1873 order redefined the reservation so that rather than defining it in terms of changeable rivers, it was defined to conform with township lines: "Commencing at the eastern mouth of the Lummi River: thence up said river to the point where it is intersected by the line between sections 7 and 8 of township 38 north, range 2 east of the Willamette meridian; thence due north along said section line to the township line between townships 38 and 39; thence west along said township line to the low-water mark on the shore of the Gulf of Georgia."[19] With the addition and subtraction of reservation lands, Grant's order resulted in an overall increase to the Lummi Reservation of 1,350 acres (2.1 square miles). Later, the tribe acquired two additional acres for the site of a school, resulting in a final area of about 12,563 acres (19.6 square miles).[20]

When the treaty was written, the government had in mind the possibility of consolidating tribes that were party to all the western Washington treaties onto a smaller number of reservations (Treaty of Point Elliott, Article 7). An 1875 report of the Committee of Indian Affairs notes that for the twelve reservations established in western Washington by the treaties of 1854, 1855, and 1856, seven had no Indian agents and few services, and only five Indian agents were in the region. The agents could not often visit distant reservations. The report estimates that only about 2,250 of the approximately 7,500 Indian people in the region (30 percent) resided on reservations, partly because they had to work off-reservation to earn a living, often fishing or logging.

Part of the government's solution was to enlarge the Lummi Reservation, where the government planned to relocate the tribes and bands "belonging to or residing on the Port Madison, Tulalip, Swinomish, and Muckleshoot Indian reservations."[21] There were already many others, in addition to Lummi, living on the Lummi Reservation. President Grant's order to enlarge the Lummi Reserve begins as follows: "Lummi Reserve, in Tulalip Agency; occupied by Dwamish, Etakmur, Snohomish, Sukwamish [Suquamish], and Swiwamish [Samamish?]." At that time there were villages at Gooseberry Point, the Portage, and at Fish Point. Fish Point Village, on the eastern shore of the Lummi Reserve, may have been formed by Indian people who relocated after the Nooksack River changed its course.[22] In 1875 Indian inspector William Vandever and the Board of Indian Commissioners recommended that the northern boundary of the Lummi Reservation be moved five miles to the north in order to enlarge the reservation. However, that recommendation remained only a proposal. (See map 9 and its caption for a discussion of changes to the reservation boundary between 1855 and 1919.)

There was no school at Lummi until the Lummi Day School opened in 1880, twenty-five years after the treaty was signed. It was open, off and on, until the BIA built a school in 1907. The only school for children of the Point Elliott tribes was at the Tulalip Reservation. The Tulalip Indian School was established in 1857 by Father Eugene Casimir Chirouse and had only a few Lummi students.[23] Father Chirouse founded the Mission of St. Anne at Tulalip, where he was based, along with missions at Lummi and Suquamish. Lummi was assigned a farming instructor, and some people did well at farming in those early years. Later there were BIA employees who came to live among the Lummi people as farming teachers, and they became excellent fishermen. They were even on the census lists that created the membership roll for the Lummi Tribe, and have ever since been Indian. Isn't that a great story? And we really enjoy their company. But back in the decades after the treaty, part of the work of the farming instructor was just to encourage Indian people to stay on the reservation. The farmer at Lummi, C. C. Finkbonner, who was also was the Indian agent-in-charge, wrote in his 1867 report to the Indian commissioner: "There are over 125 children on this reservation that ought to be at school. Rev. E. C. Chirouse has ten boys from this reservation at Tulalip, which is all he can accommodate with those he has from other places in the district. He can only accommodate about forty boys with the limited facilities at his disposal."[24]

Earlier, we saw that there still wasn't a physician for the tribes of the Oregon and Washington Territories in 1858, three years after the treaty, because of "meager appropriations" to pay one. The Tulalip Reservation was established in 1860, and it wasn't until the late 1860s that Tulalip got a physician: more than a decade after the signing of the treaty. Tulalip, functioning as a central agency, was the only Point Elliott reservation to have physician; it is sixty-six miles south of the Lummi Reservation. Seventy-six years after the treaty, in 1931, my father, Joseph Hillaire, testified in hearings held in Tacoma for the government's "Survey of Conditions of Indians in the United States." My father spoke about several problems of the Lummi Reservation, such as roads, education, reservation boundaries, and fishing rights. But the first thing he brought out was the need for health care on the reservation. He told how much need there was for a field nurse to be based there, let alone a physician. In the report Senator Wheeler and Senator Frank sounded surprised when they learned that the current field nurse had headquarters an hour away and was responsible for five reservations. My father tells of the work carried out by himself and Norbert James to minister to the sick at Lummi: "We lost two cases and barely saved the others during the influenza epidemic."[25]

After the treaties, employees of the government had to travel long distances to reach the many tribes scattered across our region, which had to be visited approximately once a year, according to treaty arrangements, to deliver annuity goods. These goods had to be transported to the tribes from government storage areas. The government employees had to do all this and put up with unscrupulous individuals along the way. There were, no doubt, government employees with high moral standards, but many opportunities existed for goods to be diverted for the profit of those responsible for transporting and distributing them. Indians were hired (perhaps, as today, at minimum wage) to transport officials to and from places in the Pacific Northwest. However, what "goods" were really needed by my ancestors, when the lands and waters had met their every need before "discovery?" Did they really need the newly introduced coffee, sugar, flour, and salt—foods that promote addiction and cancer—and, of course, the contraband commodities of whiskey and rum? Did alcohol, restrictions on freedom, and the destruction of their expansive culture change Indians from what they were before discovery to become the "depraved Indians" mentioned in the government documents? Apparently Indians in our area went from being self-sufficient to "depraved" in the fifty years between 1805 (the year of Lewis and Clark's arrival at the mouth of the Columbia) and treaty-making time, 1855.

The present-day tribes (2016) that are party to the Treaty of Point Elliott are Lummi, Samish, Nooksack, Upper Skagit, Swinomish, Tulalip, Suquamish, Sauk-Suiattle, Stillaguamish, Snoqualmie, and Muckleshoot (map 7). Tribes that were to occupy the Tulalip Reservation include Snohomish, Snoqualmie, Stillaguamish, Skykomish, and other tribes and bands that survived in small numbers. (The word "Tulalip" is not the name of a tribe; it is a Snohomish word that describes the bay there.)

Tribal members from the Nooksack Tribe, inland from Lummi, were unable to attend the Treaty Council because their river was frozen, and they could not travel there by canoe. But one or more leaders were present who represented the Nooksack, and Nooksack is a Point Elliott Treaty tribe. In 1970 the Nooksack Tribe gained title to a one-acre reservation in Deming, fifteen miles east of Bellingham. In 1973 the Nooksack Tribe received federal recognition.[26] The Upper Skagit people, east of Lummi, lived along the Skagit River and beyond. The Skagit Reservation consists of three parcels totaling just over a hundred acres near Sedro-Woolley and Burlington.

The Samish Tribe, just south of Lummi, was federally recognized as a tribe for the second time in 1996 (after having once been left off the list of recognized tribes). The Samish Tribe has a tribal center in Anacortes, but no reservation. After the treaty, people of Samish descent went to live on the Swinomish Reservation and other locations. Swinomish tribal members have ancestry representing Swinomish, Kikiallus, Lower Skagit, Samish, and other tribes and bands. These groups originally inhabited the Skagit and Samish River Valleys, the coasts around Skagit, Padilla, and Fidalgo Bays, Saratoga Passage, and islands in the region, including the San Juan Islands. The Swinomish Reservation, on Fidalgo Island near La Conner, encompasses about 7,450 acres (11.6 square miles), plus tidelands of about 2,900 acres.[27]

The inland tribes Sauk-Suiattle (Darrington), Stillaguamish (Arlington), and Snoqualmie (Snoqualmie) are federally recognized but have no reservations. The Snoqualmie tribe lost federal recognition in 1953 but regained it in 1999, after long years of effort. The Muckleshoot, descendants of the inland Duwamish and Upper Puyallup, are party to the treaties of both Point Elliott and Medicine Creek; a reservation was established in Auburn, Washington, by executive order in 1874. Today the Muckleshoot are buying back their lands and operate several economically successful enterprises.

Chief Seattle was Suquamish and Duwamish. The Duwamish were party to the Treaty of Point Elliott, yet they received no land of their own. However, the Duwamish Tribe, which has headquarters and a longhouse in the city of Seattle, still maintains its identity and traditions. In

January 2001,the Duwamish Tribe was awarded federal recognition, but it was rescinded when George W. Bush took office and overturned final executive orders that had been issued by Bill Clinton. The Duwamish Tribe has continued its fight for federal recognition.

ALLOTMENT

One of the greatest violations of Indian treaty rights was the General Allotment Act (GAA), also known as the Dawes Severalty Act of 1887.[28] The Dawes Act, named for its sponsor, Senator Henry Dawes (R-MA), dictated that the solution to "the Indian problem" was that Indian reservations should be broken up. The Allotment Act was a way to break up Native cultural ways and political systems. Some of the ideas behind it were that Indians are like, or should be like, European Americans, and that owning land and becoming an individual who competes in the economy will "build character." Senator Dawes helped to found the Indian reformers' meetings at Lake Mohonk, New York, which influenced U.S. Indian policy. A number of "Friends of the Indian" reformers groups, concerned with Indian rights, formed around 1880, but for the most part they advocated assimilation.

The Dawes Act caused the communal holdings of tribes to be cut into separate parcels of land. In general, reservation lands were divided into 160-acre parcels for each Indian head of household. Single Indian men and women over eighteen years of age and Indian orphans under age eighteen were each eligible for 80 acres. At first, married women could not receive allotments, but an 1891 amendment changed the terms so that any Indian man, woman, or child was eligible for 80 acres.[29] At most, this was only 25 percent of the amount of land received by white settlers through the Oregon Land Donation Act of 1850. According to section 1 of the Dawes Act, the number of acres could be less, or possibly more, depending on the size of the reservation and the laws and treaty stipulations that applied in particular cases.

Although the results of the Dawes Act were drastic, the act is often wrongly regarded as having created rapid policy changes. However, as Frederick Hoxie observes, the Dawes Act was not a detailed action plan, but "a statement of its sponsors' common assumptions about the Indians' place in American society," and it "gave administration considerable discretionary power."[30] The Dawes Act was an "enabling act," an item of legislation whereby a legislative body (in this case, the U.S. Congress) authorizes an entity that depends on it for authorization (in this case, the U.S. president) to take particular actions. The Dawes or General Allotment Act was *general*, in the sense of authorizing the president—without needing new legislative authorization for each reservation—to survey and divide reservation lands and, without the consent of a tribe, to allot the divided lands to individual Indians and dispose of "surplus lands." Prucha provides data about the number of allotments and the number of acres allotted to Indians in the early twentieth century. Prucha also identifies factors leading to the dissipation, by the first third of the twentieth century, of the Indian estate, which occurred because of the Dawes Act and subsequent laws that were passed for the allotment of specific reservations.[31]

When land was allotted, it was surveyed and parcels were assigned to individuals, but the land was held in trust by the federal government. After twenty-five years, the parcel could have a status called *fee simple*, meaning that the person holding title to it had the right to sell or lease it. The land also became subject to property tax. Therefore, many Indian people ended up selling their allotments because of the burden of property taxes and other financial pressures.

The Dawes Act not only greatly reduced our already small Indian reservations; it also pitted family members against each other for land inheritance. Family relationships were weakened. In many cases elders intended that land would be passed on to youth when the young people became ready to settle in their own homes. Along with policies that made it difficult to keep land in the family, bickering and alienation within families resulted. One turned against the other, fighting for the right to the better part of a specific inherited land. Some Indian persons wished to use their land, sell it, or lease it, but they could not because of poorly conceived inheritance policies. The land allotment process and an overlay of administrative rules and regulations were designed to stamp out the Indian way of life. Slowly but surely, this ate away at the dreaming capacity of Indian America.

Allotment was a way to get Indians to "acculturate" and was also a way for white America to legally (but not justly) gain Indian treaty lands. The government designated unalloted land as "surplus," and it was sold to settlers or to commercial interests, or it was taken over by the government. The allotment system violated the terms of our treaties, by which lands were reserved by tribes. The treaties did not mean that Indian land and rights were reserved unless the government enacts new legislation to override the treaty, for "all treaties made, or which shall be made, under the authority of the United States, shall be the Supreme Law of the Land," according to the U.S. Constitution (Article 6, Section 2).

Allotment was finally eliminated on Indian reservation lands in 1934, with the reforms of the Indian Reorganization Act, or Wheeler-Howard Act. This came after nearly half a century of allotment policy. From the time the Dawes Act was passed in 1887 until the reforms of the Indian Reorganization Act (the Wheeler-Howard Act of 1934), Indian America lost ninety to one hundred million acres, equivalent to two-thirds of the lands held by the tribes prior to the Allotment Act.

Allotment of land at Lummi began in 1884, three years before the Dawes Act.[32] Indian superintendent for Washington Territory, Robert H. Milroy, subdivided and allotted some reservation lands as early as a decade before the federal government passed the Dawes Allotment Act.[33] Article 7 of the Treaty of Point Elliott contains a provision for allotment:

> The President may hereafter . . . cause the whole or any portion of the lands hereby reserved, or of such other land as may be selected in lieu thereof, to be surveyed into lots, and assign the same to such individuals or families as are willing to avail themselves of the privilege, and will locate on the same as a permanent home on the same terms and subject to the same regulations as are provided in the sixth article of the treaty with the Omahas, so far as the same may be applicable. Any substantial improvements heretofore made by any

Indian, and which he shall be compelled to abandon in consequence of this treaty, shall be valued under the direction of the President and payment made accordingly therefor.[34]

Even though unalloted land at Lummi did not get designated "surplus," as occurred with lands allotted by the Dawes Act, much of Lummi land ended up being sold to non-Indians because of unworkable heirship policies, and because of Indian landowners' needs for the funds that the land sales would bring. Decades after the allotment period was over, allotment and heirship policies continued to create trouble within families. Small parcels of land could end up being owned by a number of descendants who could not use the land, nor could they easily obtain signatures from the other heirs in order to sell or lease it (see chapter 7).

> An indirect result [of the Dawes or General Allotment Act] was fractionated heirship . . . Under the Indian probate laws, as individuals died, their property descended to their heirs as undivided "fractional" interests in the allotment (tenancy in common). In other words, if an Indian owning a 160 acre allotment died and had four heirs, the heirs did not inherit 40 acres each. Rather, they each inherited a one-fourth interest in the entire 160 acre allotment. As the years passed, fractionation has expanded geometrically to the point where there are hundreds of thousands of tiny fractional interests . . . The cost of maintaining heirship records and administering the land is inordinately expensive for the BIA. Approximately 50 to 75% ($33 million) of the B.I.A.'s realty budget goes to administering these fractional interests and is, thus, unavailable for investment in productive lands.[35]

How did the Dawes Act violate the terms of our treaties? In *A Century of Dishonor*, Helen Hunt Jackson quotes American jurist James Kent: "The violation of any one article of a treaty is a violation of the whole treaty. It is a principle of universal jurisprudence that a compact cannot be rescinded by one party only, if the other party does not consent to rescind it, and does no act to destroy it."[36] Lands that were lost by Dawes Act were lands that had been reserved by treaty, the Supreme Law of the Land, according to the U.S. Constitution. Disposition of reservation lands is a function of treaties, but the Dawes Act was a way that the government found to go around the treaties.

Moreover, tribes did not have adequate representation during the assignment of allotments, and they proclaimed their objections to this. Cohen's *Handbook of Federal Indian Law* clarifies that "a tribe is not bound by a contract which is not made by a proper representative."[37] Further, the process by which the Dawes Act divided Indian lands did not allow for tribal governments to follow their own ways of conferring among their people about how to distribute available land, in order that current and future generations could sustain their lives, their families, and their culture. If the Dawes Act were not part of our history, Indian America would have been saved many assaults on prosperity and pride.

CHARRED GROUND

Our oral tradition carries the story of a "big burn." My mother told me this story when I was in the twelfth grade in Ferndale High School. In 1868, a fire got out of control at an old shake mill on Fish Point near the mouth of the current Nooksack River.[38] Once it was out of control, the Lummi Indian agent consulted with a Bureau of Indian Affairs official, and it was agreed to let it burn. It did burn; it burned much of the Lummi Indian Reservation. At that time, the trees that burned were ancient stands of cedar. The bureaucrats told the Lummi Indian Agent that the area on fire was to become the habitat of the Skalakhan (Sq'eláxen), whose descendants became part of the Lummi Tribe. They were to be removed from the San Juan Islands and the Nooksack River Valley to our Lummi land, on the mainland coast. Burning an area to create homesites may go against common sense, but the thinking of the U.S. government was to clear the ground so that our fishing tribes could become farmers. What happened was the ruination of our great cedars and firs, plus it created swampy conditions, once the trees were destroyed. Fish Point was the oldest Lummi village; it is in the Whatcom Creek area. I remember the Fish Point Village clearly, as my mother would take all of us to visit other Indian homes there. Among them were the Placids and the Browns. This is the area where the Smokehouse (Longhouse) was built, which, by the way, is still standing and is used every winter.

When I was born (in 1929, according to the Lummi census) we lived in a two-story home on the corner of what is now called Lake Terrell Road and Slater Road, kitty-corner from an oil refinery, not far from Sandy Point. We picked berries every summer and saw the Big Burn logs and stumps between our house and our grandparents' home. Only a few stumps remain. Wild blackberries, which grow well on charred ground, grow there in abundance. Before 1850, the region that became the Lummi Reservation was dominated by "old-growth forests of massive douglas fir, western hemlock, spruce, and western red cedar." The deciduous trees that now dominate were likely there too. The sources of evidence about the kinds of trees that used to grow at Lummi are early photographs, and accounts by Lummi elders and by Anglo-European explorers and settlers. Between 1850 and 1900 there may have been other fires that swept through the Lummi Reservation. The deciduous trees that are here today have almost entirely replaced the old-growth cedars and other evergreens.[39]

There were eighteen longhouses that were burned down on the San Juan Islands, our aboriginal habitation. According to Joe Hillaire and Eddie Jefferson, members of the Lummi Tribe's tribal government at that time, a Judge Griffith was judge when local agents, who were non-Indian farmers, and local BIA agents in Everett, Washington, along with the upper echelon in local government, promised Lummi Indians that they would pay them eighteen thousand dollars if they would burn down their permanent timbered longhouses, located on nearby islands. Testimonies of Lummi elders provide valuable information that, at that time, the Lummi owned all of San Juan Island, all of Lopez Island, Decatur Island, Blakely Island, Cypress Island, Sinclair Island, Vendovi Island, and Point Roberts. Joe Hillaire and Eddie Jefferson had collected testimonies from Lummi elders for the claims filed against the U.S. government in 1927 and 1951.[40] (Map 2 shows the approximate boundaries that the Lummi claimed in their 1951 Indian Claims Commission case.)

Frank Hillaire was supposedly hired by the Bureau of Indian Affairs to burn down eighteen longhouses on Orcas Island, and the tribe was to be paid eighteen thousand dollars. Frank Hillaire, born in about 1846, was my grandfather: the father of my father, Joe Hillaire. Frank Hillaire handed this information down to my father, who handed it down to me. Frank Hillaire and a company of Lummi men followed the BIA officer's orders to burn down the longhouses for that amount of money. However, not one penny was realized, because of the government policy that no money was to be given Indians. Only commodities or "gifts" were to be provided. There are no testimonies of payment or "gifts" for those burned-down longhouses. Perhaps you can consider this, along with other evidence from the decades that surround our treaties with the U.S. government, to test the truth of my claim that Indian America has been treated unjustly.

PATTERNS OF THE PAST: DELAY OF
THE TREATY'S RATIFICATION

What can we learn from patterns of the past as we look back at our tribal relations with the U.S. government? One event that we can learn from, which needs to be moved from its ahistoric status to be better known in our history, is the delay of the ratification of our treaties in the Pacific Northwest. The Treaty of Point Elliott was signed in 1855, but it was not was ratified until 1859. Why did ratification take so long? What can we learn from history, as regards our rights of today and the future?

An 1857 report from Commissioner of Indian Affairs James W. Denver states the following about the Puget Sound treaties that were still unratified:

I would invite special attention to the report of the superintendent for Oregon and Washington, from which it appears to be manifest that our relations with the Indians in those Territories are in a very critical condition, and that under the existing state of things, there is a constant liability to a general outbreak on their part from any disturbing cause, which must involve the expenditure of millions to subdue them, as well as the most lamentable loss of life and property by the insufficiently protected white inhabitants.

The non-ratification of the treaties heretofore made to extinguish their title to the lands necessary to the occupancy and use of our citizens seems to have produced no little disappointment, and the continued extension of our settlements into their territory, without any compensation being made to them, is a constant source of dissatisfaction and hostile feeling. They are represented as being willing to dispose of their land to the government, and I know of no alternative to the present unsatisfactory and dangerous state of things but the adoption of early measures for the extinguishment of their title, and their colonization on properly-located reservations, using and applying the consideration agreed to be allowed to them for their lands and to subsist and clothe them until they can be taught and influenced to support and sustain themselves. The losses and damages to the government and to the citizens resulting from another general outbreak on the part of these Indians would probably fully equal, if not exceed, in amount which would be necessary to buy out and colonize them, so that they could be effectually controlled, if not improved and civilized.[41]

Could this Indian commissioner have said it a better way? I have tried to make sense of the government's language, and I have tried to make sense of the government's mismanagement of Indians' conditions. The government was creating situations that were almost unreal to the Indians and designed to serve the government and non-Indian citizens. Perhaps it was partly owing to the government's own management problems that Washington's coastal tribes were able to remain in the Puget Sound region, rather than being removed from their homelands to east of the Cascade Mountains, plus the vastness of territory to be covered and the problem of funding such a removal.

Isaac I. Stevens was not in the Washington Territory consistently during the time that most of the western Washington tribes waited for ratification of the treaties that they had signed. Indian agents' reports from that time show how much the conduct of Indian affairs depended on Stevens's expertise and skill. For part of this time, Stevens was participating in treaty councils with the Blackfeet Nation.[42] In July 1855 he arrived from Washington Territory at Fort Benton (present-day Montana) in the Blackfeet Country.[43] Stevens sent messages to the Indians and agents elsewhere, in order to keep alive the Indian policy of which he was in charge. For this author, facts like this make it easier to understand the confusion felt by the Indian population. Some of Governor Stevens's remarks were made before the convention at Mukilteo (Point Elliott) where the treaty was signed. This description of Stevens's approach is from the book *The Life of Isaac I. Stevens* (1900), by his son, Hazard Stevens: "The success and rapidity with which he carried through these treaties were due to the careful planning and thorough manner in which he planned them, and prepared the minds of the Indians by his tour among and talks to them a year previous, 1852, and by the messages and agents he had sent among them."[44]

Hazard Stevens has this to say about the situation and about his father's efforts (although we could take this praise of his father's work with a grain of salt): "The Indian War which occurred soon after, and the delay in the ratification of the treaties, seriously militated against carrying out the beneficent policy so well inaugurated, and later the occasional appointment of inefficient and dishonest agents has proved even more detrimental; but notwithstanding all these drawbacks the Indians have made substantial advances in civilization, and it is interesting to compare their present condition, as given in the last reports of the Commissioner of Indian Affairs, and from local sources."[45]

Stevens started holding treaty councils in 1853, the year before the first of his ten Pacific Northwest treaties was signed. (His journal lists the items that he gives Indian people at these 1853 councils, including "sugar, coffee, rice, flour, blankets, tobacco, knives, axes, guns, powder, balls, hats, shirts, pants, and other essentials.")[46] The Indians' confusion resulted, in part, from messages that they received in two meetings with Stevens. In the first meeting Stevens told the Indians that the words of the treaty would become law and would outlast the nearby mountains. In the second meeting the mountains were not mentioned, but the promises were remembered by the old chiefs and headmen at the actual treaty signing. White America experienced much ado before, during, and after the treaty signing and could not fathom the situation of the Indians as a priority, because of their other pressing concerns in the Pacific Northwest.

The 1855 reports of Indian Affairs superintendents J. Cain and Joel Palmer speak of fears, on the part of both settlers and the government, of an Indian War.[47] The Mexican War (1846–48) had recently ended. Many soldiers had returned from the Mexican War and were discharged from service, leaving too few to serve in the Pacific Northwest. Perhaps this shortage contributed to the government's concerns about managing "the Indian situation" in the Northwest. Looking back, it's easy to think, "Well, of course the United States could not ratify those treaties, when the Indians weren't behaving and they were making war." But such a judgment overlooks the conditions that led up to the wars in our area: the Rogue River War, the Yakama War, and the Puget Sound "War," which was barely a war.[48]

The Rogue River War was influenced by disagreement between Isaac Stevens and the U.S. Army about how or whether settlers could just take land from Indians. In essence, Stevens said yes; the army said no.[49] Here is just one example of what occurred in that time frame. In the fall of 1855 the commander at Fort Lane (in present-day Oregon) brought Indian women and children into the military fort to save them from settlers who were attacking them. Meanwhile, settlers killed twenty-seven Indians who remained in the village. Indian warriors then killed the same number of settlers. The war continued over the winter, but by June, the Indians were sent to reservations.

Yakama chief Kamiakin did not trust Isaac Stevens's Treaty of Wallawalla, and when Kamiakin finally signed it in 1855, it is said that his lips were covered in blood, from biting them in anger. When the Yakama ceded their land, they were concerned that settlers and miners would trespass on their way west. Stevens assured them that this would not happen, but there was theft, assault on Indian women, and damage to the land, especially after gold was discovered and many miners came through with mules. Other tribes, including some from Puget Sound, joined the cause of the Yakama; confrontations included the one-day "Battle of Seattle" (January 26, 1856). The Indian men who fought in these battles were protecting their families, communities, and homes, as most people would do. In the government's thinking, and in the public mind, it seems that the Rogue River War, the Yakama War, and the conflicts in the Puget Sound area were dwelt upon to create an image of warlike tribes. The result of the Yakama War? Within a couple of years, 90 percent of Yakama land was lost. Soldiers found a letter that Kamiakin had dictated to the mission priest, Father Pandosy, suggesting an arrangement to allow certain Indian land to whites, in exchange for Indians not being forced onto a reservation. Kamiakin refused to go the reservation when it was imposed in 1858; he left his homeland to keep his freedom. After he died, his body was desecrated.[50]

Along with the destructive visits of smallpox among the Indians, problems in communication between whites and Indians, the long distance for travel and communication between the Pacific Northwest and the nation's capital, and war and fear of war, white America was also busy building its railroads to the West. The railroads provided the quickest means possible, at that time, to carry people, raw materials, and goods to and from the Pacific Coast (map 8). By then, the U.S. government was just giving land to the railroad companies. Indian title was not taken seriously by most railroad companies this far west of the Mississippi and Missouri Rivers. Sometimes railroad companies made treaties with tribes, so that they could run rails through tribal lands. However, no entity other than the federal government can make treaties that are ratifiable by Congress.[51]

The Oregon Land Donation Act of 1850 put a lot of pressure on the situation. Whites were following government policy to settle on Indian land that had not yet been ceded by treaty; this naturally led to confusion and conflict between settlers and Indians. In response to those tensions various government officials and military leaders took up time with their own conflicts about those problems. Isaac Stevens made so many changes; he was probably seen by some as too lenient toward Indians for things like allowing more reservations than the government intended; but many saw the harsh side of his treatment of Indian people.

With armed conflict occurring in places, and other tensions keeping the situation off-balance, reports from the Northwest must have discouraged Congress against ratifying the treaties. Was it stability in the Northwest that Congress was waiting for, or did the United States have other considerations? Perhaps the documents of history could help answer that question, but governmental officials didn't write reports on every thought they had. What we do know is that not until 1859—four years after signing—Congress finally ratified eight of the treaties that Isaac Stevens had transacted in the Pacific Northwest, including the Treaty of Point Elliott.[52] Only the Treaty of Medicine Creek (with the Nisqually and others) and the Treaty with the Blackfeet were ratified within a year of their signing.[53]

The first of Steven's treaties, the Treaty of Medicine Creek (with the present-day Puyallup, Nisqually, and Squaxin Island tribes), was signed in the winter of 1854 and ratified that spring. Chief Leschi, a tribal leader from Nisqually, was executed by the Washington territorial government for what the government called a murder, which he was accused of committing during the Indian War of 1855–56 in the western Puget Sound area. The Nisqually people had refused to move to the poor tract of reservation land assigned to them, which had no pastures and was far from their fishing sites. The government feared that Leschi and his brother, Quiemuth, would unite the tribes in war, perhaps joining with the Yakama. There was no evidence that Leschi had killed the white military volunteer who ended up getting shot, but what is more amazing is that the government did not regard Indian actions in this conflict as part of a military conflict, in which soldiers sometimes have to kill and die in combat. The U.S. military in this case *did* regard the white/Indian conflict as a military conflict, and so it was the county government—backed by Governor Stevens—that had Leschi hanged for murder. This was in order to teach Indians a lesson about who was in control. In 2004, a Washington State court exonerated Chief Leschi.

What messages for today and the future can we find, when we look back at those years, after the treaty? We can blame some of the failures on ignorance of, and lack of concern for, Indian people. We may also see that, for Indian leaders and citizens, and for all U.S. leaders and citizens, we need clarity in our own minds and clarity in our words with each other.

At first, Indian progress was stymied by the violent deaths of our people and our leaders. Shock waves of violence, large and small, kept Indians from progressing. President Obama is too busy with the War on Terror and the horrors of our economy to get very involved with Indian America. He has an obligation to do so, not only by law, but by kinship with his adoptive Crow family. It is vital that our U.S. president, policy makers, and citizens know our Indian history and remember our rights. Many books have been written about Indians' Americanized ending. Too few Americans know where our country is headed, and too few know how to fight it.

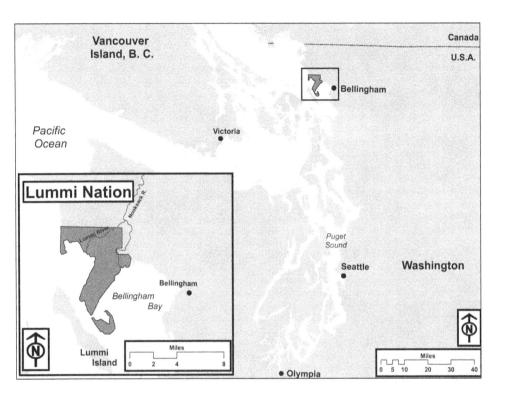

Map 1. Location of the Lummi Indian Reservation. Map by Gregory P. Fields. Cartography by Charles Yeager, 2011. The Lummi Reservation is on the coast of northwestern Washington, about twenty miles south of the U.S./Canada border, ninety miles north of the city of Seattle, and eight miles west of Bellingham, Washington. The reservation consists of approximately 12,563 acres* (approx. 19.6 square miles), plus surrounding tidelands of about 7,000 acres.**

* USGD, 1934, U.S. Court of Claims, *Duwamish et al. v. U.S.*, Sect. XXII.

** Lummi Natural Resources Department, *Lummi Nation Atlas*, 6.

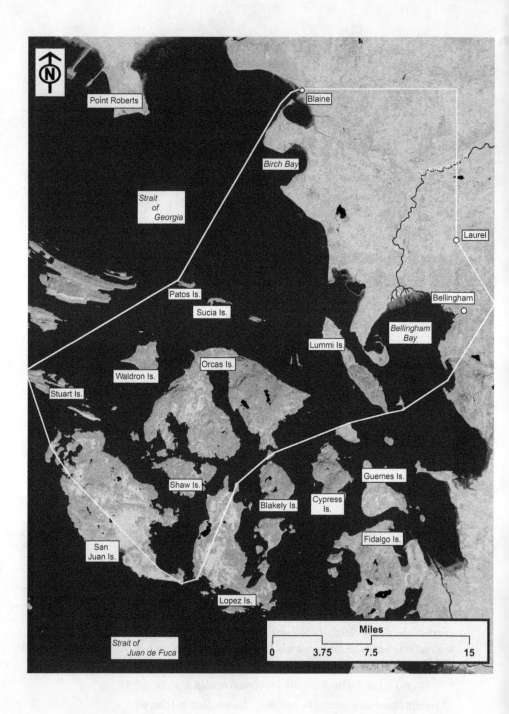

Map 2. Ancestral Lummi territory. Map by Gregory P. Fields. Cartography by Charles Yeager, 2011. Approximate boundaries of pre-treaty Lummi lands. The boundary line shows the central ancestral lands of the Lummi before the 1855 Treaty of Point Elliott. Lummi territory extended beyond the boundary shown to Point Roberts, Washington, and across the current border between Canada and the United States. The Lummi and other Straits Salish-speaking tribes, the Semiahmoo north of the Lummi, and the Samish to the south, along with tribes based on southern Vancouver Island—Saanich, T'Sou-ke, and Songhees—traveled and gathered food in the straits and among the Gulf Islands (British Columbia) and the San Juan Islands (Washington State). The boundaries on this map indicate the approximate area that the Lummi claimed in their Indian Claims Commission case *Lummi Tribe of Indians v. the United States*. The tribe's claim was for 249,800 acres (390 square miles).*

* USGD, 1952, *Lummi Tribe of Indians v. the United States*, "Opinion," 1.

Map 3.

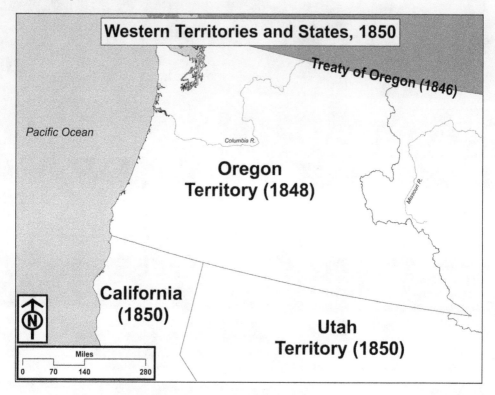

Maps 3–5. Western territories and states, 1850–70. Maps by Gregory P. Fields. Cartography by Charles Yeager, 2011. In 1846 Great Britain and the United States resolved their dispute over the Oregon Country (called by Britain the "Columbia District") by signing the Oregon Treaty. The treaty established an international boundary at the 49th parallel: the border of present-day British Columbia and Washington State. By acquiring the Oregon Territory, the United States gained the lands that would become Oregon, Washington, and portions of Idaho, Montana, and Wyoming. Statehood was attained by Oregon in 1859, by Washington and Montana in 1889, and by Idaho and Wyoming in 1890. Utah gained statehood in 1896.

References:

Trump, "The State of Oregon and the Washington Territory in 1848"; Trump, "Oregon and Washington Territories in 1853"; Trump, "The State of Oregon and the Washington Territory in 1859."

Map 4.

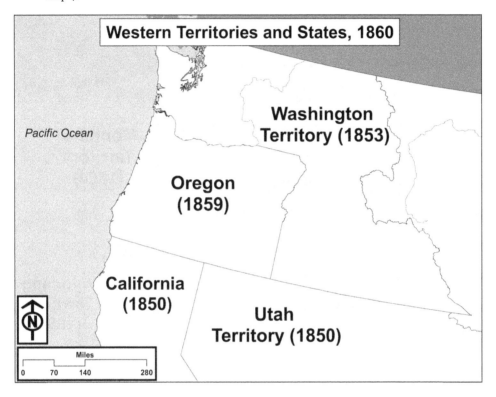

Western Territories and States, 1860

Pacific Ocean

Washington
Territory (1853)

Oregon
(1859)

California
(1850)

Utah
Territory (1850)

N

Miles

0   70   140   280

Map 5.

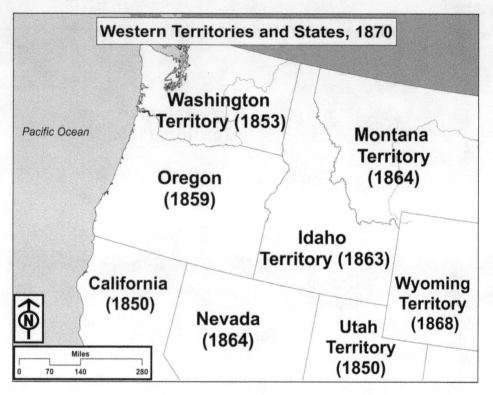

Western Territories and States, 1870

Washington Territory (1853)

Montana Territory (1864)

Pacific Ocean

Oregon (1859)

Idaho Territory (1863)

California (1850)

Wyoming Territory (1868)

Nevada (1864)

Utah Territory (1850)

N

Miles
0   70   140   280

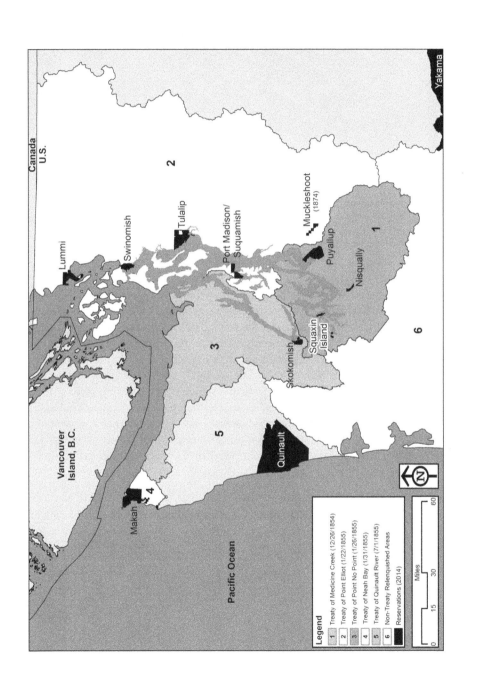

Legend

1	Treaty of Medicine Creek (12/26/1854)
2	Treaty of Point Elliot (1/22/1855)
3	Treaty of Point No Point (1/26/1855)
4	Treaty of Neah Bay (1/31/1855)
5	Treaty of Quinault River (7/1/1855)
6	Non-Treaty Relenquished Areas
	Reservations (2014)

Miles

0   15   30   60

Canada
U.S.

Vancouver
Island, B.C.

Pacific Ocean

Lummi

Swinomish

Tulalip

2

Port Madison/
Suquamish

Muckleshoot
(1874)

Puyallup

Nisqually

1

Skokomish

Squaxin
Island

3

5

Quinault

Makah

4

6

Yakama

Map 6. (*previous*) Ceded lands and reservations in western Washington. Map by Gregory P. Fields. Cartography by Charles Yeager and Zach Schleicher, 2014. Five of Isaac Stevens's ten treaties in the Pacific Northwest were transacted in western Washington. The reservations on map 6 are shown in their present-day dimensions, after enlargements and reductions. The amount of land ceded by the Point Elliott Treaty (area 2) was about 9,000 square miles—nearly 6 million acres. The original number of acres reserved by Point Elliott Treaty tribes, according to findings in the U.S. Court of Claims case *Duwamish et al. v. U.S.*, was 44,192 acres (approx. 69 square miles). After enlargements and subtractions, the final acreage reserved by the Point Elliott Treaty tribes is approximately 49,786 acres (about 78 square miles).*
Some Washington tribes have reservations that were established not by treaty but by executive order (order of a U.S. president); for example, in western Washington, Muckleshoot and Chehalis; and in eastern Washington, Colville, Spokane, and Kalispel.

* USGD, 1934, U.S. Court of Claims, *Duwamish et al. v. U.S.*, Sect. XXII.

References:

Tribal Lands: Department of Ecology, State of Washington (ecy.wa.gov); Washington Governor's Office of Indian Affairs (goia.wa.gov).

States of Oregon and Washington: U.S. Census Bureau (census.gov).

Cities: Washington State Department of Transportation (wsdot.wa.gov); Oregon Spatial Data Library (oregon.gov).

Columbia River: Department of Ecology, State of Washington (ecy.wa.gov).

Puget Sound: Department of Ecology, State of Washington (ecy.wa.gov).

Canada: Statistics Canada (statcan.gc.ca).

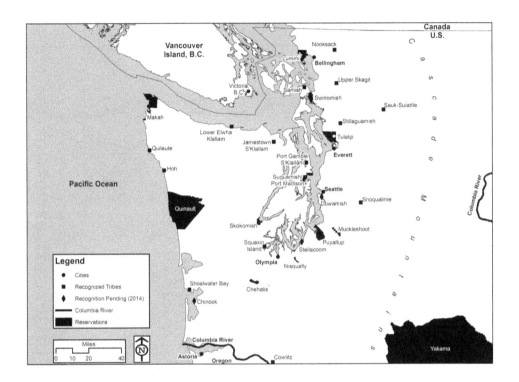

Map 7. Tribes of western Washington. Map by Gregory P. Fields. Cartography by Zach Schleicher, 2014. There are twenty-nine federally recognized tribes in Washington State, twenty-five of them in western Washington. There are four reservations in eastern Washington (east of the Cascades): Yakama, Colville, Spokane, and Kalispel.

References:

Tribal Lands: Department of Ecology, State of Washington (ecy.wa.gov); Washington Governor's Office of Indian Affairs (goia.wa.gov).

States of Oregon and Washington: U.S. Census Bureau (census.gov).

Cities: Washington State Department of Transportation (wsdot.wa.gov); Oregon Spatial Data Library (oregon.gov).

Columbia River: Department of Ecology, State of Washington (ecy.wa.gov).

Puget Sound: Department of Ecology, State of Washington (ecy.wa.gov).

Canada: Statistics Canada (statcan.gc.ca).

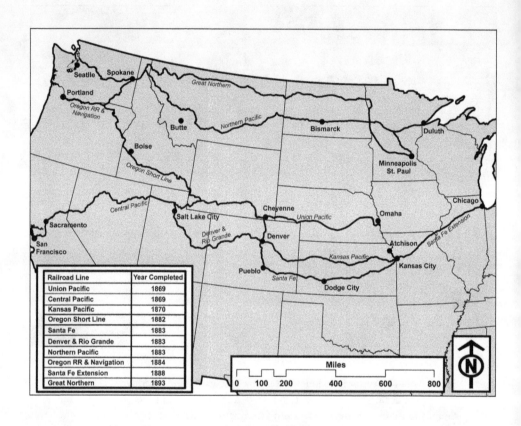

Railroad Line	Year Completed
Union Pacific	1869
Central Pacific	1869
Kansas Pacific	1870
Oregon Short Line	1882
Santa Fe	1883
Denver & Rio Grande	1883
Northern Pacific	1883
Oregon RR & Navigation	1884
Santa Fe Extension	1888
Great Northern	1893

Map 8. Railroad routes to the West. Map by Gregory P. Fields. Cartography by Charles Yeager, 2011.

References:

Stover, *Routledge Historical Atlas*, 35.

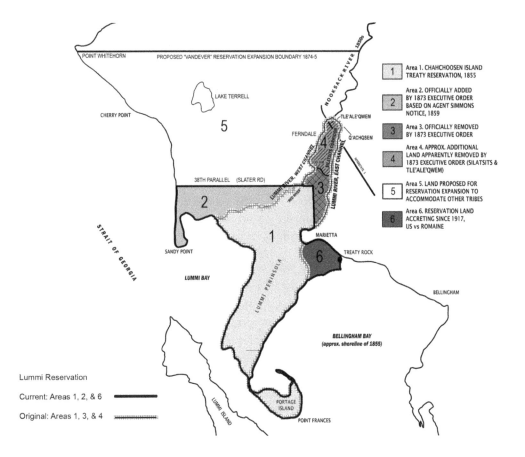

POINT WHITEHORN   PROPOSED "VANDEVER" RESERVATION EXPANSION BOUNDARY 1874-5   NOOKSACK RIVER 1850s

LAKE TERRELL

CHERRY POINT

5

FERNDALE

TLE'ALE'QWEM

Q'ACHQSEM

38TH PARALLEL   (SLATER RD)

LUMMI RIVER, WEST CHANNEL

LUMMI RIVER, EAST CHANNEL

SMUGGLERS SLOUGH

RED RIVER

2

3

4

1

STRAIT OF GEORGIA

SANDY POINT

LUMMI BAY

MARIETTA

6   TREATY ROCK

LUMMI PENINSULA

BELLINGHAM

BELLINGHAM BAY
(approx. shoreline of 1855)

Lummi Reservation

Current: Areas 1, 2, & 6 ──────

Original: Areas 1, 3, & 4 ⋯⋯⋯⋯

LUMMI ISLAND

PORTAGE ISLAND

POINT FRANCES

1	Area 1. CHAHCHOOSEN ISLAND TREATY RESERVATION, 1855
2	Area 2. OFFICIALLY ADDED BY 1873 EXECUTIVE ORDER BASED ON AGENT SIMMONS NOTICE, 1859
3	Area 3. OFFICIALLY REMOVED BY 1873 EXECUTIVE ORDER
4	Area 4. APPROX. ADDITIONAL LAND APPARENTLY REMOVED BY 1873 EXECUTIVE ORDER (SILATSITS & TLE'ALE'QWEM)
5	Area 5. LAND PROPOSED FOR RESERVATION EXPANSION TO ACCOMMODATE OTHER TRIBES
6	Area 6. RESERVATION LAND ACCRETING SINCE 1917, US vs ROMAINE

Map 9. Changes to the boundaries of the Lummi Reservation, 1855–1919. Map by Tim Wahl. Cartography and abstract by Tim Wahl, 2013. This map and its accompanying abstract provide a conservative and hypothetical assessment of historical changes to the boundaries of the Lummi Reservation between the years 1855 and 1919. The map and abstract are based on written, oral, and graphic records from those years. Not all changes to the boundaries of the Lummi Reservation are apparently documented in government publications. Pertinent government documents are cited in the notes at the end of the abstract. References to areas 1 through 6 refer only to the areas on map 9. *This map and its accompanying abstract are for informational purposes only; they are not intended for legal purposes, land claims, or any other purposes.*

The Indian Reservation that became the Lummi Reservation was identified in the 1855 Treaty of Point Elliott as "the island called Chah-choo-sen, situated in the Lummi River at the point of separation of the mouths emptying respectively into Bellingham Bay and the Gulf of Georgia." Given the language and cultural differences that existed at the times surrounding and following the Point Elliott Treaty council, it is reasonable to believe that many Lummi people understood that the extent of the Lummi River and Chah-choo-sen Island were defined by a set of diverse, often seasonally variable river courses, channels, and flood patterns. These were not well understood, let alone recorded, by non-Native record makers during and after the time that the treaty was enacted.

Area 1. Island of Chah-choo-sen: The Lummi Reservation as Established by the Treaty of Point Elliott, 1855 [1]

In 1854, before the Treaty of Point Elliott was signed, members of the treaty commission under the leadership of Washington territorial governor and superintendent of Indian Affairs Isaac I. Stevens, and acting under the authority of the U.S. Department of the Interior, met with Lummi people. The meeting was apparently held near Treaty Rock, which the Lummi regarded as a feature marking the eastern

mouth of the Lummi River at Bellingham Bay. The talk addressed the securing of a guarantee of Native rights to resources in perpetuity. These rights to resources were to be legally distinguished as retained rights to use off-reservation lands and waters for fishing, fish processing, gathering, and hunting, which would accompany a cession by the Indians to the United States of an extensive territory. The treaty was signed on January 22, 1855, at Mukilteo or Point Elliott, just south of Everett, Washington. Four reservations were established by the treaty; Chahchoosen Island was established as the exclusive land reserve for Lummi and other Native people.

The river lying mostly downstream of today's Interstate 5 was called the Lummi River; this was one of four names mapped and recorded by U.S. officials for different reaches of today's Nooksack River. The Treaty of Point Elliott states that the several tracts of land reserved by the tribes and bands who were party to the treaty were to be "set apart, and so far as necessary surveyed and marked out for their exclusive use" (Article 2).

U.S. Indian policy at the time, which was based on the presumed assimilation or demise of Indian people, could not reference a single model of what it deemed a successful Indian reservation. Congress was vested with the sole authority to approve new reservation boundaries, but the Treaty of Point Elliott also contained a provision that allowed the U.S. president to later consolidate the Point Elliott reservations into fewer, centralized sites.

Slightly over four years after the treaty was signed, Congress ratified it on April 11, 1859. Ten days later, without the consent of U.S. Indian Affairs officials, the General Land Office (GLO) contracted for a survey of a portion of upland Chahchoosen (south of the 38th parallel: today's Slater Road) for sale to U.S. settlers. The survey did not include any work that would serve to define a reservation boundary. The GLO survey was commissioned—in the heyday of the Fraser River gold rush excitement—by a prominent Bellingham Bay mineral rights owner, working in partnership with some San Francisco–based capitalists.

An ancient logjam, over half a mile in length, lies in the river just below today's city of Ferndale. Beneath it, water passed freely to today's Red River channel to Lummi Bay on the Strait of Georgia. Particularly when ice accumulated, the jam forced peak flood flows above the channel into side channels, such as Q'achqsem, today's Barrett Lake on Ten Mile Creek, and into the Silatsits floodway, a corridor of sloughs and beaver-impounded waters. Before the diversion of the

Red River to Bellingham Bay, U.S. records and local testimony show that today's Portage Island was part of Chahchoosen, connected via the emergent and vegetated Swulesen tombolo (sandbar).

Area 2. Land Officially Added by 1873 Executive Order, Based on Agent Simmons's Notice, 1859[2]

Before approval in 1860 of the GLO's township survey plat of the part of Chahchoosen south of the 38th parallel, Indian agent Michael T. Simmons had recommended saving Indian Affairs division money by using the GLO township survey lines to define the upriver extent of the reserve. The lines that he selected followed today's Slater and Ferndale Roads, along with a lower reach of the river near Marietta to Bellingham Bay. Having received no response from his superior, the superintendent of Indian Affairs for Washington Territory, Simmons published the present-day upriver reservation boundary in the *Olympia Pioneer and Democrat*. He encouraged U.S. settlers to establish claims outside that area, and he reserved Sandy Point and a portion of the Cherry Point uplands (Area 2) from sale to U.S. citizens for Indian Affairs management on behalf of the treaty tribes.

During the early 1870s, as the nation recovered from the Civil War, and as the transcontinental railways reached west, settlers poured into the region. GLO officials engaged in spirited debate with Indian Affairs officials regarding the upriver reservation boundary. Many pleas for protection of reservation boundaries had been made by tribal members and Indian agents throughout the region. Simmons's earlier notice led to confusion, fear, and conflict, especially given the excitement about the arrival of the Northern Pacific Railroad. Settlers living near or on the margins of reservations often asserted the ability of the U.S. president to eliminate and consolidate Indian reserves, as stipulated by treaty. Reservation communities were traumatized.

In August of 1871, officials of the Department of the Interior's Commission on Indian Affairs met with Lummi leaders Kwina, Whilano, and others at the church at Lummi, regarding Lummi boundary concerns. U.S. leaders promised, "The treaty will be taken and the right line run."

Two years later, a U.S. surveyor arrived to survey the reservation; his contract instructions provided for simply resubdividing the Simmons-designated reserve, this time into standard Indian allotment tracts, which were smaller than the tracts earlier offered to white settlers. The scope of the work did not involve the survey of any Chahchoo-sen boundaries.

On November 22, 1873, President Ulysses S. Grant, by executive order, enlarged the reservation according to the boundary lines that had earlier been established by agent Simmons's notice. The government map representing the enlargement does not show the area of the reservation that was removed. U.S. government records apparently do not document Treaty Rock or the location of any of the treaty-based river channels. Area 2 was later calculated to be 2,170 acres.

The area that was added included Sandy Point, the inundated back swamps of Xwe'cheyema'lh (also known as McComb Slough), and part of the Cherry Point moraine. Much of the area had been declared by the GLO as "unfit for settlement" in 1860, and the rest had poor soil unsuited to profitable farming. However, much like San Francisco, the place may have looked attractive as an American coastal city downstream from Great Britain's Fraser gold fields: a significant asset for Indian Affairs in its mission to provide for Indian people.

Area 3. Land Officially Removed by 1873 Executive Order

During the 1873 boundary controversy, and on the basis of its 1872 survey of the Ferndale Township above the 38th parallel (including Silatsits & Tle'ale'qwem), GLO officials determined that Simmons had effectively removed 820 acres from the treaty reserve fourteen years earlier. The Washington superintendent of Indian Affairs, who was briefly suspended from office during Grant's executive involvement, indicated that the area removed was at least 1,370 acres.

Curiously, the southerly discharge of the Lummi River's Silatsits channel, defining the east boundary of Area 4, *was* recorded in the 1871 Ferndale Township field notes, but *was not* mapped on the official 1872 GLO plat published for land sales. It *was* later mapped by the United States in 1880. GLO-authored maps prepared for the 1873 executive order show Area 3 lying entirely below Silatsits.

The Ferndale Township survey notes describe the removal of the Ferndale logjam by settlers. The jam and its impounded river ice had historically forced flood flows south into the Silatsits corridor at Q'achqsem. (U.S. records also indicate that the jam also conveyed primary, west channel river flows into Lummi Bay, on the Straits of Georgia.) The Silatsits corridor, particularly at Tle'ale'qwem, was initially and extensively dewatered by acts of settlers and later by the U.S. Army Corps of Engineers, who cleared the main channel below Ferndale. The west mouth river channels below Silatsits were soon scoured by the higher energy flows, released by the clearing of the channel.

Like Lummi and Nooksack people before them, settlers and U.S. government agencies favored a Bellingham Bay connection for commerce. Local records from the 1850s indicate that white men associated with the equine-powered British military at Fort Victoria, and operators of the nearby Sehome Mine, pastured horses and cut meadow grass along the east channel, above today's Marietta. In the late 1860s and early 1870s, anticipating the arrival of a transcontinental railroad, speculators purchased large tracts of marshland along both sides of the east channel, formerly the reserve boundary. San Francisco and other coastal boomtowns had demonstrated that estuarine wetlands, like those above today's Marietta, were valuable as railroad-serviced, commercial landfills, created by dredging shipping channels. The possibility of trans-Pacific trade, at the western terminus of a transcontinental railway system, motivated market speculators, both the rich and the aspiring.

Area 4. Approximate Additional Area of Chah-choo-sen Apparently Removed by Executive Order in 1873 (Silatsits and Tle'ale'qwem)

Tle'ale'qwem (the area recorded by Lummi elders in U.S. court testimony of 1917 and 1927 as the upper end of the Chahchoosen reserve) and Silatsits (the name that John Tennant recorded for the place described in his 1858 county land claim record) were somehow taken out of the reservation. The county's richest farms of the day were here, owned in part by the daughters of treaty signers Si-anelt (spelled *She-ah-delt-hu* on the treaty) and Tsi-li-xʷ (*Seh-lek-qu*), through enduring Indian/white marriages. River flows were changing, beaver dams were removed, sloughs were cleared, and swales were ditched to drain wetlands for farming. Starting in the 1860s, the Ferndale logjam was partially removed, and removal continued into the 1870s. As a result, river flows to Bellingham Bay increased below Silatsits.

By the 1870s, it was clear that the best and most accessible farmlands lay upriver around Ferndale. Earlier U.S. records also indicate a Lummi fishing village in that area, later linked by Lummi elders to Si-anelt.

The part of Chah-choo-sen reserved by the Lummi around Ferndale had also been long valued in the Native economy at the time of the treaty, owing to its mosaic of old upland prairies—suited to camas, wild carrots, deer grazing, and edge elk browsing—and its wet prairies and forest. The area was important also because it was a commercial hub, where Indian

waterways and overland trails connected at the historic, river-bridging logjam, with its elaborate system of canoe drags for portaging.

U.S. settlement efforts focused on agricultural development and the areas where alluvial soils were easiest to utilize by managing surface water. The General Land Office, steward of the nation's agricultural future, accepted the Simmons boundary. The GLO allocated the best farmland of the day for sale to settlers and allocated the wettest and the saltiest alluvium—at the west mouth of the river—to the reservation. Just above the river's east mouth, at Marietta, the GLO sold a portion of Chah-choo-sen to capitalists who were expectant of greater profits, as railway construction proceeded across Washington Territory.

Area 5. Land Proposed for Addition to Lummi Reservation in 1874[3]

U.S. immigration to Washington Territory intensified before and immediately after 1873, when the Northern Pacific Railway reached Tacoma. Advocacy for land sales to settlers reached new heights as merchants and politicians sought to enrich themselves and their communities. Indian agents working at the reservation level cited some progress in creating reservation-based economies but decried a lack of cash and administrative personnel to support their mission of service to Indian communities. Individual incentives for Indian fishing and logging were undermined by legal restrictions involving socialization of Native enterprise, and there was a shortage of staff to support reservation health, farming, and harvesting. At the federal and territorial levels, Indian Affairs officials aggressively questioned adherence to the treaties and shrilly echoed complaints of too few Indians on too many reserves, too little money, and too many isolated reserves without official U.S. oversight.

The U.S. Board of Indian Commissioners conducted a field investigation in 1874, advised by Indian inspector William Vandever. (The office of "Indian Inspector" was an office created by the Office of Indian Affairs [OIA] in the late nineteenth century, with the aim of centralizing the operations of the OIA and eventually phasing out the superintendencies. Indian inspectors were not, like superintendents of Indian Affairs, administrators based at particular locations; Indian inspectors visited various superintendencies to oversee financial, legal, land boundary, and other matters.)

The western Washington investigation by Inspector Vandever and the Board of Indian Commissioners resulted in their recommending to the secretary of the interior the closing of most of the Salish Sea reservations and the consolidating of the Puget Sound Salish and Straits Salish tribes on two expanded reserves: Skokomish and Lummi.

The agricultural prize for white economic development was to be the Puyallup Reservation in King and Pierce Counties, near the Northern Pacific Railway terminus. The residents of the Puyallup, Nisqually, Squaxin, and Chehalis reserves were to be relocated to Skokomish. The sale of the Port Madison, Tulalip, Swinomish, and Muckleshoot Reservations was also recommended, with relocation of the residents of these reservations to the Lummi Reservation, which was to be expanded five miles north, with a northern boundary running east from Point Whitehorn to the Nooksack River. A vigorous protest arose in Whatcom County during Vandever's visit. All across western Washington settlers had claimed lands suitable for the same activities that U.S. Indian Affairs policy advocated that Indians should pursue.

These settlers were poised to slam their representatives and government officials for the loss of their claims and improvements. There were also many vociferous white merchants and timber owners whose business plans were threatened. The president's

treaty-stipulated authority to consolidate the western Washington
reservations proved unworkable,
given the sense of entitlement
among the nation's settler-citizens,
combined with the nation's stated
goals for Indian country.

*Area 6. Reservation Land Accreting
since 1919, U.S. v. Romaine et al.*[4]

Between 1905 and 1907 the General
Land Office and the state of Washington surveyed newly accreting,
semi-emergent delta meadows and
tidelands at the eastern mouth of
the Lummi River. In 1908 the state
asserted title and sold these new
lands to a group of Bellingham
capitalists who anticipated creation
of a major economic port with
landfills and dredged channels. The
lands were also valuable for Lummi
fishing, grazing, and navigation.
In 1917, the Lummi Tribe sued the
state of Washington, claiming that
the treaty definition of the Lummi
River represented an understanding
with the Stevens Treaty Commission that the easterly mouth of the
Lummi River ran to Treaty Rock.
Historic records and accounts were
presented, and the U.S. Court of
Appeals declared that the accreted
lands lying west of a line running

due south from Treaty Rock were
part of the reservation. (Subsequent court actions further defined
the reservation's aquatic land
boundaries.)

Diversion of Lummi/Nooksack
River flows to Bellingham Bay
began in the 1860s, transform-
ing nutrient-rich wetlands into
arable, American-style croplands
and enhancing navigation between
upriver agricultural and timber
lands and the commercial waters
and enterprises on the bay. A
massive entrainment of sediment
continues to follow diversion
actions such as diking, channel
deepening, and removal of beaver
waters, as well as logging, land
clearing, and drainage for fields,
highways, and urban areas. As
the U.S. Army Corps of Engineers
concluded in the late nineteenth
century, physical forces in the
northeast cul-de-sac of Bellingham
Bay remain inadequate for removal
of accumulated material deposited
by river flows and marine currents
from the southwest. Wetland forest
and semi-emergent meadow and
scrubland continue to prograde
into the bay, now well beyond the
subtidal delta platform mapped in
the 1850s.

References

1. USGD, 1899, *Eighteenth Annual Report of the Bureau of American Ethnology*, 798–99. Plate CLXX: Washington Map 1 (Original Lummi Reservation: Section 350). Color map available at Library of Congress, American Memory, *Indian Land Cessions in the United States, 1784–1894*: "Dwamish, Suquamish, and other allied tribes." http://memory.loc.gov/ammem/amlaw/lwss-ilc.html.
2. USGD, 1899, *Eighteenth Annual Report of the Bureau of American Ethnology*. Plate CLXIX: Washington Map 2 (area added to Lummi Reservation by 1873 Executive Order: Section 555). Color map available at Library of Congress, American Memory, *Indian Land Cessions in the United States, 1784–1894*: "Dwamish and allied tribes." http://memory.loc.gov/ammem/amlaw/lwss-ilc.html.
3. USGD, 1874, U.S. Congress, House, *Report of the Secretary of the Interior*, 387–88.
4. USGD, 1919, *U.S. v. Romaine et al.*, 423.

Part 2
The Twentieth Century and After

ABORIGINES, U.S.A.

Buried in broken promises
Broken treaties
Forgotten genocide
Remembered rights

Iroquois Indians taught confederacy,
the Great Peace. Salish Indians taught
how to fish, what to eat
from the waters of the Great Northwest.

Chief Joseph taught his people how to travel
unseen. Chief Seattle died teaching
patience and perseverance. Chief Black Elk taught us
all Indians know spirituality.

But nothing Indians do is thought strong enough
to maintain the Red with the White and the Blue.
We either die in its glory
or live in its shame.

Pauline Hillaire
Lummi

CHAPTER 6

Legal and Land Rights

ISSUES IN INDIAN LAW

In the Civil Rights Act of 1968, Congress extended to Indians in their relationships with their tribal governments many of the provisions of the Bill of Rights (the first ten amendments to the U.S. Constitution, which protect U.S. citizens' civil rights).[1] The Civil Rights Act does not, however, override tribal sovereignty. This was tested in the Supreme Court case *Santa Clara v. Martinez* (436 U.S. 49, 1978). The Santa Clara Pueblo, originally matrilineal, had decided that tribal membership was available to children whose fathers, but not mothers, were members of the pueblo (tribe). Julia Martinez, a Santa Clara woman married to a Navajo man, sued the Santa Clara Pueblo for denying their daughter membership, on the basis of gender discrimination against the mother, a violation of the Civil Rights Act. However, the court accepted Santa Clara Pueblo's position that it was within the tribe's rights to self-government—independent of federal intervention—to establish its own laws concerning matters such as criteria for membership.

The tribes who had voted to accept the 1934 Indian Reorganization Act (IRA) had been allowed by the IRA to establish their own community-devised constitutions and bylaws (48 Stat. 984-88, Sec. 16). Some of the tribes that did not accept the IRA had to wait more than a decade before they could create their constitutions, because they needed special permission from Congress to do so outside of the IRA.

In some tribes, Indian people who were inclined toward the dominant culture's style of governance were in conflict with traditional-type Indians about tribal governance. I was a member of the Constitution Committee at Lummi in the 1980s. It was decided to update our old constitution of the early 1940s. But the tribal government of that time permitted the tribe's lawyer, a white man, to write a constitution for Lummi, and it superseded our committee's final draft. The lawyer's version was presented to the General Council ahead of the document drafted by the Constitution Committee. I did not hear of it advertised for all tribal members to vote for or against. Our years of effort toward updating our old constitution were short-circuited. I was among those who gave up.

For the most part, Indian tribes and individuals have not had the benefit of full legal protection. During treaty times in the Northwest, Commissioner of Indian Affairs George W. Manypenny recommended that the government conduct its business with tribes in such a way that Indians, as dependents of the government, would have no attorneys or agents representing them, with whom the Indians themselves had independently contracted. "There is no absolute necessity for the employment by Indian tribes of attorneys or agents to attend to their business at the seat of government. In the dependent condition of the Indians, it is the duty of the government, as their guardian, to cause all matters of a business character with them to be so conducted as to preclude the necessity of the intervention of this class of persons."[2]

Today, *laches* (pronounced "latches") is a legal principle that the government still uses to prevent attainment of justice by Indian people in suits involving land claims and other matters. *Laches* is a doctrine that denies relief to a claimant who is said to have waited too long before asserting a claim.[3] An Indian has the same right as anyone else to be represented by counsel of his or her own selection, and that counsel may not be subordinated to counsel appointed by the court. As an additional protection the U.S. district attorney has the duty to represent him or her in all suits at law or in equity.[4] These legal provisions are good; but in reality they are impractical considering the Indian position, not only in terms of the physical distance between the individual and the state district attorney, but also because many Indian persons do not recognize that they can ask the state district attorney to represent them in personal complaints regarding land, membership, complaints of racism, and so forth. We simply draw back and say, "Oh, what's the use?" And that ends that.

I encourage Indian tribal governments to keep the latest edition of the *Handbook of Federal Indian Law* on hand in their offices for reference. Felix S. Cohen's 1942 edition—written before the termination era of the 1950s—is a valuable historical edition as regards discussion of Indian rights and the law. Other valuable sources are *Federal Indian Law: Cases and Materials* by David H. Getches, Charles F. Wilkinson, and Robert A. Williams, *The Rights of Indian Tribes* by Steven L. Pevar, and *Uneven Ground: American Indian Sovereignty and the Law* by David E. Wilkins and K. Tsianina Lomawaima.[5]

The Bureau of Indian Affairs was created, in part, to help us. Instead, it facilitated Indian policy that favored non-Indian American government-protected citizens. Indian heirship policies were such that it was much easier to sell land than to keep it in the family, especially if money is shown to the poverty-stricken Indian. We have found out the hard way that even if laws of protection are in place, this does not mean that actual protection is there too. The words are there, but we have to learn how to use them.

"Plenary power" is a legal concept that is very important for Indian law. I started studying this idea in Cohen's 1942 edition of the *Handbook of Federal Indian Law*. Cohen explains that the plenary ("full" or "entire") authority of Congress: "does not mean absolute power." The exercise of power must be founded upon some reasonable basis. Therefore, plenary power does not enable the United States to give or sell tribal lands to others, or to appropriate tribal lands for its own purposes, without the obligation to render just compensation for them, as required by the Fifth Amendment to the U.S. Constitution, which concludes: "nor shall private property be taken for public use, without just compensation." For the government to do otherwise, Cohen says, "would not be an example of guardianship, but an act of confiscation." He refers to the case *United States v. the Creek Nation* (295 U.S. 103, 1935), a case that illustrates how plenary power works in connection with the Fifth Amendment's principle of just compensation:

> Thus, while Congress has broad powers over tribal lands, the U.S. does not have complete immunity from liability from the actions of Congress. If Congress takes tribal lands from the Indians without either their consent or the payment of compensation, the United States is liable under the Fifth Amendment to the United States Constitution for the payment of just compensation, which must include payment for the minerals and timber. But the right of the Indians to just compensation is legally imperfect unless Congress itself passes legislation permitting suit by the Indians against the United States, as the United States is not liable to suit without its consent.[6]

The United States is bound by the U.S. Constitution and is also bound by Supreme Court decisions interpreting the Constitution to pay fairly for Indian lands and to pay for the resources in and on those lands, such as minerals and timber. In the early days of the nation the right to file suit against the United States required the permission of Congress. In 1855 the United States established a Court of Claims, to permit suits against the federal government. However, in 1863 the government prohibited the Court of Claims from considering claims related to treaties with foreign nations or Indian tribes. Therefore, a special act of Congress was required before an Indian claim could be brought before the court. Of the nearly two hundred cases filed by tribes before 1946, only about 15 percent received awards; most of the other cases were dismissed on technicalities.[7]

In 1946 tribes gained the right to file suit against the United States, when Congress enacted the Indian Claims Commission Act (ICCA).[8] The ICCA authorized any tribe, band, or identifiable group of Indians "to seek compensation for the value of land or other property conferred by a treaty that was later taken by the government through fraud, force, or mistake." In 1978 all Indian Claims Commission cases were transferred to the U.S. Court of Claims (now called the Federal Court of Claims).[9]

In recent decades Native law experts and scholars have created organizations and resources to help explain ideas and processes that are important for the protection of sovereignty, treaty rights, and other Native rights. Wilkins and Lomawaima's book, *Uneven Ground: American Indian Sovereignty and the Law*, analyzes different meanings of terms such as "sovereignty" and "plenary power": how these concepts are related, and how they have been used—and misused—in Indian law cases. For example, the United States has claimed plenary power over tribes, while at the same time acknowledging tribal sovereignty. How can both of these principles apply? Wilkins and Lomawaima give examples to show how plenary power does not mean *unlimited power*, as the court interpreted "plenary power" in the 1903 case *Lone Wolf v. Hitchcock*, when Congress acted as if it had the power to unilaterally abrogate treaty rights. However, plenary power can legitimately mean *exclusive power*, for instance, in the context of the Commerce Clause of the Constitution, which states that *only* Congress has the power to regulate commerce with Indian tribes. Plenary power also has the legitimate meaning of *preemptive power*, in the sense of federal powers "preempting" or *superseding* state powers. The preemptive sense of plenary power was exerted by Congress in the treaty-making era. In contemporary times the preemptive power of Congress can have applications, for example, in preventing a state's efforts to tax the income of Indian residents of a reservation.[10] Reviewing these ideas, one realizes how confusing the law can be. Keeping focused, for me anyway, is difficult. Now, that is why I am not a lawyer.

DUWAMISH ET AL. TRIBES OF INDIANS V. THE U.S., 1927

Until 1946 (when the Indian Claims Commission was established) an act of Congress was required for a tribe to file suit against the United States. A jurisdictional act of Congress was passed February 12, 1925 (43 Stat. 886, ch. 214), by which approximately twenty western Washington tribes, including the Lummi, were able to file a claim against the United

States. *Duwamish et al. v. U.S.* was filed in the U.S. Court of Claims in 1927, and the case was decided in 1934. The cases of the tribes were consolidated and evidence was heard from each tribe separately. One hundred fifty-five members of tribes who were party to the Treaty of Point Elliott, including ten Lummi, testified regarding U.S. failures to honor the treaty of Point Elliott and the tribes' loss of lands to non-Indians, who obtained Indian lands by means of the Oregon Land Donation Act before the treaty was signed and ratified.[11]

The First Cause of Action was that (1) the treaty had not been honored in the manner that it had been understood by the Indians who attended the Treaty Council and by their descendants, (2) that Article 6 of the treaty had promised $150,000 to the tribes for ceded lands, which had not been fully paid, (3) that the goods and services provided as annuities (commodities provided annually for a period of twenty years) were valued by the government at excessive rates, and (4) that the operating costs of the government's Indian services should not be deducted from the amount that the treaty promised to pay the tribes. (See appendix 1; see also fig. 7.) The Lummi Tribe claimed $7,000.

The tribes claimed in their Second Cause of Action that the lands of particular tribes were lost when the reservations established by the Point Elliott Treaty were reduced and enlarged by executive order. In the Third Cause of Action, the Lummi Tribe claimed that the $15,000 promised by the treaty for clearing reservation land for farming had never been paid. In the Fourth Cause of Action, the Lummi Tribe claimed damages of $350,000 on grounds that the school, physician, and services of a blacksmith, carpenter, and farmer promised by the treaty had been inadequate, and that few Indians had received these services. The Fifth Cause of Action concerned Article 7 of the treaty, which promises compensation from the government for improved property that the Indians were forced to abandon. The Lummi gave evidence of loss of twenty-six longhouses, with a total of 211 living compartments, each compartment worth an average of $900, for a total value $189,000. They also claimed $14,972 for eighty-five half-acres of cultivated land, bringing the total claim to $204,972, plus $350,000 for injury and damages.

The Sixth Cause of Action concerned the land area received by the tribes. First, the tribes claimed that the Chinook Jargon was inadequate for the treaty deliberations, and that both the Indian leaders and their present-day descendants understood that the Indians would later receive a large reservation, and that, as specified in Article 7 of the treaty, the land would be allotted as it had been in the Omaha Treaty: 80 acres for a single person and 320 acres for a family. Lummi claimed that they should receive 52,480 acres (80 acres per person) but had received only 12,563 acres. They valued the loss at $3,991,400, and claimed damages of four million dollars.

This is what my father wanted me to research! Eighty acres per person, as per the Omaha Treaty, as mentioned at the initial meeting of Governor Stevens and the tribes and in Article 7 of the treaty. Joe Hillaire, Frank Hillaire, and others had noted that the Omaha Treaty was the model for the Point Elliott Treaty of 1855. The average amount of land reserved for the Point Elliott Tribes was about 6 acres per person (44,192 acres, before adjustments, for an estimated 7,559 persons at the time of the treaty). Six acres may sound like a lot by today's standards, but it was not all usable land, and not large enough for hunting, gathering, and growing food to support life in the days when people supported themselves—along with elders and children—from the resources of the land and waters. Immediately after the treaties, Indian people were not part of the new nation's economic system, and their homes were gone. But still, they relied in part on their former means of subsistence, on lands and waters that were no longer sufficient for it. Land—and the resources of the land and waters—was the only wealth. Chief Seattle, present at the treaty negotiations and the signing, claimed that they were promised a big reservation. No large reservation was ever established, and the small amount of available land allowed only a small number of persons to later receive allotments, as Lummi elders testified in the case.[12]

In the Seventh Cause of Action, the tribes claimed damages resulting from the Oregon Land Donation Act, which had given white settlers a means to occupy and gain ownership of Indian lands used for living and food-gathering. Settlers, according to the United States, did not receive formal title to the land until after the treaty was ratified. But they staked a claim to it, occupied and farmed it, and ultimately gained ownership—all the while displacing Indian people from their own homes and resource places. The Lummi claimed damages of $75,000. In the Eighth and final Cause of Action, Lummis claimed $928,000 for the government's reduction of the reservation by 9,280 acres.

When the case was decided in 1934, no compensation was awarded. Regarding the First Cause of Action, the court determined that during the twenty-year period after ratification, over which the United States had committed by treaty to pay the tribes $150,000, it had spent $150,124, presumably for the benefit of the Point Elliott tribes. The Point Elliott Treaty tribes, according to the court, had therefore been overpaid by $124.[13]

One of the government's defenses, applied to both the Second and the Eighth Causes of Action, was that the total lands of the Point Elliott Treaty tribes had been increased, owing to the enlargement of the Port Madison/Suquamish Reservation in 1864 and the enlargement in 1873 of the Lummi Reservation plus its tidelands. The enlargement of Port Madison (by 6,004 acres, from 1,290 to 7,284 acres) did not help Lummi people with land on which to live and obtain food; Port Madison is too far away to be of use to Lummi tribal members. The Port Madison Reservation is not even in Lummi Country; it is home of the Suquamish Tribe, about a hundred miles south of the Lummi Reservation. To get from Lummi to Port Madison requires a couple of hours travel south by highway to the Seattle area, then a short ferry ride from Edmonds (near Seattle) to Port Madison.

As regards tidelands, they are valuable for cultivating and harvesting food from the ocean, but they are uninhabitable. Our tribal ownership of tidelands, which the Lummi Nation later developed for aquaculture, was upheld in the 1919 case *U.S. v. Romaine*.[14] After the Lummi Reservation was allotted, a number of Lummi sold their allotments to white people. Some of these white people, including a Mr. Romaine, purchased lots bordering the tideland and claimed that they owned the tidelands, too. The Supreme Court ruled that the reservation lands included the tidelands, down to the low water mark. Our tribe has had to continue to defend the tidelands in court, but we have prevailed.[15] Vine Deloria Jr. tells of early tideland controversies and how the Lummi aquaculture project got its start, in his book *Indians of the Pacific Northwest*.[16]

Regarding the Third Cause of Action, the court found that of the $15,000 promised by the government to the tribe for clearing, fencing, and breaking up land for farming, only $13,340 had been paid, so Lummi should receive the remaining $1,535. When it came to the Fourth Cause of Action—that few Point Elliott tribal members had received the promised education, medical care, and technical services and instruction—the government argued that the treaty did not specify how much was to be spent and that no evidence existed to prove how many children there were or whether their parents had wanted them to attend school. Lummi farming agent Finkbonner had noted—twelve years after the treaty was signed—that 125 Lummi children were in need of a school. But the court agreed with the defense, and dismissed the tribes' claim.

In the Fifth Cause of Action, concerning the value of lost Lummi houses and improved lands, the court judged that the 211 compartments in the nineteen Lummi longhouses were worth only $250 apiece, so the total value of the lost homes was not $189,900 as claimed, but only $62,750. As for the important Sixth Cause of Action, involving the promise of "a large reservation" and allotment of eighty acres per person as in the Omaha Treaty, the court judged that the use of Chinook Jargon did not prevent the Indians at the treaty negotiations from understanding the terms of the treaty, and that the treaty's terms had been sufficiently clear to them. Furthermore, the court found that the treaty's reference to a large reservation and allotment of acreage, as per the Omaha treaty, was stipulated in the treaty as an *option* of the U.S. president, not as a commitment. The Sixth Cause of Action was dismissed.

The Court of Claims also dismissed the Seventh Cause of Action, concerning the Oregon Land Donation Act. First, the Court said, the boundaries of Indian lands had not been surveyed, and some lands had been shared with other tribes; therefore, determining the land claims of particular tribes was not possible. Secondly, the court could only address *treaty issues*, not matters that Congress had enacted *prior to the treaties*, such as the Land Donation Act. The Eighth Cause of Action was also dismissed: the claim that the boundary of the Lummi Reservation had been reduced by 9,280 acres was met with the government's defense that, although 820 acres had been excluded, the total gain was 1,350. The court agreed with defense, and the final claim was dismissed.

The court found the claims without merit, except for the Third and the Fifth Causes of Action: Lummi was entitled to $1,535 for farming assistance that had not been paid, plus $62,750 for nineteen lost longhouses: a total of $64,285. The allowance for "setoffs" was one of conditions the Congress had set, when it permitted plaintiffs to assert claims against the United States arising from treaties.[17] In this case, the setoffs were deductions from the amount awarded of amounts that the government had spent on supplies and administrative costs for its functions related to the Point Elliott Treaty tribes. The total setoffs against the Point Elliot claimants, according to the court, was $2,153,074 ($2.2 million). So, no claim was paid any of the Point Elliott Treaty tribes.[18]

David E. Wilkins discusses *Duwamish, Lummi et al. Tribes v. U.S.* as an example when he writes: "fatal to recovery is the allowance of a setoff of all the money the government had spent in the administration of governments agencies, as for superintendents, interpreters, teachers, Indian police, and so forth . . . on the ground that these things are beneficial to Indians."[19]

Across different tribes' cases in the U.S. Court of Claims the court was not consistent regarding which types of expenses could be deducted as "gratuities" from the amount awarded to a tribe. In some cases, the court did not categorize the government's administrative costs as funds spent to benefit the tribes (*Assiniboine Tribe v. Uintah Tribe*, J-31, April 10, 1933). In such cases, the court excluded the government's costs of performing its own functions—the government having incurred obligations to administer Indian policies that it had created—instead of categorizing its administrative costs as payment to the tribes for their lands.

After the Indian Claims Commission was created, the Lummi Tribe filed an action in 1951. Tribal leaders remembered our rights by using the justice system to make a claim for the value of lost lands in behalf of future generations. In *Lummi Tribe of Indians v. the United States* the Lummi claimed that they had ceded 249,800 acres (390 square miles) for their share of "the completely inadequate and unconscionable sum of $150,000" promised to all of the twenty-two-plus tribes and bands that were party to the Treaty of Point Elliott.[20]

Indian Claims Commission Docket 110, *Lummi v. U.S.*, contains over twenty court documents, such as Findings of Fact, that provide details of this complicated case. Here, as for *Duwamish et al. v. U.S.*, we provide just the skeleton of the case. The ICC documents are interesting in terms of both their legal reasoning and for information about the western Washington tribes provided by ethnographers of the time.[21]

When Lummi filed its petition in the mid-twentieth century, there were eleven remaining and federally recognized Point Elliott Treaty tribes. According to a 1952 opinion of the court, presuming that the government had compensated those eleven tribes together with $150,000, Lummi would have received one eleventh of that amount: $13,636. Lummi submitted a claim for the current-day value of the land: $30 million, plus interest.[22] The case began in 1951 and continued for over twenty years. Below is Ann Nugent's summary of the case (pertinent Indian Claims Commission volumes have been added in brackets):

> The first part dealt with whether the Lummis had a right to sue the United States over this issue [vol. 2, 1952, 1953]. The second part of the case dealt only with the determination of acreage of land the Lummis possessed [Vol. 5, 1957]. The third part dealt with determining the value of the land [vol. 10, 1962]. The fourth part dealt with how much money was already paid the Lummis [vol. 13, 1964]. The fifth part was important because the Indian Claims Commission decided the Lummis had been fairly paid for their loss of land, and therefore the case was dismissed [vol. 16, 1966)]. But the Lummis decided to

appeal the case (part six), and that court [the U.S. Court of Claims] decided to reverse the decision of the Indian Claims Commission [181 Ct. Cl. 763 (December 15, 1967)]. The case was sent back to the Indian Claims Commission for reconsideration. In the seventh part the Indian Claims Commission, having reconsidered, decided that the Lummis had been unfairly paid for their land, and they were entitled to a sum of money [vol. 21, 1969)].[23]

The eighth part of the case (vol. 24, 1969, 1970) dealt with "setoffs": subtraction of an amount awarded from an amount presumably already spent by the government on expenses related to treaty tribes. After consideration of factors such as land boundaries, market value, and setoffs, the Indian Claims Commission determined that the Lummi were entitled to $57,000 (affirmed, 197 Ct. Cl. 780, 1972). The tribe declined to accept such an insignificant settlement.

Refer to the testimonies of Lummi tribal members in *Duwamish v. U.S.* (1927), reprinted by Nugent in *History of Lummi Legal Action*.[24] Lummi elder Albert Descanum (born ca. 1840) testified: "And . . . we are still waiting, we haven't seen those promises which was made at that time by Governor Stevens and the people that was there present at the treaty; the chiefs, they were waiting up to the time they were all passed away and never received all those that was promised, and it was almost a daily discussion among the people. When is those promises going to be fulfilled?"[25]

Sufficient "payment" for lands ceded by treaty, as the U.S. government would have us understand in the 1927 Court of Claims case *Duwamish Tribe et al v. U.S.*, had already been given to the tribes, in the form of unrequested commodity items and in the form of the government's costs for operating the Indian Service/BIA. Lummi elder John Andrew Williams (born ca. 1846) testified in the 1927 case. He was asked, "Did they get many goods when they did get annuity goods?" He replied: "What they receive is just little small garden hoes and garden outfits and small little articles."[26] We do not accept such a transaction as just, nor did Chief Seattle, nor any tribal chief since. The lands of the great Pacific Northwest are far more valuable than any price ever placed on them by government officials, certainly more valuable than ten cents an acre, the top price the government was willing to pay tribes at that time, when they would pay money at all.[27] True, it was wild country, but it produced all that any culture could ask for, for the sustenance of families, communities, and visitors.

Similar to our 1927 case, but on a larger scale, the Lakota Sioux filed suit in the U.S. Court of Claims in 1923 for violation of the 1868 Treaty of Fort Laramie and the loss of an enormous amount of Indian land. Lands originally amounting to more than a million acres were reduced by approximately 90 percent in the first twenty years that "surplus lands" were opened to settlers. Part of the land that was lost was their sacred Black Hills in South Dakota. The claim was dismissed in 1942, but the Lakota sued again, after the Indian Claims Commission was established. In 1974, the ICC decided that the U.S. government had violated the Fifth Amendment by taking the lands without just compensation. More litigation followed, and the case went to the Supreme Court, which upheld the ICC's decision to award the Lakota Sioux $17.5 million plus interest: slightly more than $106 million. The Lakota people would not accept the money. It remains in a BIA account, collecting interest, and is now worth hundreds of millions of dollars.[28] In this way, the people remember their rights: no amount of money can replace the land, or replace justice.

When our Lummi case went on during the 1950s, the Indian Court of Claims, established in 1946, was fairly new. Federal Indian policy in the 1950s was leaning toward termination of U.S. tribes' relationship with the federal government. The establishment of the Indian Court of Claims might seem like a move toward greater justice for America's tribes on the part of the United States, and likely, in the minds of some government leaders, it was. But overall, the trend of Indian policy at that time was toward termination of the government's relationship with the tribes. Many tribes were terminated, although most were later reinstated, including the Klamath in Oregon. So it makes some sense

to think of the Indian Claims Commission as another way of conclud-
ing business with the tribes in order to get them out of the way—a
financial relocation, so to speak. Even though our Lummi leaders were
denied their claim for compensation, their efforts—and the efforts of
the other tribal leaders—were part of keeping our rights alive in those
dangerous times.

LUMMI HOMELANDS

The Lummi Reservation is on the coast of northwestern Washington,
about twenty miles south of the U.S./Canada border, ninety miles north
of today's city of Seattle and eight miles west of Bellingham, Washington (map 1). The reservation consists of approximately 12,563 acres
(approximately 19.6 square miles).[29] The surrounding tidelands consist
of about 7,000 acres, according to the 2008 *Lummi Nation Atlas*.[30]

For the government to return lands north of the Lummi Reservation,
an area that, unlike our reservation, is not yet heavily populated, would
be merciful for our recent and future generations. In the testimonies
given in the 1927 U.S. Court of Claims case *Duwamish Tribe et al. v.
the U.S.*, Lummi elder Louis Mike (born ca. 1847) testified that he had
seen the original surveyors' posts at "Ballard's" (Barrett) Lake and Bay
Station, and that the reservation boundary had been reduced by about
two miles from the north and about one mile from the east.[31] This
reduction of reservation boundaries was also stated in the testimonies
of John Andrew Wilson (born ca. 1846), Frank Hillaire (born ca. 1846),
and Albert Descanum (born ca. 1840). See map 9, which shows various changes to the reservation boundaries over time. One of the areas
identified is the proposed "Vandever Extension," a large area with a
border five miles north of the current northern border of the reservation. In 1875 the Board of Indian Commissioners recommended adding
this large area and extending the reservation to the north, but the plan
was not carried out.

Currently non-Indians own 23 percent of land on the Lummi Reservation. This shows how land-poor our tribe actually is today. The number
of Lummi people has increased from an estimated 250–624 persons

when the treaty was signed (1855) to well over 4,000 persons as of this writing. Such growth in population illustrates why the tribes' Court of Claims cases are important to modern communities. The 2008 Lummi census shows approximately 4,200 enrolled members of the Lummi Tribe, about 2,400 of whom live on the reservation. In 2005 the total population of the Lummi Reservation was 6,590. Only 2,564 of these persons were enrolled Lummi tribal members (39 percent). In addition there were 655 persons (10 percent) related to tribal members, but not enrolled members of the Lummi Tribe. The remaining 51 percent (3,361 persons) were nontribal members.[32]

The Indian population nationally suffers a low employment rate. In 1993 the rate of unemployment for working-age members of the Lummi Tribe was 56 percent, mainly because of the decline in the fishery (see chapter 8) and conditions that led to closing and restructuring the tribe's casino. A 2003 survey by the Lummi Indian Business Council reported that 28 percent of tribal members between age eighteen and retirement age were unemployed, and up to 14 percent were underemployed.[33] Some individuals are employed seasonally, and rates do improve when fishing season is open. Education is very weak on most Indian reservations; it is caught in a "white society" model when it comes to curriculum, evaluation, and, ultimately, employment.

Since the signing of the treaty in 1855, Indians in our area waited until the 1970s for permanent homes. In the early years after the treaties, many Indians lived in temporary shelters or shacks. Our ancestors bravely prayed for the Great White Father and to the Great Spirit for the promises to be kept, for land to settle on, and for supplies with which to build permanent shelters from the relentless coastal weather. Had any of us been born in those days, could we have waited for what we thought were promises made by good men, while we continued to live in cold temporary shelters, waiting for the treaty arrangements to be honored?

The housing that was finally received came only to their descendants, living over a century later. HUD (Housing and Urban Development) homes came to Lummi in the early 1970s, two or three at a time, starting with the tribal government members' families. I moved into my home on Lummi land in 1996. This seems like a deadly game, but in reality it reflects the same slow pace that the 1855 treaty-signers felt in their time, which we still feel today. There are homeless Northwest Indian people all over the country, living under bridges and the like, or confined to small homes with tiresome relatives, instead of living in decent homes of their own.

In earlier history, our ancestors were photographed in front of their temporary shelters, instead of showing them at home at the great longhouses that were our original, permanent homes. This has created a pictorial misrepresentation of our culture in the records of history. It has been so degrading for my ancestors, myself, and my descendants, given that my generation has experienced living in beautiful timbered longhouses. Why were we not pictured in our beautiful red cedar timbered homes, which the government ordered burned, instead of the temporary shelters shown in many books on Pacific Northwest Indians? At least Northwest Indian life has been depicted in some books that contain truthful histories. See, for example, the pictorial history *The Nisqually Indian Tribe* by Nisqually historian Cecelia Svinth Carpenter, Maria Pascualy, and Trisha Hunter.[34] We are thankful.

Marlene Dawson, a non-Indian resident on our reservation, joined with Senator Slade Gorton (R-WA) and threatened my tribe with abrogation of treaty rights in her letters to the *Bellingham Herald*.[35] Non-Indians have attacked many tribes in the United States by various forms of communication and attempted takeovers. If this is not dishonorable conduct toward a federally recognized tribe in this day and age, I don't know what is, when a non-Indian suggests treaty abrogation once they own property and a home on the reserves. It worries me no end. These kinds of threats to our sovereignty promoted my research into the subject, and such problems require brilliant minds for solutions. Attacks on our sovereignty occurred not many decades after documented massacres conducted by the United States, such as the 1864 Sand Creek Massacre in Colorado, in the gold rush times. A hundred or more Cheyenne and Southern Arapahos—mostly women and children—were killed and mutilated by the Colorado Cavalry. This occurred while the people were camped on land set aside for them—land that was supposed to be under the protection of the government.[36] Less well known is a similar event in the Northwest: the Grande Ronde River Massacre. In 1856 Colonel Benjamin Shaw, leading a detachment of volunteers, went looking for Cayuse soldiers and instead killed dozens of Cayuse people at home in their village—mostly elders, women, and children. Then he and his soldiers burned down their village.

One advantage for non-Indians living on Indian reservations is that they do not have to pay taxes for the reservation land that they occupy. In addition, the law rarely touches them if they are living on the reservation. This is partly because Indians do not report them, but if they were living off-reservation, they would be more aware of the need to behave. Violent crime such as assault and rape, often committed by outsiders who come onto the reservations, was partly addressed by the Violence against Women Reauthorization Act of 2013.[37]

Many non-Indian residents speed down our roads without a lick of care. At least one Indian in our area was killed this way in recent years. One is too many. Perhaps there were others before I returned to live on my own reservation. The non-Indian reservation residents feel protected, and that affects their behavior. They get an "attitude" of superiority, and believe me, it shows. The Indian attitude tends toward a "laid back" attitude, where the non-Indian is seen to hold power when it comes to the law. White culture and government also provide models of violence. This is a bad example for our poverty-stricken Indian youth looking for excitement. Some can only find excitement when they present themselves as white people do in the greater communities, or beat up a fellow Indian. Sure, they'll be in trouble for the rest of their lives; violence is just as addictive as drugs or alcohol. Such young people are not able to recognize a good role model even if one is living right next to them.

Wards of the government.[38] This phrase came from Chief Justice John Marshall in the 1831 Supreme Court case, *Cherokee Nation v. Georgia.* "Wards of the government" has suggested to some Americans that the government took care of individual Indians, as well as tribal groups, all across America. We are not "wards of the government," but what it really implied was that the U.S. government should make decisions for us, as if we could not. The United States has made many decisions, especially where our lands are concerned, in its own interests. We also hunger for the American dream of life, liberty, and the pursuit of happiness, but on our own turf. We have geniuses in our tribal membership; we have teaching and the sharing of skills and arts. We have everything it takes to succeed. We deserve conditions for our minds to become unshackled from prejudice and acts of racism; these have a way of haunting us through generations.

Take courage. Our school is a fantastic place in our world. Our casino is a great opportunity to help us out of the cycle of poverty. Our college, Northwest Indian College, is growing and taking hold for us in higher education.[39] The enhancement of the habitat of our salmon, and the re-creation of the reverence we once had toward all sea life—all these show that more and more encouraging things can happen. It is catching on. Poverty, let my people go! Once poverty does let us go—once our attitudes have graduated from those "crabs in the bucket" that will not let each other get ahead—once we fully believe we can do it, we can. Put a bunch of crabs in a bucket, they will hold each other down. The attitude is, why let someone else get ahead when, after all, you are the one who really wants to get ahead? So hold him or her back; you want to get there first. Now you are living the real life of an Indian today.

Our children, grandchildren, and great-grandchildren are so beautiful. They deserve good lives; that is my hope, my dream, my prayer. The acreages were too small at the time of the treaty to provide home sites and an economic base, even for the small numbers of Indian people who survived the epidemics and the other changes brought by the New Americans. Our numbers have recovered, and now the need for land is the same and stronger: for homes and for an economic foundation. And the need continues, that we may preserve our sacred lands and our relationships with them.

CHAPTER 7

A Shrinking Land Base, Persecution, and Racism

Today I see some young women with earrings in their eyebrows, rings in their noses or lips, many earrings on their ears, and even jewels on their clothes. Such a difference in the way many dress today; what is sacred anymore? Some American Indian women try to keep up with non-Indian America in matters of dress and adornment; Indian men, too, try to keep up with contemporary America's many styles. Yet are our spirits anywhere near alike? Are our hearts in the right place yet? Can we be holy men or women? Let's try at least for understanding, logic, and common sense, especially where it concerns Mother Earth and all she produces, Father Sea and all he produces, and the Great Spirit's space. Maybe one day we will even enjoy our diversity, which would be unlike what many of the first European Americans did. Racism and prejudice still rule in many regions of our nation and world. Watching documentaries on Native people in Africa today and how they are treated, I see how ungodly racism is, and the little sibling to "ungodly" is prejudice.

FORCED TO SELL

When I was about ten to nineteen years old, I lived in a big two-story home at Gooseberry Point on the Lummi Indian Reservation. Our beach was about a mile long and there was a two-level spring that provided us with what Chief Seattle would call "living" water. For a decade I enjoyed that paradise: the freshest spring water, the mile-wide open beach with no crowds. For many years we logged for our sustenance, and we had had a large garden beneath our orchard. I fished with my elders, mostly with my stepfather, drifting on the Nooksack River in front of the village (we remember this and we all smile). We cared for chickens and cows, and we always had workhorses purchased from local farmers. These horses competed in weight-pulling contests at the Pioneer Days Picnics. Our work, and our play, was tireless as well as endless. My brother Ruben and I built a fence below the house, in a giant field.

My stepfather, Bill Scott, had inherited the house and land from his first wife. Eventually all of my mother's children—my brothers and sisters, my stepsisters and I—grew up and left home for education or marriage. After my stepfather was killed in a car accident in 1951, the "Welfare Department" as we knew it (the Department of Social and Health Services) made my mother sell the house and the land for fifty dollars an acre. Today that same land sells for many thousands of dollars per lot. Forcing my mother to sell that part of heaven for fifty dollars an acre was a travesty of justice. Who is guilty? The man who built the grocery store on the reservation-land side of the Lummi Island ferry dock also built a large water tank, just yards below our two-level spring. He was responsible for drying up our spring, thus helping the tribe label that little heaven a "condemned property," and therefore worth only fifty dollars per acre. That the DSHS required my crippled mother to sell that beautiful shoreline in order to receive health services was unfair beyond words.

The Lummi Indian Business Council would not help my mother or me, for I wrote them in 1971, when I came into the Smokehouse spiritual tradition, pleading with them to help us right this wrong. I was taught how to tell right from wrong at home and in college. But no. The man who bought the property from my mother had to know that he was unjust too, yet said nothing. My sister, Mary Ellen Hillaire, also remembered our mother being told that in order to receive health care she would have to sell that little heaven for fifty dollars an acre. When my mother sold that property, we all grew sad and despondent, lonesome for that little piece of heaven. We knew she would not otherwise receive health services, as she was told by her caseworker. I still think it was a sin to ask a crippled, old, helpless woman to sell her home and family's land in order to receive health care. My mother had no one to help her. Not even her tribe would help her keep her land. It was an injustice: government against its people, not protecting its own membership, Indian against Indian. Greed for land was learned. These memories hurt, even today.

HEIRSHIP POLICY

After the Dawes Allotment Act of 1887, Indian land heirship became extremely tangled for all the generations. Land allotments had begun even before that, such as allotment of the Lummi Reservation, which began in 1884. The U.S. government's *Indian Heirship Land Study* (1961) reported the following:

> As the original allottees died, the estates were probated by the Federal government and the heirs were notified that they owned a certain fractional interest of the tract. . . . The years since the passage of the General Allotment Act have witnessed the decrease of not only original allottees, but heirs who have inherited from them, and in turn, the increasing fractionalization of interests. This, then, is the heirship problem as we know it today, a tract of individual trust land is owned by up to several hundred Indians with the resulting problem of administration for the Federal Government and utilization by the heirs. . . . One heir (#49030) stated that his grandmother (now living), has 116 grandchildren and five generations in the family now, and one of the examiners of inheritance referred to a case which is now being probated where there are approximately 245 heirs.[1]

Some of the problems of Indian heirship were addressed in 1963, in an amendment to Senate Bill 1049. The amendment begins with a provision that "owners of not less than a 50 per centum interest in any land, where ten or fewer persons own undivided interests . . . may petition the Secretary of the Interior . . . to partition the land in kind, or to partition part of the land in kind and sell the remainder, or to sell the land if partition is not practicable."[2]

As we understood it, in order to sell an allotment, only 51 percent of heirs had to approve, but in order to settle and build on allotment land, signatures of 100 percent of heirs to the allotment were required. But nobody could collect 100 percent of the other heirs' signatures. Many of our ancestors here at Lummi had long ago ventured about and found places off the reservation to settle. For reasons including military service, Lummi heirs were scattered all over the nation and the world. Of course it would be easier to get 51 percent of the signatures and sell than to get 100 percent and stay, especially since earlier generations had little assistance from the BIA in settling heirship cases until a few years ago. But, this assistance was too late and too little.

Various types of pressure led to tribal members' selling tracts of allotted land in order to receive social or health services, or to get money to survive, as poor people throughout the country had to do, no matter what race. Nowadays, white settlements on the Lummi "Indian" Reservation are all over the place and growing. Lummi is now about 23 percent white-owned and has a non-Indian population of approximately 51 percent. Sandy Point is one such place; now it looks like a city from across the water. The same goes for Formosa Beach on Bellingham Bay and the McKenzie Road area, where our two-story home was located. There are lots of white settlements crowded in on the same area, just like white settlements in non-Indian areas. The fishing site of Marietta used to be considered an Indian village off the reservation site; it was considered Indian territory because of the Indian settlements there. The number of non-Indian settlements shows why we say that the Lummi Reservation is a quarter to a half white-owned and occupied. Encroachment upon trust territory was facilitated by U.S. policies regarding land. This left a pinch of land for me and my four-generation family and our extended family, here and there, on this Indian/white reservation of about twenty square miles.

I tried for years to eke out some justice regarding another Indian allotment, which once belonged to my father, Joseph Hillaire. Relatives who had gained possession of the land refused to let Joe Hillaire's and Edna Hillaire Scott's children settle on our birthplace. Joe Hillaire and Edna Hillaire were married in the Lummi culture way and in the white man's court. Then they divorced in the Lummi culture way and by white man's court. The white man's court awarded to my mother all eight children and also the land deeded to Joe by his father, Frank Hillaire. My father remarried. When he divorced my mother he had a signed-by-himself-alone deed to that land, signed over to my mother, as the white divorce court asked him to do. Because of this, I found that I had a basis for my claim. So I carried on that battle for twelve years. I kept the pertinent documents and tried hard to obtain justice for my family and myself. A Lummi Business Council representative said that he had "studied the case" and what he had come up with was this: "Give unto Caesar that which is Caesar's." For twelve years I preserved those papers and thought I had an argument for acreage and a home. After a long struggle to gain justice for land and a home where my mother, father, and brother Ben wanted me to live and build, the heirship policy beat me, and the rest of my brothers and sisters, out of land enough to build homes. I was crying miserably when I left there for the last time.

In 1983 the Indian Land Consolidation Act was passed to authorize tribes to create plans for sale and exchange of lands and to adopt their own probate codes. Senator Ben Nighthorse Campbell (D/R-CO) introduced the 2004 American Indian Probate Reform Act, or AIPRA, which amended the Indian Land Consolidation Act and amendments made in 2000. AIPRA facilitates the passing of individual Indian land from one generation to the next.[3]

INDIAN PERSECUTION

Because I lived on an Indian reserve most of my life, if I thought at first that it was mainly white America that commits injustices against Indians, I was wrong, because there is also injustice committed by Indian against Indian. True, there has always been competition and conflict among particular tribes; but I suspected that Indian America learned how to persecute individuals of the same race from the way that white America treated Indians across the continent. But I rethought this and figured out that if an Indian were to become successful in the white world, one had to be like those in the white world. Bullies in the white world persecuted some of us in Indian America and that is where Indians learned how to hate.

How can we beat that "beaten down" attitude for the Indian? By giving him back his mind: unshackle his mind from prejudice and racism, especially on his homeland, the Indian reservation. Racism is not just on the reservation; it is everywhere. In addition to the prejudiced attitudes and behaviors of white people, it is Indian against Indian. If an Indian feels "down," that is the easiest time for another Indian to kick him. "Kick him while he's down" is the feeling and freedom some Indians feel regarding persecution of one another. Our better option is to help unshackle another's mind, so that person can perform at his or her best. It cannot, otherwise.

One way that exclusion of Indians occurs is by means of particular reservation ordinances: if a resident is found to be in violation, that person can be banned from his or her trust property and denied his membership. The excluded person might be separated from his or her children, who are allowed to stay on the reservation. The excluded person may have to go on welfare for the rest of his or her life, usually without a badly needed education. The excluded individual is then ridiculed for having been kicked off the reservation, sometimes because of drugs or alcohol. Someone may be "excluded," while another tribal member, who has the same problems, is not.

When it is non-Indian against Indian, that is prejudice or racism. When it is Indian against Indian, that is persecution. Those who are persecuted are isolated, because there is nowhere to turn for justice or comfort. They are isolated until they make up their minds and stick to better, more powerful thoughts. There are too many things in this world that are of greater interest than your neighbors' faces of hate and persecution. Let them go. Just do what you think is better, stronger, and more helpful to yourself and your immediate family members, and show them the powers against Indian persecution. It works!

In the twentieth century, films and popular culture portrayed us as savages, or as beneath the white man star of the show. Indian America needs its place in a genuine history of the United States, other than the type we see in sports mascots, cartoons, programs such as *The Lone Ranger*, videos such as *500 Nations*, and movies such as *Last of the Mohicans* and *Dances with Wolves*. We love America just as much as anyone else — always have. We are devoted to our aboriginal histories and cultures, which are still not adequately represented in popular culture or public education curricula. Non-Indian friends of mine ask me, "Why didn't I learn about Indian history when I went to school?" Well, I do not know, but that also happened to me. I wondered the same thing; yet I was living proof that we did exist.

The Iroquois tribes influenced democratic ideas in the U.S. Constitution and the American concept of confederacy. This influence remains ahistorical in most public education systems. But why have such a prideful attitude? In another instance, the Code Talkers of the Navajo Nation helped the United States win in World War II. They spoke their language to each other within the military communication systems, and the enemy could not break the code. Some of them gave their lives in the line of military duty overseas. I am so proud of them, but the history books in our public education systems do not emphasize this story from America's life. Such accounts would help to reverse stereotypes perpetuated by anti-Indian caricatures and mascots. What a relief that would be for our future Indian generations. We have never accumulated in numbers like African Americans and Hispanic Americans. Indians have been the most abused race of America, at least longer than black Americans and Japanese Americans. I do not intend for it to be understood that I am bragging; no. We survived: 519 years, so far.

Nations beyond the United States have shown respect for American Indians: European scholars were interested in American Indian cultures centuries ago and invited Indians to Germany, for example, to obtain a better understanding of Indian music, such as the Bella Coola who toured Germany in 1885–86, and whose songs were studied by Franz Boas and Carl Stumpf.[4] Russia has invited Indian persons and groups to make presentations for greater understanding of aboriginal America and its cultural knowledge. Japan has invited Indian groups to visit and share cultural arts. Ferndale, Washington, has a sister city in Miyoshi, Japan. Kobe, Japan, is Seattle's sister city. My father, Joe Hillaire, carved a sister city totem pole for Kobe in 1962 to help unify citizens of Japan and the United States after World War II.[5] Exchange students in the United States sometimes learn about Indian America. In Bellingham, Washington, there are students from all around the world; the curriculum for international students invites Indian citizens into the classroom. I was one of those presenters; I told Indian legends. Such programs provide exposure to the best of Indian America.

When we were young, school-aged white bullies showed some petty, childish meanness against us Indian children, but those situations were quickly resolved by our older siblings. What hurt the most was after my brother returned from World War II. Each of my brothers served a four-year term in that war. I was with one of my brothers, and his wife and children, in a public restaurant that refused to serve us. We sat and sat and sat, and waited and waited and waited, until my brother said, "I guess they're not gonna serve us," and with that we just filed out of there, as they watched us out of the corners of their eyes. Prejudice? It is not pretty. In this instance it was not healthy either, because our children were hungry and had to leave hungry. There comes a time in every person's history when one must turn back the clock in order to find the future. My family elders used to say: "You can't have a future without having a past." It took time, but I did realize that these teachings are tried and true.

In order to set down the beginning of a written history of my tribe, I have gathered information that would help establish in your mind the setting, the background, the sense and the feel of Indian America and how it continues across the land, from the Iroquois tribes on the East Coast to the Coast Salish tribes on the West Coast. Imagine that the North American continent was one great village, and in each house was a separate people, born of the Great Spirit, one Creator—an entire village of innocent people, being taken over by strangers among strangers from the other countries: Spain, Great Britain, France, and others. But it was not just strangers. In the Northwest it was disease that was felt most, along with the vicious cycle of racism and prejudice. Across America, Indian orators spoke of peace and understanding; some of their speeches became famous. Even when they spoke harshly to defend their land and people, they did not speak from a mindset of prejudice based on a false sense of superiority.

What variety of views of Indians can we find in the Bureau of Indian Affairs documents? On the one hand we read respectful remarks such as this one, from an 1865 report by Indian commissioner George Manypenny: "He has noble impulses and possesses in a high degree the finer feelings and affections, and there is no lack of evidence that he can be elevated and highly civilized. Erroneous opinions and prejudices in relation to the disposition, characteristics, capacity and intellectual powers of the race, have almost excluded the Indian from the public sympathy. Statesmen and philanthropists but slightly regard him."[6]

In contrast, Indian commissioner Luke Lea's 1852 report contains racism, uses racism to rationalize, and might have added to further racist thinking:

> When civilization and barbarism are brought in such relation that they cannot co-exist together; it is right that the superiority of the former should be asserted and the latter compelled to give way. It is therefore, no matter of regret or reproach that so large a portion of our territory has been wrested from its aboriginal inhabitants and made the happy abodes of an enlightened and Christian people. That the means employed to effect this grand result have not always been just, or that the conquest has been attended by a vast amount of human suffering, cannot be denied. Of the Indian's wrongs there is, indeed, no earthly record. But it will not be forgotten, by those who have a correct understanding of this subject, that much of the

injury of which the red man and his friends complain has been the inevitable consequence of his own perverse and vicious nature. In the long and varied conflict between the white man and the red—civilization and barbarism—the former has often been compelled to recede, and be destroyed; or to advance and destroy. The history of the contest, however, bears witness to the fact that the victor has, in general, manifested a generous desire, not only to spare the vanquished, but to improve his condition . . . to reclaim and civilize the Indians within our limits; and who can fail to remember, with reverence and regret, "the noble army of martyrs" who have sacrificed themselves in this holy cause?[7]

With the self-contradiction in the statement above, it is plain to see the ambivalence of the U.S. government and society toward Indian America, but also why Indian America was ambivalent toward white America. One civilization was too slow and the other too fast, but there was good and bad in each. The pride and patience of the Indians and the speed and greed of the white man can coexist; at least we have for centuries. We, Indian and white in America today, are proof of it.

Today racism wears a mask, but back when my parents were required to attend the Tulalip Indian School in the early 1900s, racism wore its real face. These military-style schools were different from the old mission schools that followed them. The school was extremely strict. Our Indian cultural ways were prohibited, never (supposedly) to be used again.[8] The Indian School at Tulalip applied the rules of Indian cultural assimilation. Remember the slogan of Colonel Pratt, founder of the famous Carlisle, Pennsylvania, Indian school? "Kill the Indian, but save the Man."[9] The Indian schools aimed to remove all Indianness from Indians. My mother, born in 1894, used a dozen or more local Native dialects. She attended Indian school in the first decade of the twentieth century, when our Native languages were supposed to be removed entirely. Her relatives and friends told her that Native languages were not allowed at school; only English was to be spoken. My mother's age group knew extremely little English. They knew, however, that they would be learning English in this school. She and her schoolmates talked in near whispers, but in their Native languages. They understood each other, no matter which local tribe they belonged to. One day, a teacher caught my mother talking in her Indian language and reported her. The school disciplinarians walked her to the nearby beach and shoved her in a cave (which is there to this day). There were bars that pulled shut. The school disciplinarians closed the bar doors behind my mother and padlocked her in. Looking around the cave cell, she saw no place to sit, no place to lie down. They left her there overnight. The tide came in; she could feel the things she knew were there, but at night they felt different, especially because she was still a little girl (I believe the school went from first to sixth grade). Imagine what this could do to a little child's mind: the seaweed, small creeping creatures, and buzzing of what she guessed were mosquitoes. There was nowhere to escape the feeling of slippery seaweed and the creeping creatures, maybe small crabs, at night. The next morning the school disciplinarians came after her, and she was told again never to speak her Indian language. She did not, even at home, later in life.

She would whisper instructions to us, telling us to go after some Indian medicine or berries nearby our home, and she was old by then. Old in those days might be fifty-five years of age. When we lived at Gooseberry Point when I was in my teens, she would still whisper orders to us, especially when she needed some medicine, which we gathered from near the shores at Gooseberry Point. She gathered her own herbs, roots, and barks for her medicinal juices and teas. She would just whisper a few words in Indian, "Go get me some of that *xexmein*" (*q'əxmín*: wild celery, Indian consumption plant, *Lomatium nudicaule*). That is how the Indian school at Tulalip affected her. Years went by, and the school got beyond its cruelty and became a different kind of school; I do not remember if it became a mission school or just a regular day school.

My father, born in the same year as my mother, 1894, also attended the Tulalip Indian School. His experience, with different details, was the same thing: racism. He learned from his classmates how strict the school was against Indian languages and culture. He outwitted the school officials from the start, being very watchful and protective of his classmates as well. Then one winter he was called into the school office. He was worried, but what they wanted of him struck him as extremely puzzling. They wanted him to sing. The instructors told him that his classmates from Lummi had told them that he could sing, that he always sang at Lummi. Well, my father knew they did not want to hear "Indian languages," even in song. So, after days and nights of thinking about it, he came up with an answer. He was a very creative person and must have been that way all his life. He and his classmates practiced a song that came to him. They practiced the song and the choreography. It went like this, to the rhythm of the four count: "Hello, hello, one-two-three; hello, hello, A-B-C." They pounded sticks for the rhythm. He and his classmates stomped around the room to the rhythm of this song, boys with a stomping march, and girls with a light-footed step, all with arms raised in the traditional Native greeting. Once around the room, and the instructors were satisfied, but whenever we sing it in our dance group, we are reminded of this story, and we all smile. He had satisfied the racist school instructors by not using his Indian language in the song, and the Indian rhythm and choreography pleased them, too. Today I still think how clever he was at every turn. And I think of those racist instructors; I bet they smiled, too, after they saw and heard this song and dance. But how disappointed they must have been that they could not punish him, as they did my mother.

Years later, after my parents married, they applied for the famous commodities made available through the BIA. Indian families were to receive farm equipment, supplies, and domesticated animals. The supplies consisted of cloth, pots and pans, silverware (probably surplus from the military). Well, everything went well for the pots and pans, but the farm equipment would not work. As a bunch of kids, we all played with the broken-down tractor, especially. Oh, it was fun to pretend to be a farmer. The farm machinery was no good for anything but special toys for us. Wild. My mother examined the little squares of material of all colors on a ring. We got to watch her make a quilt out of at least one. I am not sure what the government meant for her to do with those small squares of different colored material, but she saw that it made a good quilt blanket. It was great big, too; it covered the three boys who slept in one room upstairs. My father did a good job of raising pigs; he even got a prize for raising the biggest pig in the county at the county fair (Pioneer Picnic Days) in Ferndale, Washington. One year my mother won a prize for her bread. Events like these filled us kids with great big pride! How did I find out he won a prize? Mom, too? Well, I dug into the school records at the Sandpoint National Archives in Seattle, where records were kept of the children who attended the Tulalip Indian School. In the archives at Sandpoint, I saw a picture of the school and the students in their uniforms. But turning us into farmers did not succeed. It was just not in the blood. Vine Deloria Jr. gave this account of the government farming program at Lummi:

> The men were recruited to cut and burn the trees, some of them the finest cedar in the country, so that all the land would be clear for farming. But since the land was really an island, clearing the trees resulted in the creation of many swamps and pools of almost perpetual duration. While the agents gave an optimistic report on farming at Lummi every year, listing, as we have seen on other reservations, bushels of wheat, corn, and other crops, it was apparent from the first that farming was not an occupation that would be very profitable on the reservation.[10]

I think it was the destruction of our cedars and firs, along with changes in the river, that led to about four thousand acres of the reservation, plus some of the allotments, eventually getting flooded every year, some with ocean water. This led to a land reclamation project in the 1920s.[11]

I remember also how my mother had to stand in a commodity lineup near the old city hall in Bellingham. She received long brown stockings for us girls, pants for the boys, trapdoor underwear for all of us, and lard, flour, and sugar. But the lineup consisted of many white people and just a few Indians, because Indians were told that Bellingham was out of bounds for them. As a result of this, and the fact that the church we attended was in old downtown Bellingham, we would walk past, but never go into, the old Sears store (at Holly and, I believe, Bay Streets). Our experiences with these clothes were comically dramatic, especially the trapdoor underwear and high ankle shoes. I do not think that goods such as these could be claimed as "payment" for the lands beyond our miniature Indian reservations—a very vast region, and beautiful, too.

My father was a natural-born carpenter, born on Christmas Day in 1894. He built the barn and our two-story house on the corner of Slater and Lake Terrell Road (once called Hillaire Road). He never went to school for that; he just looked at the pictures of homes in catalogs. Those old catalogs served many a purpose for Indian families—not for ordering things, but for making fires, and so forth. And I believe some good things came from those "government gifts" that accompanied the broken-down tractor. They gave my mother seed for our hayfield. My mother was a survivor! As she raised us, after divorcing my father, she built a spring for our fresh water and sold gravel from the gravel pit in our nearest field. We had fun going to the spring that Mom built so we'd have water for the house, and we swam in the gravel pit swimming hole. Because of her, we were one of the first Lummi families to have a car. The first one was a Model T Ford; another one was an old Essex. More fun! My brother Ruben bragged about our Model T to someone visiting us at the mansion (old house). He said, "Our car goes fast . . . downhill." One time Mom drove us younger ones to town, Ferndale, in her old Model T. As she braked on a hill, a front wheel came off, and we watched, shocked, as the car slowly rolled down a sloping field. Talk about laughing, even years later. The car did not topple; it just kept rolling. It must have been perfectly balanced. Mom taught us how to survive.

CHAPTER 8

Aboriginal Fishermen

The right of taking fish at usual and accustomed grounds and stations is further secured to said Indians in common with all citizens of the Territory.
—Treaty of Point Elliott, Article 5

During my seventeen years of leading the Lummi Indian dance group Children of the Setting Sun, I told stories from Lummi oral tradition and from my research. Here is one of the stories about our aboriginal fishermen. Why weren't our coastal tribes "removed" to east of the Cascades according to the U.S. government's original plan to take over all of coastal Washington?

In 1841 President John Tyler and his secretary of war expressed the government's "indisputable" intent to occupy the vast Pacific Northwest.[1] Joseph Lane, the first governor of the Oregon Territory, had urged Congress to "extinguish" Indian title to land in the Northwest and remove Indians to make way for white settlement (he argued that this would help Indians, whose lives had already become so deprived and miserable, as settlers continued to arrive). A congressional delegate from the Oregon Territory by the name of Samuel R. Thurston convinced Congress to act, and the House passed a resolution on June 5, 1850, to make treaties and to extinguish Indian claims to land west of the Cascade Mountains.[2] White Americas wanted the coastal regions all to themselves.

It was decided that the Indians of coastal Washington should be removed from west of the Cascades to the eastern side of the mountains.

Our Washington coastal tribes were to become enrolled members of either the Yakama or Colville Tribes. The plan was that a U.S. military force would remove our ancestors from west of the mountains to east of the mountains in these later years of Indian removal. So, how it started was that the fishermen were told to gather up their families, pack their belongings, and go with these regiments over the Cascade Mountains to their new homes. The aboriginal fishermen obeyed the military forces. Together, the military and the fishermen with their families headed over the Cascade Mountains. Far into this long, rugged journey, the military lost their way. The Indians had been over the Cascade Mountains time and again for hunting, gathering berries, roots and cedar, or on their journeys to find wives or husbands. So, the Indians picked up on the journey and led the military over the mountains.

Very near their destination, the military men ran out of rations. Because the Indians had hunted those mountains for all the years of their history, they hunted food for the soldiers and officers. After everyone ate, they reached their destination, near Wenatchee. The soldiers were relieved that they had arrived. The encampment was to hold the Indians until arrangements were made for these aboriginal fishermen's new homes with the Yakama and Colville Tribes. Everyone slept. The Indians, being fishermen, arose early, earlier than the military; the military men were tired because they were not as accustomed to this type of journey as were the Indians. The Indians left the encampment the very next morning while the soldiers slept soundly. They came back home to the coast. When the military returned to the villages on the coast side of the mountains, they found the Indians in their usual fishing grounds. Once more they ordered the Indians to pack their families and belongings, telling them that they must obey orders of the U.S. government and the superintendent of Indian Affairs, and that they would be better off on the east side of the mountains.

Once more the Indians left and came home to the coast. This happened a third time, too. After the fourth time, the Indian commissioner concluded that it was getting expensive trying to keep the Indians on the east side of the Cascades. The Coast Salish Indians had permanent homes, canoes for travel, clothes for every season, twenty-six kinds of berries, nine species of fish, and countless shellfish; in fact, it was a fool who could not find food in the abundant land of the coast. The pioneer Ezra Meeker later wrote: "I have seen salmon so numerous . . . as to literally touch each other. It was utterly impossible to wade across without touching the fish."[3] Finally, the Indian commissioner said, in essence, "We might as well leave the Indians on the coast; they will just keep returning to their old haunts." It was due largely to the steadfastness of our fishermen that our tribes were permitted to stay in their coastal homelands, rather than being removed inland.

OUR ANCESTRAL FISHING COMMUNITIES

In prehistoric times our ancient ancestors established communities based on fishing, and by the strength of the fishermen, our people have continuously inhabited our area for thousands of years. Our ancestors were here 8,000 years ago, and possibly as long as 11,500 years ago. Scientists have documented that the Gulf of Georgia and the Point Roberts Peninsula (map 2) had a regional settlement of aboriginal people 8,000 years ago—that is, about 6,000 BCE. Prehistoric occupation of Point Roberts might have occurred as early as the end of the late Pleistocene glaciations: approximately 11,500 years ago (9,500 BCE).

The fishing culture in our region is a central feature of our aboriginal culture, according to a report prepared for nomination of Lily Point, on Point Roberts, as a Washington State Historic Site. The report was researched by Al Scott Johnnie, director of the Lummi Culture Department, and Leonard Garfield. "Evidence suggests that the earliest inhabitants were hunters oriented toward land based resources, but over the last 5,000 years, fish, shellfish, and marine mammals became important resources, as maritime adaptations developed."[4] Lily Point is also known as Chelhtenem or Chehelhtenem, from the Lummi word *tsalhten*, which has to do with hanging salmon to preserve it.

Chelhtenem is associated with supernatural beings called Transformers, whose powers prepared the world for the coming generations of human beings. Anthropologist Diamond Jenness transcribed accounts such as this one, given by a Katzie elder, Old Pierre. (Old Pierre is father to Joe Washington's second wife, Martha Pierre. Joe Washington was one of the leaders of our Lummi Setting Sun Dance Group. I am proud to say that Martha, too, was a magnificent and spiritual person.)

> Three brothers accompanied by twelve servants . . . appeared suddenly at Chelhtenem. . . . In front marched the eldest of the three brothers, a being of marvelous power named Khaals (x̣eʔəĺs) who could transport them wherever he wished by his mere thoughts. Khaals approached an Indian and his wife who were sitting on the beach, and swept his right hand upward, restoring their souls to the Lord Above and changing their bodies to stone. To the woman he said: "You shall help the people who come hereafter. If they speak fair words to you, you shall grant them fair weather." What he said to the man, who sank deeper into the ground than the woman, we no longer remember.[5]

Two stones remained, like those around which the young men of present generations march during their part of the First Salmon Ceremony. According to the legend, the original stone figures have reappeared over time, and it is said that they have special powers.[6]

During the fishing season in late summer, many tribes from both Washington and Canada would gather at Chelhtenem—right into the earlier decades of the twentieth century. The Lily Point historic preservation report notes that "Chelhtenem is widely considered the most important reef net fishery, and one of the most important salmon fisheries, for the Central Coast Salish."[7] Some of the evidence in the report is from the Jesup North Pacific Expedition, directed by the anthropologist Franz Boas. The Jesup Expedition took place in 1897–1902 to investigate the prehistoric peoples of the Bering Strait area. The report gives this summary of archaeological studies of Chelhtenem:

> Evidence of prehistoric occupation of Chelhtenem (Lily Point) at the southeastern tip of the peninsula was first recorded nearly a century

ago during one of the earliest archaeological surveys in the Pacific Northwest. In 1898, archaeologists Harlan Smith and Gerard Fowke found a series of "cairn-like sepulchers" at "the southern end of the shell heap situated at the eastern end of the bluff . . ." Since that time, Chelhtenem has been surveyed several times (Grabert 1984; Reid 1984; Roulette 1984; Campbell and Miss 1990) and tested once (Millar 1978). A recorded site (45-WH-218) includes prehistoric shell midden, other faunal remains, fire-modified rock, and other features and cultural deposits significantly associated with prehistoric Salish settlement.[8]

"Midden," by the way, is a term that archaeologists use for material that has accumulated around a dwelling, which gives information about a people's food, tools, housing, and so forth. For more on archeological studies of the Straits Salish people of Washington's San Juan Islands (west of the Lummi Reservation and south of Point Roberts), see *Exploring Coast Salish Prehistory* (2000) by Julie K. Stein.[9]

As early as 1791, European explorers encountered and described Native American utilization of the Point Roberts/Chelhtenem area and commented on the large and productive fishery and the seasonal occupation that attended it. Pantoja, a member of the Spanish expedition led by Francisco de Eliza, visited Lily Point in July of 1791 and reported "an incredible quantity of rich salmon and numerous Indians." A member of George Vancouver's expedition, Menzies, recorded that in July 1792, Captain Vancouver observed a large village at Lily Point with longhouses that he mistakenly thought had been abandoned (owing to the seasonal fishing culture of the aboriginal fishermen). The report estimated that four hundred to five hundred persons lived in longhouses arranged in three rows, with four to six longhouses in each row. Ethnologist and surveyor George Gibbs noted an "'Indian fishery' at Lily Point in 1856, and the General Land Office map of 1859 notes an Indian fishing village at the same location."[10]

My personal memory is that my brother, born in 1918, would drive us to Point Roberts, Washington, where we would dig for horse clams.

Horse clams make good clam chowder; in fact, the best. Every year we would go there; it always seemed to me like an exclusive vacation site, a place where many tribes came to camp, harvest foods, have a good time, and then go back home. The book *Lummi Elders Speak* (1982) contains testimonies of Lummi elders born between 1886 and 1910 who remember that Point Roberts was a vast gathering place for local tribes of the entire region. A classmate, my age, remembers that she used to get camas from the upland bluffs. My family and I visited Point Roberts many times when I was a child of five to seven years old; I remember seeing some old, run-down buildings there. We always drove around the community; this was our chance to hear stories about Point Roberts from my mother and stepfather. The oral history that I know goes back to the early eighteenth century. Ancestors have passed down oral history about camping at the Point Roberts site for fishing and gathering shellfish and berries. By custom of oral tradition, Lummi elders older than me have witnessed and told of campsites even earlier than those spoken of by my elders. Their testimonies align with researchers' findings about the area. In *Lummi Elders Speak*, Lummi elders born around the beginning of the twentieth century recall the days they camped at Point Roberts to fish in the manmade channels, to pick berries on a nearby plateau, and to gather shellfish.[11]

For readers who may not be familiar with Coast Salish life, please understand that fishing was not a pastime, or just for feasts and ceremonial purposes. Our fishing tribes absolutely depended on salmon for food and for livelihood, and today salmon remains a foundation of our cultural life and our tribal economies. Anthropologist Barbara Lane wrote in a report for our famous federal fishing rights case, *U.S. v. Washington* (the Boldt Decision, 1974): "throughout most of the area, salmon (including steelhead when available) was the staple food and the most important single food resource available to the Native population."[12] (The steelhead is an oceangoing trout, with a lifecycle similar to the salmon.) In earlier history, when Native people of the Pacific Northwest obtained all their food from the lands and waters, the heavy growth of the coastal forests made it difficult to hunt enough wildlife to sustain communities of people, but the open waters of the ocean and rivers provided an abundance of food. During the Lewis and Clark expedition, William Clark recorded that "the multitudes of salmon were "almost inconceivable" and that "they could readily be seen at a depth of fifteen or twenty feet."[13] In today's times Indian America suffers a lack of sufficient economic opportunities, and in the Northwest the salmon fishery remains essential to economic survival for families and communities. More than that, salmon is one of the main roots of our cultural life. Lane described the Indian spiritual reverence for salmon: "The symbolic acts, attitudes of respect, and concern for the well being of the salmon reflected a wider conception of the interdependence and relatedness of all living things, which was a dominant feature of Native world view. Such attitudes and rites ensured that salmon were never wantonly wasted and that water contamination was not permitted."[14] (See chapter 11 for an account of the First Salmon Ceremony; see also fig. 8.)

We have five species of pacific salmon: *chinook* (also called king, tyee, and quinnat), *coho* (silver), *chum* (also called dog salmon, because of its use as food for sled dogs and its canine snout), *pink* (humpback, the smallest salmon), and *sockeye* (blueback or red salmon). The *steelhead* is a salmon-like trout that also travels between river and ocean.[15] Lummi has historically been a major fishing tribe among the western Washington tribes. The main method of Lummi fishing was reef netting. Lane explains: "Lummis primarily fished by reef netting. They individually owned specific locations on the reef, which they received by heirship. Owners of locations then hired relatives and friends to work with them in preparing the gear and fishing the site."[16] It took a lot of knowledge, skill, and effort to place nets in the oceans where salmon are traveling back to the spawning grounds in their home rivers.

Reef nets were held in place by heavy anchor stones and attached at the top between two canoes (fig. 11). When the fishermen signaled that the salmon were in the net, the canoes were released from the anchors and the weight of the net—full of fish—pulled the two canoes together. The salmon were brought up into one canoe and the net into the other canoe.[17] Vine Deloria says of reef net fishermen: "With such split-second timing necessary, the leader of the fishing expedition had to have an almost mystical sense about the salmon, the current of the water, and his men's ability to the raise the net quickly. Reef net fishing required an incredible sense of timing and an intimate knowledge of all the factors that affected fish life. Leadership of reef net fishing expedition was so intuitive that those men who had continued success as reef netters were considered to be possessed of a supernatural ability and religious power over the salmon."[18]

There were reef net sites at Orcas Island, San Juan Island, Point Roberts, Village Point on Lummi Island, Fidalgo Island, and Sandy Point (map 2). Point Roberts was the largest. The Straits and Sound were used for fishing in common by all the tribes of the region. Lummi fishermen originally fished from the Lummi area south to Seattle and north past the Canadian border to the Fraser River. Today the colorful sight of reef net canoes, silhouetted against the sun and water, will never be seen again. Never again will the waters echo the aboriginal fishermen's excited cries, "Sockeye! Sockeye!" At those times we stood in awe, watching the fishermen pull in their nets, loaded with beautiful salmon. No one can turn back the calendar, but what wonderful memories of my childhood.

THE STRUGGLE FOR TREATY FISHING RIGHTS

Records kept by the Hudson's Bay Company state that on August 20, 1829, there were "at least 200 canoes of Indians assembled at the site" (the Lily Point village).[19] Two hundred canoes! It is hard work to carve one canoe; these Indian people could not have been "lazy," as some Indian Affairs officials claimed. In the mid-nineteenth century the landscape began to fill with non-Indian activities, after the pattern of land takeovers across Indian America. Speculators, traders, and corporations located the resources, found out where the Indian population was operating, and took things over. In our area the first major companies were the American Fur Company, which built its main trading post in 1811 (in Astoria, present-day Oregon, at the mouth of the Columbia River; map 7), Canada's North West Company ("The Northwesters"), and the British Hudson's Bay Company (HBC), which had trading posts on both the

U.S. and the Canadian sides. The HBC ultimately took over the other two companies.[20] After the fur trade was no longer profitable, white people discovered that there was money in fishing. When white fishing interests got underway in our ancestral fishing areas, the Bureau of Indian Affairs was mostly silent regarding protection of the Indians. It was similar to what happened in earlier generations, when the military was ordered to protect—for the most part—white people against Indians, but not vice versa, while white Americans were encouraged by the government to "emigrate thither" (this phrase is scattered here and there in the government documents of the time).

Fishing rights is a major treaty issue for the Northwest tribes and the U.S. government, historically and for the future. In Governor Stevens's report about the Washington coastal tribes written the year before the 1855 Treaty of Point Elliott, he says: "The subject of the right of fisheries is one upon which legislation is demanded."[21] In the Point Elliott Treaty and other treaties in our region, fishing—both on and off the reservations—is a right that the tribes reserved as part of their survival and their identity. When settlers started inhabiting the Pacific Northwest, at first they just acquired fish from Indians, but soon they began to fish for themselves. White fishermen experimented with fishing techniques for years before they could come close to matching the success of Lummi reef netting. Traditional Indian fishing was disrupted by white commercial fishing starting in the late nineteenth century. When commercial canning made fishing a profitable business, there was a rapid increase of non-Indian fishing and encroachment. Salmon canning quickly became a big industry in the Northwest. The first cannery in Washington was built on the Columbia River in 1866, and in 1877 the first of many canneries went up in Puget Sound. Commercial fishermen—including new immigrants from Europe who were expert fishers—used costly fishing equipment to fish far out at sea, where they reduced the number of fish that could reach Indian fisheries closer to shore. Immature fish were being harvested before they had opportunity to reproduce. As the methods and the extent of commercial fishing expanded, the states of Oregon and Washington grew concerned about the security of the fish runs. In 1877 the Washington State legislature, without much knowledge or guidance concerning the lifecycle of the salmon, began restricting fishing. Over time more restrictions were placed on fishing seasons, locations, and methods. In 1887, 1899, and for several years following, the state placed restrictions on fishing in Puget Sound's rivers and tributaries, including saltwater adjacent to the rivers. All these were places that Indians traditionally fished.[22] These restrictions did not actually help the salmon, and they certainly harmed the fishing tribes. A century later, an article on the economics of fishing rights in Washington observed, "the Northwest commercial fishery has been managed by myths, symbols, and ethnic politics, not by science."[23]

Garfield and Scott Johnnie report: "in 1893, the Alaska Packers cannery built a trap that blocked the Lummi net locations." In the years before World War II those same kinds of traps were used outside the Village Point reef net site at Lummi Island. The design and large size of the traps permitted enormous catches. A government fisheries report for 1895 indicates that approximately 5.2 million pounds of salmon were caught at Point Roberts, most of it by commercial traps; the amount caught by Indian reef nets was 184,239 pounds (approximately 3.5 percent of that amount).[24] In 1894 Lummi tribal members had called upon the commissioner of Indian Affairs for help in protecting their treaty rights to fish at Point Roberts. They requested that the commissioner instruct the U.S. district attorney in Seattle to prosecute the commercial fishers who were depriving the Lummi of their fishing grounds, their fish, and their rights. The BIA did not help, so the Lummi hired legal counsel that pressured the state attorney general to prosecute.

In the case *U.S. v. The Alaska Packers Association*, Judge C. H. Hanford ruled against the Lummi, saying that under the Treaty of Point Elliott, Indians retained equal fishing rights, but no "special privileges." Furthermore, the judge said, there were still fish to be caught, and closing the cannery would be a disservice to Indian fishers, who sold some of their catch to the cannery.[25] In 1897 the Lummi again requested the help of the BIA. This time the case reached the U.S. Supreme Court. But the U.S. attorney general advised the BIA to drop the case, and the Supreme

Court granted a motion to dismiss. So, Indian fishers lost their traditional fishing grounds at Point Roberts and Lummi Island. Indian fishing was thus restricted to small-scale subsistence fishing, on and adjacent to the reservation. But even there, non-Indian fishermen trespassed on tidelands and sometimes on the uplands of the reserve.[26]

For quite some time I kept track of just which fishing spots were lost, but there got to be too many for me to keep track of, so I gave up. Our loss of fishing sites was one of the last low blows. In addition to the gigantic traps that white fishermen placed to catch fish around reef netting sites, they also put pilings in place, so as to prevent Indians' entry to the fishing sites. The traps eventually overcame the picturesque reef net fishery. Reef net fishing was a stronghold for our ancient fishermen, but when overcome by the white men's traps and barges, Indians became discouraged. Even tourists lost interest.

The state of Washington was inconsistent concerning whether Indians had to have licenses to fish off-reservation. In 1913 Judge Ed E. Hardin ruled for the State Supreme Court that Indians could fish in their "usual and accustomed places" without licenses, because the treaty was an agreement with the federal government and thus outweighed state requirements. But not all courts in the counties of Washington State followed Judge Hardin's ruling. State fish commissioner L. H. Darwin ignored it, and he instructed wardens to arrest Indians who fished off-reservation without licenses. White fishers sometimes complained when Indians fishing off-reservation did not have licenses: for them, this was a problem. Some Indians reluctantly got licenses to avoid conflict with white fishermen and wardens, but many could not afford to. This further confined Indian fishers. Darwin continued to arrest Indian fishermen, even after he promised he would not do so without first consulting Indian superintendent Charles Buchanan. This led to the 1915 court case *Dan Ross, John Alexis, George Boone, Frederick Pearson, Michael Kwina, Julius Charles, Peter Victor, Matt Paul, John Horn, Peter Kwina, Harry Swalton, William James* (Lummi tribe members) *v. Darwin*. The state court would not issue an injunction against Darwin, so he continued to have Indian fishermen arrested for fishing off-reservation without a state license.[27] The arrests included confiscation of fishing gear and canoes, thus interfering with future fishing by Indians who had been arrested.

Austrian fishermen created a legend by trespassing on an Indian fishing site. In 1916 Lummi fishermen defended one of their fishing sites, and on that occasion, they received the support of the Indian Agency. "About April 10, 1916, a half dozen Lummi fishermen, led by August Lane, seized a purse seine net belonging to an Austrian fisherman by the name of A. Galinovich, who was fishing for herring in Hale Passage above the low water mark, which the Lummi claimed was within the reservation boundary. The Lummi cut the Austrian's net, releasing the herring catch, and they confiscated the net." On April 21 Charles Buchanan, superintendent of the Indian Agency at Tulalip, gave orders to farming agent McCluskey at Lummi "to arrest and prosecute any non-Indian fishermen fishing above low water mark."[28] Vine Deloria's account tells that the Lummi fishermen took several Austrian fishermen back to the reservation as prisoners, which would have created bad press for the United States, with World War I beginning in Europe. When the story of fish commissioner Darwin's ongoing harassment of Indian fishermen became public, he finally stopped.[29] In that instance the scale of justice tipped in favor the Indian fishermen. Superintendent Buchanan was also an exception to the rule by his helping to defend Indian fishing with an article, "Rights of the Puget Sound Indians to Game and Fish," published in the *Washington Historical Quarterly* in April 1915.[30]

Indian tribal governments undertook extensive efforts to raise money for lawyers to stand up for their treaty rights. But most often, the decisions of state courts benefited commercial and sports fishermen. Tidelands were an issue between Indian and white fishermen, along with the timeless trading practices of Indian fishermen. Deadlocks were created by interference initiated by white fishing organizations. This involved factors such as conjured-up boundary lines in the waters of Bellingham Bay, between Point Frances (on Portage Island) and the Treaty Rock, located at the mouth of the Nooksack River (map 9). The problem of trespassing by non-Indians came up again every few years, sometimes on the east side of the Lummi Reservation boundary.

Tidelands around Point Frances Island were hotly disputed over and again. White fishermen did not know or accept the border from Point Frances across Bellingham Bay to Treaty Rock. They fished that area, and the Lummi claimed they were trespassing. In 1919 the case *U.S v. Romaine et al.* (255 Fed. 253 [1919]) resulted in the decision that the reservation boundary went from Treaty Rock to the east side of the Nooksack River, which over time had changed its course (see map 9 and caption). Often the chance to settle disputes just faded over time. Court battles were taking much of the fishing families' money. When borders were disputed in court, it cost Indians money they did not really have, but they collected it from friends and family. The Indian fishers suffered through all this, but they maintained their legal stand.

In the 1920s and 1930s, Indian fishermen in Washington had difficulty obtaining food and livelihood for their families, owing to lack of federal support from the BIA and threat of arrest by state wardens. Fish could be sold openly only during regular fishing seasons; at other times fish were sometimes shipped to processors undercover.[31] A serious hardship arose for the tribes in 1925, when the state, pressured by sport fishermen, designated steelhead a "game fish" once it reached fresh water, so that it could be caught only by hook and line, and not by net, as Indians had always fished. The winter steelhead catch provided about half the food supplies for the fishing tribes and a portion of their trade. At first Indians who fished in reservation waters were exempt, but by 1927 the ban covered the netting of steelhead on reservations.[32]

In 1934 Washington voters approved Initiative 77, the "antitrap legislation." Initiative 77 made it illegal to use fixed gear, such as traps, fish weirs, fish wheels, and set nets. Along with restricting methods of fishing, Initiative 77 placed limits on the areas and times that fishing was permitted. Some said that Initiative 77 made fishing more fair, but it imposed more regulations. Indians fishing under federal regulations were supposed to be exempt from Initiative 77, but sports fishermen pressured the State Department of Fisheries to arrest Indian fishermen who were considered to be fishing in violation of state law. The state took the position that Indians who fished off-reservation (as the treaties allowed) were infringing on the state's rights. The state restricted Indians to fishing on, or near, their reservations. This seriously compromised the ability of Indian fishermen to be at the right place and time for the salmon runs. Our Indian fishermen had to identify themselves as Indians from a federally recognized tribe, identify their boats, report their catches, and follow, follow, follow the Indians' side of the line.

Traps became a strategy tool of the white fishermen. Confusion existed about whether Lummi reef netting involved "fixed" (permanent) gear and locations, and whether reef netting was thus illegal according to Initiative 77. Therefore, many Indian fishermen lost their reef netting sites. White fishermen quickly moved into the Indian reef netting sites. Soon most of these sites were owned by non-Indians. Indians were edged out in every way. Oh, the battle became atrocious. Reef netting was the main source of the Lummi economy. Lummi fishermen became unable to make a living for their families while court hearings increased, and they continued to collect monies between them to hire lawyers to fight for their treaty rights. BIA red tape made the application of protection measures extremely slow. Indian fishermen had to contend with the State Fish Commission, the BIA, sports and commercial fishing organizations and fishers, and state fish and game wardens (game wardens were in charge of the steelhead; the state fisheries department controlled the salmon). The Washington State courts usually sided with every group except the Indian fishermen, even opposing the federal courts at times. Courage had to match the ungodly.

The loss of Lummi reef netting sites, which had occurred during the 1930s because of Initiative 77, was still an issue for Lummi fishermen decades later. In the 1960s it was under discussion between tribal fishermen and the BIA. A 1961 BIA report describes how non-Indian fishermen at that time controlled the reef net sites, and how their way of doing business continued to keep Lummi fishermen from their ancestral occupation: "Sites are only sold with the gear included, which could be between $10,000 to $80,000 each, a price too expensive for Lummis. Agents from the BIA inspected the sites September 28, 1962. The Lummis stated they would like about fifteen sites. Nothing was done about this."[33]

Seven Pacific Northwest fishing rights cases reached the United States Supreme Court. The first six were *U.S. v. Winans* (198 U.S. 371 [1905]), *Seufert Brothers Co. v. U.S.* (249 U.S. 149 [1919]), *Tulee v. Washington* (315 U.S. 681 [1942]), *Puyallup Tribe v. Department of Game* (391 U.S. 392 [1968]), *Department of Game v. Puyallup Tribe* (414 U.S. 44 [1973]), and *Puyallup Tribe, Inc. v. Department of Game* (433 U.S. 165 [1977]). The seventh case, *Washington v. Washington State Commercial Fishing Vessel Association* (443 U.S. 658 [1978]) was a review of *U.S. v. Washington* (the Boldt Decision), which had been decided in 1974 in the federal district court in Tacoma, Washington.

In the first case, *United States v. Winans* (1905), the U.S. government sued in behalf of the Yakama, a Stevens Treaty tribe of eastern Washington. The Winans brothers operated a fish wheel, a device that caught a huge quantity of fish, thus interfering with Yakama Indians being able to obtain enough for themselves. The Winans also prevented the Yakama fishers from crossing the Winans' homestead land to reach usual and accustomed Yakama fishing grounds. The Supreme Court affirmed the Yakama's treaty right to have access to their fisheries. The ruling in the *Winans* case was important for several reasons: It rejected the defense's argument that since Washington was now a state, and no longer a Territory as it had been when the treaty was made, that the treaty was no longer binding. The *Winans* ruling is also an important case because it clarified the *reserved rights doctrine*. Associate justice Joseph McKenna wrote the majority opinion for the court: "the treaty was not a grant of rights *to* the Indians, but a grant of rights *from* them—a reservation of those [rights] not granted." Justice McKenna made other points in the opinion that became important for future cases of treaty interpretation. To summarize: (1) A treaty should be interpreted in ways that are appropriate to the ways that the Indian signatories likely would have understood the treaty, and (2) the U.S. government should not get so caught up in technicalities that its interpretation of a treaty fails to embody justice and reason. These principles of the Winans case were applied in the 1919 case, *Seufert Brothers v. U.S.*, which upheld Yakama fishing rights in areas on the south side of the Columbia River. The difficulty with the Supreme Court's decision in the *Winans* case was the court's allowing that the state should not be unreasonably restrained in regulating Indians' treaty right to fish.[34] In the decades that followed, the state of Washington would utilize this allowance to its maximum advantage and against the interests of aboriginal fishermen.

In 1916 the Washington State Supreme Court heard the case of Lummi Indian fisherman John Alexis, who was reef netting at a usual and accustomed Lummi station, during a state closure and without a license. This was one of several cases in which a state court went against the U.S. Supreme Court's position. The state argued that that the Treaty of Point Elliott, which protects fishing rights, was abrogated by the Enabling Act under which Washington was admitted as a state.[35] Judge Ed Hardin listened to testimonies of elders who had attended the Point Elliott Treaty Council. His ruling presumed that the tribes' only treaty fishing right was the right of easement over private lands, in order to reach their traditional fishing grounds. He ruled that Alexis was subject to the same state laws as all other citizens of Washington, but he imposed the minimum fine. Alexis could not pay it, so he went to jail. Following the Alexis case, the state imposed increased restrictions on off-reservation fishing. Johnny Alexis's case was a living example of the power of white law. Alexis withstood his own individual battle with the powers of the state. He and his property suffered: his land, his farm, and his home were left uncared for while he spent nearly five months in jail. Finally the governor pardoned him in June 1917. On June 27, 1917, a letter from Alexis appeared in a local paper: "In the Treaty of 1855 between this government and the Indians, Uncle Sam agreed that in consideration of the surrender of large landed tracts the Indian was to be provided for and have a small home . . . he was granted, according to that treaty, the right to fish and hunt whenever and wherever he pleased. . . . If this is a sample of the justice we are to receive then I fail to comprehend the true meaning of justice."[36]

That same year Yakama fisherman Alec Towessnute was arrested for fishing—with a prohibited gaff hook—off-reservation and without a license. The opinion of Washington Supreme Court justice Bausman exemplified the state's view in that era: "The principle of sovereignty we reject. The treaty is not to be interpreted in that light."[37] Pacific Northwest fishing cases ended up in the Supreme Court for a run-up of seventy years until the Boldt Decision in 1974. The state court cases of these early twentieth-century fishermen point to issues that would continue to need resolution: How should the state's fishing regulations be seen in relation to the rights reserved by tribes in their treaties with the federal government? How should the treaties be understood regarding Indians' right of "taking fish . . . *in common* with all citizens of the Territory"? These and other issues would be addressed in detail in the 1970s, when federal Judge George H. Boldt entered the picture.

In the 1940s, concern about depletion of the salmon runs became an issue about which Indian and non-Indian fishermen could agree. But they didn't agree about the causes of the problem. Non-Indian fishermen and organizations and the state spoke as if the salmon runs would be fine, if only Indian fishing could be minimized. The salmon population continued to be damaged by overfishing, pollution, and dam construction throughout all these cases and debates about regulations. Indian fishermen had fished for thousands of years, but they never fished for more than what they needed for themselves, for trading with other tribes, and for people passing through. They taught me a lot when I was fishing. Never waste; never pollute. Yet no matter how we advocate for our aboriginal fishermen and their lifestyle with the waters, the big spending in the larger world, along with damage to the environment, hurts our salmon populations. Aboriginal fishermen had no poisons and no reason to pollute the land and water, nor any reason to bite the hand that fed them.

The 1940s did bring some progress. In 1942 the case of Yakama fisherman Sampson Tulee was heard in the U.S. Supreme Court. In *Tulee v. State of Washington*, the court determined that Tulee was not required to obtain and pay for a state license because he fished under the provisions of the 1855 Treaty with the Yakima. The Tulee case showed the invalidity of the state's claim that Indian treaty fishers must have state licenses. Along with the Winans case, the Tulee decision also upheld that treaty fishing rights include off-reservation sites.[38] However, the court maintained in the Tulee case that the state could still impose regulations that were "indispensable to the effectiveness of a state conservation program."[39] This "conservation criterion," when it was applied without a real basis, was another hurdle that Indian fishermen had to overcome as they continued their stand for fishing rights.

In the 1950s, when U.S. Indian policy began to terminate the federal status of some tribes, organizations such as the National Congress of American Indians and the American Friends Service Committee worked to increase public awareness of the threats that faced Indian people across the United States, such as the elimination of health and education programs and the selling off of reservation lands. In the Northwest, fishing families—men, women, and young people, both boys and girls—put their personal safety at risk, along with their valuable fishing equipment (which was sometimes confiscated, according to the state, as evidence), in order to bring national attention to injustices that would later be addressed in court.[40] Washington state courts defeated Indian cases many times, but usually federal courts overruled those decisions.[41]

The case *State v. Satiacum* (314 P.2d-400 [1957]) was one of the first major events in Washington State's fishing rights activism. The sit-ins and civil rights activism of the 1950s and 1960s provided inspiration for the "fish-ins" in the Northwest. Some of the main leaders in Washington State were Billy Frank Jr. of Nisqually, Nugent Kautz of Nisqually, Ramona Bennett of Puyallup, Janet McCloud of Tulalip, and Hank Adams (Sioux-Assinaboine), a young man from Montana who grew up at Quinault.[42] The stands made for treaty fishing rights in the Northwest became a national focus in the American Indian activism that was gaining strength in those years. In 1957 tribal leader Robert Satiacum, along with James Young of Puyallup, intentionally fished out of season and were arrested. The issue at stake was whether the treaty right of fishing would be honored. The state of Washington focused on defending its claim that state regulations had to be enforced. The court looked into questions such as whether the state regulations enforced against Satiacum were genuinely necessary for conserving the fish runs; the state failed to present compelling evidence for that.

The Washington State Supreme Court sustained dismissal of the charges against the defendants. However, the court was split four to four on the question of treaty rights, so no decision was handed down. After the case, restrictions on tribal fishing by local and state law enforcement increased. However, the case also encouraged tribes to assert their rights. In 1964 Robert Satiacum was intentionally arrested—with Episcopal clergyman John Yaryan and actor Marlon Brando—gaining national media attention.[43] Sometimes the scales of justice tipped in favor of the Indians, and what a relief. However, this angered some white fishermen, and at times they tried to intimidate the Indian fishermen by acts of violence. Blame was often placed on the tribes for depletion of the salmon runs, and at that time the *Seattle Times* often promoted such a view. But the fishing tribes in western Washington, with their small number of fishermen and their limited fishing equipment, could not possibly deplete the salmon. Besides, it was not their way.

In response to the fish-ins, the state legislature petitioned the U.S. Congress to enact legislation that would resolve the controversy. Senator Warren Magnuson (D-WA) introduced Senate Joint Resolution 170, which recognized the treaty right of off-reservation fishing but allowed for state regulation of Indian fishing at those sites. Senate Joint Resolution 171 was intended to extinguish by purchase (to "buy out") the tribes' right to off-reservation fishing. Tribal members at the hearings felt that they were being unfairly blamed for the mismanagement of the fisheries. No one present could provide evidence to dispute the Makah Tribe's estimate that the Indian catch at that time was 5 percent, or less, of the total.[44] The bills died in committee. Court decisions in the state of Washington came to different conclusions about whether state regulations on Indian fishing could be enforced.

A series of three cases that went to the U.S. Supreme Court and came to be known as Puyallup I, II, and III (the Puyallup Trilogy) focused on state involvement in the regulation of Indian fishing. In *Puyallup Tribe, Inc. v. Department of Game* (Puyallup I), Justice William O. Douglas wrote the opinion that the state could regulate Indians' off-reservation fishing if "reasonable and necessary" for conservation of the salmon, as long as the rules did not discriminate against Indians. In Puyallup II, the Puyallup returned to the Supreme Court, claiming discrimination. This occurred after two important events: the Department of Game banned Indians from catching steelhead on the rivers, and the *Washington Law Review* published an article by University of Washington law professor Ralph Johnson that showed how the state's fishing regulations were discriminatory, incompatible with the treaties, and actually unnecessary for conservation. In Puyallup II, the Supreme Court rejected the state's "conservation argument." Officials from the Department of Game had argued that Indians' share of fish should not include fish that originated in hatcheries that were financed largely by license fees paid only by non-Indians. The court did not rule on the hatchery issue in Puyallup II.

In Puyallup III the justices were asked to assess the state's decision to allocate 45 percent of the steelhead run to Indian fishers. Puyallup III was puzzling in that, contrary to the Supremacy Clause of the U.S. Constitution, which establishes treaties as the supreme law of the land (meaning, among other things, that state courts are bound to observe them), the Supreme Court upheld state rather than federal authority. State policy did not accord with the federal decision, based on treaty rights, that was handed down in *U.S. v. Washington*, of a 50 percent allocation to Indian fishers.[45] The hatchery issue was not addressed in Puyallup III, nor by Judge Boldt in *U.S. v. Washington*; the issue remained to be determined by Judge William Orrick in Phase II of *U.S. v. Washington*.[46]

Fishing treaty rights were defended by fishing treaty tribes throughout the Northwest in Washington, Oregon, Idaho, and Montana. Tribes in California and the Great Lakes area were also fighting to protect their fishing rights. The struggle taking place for the fishing tribes on the Columbia River helped bring Northwest fishing rights into federal court. In 1968 a highly decorated army veteran named Richard Sohappy, of Yakama, and his relative David were arrested for fishing with gill nets, and they brought a test case. The case *Sohappy v. Smith* (Smith was the Oregon state fish commissioner) was consolidated with *U.S. v. Oregon*, in which the U.S. government filed suit against the state of Oregon on behalf of the Yakama, Umatilla, Nez Perce, and Warm Springs Tribes.[47]

Federal district court judge Robert Belloni ruled that the Oregon would continue to regulate Indian treaty fishing in the interests of conservation but must do so in a way that Indian fishers could harvest "a fair and equitable share."[48] In 1969 Washington State announced that it was adopting this "Fair Share Doctrine." But "fair and equitable" was not specific enough, and conflict continued.[49]

The Puyallup River in the southern Puget Sound area and, in particular, Frank's Landing—the Frank family's land on a bank of the river—became a center of treaty rights activity in the Northwest. The first major state raid on fishing families to occur at Frank's Landing was in 1962. In the book *Messages from Franks Landing: A Story of Salmon, Treaties, and the Indian Way*, Charles Wilkinson describes the raids:

> The game wardens—a dozen to more than fifty—would descend the banks in a stone-faced scramble toward a few Nisqually men in a canoe or skiff unloading salmon from a gillnet. Usually the Nisqually would give passive resistance—dead weight—and five officers or more would drag the man up the rugged banks toward the waiting vehicles. The dragging often got rough, with much pushing and shoving, many arms twisted way up the back, and numerous cold-cock punches. The billy clubs made their thuds. Sometimes the Indian men struck back. Sometimes Indian people on the banks threw stones and sticks at the intruders. The stench of tear gas hung in the air.
>
> The Nisqually women got involved too. Film footage shows Maiselle Bridges [Billy Frank's sister and the wife of his fishing partner, Al Bridges] and Billy's wife, Norma, clinging desperately to the nets as the officers dragged them forcefully up the rocky river bank. As with all the blood struggles of minority people for freedom in the world over, a sorrow, a poignancy shared the air with the tear gas.[50]

After two decades of effort, Indian fishing rights activists saw little improvement in the attitudes and actions of the state of Washington. Protests and repeated requests for federal intervention went unheeded. In 1970 assistant solicitor George Dysart of the Department of the Interior (Northwest Regional Office, Portland) urged the U.S. government to intervene, but his message was initially disregarded. That summer armed Indian protestors had established an encampment on the Puyallup River. Only after a three-hundred-man state police force arrived and surrounded it, firing tear gas and shotguns, in order to arrest the sixty-two Indian occupants, did the federal government intervene. In 1973 the U.S. government filed suit in behalf of the fishing tribes to force the state of Washington to respect their treaty fishing rights.[51]

THE BOLDT DECISION, 1974

In 1973 the United States, on behalf of fourteen Indian tribes in western Washington, sued the state of Washington. The case *U.S. v. Washington* was heard in the federal district court in Tacoma, Washington, with Judge George H. Boldt (1903–84) presiding.[52] The case not only helped resolve issues surrounding treaty rights of fishing, but it also helped clarify treaty rights issues in general. Along with questions about rights to treaty resources, at stake were sovereignty issues concerning the rights of tribes to regulate their own affairs.

In *U.S. v. Washington* the state was represented by Attorney General Slade Gorton (b. 1928), who later served in the U.S. Senate (R-WA). Senator Gorton, we should note, as a descendant of the founder of one of the biggest seafood companies in the nation, Slade Gorton and Company, was not impartial about the fishing industry.[53] Other attorneys for the state represented the Department of Game and the Department of Fisheries. Also represented in the case was the Washington Reefnet Owners Association. Other commercial fishing groups and several sports fishing organizations—although they were not represented in the case—submitted briefs opposing Indian treaty fishing. The federal case was presented on behalf of the tribes by George Dysart, assistant regional solicitor of the Department of the Interior, along with government attorneys from the U.S. Attorney's Office of the Department of Justice. Eleven of the fourteen tribes represented in the case were represented also by attorneys whom they had retained.[54] Hank Adams and Janet McCloud arranged for legal assistance to be provided by the Native American Rights Funds (NARF).[55]

The fourteen plaintiff tribes were parties to six treaties: Treaty of Quinault (Hoh, Quileute, and Quinault), Treaty of Point Elliott (Lummi, Muckleshoot, Sauk-Suiattle, Stillaguamish, Upper Skagit), Treaty with the Makah (Makah), Treaty of Medicine Creek (Nisqually, Puyallup, Squaxin Island, and Muckleshoot; Muckleshoot is party to two treaties), Treaty of Point No Point (Skokomish), and Treaty with the Yakima (Confederated Tribes and Bands of the Yakama Nation).[56] The decision covered the waters of Puget Sound, much of the Washington coast and adjacent ocean, and all the rivers flowing into the ocean in that region.[57] The Washington Department of Game (responsible for management of sport fishing) took the position that the treaties did not entitle Indians to any fishing rights beyond the rights held by other U.S. citizens. The Washington Department of Fisheries accepted that Indians had treaty rights and proposed that the fish supply should be split equally three ways: between Indian fishers, commercial fishers, and sports fishers. The tribes held that the treaties intended to preserve the tribes' rights to livelihood as cultures that depended on their fisheries, and that therefore they should be entitled to whatever percentage of fish was necessary for their livelihood. The focus of the federal government was the Indians' right to fish according to their rights as stipulated by treaty: "the right of taking fish, at all usual and accustomed grounds and stations, is further secured to said Indians, in common with all citizens of the United States." Government attorneys, therefore, suggested that Indians be entitled to "an equal share" of the fish.[58]

"In common with" was controversial wording in the treaty. "Fair and equitable share" had proven to too vague when Washington tried to apply the principle of the Belloni decision, and the state of Washington had regarded "in common with" to mean that everyone in the state would fish under the same regulations: state regulations.[59] Newspapers carried many articles, pro and con, regarding Judge Boldt. Many Indians in Washington State testified during *U.S. v. Washington*. Among the Lummi Reservation residents who testified was Forrest Kinley, a former fisherman who had served as chair of the Lummi Indian Business Council (tribal chairman) and as director of Lummi Fisheries. Anthropologist

Barbara Lane, PhD, testified as an expert witness for the U.S. government in behalf of the fishing tribes. Lane submitted to the court two reports: "Anthropological Report on the Identity, Treaty Status, and Fisheries of the Lummi Tribe of Indians" and "Political and Economic Aspects of Indian-White Culture Contact in Western Washington in the Mid-Nineteenth Century." Her research on Pacific Northwest Indian culture provided important evidence in behalf of the tribes.[60] Between three and four hundred documents were entered into the record as exhibits, and the several attorneys involved presented proposals for more than five hundred conclusions concerning fact and law. Three years of pretrial preparation preceded the hearings, which continued six days a week for nearly a month. After that, Judge Boldt took several months to review the evidence and arguments and to deliberate before announcing his decision.

On February 12, 1974, the *Seattle Times* carried the headline "Indian Tribes Win Fishing Rights Case." Judge Boldt's opinion was 203 pages long. He had determined that the crucial phrase "in common with" meant that the tribes were entitled to the opportunity to catch 50 percent of the harvestable fish and shellfish in those tribes' "usual and accustomed fishing grounds and stations." "Harvestable" fish excluded the fish that must be left to return to their home rivers, where they spawn, to ensure the continuation of the species.[61] *U.S. v. Washington* recognized tribal sovereignty by ruling that the tribes were entitled to regulate fishing for their own tribal members. Tribes that qualified for self-regulation would not be regulated by the state, and the state could not impose regulations on them without tribal consent or court approval. The state and the tribes would be required to exchange data and proposed regulations, and fisheries management procedures would be put in place.[62] Soon after the Boldt Decision the fishing tribes formed the Northwest Indian Fisheries Commission, chaired by Billy Frank Jr. (1931–2014).[63]

At the time of Judge Boldt's ruling, the Indian fisheries counts were very low: perhaps 5 percent of the total catch. How could they up their counts to 50 percent? In consideration of all the factors involved, the question was asked: Is 50/50 a fair deal to Indians? But the Boldt Decision remembered Indian rights and recognized tribal sovereignty. It restored the rights of tribes to regulate their own treaty resources. The ruling resolved many legal questions, but it was difficult to enforce. Some disputes still continue. Immediately after the Boldt Decision many non-Indian fishermen were drastically upset. Some complied with the law, whether they agreed with it or not, and some fished illegally, while the state did little to stop them. Sometimes Indians fished illegally. Even when they fished within the law, conditions on the water could be tense; violence sometimes broke out. Legal disputes continued between the state, the tribes, and the federal government. In 1975 the U.S. Court of Appeals for the Ninth Circuit affirmed the Boldt Decision, but controversy continued. In 1976 the Supreme Court denied a request for a review of the decision. In 1977 the Washington State Department of Fisheries adopted regulations that did not comply with the Boldt Decision, and Judge Boldt placed the fisheries under federal control, utilizing court orders and federal marshals. In 1979, for the first time in its history, the U.S. Supreme Court reversed its decision against a review. In the Supreme Court case *Washington v. Washington State Commercial Passenger Vessel Association*, the Boldt decision was upheld, with the addition of an allowance that adjustments might be made in the future.[64] Thus the state and the fishing tribes of Washington have had to focus on fisheries management, in the best interests of the salmon and of the people involved.

IMPROVING OUR FISHERIES

What was the result for Northwest fishermen, after all their years of resistance and after the gains of the Boldt Decision? The salmon runs were badly depleted by commercial overfishing, by dams that interfered with the salmon migration, by pollution from farm fertilizers and industrial toxins, and by the by-products of logging, which ruin oxygen needed by salmon—especially the young ones. Planting fish had been started by both Indian and non-Indian fisheries. This helped somewhat, but artificial propagation is no substitute for healthy habitats. Salmon depletion continues today. Perhaps in the near future the salmon runs will pick up, and people will fish with common sense, rather than the rush of greed. Rivers need to be cared for by loving hands to restore the wasting salmon habitats. One river, the Nisqually, has undergone river and salmon habitat restoration and enhancement. It is absolutely the most living, beautiful sight I have ever seen as far as Washington rivers go—more, more![65]

In 1978, four years after the Boldt Decision, the Regional Team of the Federal Task Force for Washington State Fisheries issued a report titled *Settlement Plan for Washington State Salmon and Steelhead Fisheries* (1978).[66] My comments on a few items in that report may offer perspective on the imbalances that can exist between policy and regulation, and point to the need for open communication between the state and the fishing tribes. The report notes that, compared with the early 1900s, when record catch levels were at their highest, catches of the five species of pacific salmon had significantly declined. Overfishing, habitat destruction, and poor resource protection and management all played roles in the decline. The main problem was too many fishermen. It was earlier, in the 1960s, when the human population had reached a high point, and salmon such a low point, that supply could not meet demand. In order to counteract the decline, the state, the federal government, and the tribes had increased artificial production and management practices for fishery habitats. In many cases, according to the report, these efforts halted the dramatic decline in run sizes.[67] Although management efforts are essential, the artificial hatcheries have not always been as successful as was hoped. Regarding management challenges for the state and the tribes, the regional team observed: "If this disjointed management of the salmon and steelhead resource is allowed to continue it will be difficult, if not impossible, for the resource to be restored, maintained and enhanced. A coordinated management system involving the State and the tribes, which will promote closer working relationships and greater unity of purpose, is essential for the long-term well being of the fishery."[68] An example of necessary cooperation is coordinated hatchery releases.[69]

I would like also to point out that the scale of commercial fishing that developed in Washington State was not anticipated during treaty-making days. Consider these figures from the 1970s: "During the preceding decade, the number of non-treaty vessels has rapidly increased. For example, in 1965, there were 1,822 trollers licensed by Washington State. By 1977, the number had increased to 3,232. During the same period, the Puget Sound gillnet fleet increased from 906 vessels to over 1,500; the Columbia River gillnet fleet increased from 237 to over 700."[70]

I was surprised to learn that fishing is the sole source of family sustenance for many non-Indian commercial fishermen too. All small-scale fishermen face financial pressures and hazards. But Indian fishermen, overall, have greater economic challenges, and they have rights that existed before any fishing policies.

Visiting the fish docks in Seattle one day with my son, I met a number of non-European American fishermen readying their boats and nets to go out onto the big waters. Their numbers increase the number of non-Indian license holders. White Americans are not the only ones included in the 50 percent non-Indian slice of the pie. The numbers of future U.S. immigrant fishermen, plus sports fishermen, were not considered in the equation when the treaties granted Indians "the right of taking fish at usual and accustomed grounds and stations . . . in common with all citizens of the Territory."

Ann Nugent's book *The History of Lummi Fishing Rights* (1979) describes the trauma that Lummi fishermen withstood for their people against white fishermen, from the time of the Point Elliott Treaty of 1855 until *U.S. v. Washington* in 1974. Nugent describes the battles fought by Lummi fishermen for their treaty rights: against non-Indian commercial fishers and sport fishing interests, and against state courts that sided mainly with non-Indian fishermen. Nugent makes this point about treaty fishing rights: "The purpose of the Treaty of Point Elliott was to cede land to the non-Indians from the Indians legally, so as to avoid friction between the two."[71] The non-Indians made promises of protection from white encroachment and of minimal compensation. But in the beginning the United States and white settlers were not concerned with the great waters or its resources. This is apparent from the fact that the treaties make no compensation to Indians for water rights: Indians did not cede water rights to non-Indians. In treaty-making times, water resources were not seen as very significant to the non-Indians. But Indians depended primarily on the waters for their food resources. Nugent refers to Article 5 of the Point Elliott Treaty and observes: "There is no mention of restrictions of manner or place of taking fish. It was clearly evident that the authorities who recorded evidences regarding the negotiations of the treaty wanted the Indians to continue in their fishing."[72] Lane explains the motivation of the U.S. government at that time: to support Indian fishing for the sake of Indian livelihood and trade with settlers. This in turn, would help Indian prosperity and the prosperity of Washington Territory.[73]

I think that the Fifth Amendment in the Bill of Rights applies to non-Indian use of waters around Indian lands. It states: "nor shall private property be taken for public use without just compensation." My parents and other tribal members received government commodities such as misfit clothing, surplus kitchenware, a broken-down tractor, and cows and pigs (both animals are foreign to our soil). These items were similar in value to the annuity goods provided to the generation of my great-grandparents as payment for our ceded lands. This exchange did not fulfill the letter, or the spirit, of the Fifth Amendment as "just compensation" for our share of the large territory ceded by the Treaty of Elliott (map 6). The government has failed to compensate us for the use of our water areas, which the nation has used, and continues to use, for public fisheries and other purposes. Compensation for our water space is still needed, whether done through zoning, permits, a licensing plan, or otherwise.

Our fisheries used to be an open book in this small community, but no more. It used to be fun to congratulate the fisherman who was known to have caught the most fish. Now we get used to going without fish, spend our money in town for meat, and are grateful for the salmon we get for tribal gatherings. Since fishing is part of the tribe's trust status, and also because our membership has treaty trust status, shouldn't the fishing sites for tribal fisheries be a tribal agreement? As for the cutbacks on "open fishing days" for tribal fisheries, because fishing is a treaty right, shouldn't this be reason for notification to the whole tribe? We must pay more attention to trust property status for land, fishing, membership, and other such matters.

One of the unresolved issues for the Pacific Northwest tribes concerns whether the treaties transacted by Isaac Stevens and Joel Palmer impose an obligation on states to protect the habitat of fish.[74] Courts *have* imposed on the United States to protect treaty resources, warranted in part by the U.S. trust relationship to tribes.

> This trust responsibility is an overlay on Indian treaty obligations. The federal trust responsibility to Indian tribes applies to all federal entities. It imposes its own obligations with regard to enforcement of Indian treaty rights. A tribe is "entitled to rely on the United States, its guardian, for needed protection of its interests" (*U.S. v. Creek Nation*, 295 US 103, 110 [1935]). A tribe is not required to prove to what extent and how its property needs protection. Federal agencies have a duty to investigate potential adverse impacts on treaty-secured resources thoroughly, and not simply make a "judgment call" or balance competing interests, in choosing the appropriate course of action. The trust responsibility has also been held to require strict compliance with administrative policies, such as consultation with Indians, that are intended to protect Indian interests.[75]

In 2007 the Northwest Indian Fisheries Commission achieved a thirty-three-million-dollar settlement of state and federal funds for the purchase and enhancement of tidelands for shellfish harvesting. This helped to resolve a century of injustice, during which non-Indian commercial shellfish growers had been allowed to buy some of the best treaty-protected Indian tidelands.[76]

So, progress continues. But our communication and cooperation need on-going attention. Through all the hardships we have experienced in the past century and a half—with a new government moving in and taking over, continual changes in fishing regulations, unfair restrictions and penalties, expenses, jail terms, and the depletion of the salmon—our aboriginal fishers are still there. They are still there, on the Indian side of the enormous structure of white fisheries management. I am so proud of these aboriginal fishermen and women that I say: Let's survive together, as we have from times before history.

CHAPTER 9

Break Through Ahistory

How do we break through ahistory? In order to break through ahistory, we must study the patterns of the past. Breaking through ahistory starts with knowledge. But it does not stop with knowledge. Knowing about events and remembering rights are just the start of righting wrongs. We need respect and effort, along with knowledge, to make things right. This chapter is about how we can break through Indian ahistory, and how the best of both worlds, Indian and non-Indian, could work together.

DREAMS OF OUR ANCESTORS

Of course, I know very little about the many tribes in Indian America, let alone their chiefs, subchiefs, holy men and women, elders, healers, artists, skilled fishermen, hunters, gatherers, and others. I have read many books about them, and I have met many of today's citizens of Indian America. I believe that today's elders are much like the Indian elders of the past: courageous, generous, and skillful. But our ancestors had more freedom to act their best conscience, unlike us American Indians of today. How I would love to carry on from our ancestors' best ahistoric moments to a place where their dreams could be realized by our efforts. But to get there we must break through the dominant versions of "American History." We must break through the well-established "programmed failure" meant for our Indian ancestors and the built-up racism of a forgotten genocide.

Particular eras of Indian policy were different from one another and different from the Indian policy of today's U.S. government. Like that long-ago U.S. government, which has changed its Indian policies over time, non-Indian America at large has changed also. Indian America has changed too, and curious people of today want to know about our yesterdays. Like myself, there are those who want to know Indian America's dynamics of survival throughout the traumatic changes of history. Are we ready to give the American Indians of history the honor they deserve? In the Northwest they did not just sign treaties to cede and reserve land; they signed treaties of peace. In the great Northwest the region ceded to the United States is vast and includes the best land and beaches, comparable in size and beauty to those in many states and countries.

Indian citizens lead America in high death rates, high dropout rates from school, lowest-paid jobs, and being easy targets for middlemen. Other Indian authors have more to say regarding the government-created ghettos called Indian reservations. But we remain ever grateful to the U.S. government for correcting some of the wrongs of the past that were dealt to the aboriginal tribes of every region. Our future may yet outweigh our past when it comes to freedom and justice for all. Fairness is all that Indian America has ever asked for, from the historic "talkers" like Canasatego of the great Iroquois Confederacy on the East Coast to Chief Seattle on the West Coast.

From my first notes of forty-three years ago, when I lived on the Hood Canal—a time when I had opportunity to study the government documents—I wrote this:

As one pores over the government documents, one sees why the President of the United States was held in esteem and awe by the Indians, as though he were a spiritual being. His actual name was never mentioned. Whenever he was referred to, only the title "Great White Father" or "our chief" was used in place of a name. It becomes easier for me to understand the perplexity of the Indian people in this regard, because they were spiritual. Thereby, the men assigned to the Great Father's or chief's duties came in a guise to the Indians, who regarded them as spiritual disciples, as described in the Bible.

Indians were subjected to trial and error as regards assimilation. The agents were enjoined to reside among the tribes to make the personal acquaintances of the chiefs and headmen, to inform them fully respecting the power of the United States military and the readiness of the president to treat them with kindness and magnanimity when they did right, and his ability and purpose to punish them when they did wrong: the blind leading the blind. Just reading through the government documents, I can sense the absence of spiritual forces in the new government's approach and the presence of Indian America's inner spiritual forces.

As I read my thoughts on U.S./Indian history from decades ago, I feel that my words still hold the life of truth in them.

FAIRNESS AND UNITY

There were philosophers during the conquest era, like Francisco de Vitoria, who believed Indians had rights to their lands.[1] So in the more enlightened minds Indians were not counted out of the game. I do not excuse torture on your side of the fence or mine. We must both admit that it occurred, in one form or another. The papal bulls and the Doctrine of Discovery gave our conquerors the expectation that we would not survive this long. Think how much farther ahead we would be if our two cultures, from the start, had each formed a constitution and a confederacy, as the Iroquois did. In the early years of conquest the land had a lot to offer. We should understand by now that the new arrivals' predominating doctrine supposed that the land was rich and vacant, and that the aboriginal peoples of this continent were unworthy of being counted as human beings. Our Indian past was just another participle in the grand entry of the English. So why are we still here?

Our earliest philosophers, the great Indian leaders of long ago, had the right idea: that both cultures could share what was here. Ideas of from the Confederacy of the Five Nations (the Haudenosaunee or Iroquois) were conveyed to Benjamin Franklin and some of the founding fathers. Whether the Five Nations way of Great Peace took hold in America by osmosis, or by the planning expertise of the founding fathers, it did take hold, and it remains alive today.[2] America's written history does not give the philosophy of the Iroquois' Great Peace much consideration one way or another. The Constitution of the Five Nations is not as expansive as the U.S. Constitution. But you may find, as I did, that the Iroquois Constitution carries a bit more humanity and justice. For example, the women of the Iroquois had power from the beginning. The Iroquois philosophy offered cautions for the Great White founding fathers to not fall out with one another. And despite their differences, overall they stayed united. Their successes in the American Revolution and the War of 1812 are proof of that. Democracy, the division of powers, and the centrality of the people—government of the people, by the people, and for the people—were new concepts for white America at first. Today, members of the top administration fall out with one another, and the nation sometimes teeters on self-destruction. We must, once again, warn our leaders to remain united. Let us keep in mind the well-being of the people of the United States as a whole; this is our unity, whether or not our leaders agree each step of the way. The Great Peace of the Iroquois is all but forgotten, deep in thousands of yesterdays. For all of us to live peacefully, we must dig deep to remember the ways of peace.

Immigration has nearly swallowed us entirely. The world news tells us that couples can have but one baby in the cities of China. Perhaps that is why the move here is so significant, so they can freely have a family. Every day we hear of unrest in Mexico because of drug trafficking. Some Eastern cultures are looking for more space to spread their religions, and America's doors are open, especially for the oppressed. Many African countries suffer treachery from their own governments, and America's doors are open to their citizens. We hear of troubles in some countries every day, but not much about the less troubled countries, whose citizens also immigrate to the United States. Look at all the ethnic restaurants and communities in our American cities. They are not in the news every day, but they exist in our larger and smaller cities. Therefore, it is the United States of the World, for now. Will it become the United World in America? Or the World in the United States, or America: Atlas of the World? Is there no common sense in compassion? The ideals of democracy that North American and other nations have shown the world can exist throughout the world, even if peoples from every corner of the world don't live on the North American land base. In the future, we may hope that immigration laws will be more compatible with the nation's resources and growth, and that we can live together as people united.

SUBJUGATION

Some people think that the papal bulls, which directed domination of indigenous peoples, had power only back in the time of the "discoverers," or that the Doctrine of Discovery is a part of history that is over, but no. Some may believe that the thinking behind "conquest" continues today only at a personal level, and not in policy and law. True, policy and law have come a long way since the earliest U.S./Indian relations, but early Indian policy shows that the "discoverers" took for granted their "right" to take over lands and to set the rules. We can see from the Indian Affairs documents, and the events that occurred after treaties were enacted, how the early laws and policies formed a basis for the ones that followed.[3]

The papal bulls and the Doctrine of Discovery contained the authority to "enslave" aboriginals in "the New World" (i.e., the Americas, Africa, and wherever they might be found). This way of thinking must be overcome. Otherwise, a sneaky or roundabout way of law is enforced: justice for some, but not all, of the people. Slavery is not just a black servant; it is a bad concept. Many persons believe that American slavery went out with Abraham Lincoln. But many who are enslaved today are enslaved by injustice, usually in a cunning manner, hidden from the view of the population at large. If we did not have human nature, we would be gods. But we do have human nature, and it stands to reason that the weaker we are to ill-gotten gains, the more susceptible we are to subjugating others.

The International Council of Thirteen Indigenous Grandmothers traveled to the Vatican in 2008 and presented a letter (dated October 22, 2005) calling on Pope Benedict XVI to rescind the papal edicts and doctrines that give foundation to the oppression of indigenous peoples:

> While these papal bulls and edicts were written over five hundred years ago, they remain the spiritual, legal, and moral foundation for the exercise of jurisdiction over tribal nations by nation-states today. Given the inherently unjust moral and legal basis for their authority, nation-states have only been able to exercise their rule over tribal nations through warfare and acts of violence.
>
> Were these acts of violence—physical and cultural—confined to history, perhaps we would focus our collective efforts on other concerns. But unfortunately, this is not the case; they persist into the present. Our peoples must still live with the continuing legacy of this first denial of our right to be treated as equal participants in the community of nations. Our peoples are still struggling for the right to live on earth and practice our cultural and spiritual traditions as our ancestors did.
>
> Revocation of these bulls and other papal edicts will remove the keystone of legal authority upon which the doctrines of conquest and discovery were constructed.[4]

The Episcopal Church has been a leader in repudiating the Doctrine of Discovery, acknowledging its own history as a colonizer, when William Penn came to America under a Doctrine of Discovery mandate issued by King Charles II. The Religious Society of Friends (Quakers), inspired by the Episcopal Church, issued a resolution in 2009 renouncing the Doctrine of Discovery as incompatible with the teachings of Jesus and "inconsistent with Quaker testimonies of Peace, Equality, and Integrity." The Haudenosaunee (Iroquois) sent a delegation to the 2009 World Parliament of Religions in Melbourne to seek a resolution repudiating the Doctrine of Discovery.[5] The "Indigenous Peoples' Statement to the World" that was presented at the Parliament addressed the earth's waters, climate, and other matters, and called for healing of cultural life and languages: "This oppressive tradition is what led to the boarding schools, the residential schools, and the Stolen Generation, resulting in the trauma of language death and loss of family integrity from the actions of churches and governments. We call on those churches and governments to put as much time, effort, energy and money into assisting with the revitalization of our languages and cultures as they put into attempting to destroy them."[6]

I believe that the Dalai Lama came closest to what our Indian elders still teach, and that is compassion. This is probably why the Iroquois allowed women power: because women have compassion. And it wasn't learned by books, it was learned in their role as the Givers of Life. Men are warriors, and many of them don't know when to stop whatever punishment is required. My father was not permitted to punish any farther than my mother wanted him to punish. Such a concept is woven throughout our civilization, as Indian people.

American Indians are kept at a certain level of advantage and are excluded from the world of the rich and powerful, even though it was mostly the resources of Native America that allowed rich and powerful Americans to become rich and powerful. White America evidently believed that what this land produced was there for their bold taking, taking, taking: land, resources, knowledge, and power. And for the most part, they maintain these goods out of the reach of others. My message here is that the state of being denied access to resources can be called a form of enslavement. As things now stand in Indian America, the world around us remains confusing—but in different ways from the confusion that existed in the times of colonization. And now, the country's resources are immensely depleted.

UNITED STATES OF THE WORLD

Why United States of the World? Perhaps not many people would agree. Count the cultures and individuals that have come to America. What are the numbers? It would be difficult to count. So, when I say "United States of the World," I mean the United States of Many Cultures entering and settling here. As the aboriginal people of this continent, we have survived a great deal, and believe me, it's been an uphill battle. Our survival is a blessing. I believe we are looking for the same thing in America that people of other cultures are seeking. Many of the founders of the new America came here because they were oppressed in their old countries: politically, religiously, or economically. But once they arrived here, the newness of the abundant land captured many a greedy heart. Higher purposes wore thin, and many people missed the target of life, liberty, and the pursuit of happiness. The cycle of oppression began again. Indian America survived it, but Indian cultures, as total cultures, did not. None of this has been easy for you or for me. What many Americans from Europe experienced in their old countries was dreadful. The founders of the new America created a great nation, but a nation that is not great in every way, if we look honestly at history and current conditions. Like a most important game, they thought that there could be only one winner. Ultimately there was destruction for one group and advantage for the other. Those who are wealthy stay wealthy, and those who are poor stay poor. The fear that it will continue this way for our future generations is what drives me to do the work that I do.

IMMIGRATION AND THE AMERICAN DREAM

People from all around the world still flood into America, expecting their dreams to become a reality here. They are interesting people. I belonged to an organization called Folklife in the Schools, and I traveled to many of our United States, intermingling with people of all colors, styles, and backgrounds. My heart melted when I was able to meet them, talk with them, watch their performances, understand where they came from, and read about all this in the newspaper: fascination upon fascination.

My father once told me of one of his best visions. We were standing above his garden of flowers: wildflowers, with domesticated flowers planted among them. He said, "See; look at the beauty, the strength, of these plants. Imagine, if you will, that they were all people." I did, and I understood the depth of his meaning. He was talking about Indian tribes at the time. But as years rolled by, I could see his vision clearly in all the people coming to the United States: every hill, a new world; every valley, a different civilization. Imagine; here in the United States we can go around the world as fast as any jet could take us, without running out of fuel, education, or entertainment. An innocent little baby once looked at me: wondering, learning. I could see the dependence in her eyes. By the hand of a little child, I followed, leading that child down the best path I knew, with the considerations of love, faith, and charity. If only we could look at each other in this sense: no matter the color of our skin, but according to the texture of our spirits.

Immigrants have continued to arrive, seeking prospects for their success. They are reaching the prize much faster than Indian America is, especially since our solemn treaties have been broken. We are still at a place of beginning, and they are reaching their goals: citizenship, voices, rights, and prosperity. How do they get their money ahead far enough to make a lasting light for their futures? Here we American Indians are, "sitting on the shelf," waiting for some order of respectful response to our long-standing questions. Yes, you helped us survive, but we need the conditions for life, liberty, and the pursuit of happiness, too. Instead, we began on the brink of annihilation, and we are still kept close to that starting point by circumstances almost beyond your control, and far beyond our control. Aboriginals deserve as much as any other American on this continent. Our memories hold and withstand all the torment of our past histories. No matter how you look at it, we have paid our dues for success here. I love this land, whether it is called America, the United States, North America, the United States of America, or the United States of the World. And I know it: the land, anyway, loves me.

JUSTICE FOR THE EARTH AND HER CHILDREN

On Christmas Eve on the National Geographic Channel, I watched a movie with Queen Elizabeth portrayed in it. They showed a scene where a man was being punished in a Judas Cradle; in another scene, a woman's head was chopped off. Terrifying!—and so depressing. I changed the channel, but the next program was about the Romans' wars. One of the Roman leaders shouted: "Come, all you Leagues of Christians: Forward into battle!" and they attacked. I don't believe today's Christians would do that. I changed the channel again. On the Discovery Channel a Brazilian leader was asking for help to let the world know of their plight in Brazil: disease, land destruction, and depletion of resources. The Brazilian leader sounded so much like Indians here in America. I figured, well, this wrong-direction lifestyle is going around the world. Sure enough, the next channel showed a country in Africa and the destruction of the land, the people, and diamond resources there. Greed is a terrible bed partner. Should our future be blessed with the intelligence that we desperately need to take care of what we have now, so that all Americans can help with the current balancing act of our government, we must be ready. There was a time in the past that I thought I could help, but I just couldn't break through our aboriginal people's ahistory.

There are great things in Indian history that can help the United States create a better future. We cannot look at the condition of our world while excluding ourselves. Instead of saying, "It's a good day to die," let us learn to say: "It's a good day to kick bad, hurtful habits." He taught peace. And He is on our side. I am in the game as long as He is in the game. We must keep an eye on our leaders. Our goal is justice for Mother Earth and all her children. For Indian America, justice starts with land rights. We are people who want to see our best dreams a reality too, just like America's immigrants.

RIGHTED WRONGS

Dare we hope that the U.S. government will continue righting the wrongs that have occurred, whether by accident or on purpose? I would like to mention some of the wrongs that have been righted, as examples of the countless issues that we have faced as Indian people, and also in acknowledgment of the government's righting of wrongs. Felix Cohen's *Handbook of Federal Indian Law* (1942) spells out many of the wrongs righted by the federal government in early Indian policy.[7] Following are some examples from the important historic period of the 1930s—the Indian America that I was born into—which was the decade of 1934 Indian Reorganization Act (the IRA or Wheeler-Howard Act).

The legal reforms of the IRA were put in place shortly after the

1928 Meriam Report, in this important timeframe when tribes began to recover their self-determination. The *Report on the Problem of Indian Administration*, generally known as the Meriam Report, published by the Institute for Government Research, was part of the government's response to the failures of the Dawes Act and policies of assimilation.[8] The Meriam Report was evaluated in a publication of the American Indian Defense Association:

> The report of the Institute for Government Research is the most important single document in Indian Affairs since Helen Hunt Jackson's "The Century of Dishonor" published forty-five years ago. It contains three sections, which intrinsically are very fine ("Health," "Education," and "Family & Community Life and the Activities of Women"). Its 847 pages of text are a result of teamwork between ten specialists. The studied moderation of its language; the avoidance of a suggestion even as to where responsibility shall be placed; the omission (save in regard to health and education) of most of the facts which give a quality of sinister deliberateness to the wrongs suffered by Indians; its nearly total avoidance of those skeleton closets; the handling of individual Indian trust monies and reimbursable indebtedness; these qualities of the report increase its convincingness and usefulness.[9]

A number of policy reforms took place after the Indian Reorganization Act and the Meriam Report. One reform was the Leavitt Act of July 1, 1932. Indians and Indian tribes were being charged for high construction costs of irrigation projects, even though they didn't request such construction. The tribes benefited little, or not at all, from the construction. The Leavitt Act "authorized the Secretary of the Interior to adjust or eliminate reimbursable charges of the government of the U.S. existing as debts against individual Indian or tribes of Indians in such a way as shall be equitable and just."[10] There were many irrigation projects on the Colville Indian Reservation. During the years that this author worked for the Colville Confederated Tribes, irrigation problems arose just about every year. Flumes were adjusted by Indians and non-Indians nearly every day, and the arguments got pretty hot. This was between 1951 and 1958, twenty years after the Leavitt Act was passed.

During the Great Depression, one of the measures applied by President Roosevelt to help the economy was the National Industrial Recovery Act, passed by Congress in 1934. One of its branches was the Civilian Conservation Corps (CCC), which had an Indian Division. It was extremely important to Indian tribes throughout the land. Our tribe, the Lummi, benefited by this act, and we are grateful. Another act that gave relief to tribal members freed them from having to refund monies when buyers defaulted on purchases of Indian heirship lands: the act of April 30, 1934, provided that installments on a defaulted contract would inure (build up) to the benefit of the vendor. The act made this protection applicable to Indians who sold land, just like everyone else (An Act to amend section 1 of the Act entitled "An Act to provide for determining the heirs of deceased Indians, for the disposition and sale of allotments of deceased Indians, for the leasing of allotments, and for other purposes"). The act of May 21, 1934 (48 Stat. 787), repealed twelve sections of the United States Code that restricted Indians' civil liberties. However, the statutes repealed were only some of the oppressive laws that existed at that time. The only regulation that this author remembers vividly is a requirement that involved the use of vehicles purchased by the BIA for specific uses, whereby the driver had to inspect the physical aspects of a car—the tires, the condition, and so forth—before getting in the car to drive it.

Now, to mention the extensive Johnson-O'Malley Act of April 19, 1934: this act authorized the federal government to contract with states for "the education, medical attention, agricultural assistance, and social welfare, including relief of distress of Indians," through qualified agencies of their particular state or territory. It is not clear that tribes fully benefited from Johnson-O'Malley federal funds that were managed by the states, especially at first. Use of JOM funds was a cause of dispute between federal and state adminstrators.[11] Our Lummi Tribe has benefited from the Johnson-O'Malley Act during floods and earthquakes and in education (whereby our Indian students receive supplies). Lunches have been provided through this program for many years. I clearly remember the types of lunches that Indian students had to accept in earlier years; now the lunches are better. But, as always, we should leave room for improvement. We should also keep in mind how long Indian students have suffered on poverty-stricken reservations; student lunches have become essential because of the resource limitations of tribal governments. Native Americans don't hunt, gather, or fish as we did before the signing of the treaties and loss of our lands. This economic reality affects our students, in that many do not receive the nutrients they need and deserve, due to the current economic limitations that exist for tribes. A fundamental problem suffered by our people now is our economic survival. Amid each tribe are poverty-stricken individuals who cannot afford money for gas or the new foods market. Add to this our inability to harvest in our usual and accustomed places, for some tribes, a right preserved by treaty. In these ways, restrictions on our total culture continue. Losses to our cultural knowledge and practices, along with economic disadvantage, feel to some of us like a double indictment.

When Indian self-determination starting gaining strength in the 1960s, a number of positive items of legislation followed, such as NAGPRA, the Native American Graves Protection and Repatriation Act. Some other major items of legislation are listed on the timeline in appendix 3. Last and not least, our religious freedom was restored to us with the American Indian Religious Freedom Act in 1978.[12] The United States government prohibited our ancestors and tribal elders from practicing a complete knowledge of our way of life (what many people call "religion"). Our way of life—banned by the BIA in 1883—has never fully come back to us, due to the length of time it was banned.[13] The real harm done by this restriction spreads farther than the ordinary person can imagine. The way of life in my grandfather's youth was highly disciplined and involved expansive distances. Denominations outside our reserves do not suffer these restrictions. It was not our fault that white America has never understood Indian spirituality in connection to Mother Earth, Father Sea, and the Great Spirit, but that is how it has been. I have excluded important details about our old, and now new, way of life, for the protection of tribal people and traditions. Perhaps in the future more can be shared. But that's up to our next generations. Until then, never lose your common sense or logic, young people. We older people will build up your strength, and our own, for the days to come.

THE BEST OF BOTH WORLDS

This book aims to place U.S. history and American Indian history together in the endless cycle of history. We can all benefit from both the Indian and non-Indian worlds, harvesting the best of each for our future generations. With the new era of technology, and the wisdom of men and women of the past, present, and future, we can succeed, with reason and understanding leading the way. Our cultural diversities fit with the democratic principles expressed in the U.S. Constitution. We can, and should, complement each other's cultures and missions for the world.

INDIAN CONTRIBUTIONS

America has pride in its citizens' accomplishments in medicine, law, and all other professions. We American Indians also have great respect for America's professional people. Two white doctors saved my life: once for a dangerous case of thrombophlebitis, and another time a doctor from Germany helped me recover from two broken legs. I had been in a serious car wreck and my right foot had come off. That German doctor reattached it, and it healed back on. Because it healed as a clubfoot, he returned and straightened it out. It took lengths of time for both healings, but I do have use of both of my legs now, although they are not the same as they used to be. I am extremely grateful to those white doctors and their staffs of white nurses, too. White professionals, inventors, and discoverers of healing medicines and procedures, mechanics: so many, I cannot count. May I always keep the deepest respect for them in my personal history. At first the medical field ignored Indian America during plagues of smallpox, tuberculosis, typhoid fever, measles, and the serious flu of years ago. However, many American Indians helped save white Americans from starvation and from some diseases in this, their new land. But when diseases brought by the newcomers first afflicted

Indian people, for the most part whites refused Indians hospitalization or any kind of medical treatment. Today it is different, and this should be acknowledged in history, because it shows a great change of heart on a government-to-government basis. I am elated when I think of the positive changes that have taken place between white America and Indian America.

It is a right of American Indians to have their contributions remembered by all generations of Americans. We have proven ourselves as upright citizens in our country and have contributed to America's civilization in military service, public service, education, sports, music, art, and other high achievements. My three brothers were in World War II. I had two stepfathers and both served in World War I: one in the navy and one in the army. Four of my grandsons served in the Iraq War, two in the marines and two in the army. Countless relatives have been in all America's wars of the last century: cousins, nieces, and nephews in all branches of the service. Among the well-known heroes in Indian country are military servicepersons, such as Ira Hayes of the Pima Tribe, the marine shown in the famous photo of U.S. soldiers raising the flag at Iwo Jima. Charles Curtis, U.S. vice president under Herbert Hoover from 1929 to 1933, had significant Indian ancestry. Curtis served in the Kansas Senate and House of Representatives. As a boy, he lived for some years on the Kaw Reservation. His background was mainly Kaw, Osage, and Pottawatomie, on his mother's side.

A few exceptional Indian people have received national honor for their athletic accomplishments, such as Olympic gold medalist Jim Thorpe, of the Sauk and Fox. Discouragement seems to shackle the minds of Indian America's athletes, for they have not met their potential to excel in sports. Sports show us that athleticism and teamwork are superior to gang competition. I am certain that some athletes who have made it to the top have small amounts of Indian blood but have hidden it, because of the shame placed upon Indian America. Oh, I admired the Sonics when they were in Seattle, and I admired boxers like Joe Lewis, a Black American hero. My first husband, Ed Covington, was a boxer on his ship in the navy. My whole family kept up on all sports, and I had special ones that I kept track of. Billy Mills, an Indian runner, reached the top. Osage ballet artist Maria Tallchief was the lead ballerina for the New York City Ballet. Other top performers who carried some Indian blood hid it well. I read somewhere long ago that Charles Bronson was part Indian. Cher, the singer, is part Indian and is not ashamed of it. Nick Ramus, a Blackfoot Indian, achieved notoriety in the movies, bringing more grace to Indian America. Adam Beach of the Saulteaux, in Canada, is an Indian actor nowadays. We are grateful for all of these people. Although I name these few from my lifetime, there are others.

Lucy Covington of Colville Confederated Tribes was one of our leaders for Indian rights; she worked successfully against the termination of the Colville Reservation in the 1960s. My sister, Mary Ellen Hillaire, gained fame in her field as a professor at the Evergreen State College in Olympia, Washington, especially for her Native American Studies program. It was one of the first of its kind. She made it to the top in her generation and was listed among the top twenty Indian professional women in our region. When I was doing research at the University of Washington's Suzzallo Library, I saw a multivolume set of books on Indian contributions to the civilization of America. Such information should have a greater role in America's high schools and institutions of higher education.

SUBSTANCE ABUSE PROGRAMS

Thom White Wolf Fassett (Seneca) states in his book, *Giving Away Our Hearts: Native American Survival*: "Who can say everything happening to Indian America is good when alcoholism in Indian America is 950% greater than any other's America, when tuberculosis is 630% greater in Indian America than in any other's America, when diabetes is 350% greater in Indian America than in any other's America, when suicide in Indian America is 70% greater than in any other's America? Death from alcoholism, alone, is seven times higher in Indian America than in any other's America."[14] This information comes from our friends at the Garden Street United Methodist Church in Bellingham, Washington. The Methodist church has a long history of advocacy for Indian America, beginning, I believe, in Oklahoma with the Cherokee.

In Indian Country the counteracting of drug and alcohol addiction and programs for recovery are consistently and notoriously underfunded and understaffed. It's as if white America wants an advantage to stay ahead in fighting that plague. Drugs and alcohol claim many lives in Indian country, and Indian people are so often downtrodden, ignored by the government, and publicly brought out as drunks and addicts beyond the possibility of recovery. This occurs, although I realize that compassion does exist in white American society. Some of us recover on our own, basing that recovery on Indian traditional teachings and practices.

EDUCATION

Gathering definitions of education from my elders proved one of the most interesting parts of writing this book: (1) "Book Learning" was one of the very first descriptions of education that I remember; my stepfather used this term. (2) "You're born learning, learning to eat. You learn all your life. You even die learning, or, you learn to die," was my paternal grandfather's definition. (3) "Learning from the living example" is from our timeless Indian cultural teachings. (4) "Growing up" or "maturity," from my mother. (5) "Empowerment," a definition learned from my experience as a teacher. (6) "Growth" is a definition of education from my father. Education has been on our minds since way before the Tulalip Indian School that my parents attended in the early twentieth century.

It is astounding to think of the foresight of my sister, Mary Ellen Hillaire, when it comes to the insights she conveyed to audiences of white American educational leaders:

> What has happened, is happening, and will continue to happen, is that Native American people interested in and capable of education will, at worst, become victims of institutional racism through educational success; unresolved cultural contradictions having responsibility to do, without the authority to validate, and what appears to be, at best, statistically listed educational failure, a condition that defines

the negative or non-position of Native American people in a plural society, denying them a voice in educational direction and choice in educational selection in the determination of what is worth knowing and what is worthy to know through institutional learning. This situation makes a hard to beat team of white Indian experts and educationally successful Native American people, who then establish direction, set up objectives, and evaluate progress of education and training of Native American People based on the values and standards of white people.[15]

I understand her choice and usage of words in this testimony to the Coalition of Indian Controlled School Boards (CICSB). One more Mary Ellen Hillaire whammy:

Over all, this historical educational situation has generated a fairly large body of diverse materials that reflect various attempts to serve Native American people, such as Indian Studies, teacher corps training, leadership training, multi-occupational projects, aquaculture, treaty workshops, special workshops and institutes concerned with the "Indian problem," and other programs designed to help Native American people get into the mainstream of society, such as employment, counseling, relocation, and various outreach programs, such as community workers and community health representatives, which seem to keep the Native American people employed at a poverty level with little or no upward mobility.[16]

My sister said so much about Indian and white American history in these two statements that need I write this book? If only she had survived cancer: I can visualize her advocating for Indian education regarding Washington State test materials for grades one to twelve and showing the ways that these tests are irrelevant to the Indian American population.

Mary Ellen Hillaire, our father Joe Hillaire, and I have had many white friends and neighbors, and many of them advocated for Indian rights. Some Indian families make it to the top, unrecognized by school systems. We are surviving and have been in full bloom with the rise of recognition of Indian people in the United States. But legal reforms in behalf of Indians are far too low-key in America, and here we have "in common" history, economy, and federal government.

TRIBAL ARTS AND MARKETING

Members of the Lummi Tribe have made it to the top with specialized skills in the arts. To name a few: Bill James (b. 1944) and his mother Fran James (1924–2013) made baskets and robes by the hundreds each year, in addition to other important works of art, as well as having possession of Lummi history, lore, and legend. Ted and Marina Plaster excel in cedar basketry and have gained fame in their accommodation of Indian families who have lost a family member. The Plasters also provide cedar roses, wreaths, and other carvings. Many artisans qualify for fame, but they go unrecognized. These artisans' creations are displayed in some of the nation's greatest museums and galleries. Soon we will have a building next to Interstate 5, where our many artisans can sell their artwork and crafts. All this can be added to our history, as Indian America rises to the economic level of Americans in general, in the best of both worlds.

CULTURAL AND ENVIRONMENTAL COOPERATION

Entire communities in Seattle are made up of the various cultures of the world. Beacon Hill stands out in particular. It is a beautiful place for the diverse colors of its people, their friendliness, and their focus. The entire community makes one big happy family and shows it. Entire schools for Hispanics, African Americans, and Asians are scattered throughout Washington State. I have visited quite a few, and they accept me, listen to my stories, and ask me questions. And I accept them, many times having lunch with them. In fact, these students, I can bravely say, paid closer attention in listening to me than students at white or Indian schools. How can cultural cooperation be reflected in our schools? Teach youth about the diversity around them, about humanity across the nation and world, about the partnerships that have been created and the fast friendships that can be enjoyed by all. This book is my way of putting all my American neighbors in my personal library. This kind of history complements my intentions, as well as the intentions of my family and friends. The United States of the World: my world, too.

As for the people of the Great Plains and deserts of these United States, there are many. In order to have more livable land for our growing numbers, we could irrigate the dry lands and deserts with water carried from our rivers and the flooded areas of the United States. Not long ago, when I spoke with an engineer for our tribe's new aquaculture project, he told me, "Yes; that could be managed with our new technology." Maybe such a "flood transfer" is already happening; I do not know. I just pray that the right innovators hear my plea. Our growing nation needs more living area that we can maintain and enhance as years pass. This will take both ingenuity and compassion. Lummi is one of the tribes working on forms of renewable energy that are compatible with a healthy environment for the earth, waters, air, and living beings. Solar-powered lights and geothermal energy are already in use, and more ideas are being studied.[17]

U.S. government, you cannot just take, take, take, and build, build, build. If we have sufficient resources, Indian America will use old and new methods to protect the land, water, and air. The United States can, too. Cooperation between Native and non-Native Americans will help tribes toward self-sufficiency in their needs for energy, and it will help the environment and economy for everyone. Together, we can do it; it will be the best of both worlds.

Although I am proud of America, and of being American, because of what our ancestors—Indian and non-Indian—created here, I have reason to ask, are we really equal? Do Indians have equal standing yet in the total diversity of the United States? So many cultures are blooming and creating businesses across America. There is so much empowered diversity, and all this before Indian America's treaty-based government-to-government relationship is totally complete.

God created our diversity, but humankind created the division of our races, which, to me, is all right. But we have regarded our diversity either superficially or in terms of unsolvable cultural contradictions.

A problem exists when we don't allow both cultures to grow: white America sticks to their old cultural ways, and Indian America sticks to theirs. We need an American culture that blends both: one that might soften the violence of one side, and sharpen the other side toward more contemporary methods. This new culture could empower Indian America and all of America, and it could ultimately save Mother Earth. In this way, we would have the best of both worlds.

Breaking through Indian America's ahistory requires knowledge as a foundation. Remembering that many peoples were here—before Columbus—may be hard for some to accept. Today education is a door to our future. Getting an education can mean that our freedom is in hand. Who could hold us back? Education leads us into a timeless future; use it right. This is connected with the endless circle of life and the lesson of the drum.

3. Chief Siʔaɫ/Seattle (Suquamish and Duwamish), ca. 1865. Siʔaɫ (178?–1866) was a leader and speaker on behalf of survival, peace, and rights for Coast Salish people during the era of the Point Elliott Treaty. His signature appears first among the signatures of eighty-two Native leaders who signed the treaty. Photo by Joseph Thwaites. Reprinted with permission from Washington State Historical Society, #2005.0.145.

4. Isaac Ingalls Stevens, in Red River Métis jacket, 1857. Stevens (1818–62) served as governor of Washington Territory, superintendent of Indian Affairs, major-general of the Territorial Army, and leader of the Northern Pacific Railroad Survey. In this image Stevens is wearing a Red River Métis jacket and bandoliers given to him by the Nez Perce during the Northern Pacific Railroad Expedition. The hands and cuffs of the jacket were sketched in at some point. Photographer unknown. Reprinted with permission from Washington State Historical Society, #2007.0.8.

BRIGADIER GENERAL I. INGALLS STEVENS.

5. Brigadier General Isaac I. Stevens, in Civil War officer's uniform, 1861. Stevens died in 1862 in the American Civil War in the Battle of Chantilly. Photo by J. H. Buford. Reprinted with permission from Washington State Historical Society, #2006.0.507.

6. A page of the handwritten notes from the Treaty of Point Elliott: portion of the treaty speech in Chinook Jargon and English, 1855. The notes from the Proceedings of the Treaty of Point Elliott were written by George Gibbs, an ethnologist, surveyor, and lawyer. Gibbs was a major figure in the writing and transacting of the treaty. This page shows a portion of a speech by Colonel Michael T. Simmons. At the top is the conclusion of Simmons's speech, which he first gave in Chinook Jargon. Ratified Treaty No. 283. Documents Relating to the Negotiation of the Treaty of January 22, 1855, with the Dwamish, Suquamish, etc. U.S. National Archives. Available at the University of Wisconsin–Madison Libraries Digital Collections Center, http://digital.library.wisc.edu/1711.dl/History.IT1855no283.

Konaway kwaish kumtuy nika tumtum klip Boston yuka wa. Wake
close nika na wawa koha Suwash? (Cose kokit alta, Alta mesika
wawa Governor Stevens pe kwaish tyee."

English

"My Brothers. I have known you a long time, and you have known me.
Your hearts have always been good towards me, and formerly, they
were towards all Americans. Since then bad White men have come
who sell you rum, so that people cheat you of your money and
Indians become poor. Nowadays some Indians ill treat the Whites.
In my opinion rum is the cause of this — such is my real mind.
I now give my true heart to you — Do you stop buying rum
of bad white men, and it will soon be well with all Indians.
All your children will be like American children. My heart has one ise for a
long time. The Whites tell me the Indians are always stealing their ~~that I am~~
~~Whitemen~~ goods, their axes, blankets, shirts, pantaloons and potatoes
and bad white men are always beating Indians. The Indians are always
telling me that some Whitman or other beats them. My heart is sick all
the time. If you Indians will stop drinking liquor, stop going to
the houses of bad white men, it will be good for you.

"Your father in the American country, his heart is not to do
ill to you. He will hereafter always take care of you. As soon as the
Indians and Governor Stevens have agreed on the paper. Our chief will
see it. If he thinks the paper good, he will put his name to it.
When he has signed it the paper will be returned and the money
will be sent for your land.

"The goods that are given to day are given as a present. You
all know what my opinion was before other Americans came here.
Did I not tell you the truth? Now then the Governor will speak
again and then the Indian chiefs. [Cheers.]

Governor Stevens resumed. "All this rejoices my heart, my heart
is right and I am glad yours is. Our hearts are all the same. The
Great Father wishes you to send him back a paper showing your desires
and wishes. The Great Father thinks you ought to have homes
as I before told you. The Great Father knows that you are Christians,

150. ww.

3.ww –   1 – 15. ww   21.ww
              2, 24. ww – 12. ww bezem   12.9. ww
              3.   20. ww – 10. ww bezem
              4.   30. ww – 7.50 bezem
              5.   30. ww – 6. ww bezem
              5.   21. ww – 4.250 bezem
              150. ww

4. + 15 ww.
2–3 (2) (12 ww) 24. ww
3 7 (4) ( )

              1 ——— 15. ww
              2 ——— 12. ww
              3 ——— 12. ww
              4 ——— 10. ww
              5 ——— 10. ww
              6 ——— 10. ww
              7 ———   7. ww
              8 ———   7. ww
              9 ———   7. ww
             10 ———   7. ww
             11 ······ 6. ww
             12 ———   6. ww
             13 ———   6. ww
             14 ———   6. ww   29. ww
             15 ———   6. ww
             16 ———   4. 250
             17   4. 250
             18 —   4. 250
             19 —   4. 250
             20 —   4. 250

                              150. ww

25°

7. A page of the handwritten notes from the Treaty of Point Elliott: calculation for distribution of payments for lands, 1855. This page of George Gibbs's handwritten notes from the Proceedings of the Treaty of Point Elliott calculates how $150,000 would be paid to the treaty tribes in annuities over a twenty-year period. Ratified Treaty No. 283. Documents Relating to the Negotiation of the Treaty of January 22, 1855, with the Dwamish, Suquamish, etc. U.S. National Archives. Available at the University of Wisconsin–Madison Libraries Digital Collections Center, http://digital .library.wisc.edu/1711.dl/History.IT1855no283.

8. Haeteluk, Frank Hillaire (Lummi, 1846?–1937), with Lummi people at a salmon ceremony in front of old-style cedar plank house, ca. 1915. The author's paternal grandfather, Frank Hillaire, is on the left, wrapped in a blanket and holding a fish aloft; Peter Kwina is sitting in the foreground, holding a drum; Thomas Squiqui is standing second from right. Photo by L. R. Corbett. Howard E. Buswell photographs, image #203, Center for Pacific Northwest Studies, Heritage Resources, Western Washington University, Bellingham, Washington.

9. Wedding photo of Edna Hillaire (Lummi, 1894–1958) and Joseph R. Hillaire (1894–1967), ca. 1920. Pauline Hillaire Archives; Center for Pacific Northwest Studies, Heritage Resources, Western Washington University, Bellingham, Washington.

10. Frank Hillaire and grandchildren, the Setting Sun Dancers, 1930s. Pauline Hillaire Archives; originally appeared in *Lummi Indian How Stories*, by Edith Fyles Beck (Caxton Press, 1955).

11. Lummi reef net fishermen, early 1930s. See chapter 8 for a description of reef net fishing. Photo by Eugene H. Field. Reprinted with permission from University of Washington Libraries, Special Collections, #NA1810.

12. (*above*) Edna Hillaire and children, ca. 1940. To the right of Edna is Pauline, then, counterclockwise, Mary Ellen, Ben, Dorothy, Joe, Bert, and Ruben. Pauline Hillaire Archives.

13. (*opposite*) Bellingham Centennial History Pole, detail, 2011. The Bellingham Centennial History Pole was carved by Joseph R. Hillaire in 1952 for the city of Bellingham, Washington. In 2007 restoration of the pole was completed by Lummi master carver Felix Solomon, Scott Jensen, and Andrew Todd, and it was reinstalled at the Whatcom County Courthouse. The pole documents the history of the relationship of the Lummi people with the Anglo-Americans who arrived in 1852 and founded the City of Bellingham. Pauline Hillaire explains one of the meanings expressed in the carving: The cattails at the top of the pole represent the Lummi people. The artist chose cattails because cattails never die. However, the serpent that is wrapped around the cattails can symbolize control of the people by the new government and the Bureau of Indian Affairs. Photo by Gregory P. Fields.

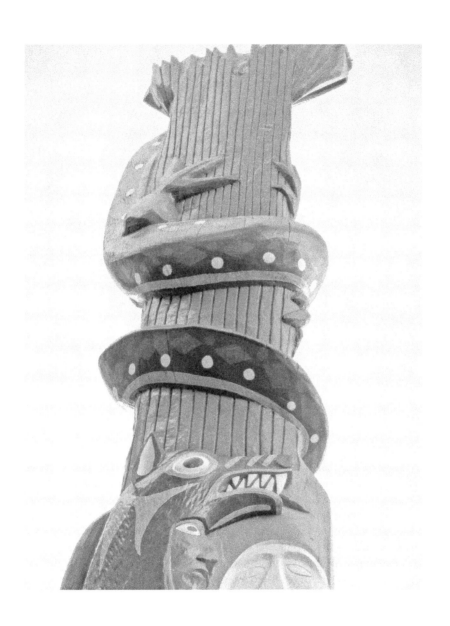

14. (*above*) The author's father, Joseph R. Hillaire, a noted cultural leader and carver, with Senator Henry Jackson (D-WA) (left) and Secretary of the Interior Stewart Udall, at the Century 21 World's Fair Exhibition, Seattle, Washington, 1962. Stewart Udall represented Arizona in the U.S. Congress and then served from 1961 to 1969 as secretary of the interior. Udall worked to preserve American wild lands and defended tribal self-determination. Joe Hillaire carved the Land in the Sky totem pole for the 1962 World's Fair in Seattle, and he did part of the carving in a specially equipped moving van on an 8,470-mile goodwill tour of the United States, with stops in twenty-five cities, including the nation's capital. Photographer unknown. Reprinted with permission from University of Washington Libraries, Special Collections, #HMJ0776.

15. (*opposite*) Mary Ellen Hillaire (Lummi, 1927–82), the author's sister, a leader in education, ca. 1973. Mary Ellen Hillaire founded the Native American Studies program at the Evergreen State College (Olympia WA) and began the work that established the college's Longhouse Education and Cultural Center. Evergreen State College Photo Services.

16. (*above*) Pauline Hillaire uses cedar and water to ask a blessing on Isaiah Francis of Seattle. Holding the bowl of water is Scälla's grandson, Benjamin Covington (Lummi/Colville, b. 1980). Scälla was the main organizer of the Grandmothers' Project Northwest, held in June 2003 at the Whidbey Island Institute in Clinton, Washington. The grandmothers who spoke represented traditions including Native Canada, Hawai'i, New Zealand, and Tibet. Photo by Meryl Schenker. Reprinted with permission.

17. (*opposite*) Benjamin Covington, Cuth Sells (Lummi/Colville, b. 1980), speaks on behalf of his grandmother Pauline Hillaire at the 2013 National Endowment for the Arts Concert in Washington DC. Scälla, Pauline Hillaire, was awarded a National Heritage Fellowship, and among the Heritage Fellows that year she was also designated the 2013 Bess Lomax Hawes National Heritage Fellow for her contributions to preservation of her tribe's—and the nation's—cultural legacy. Ben has said of his grandmother, "Her name, Scälla, means of the Killer Whale. The Killer Whale is the pillar and guardian of the sea, and so also my grandmother is a pillar and guardian of our traditions." Photo by Mark Carde. Reprinted with permission.

18. Members of the Children of the Setting Sun sing to welcome people to a 2013 presentation at Western Washington University on Pauline's book *A Totem Pole History: The Work of Lummi Carver Joe Hillaire* (Lincoln: University of Nebraska Press, 2013). The adults pictured (from left to right) are Jolene Armstrong, Lila Covington, Richard Solomon, and Benjamin Covington. The five boys are sons of Lila and Ben Covington. Pauline Hillaire is in the foreground. Photo by Gregory P. Fields.

19. Seventeen members of the Lummi song and dance group Children of the Setting Sun, representing four generations, sang and danced at the 2013 National Heritage Concert in Washington DC. Pictured are (seated) Wilma Olsen, (from left) David Alexander, Richard Solomon, Audrey Chicone (daughter of Pauline Hillaire), Loretta Olsen (daughter of Wilma Olsen), and Lois Cadiente. Photo by Michael G. Stewart/ NEA. Reprinted with permission.

Part 3
Oral History and Cultural Teachings

Lesson of the Drum

Everyone in the Smokehouse, where I was brought into the secret society, dances with the universe: against the clock, with the universe. And as everyone dances, their song is sung four times, honoring every corner of the room. East, north, west, and south are four directions; four members of the family: mother, father, daughter, son; four elements: fire, water, air, and earth.

The drum is a sacred object; treat it with respect. When drumming, you hold the drum next to your heart. The sound of the drum is like a heartbeat. As I remember this lesson of the drum as told by a teacher in Prince George, British Columbia, the position of your hand is loosely holding the drum. Remove your hand from the drum and hold it before you. The position of your hand is like the way your hand was at your birth. This is a sign of your purity.

The spokes of your drum represent the pathways of your life. Sometimes there are few; sometimes there are many. One spoke may represent education, another may represent religion, another a job. Each spoke leads you to maturity and encouragement, whether it's education, religion, or however you receive it; you have to finish that road in order to get to the endless circle of life. These spokes lead from your hand to the rim of your drum, and the rim of your drum represents the endless circle of life.

No matter what story your drum tells, of a complicated life or a simple life, it shows your purity when you hold it like this; a drum takes you back to your purity. Don't be afraid to show it when you use a drum, don't be afraid to show your purity. This is a teaching that we have for young people, to encourage them, to show that this is a place where you will end up: after school, after you've grown to adulthood, after you've had a family, after you've matured in mind, body, soul, and spirit. This is the endless part of your life. This encouragement of endlessness is yours, and you earn it from your purity. This is one of the things that I want to leave with you.

CHAPTER 10

Scälla—Of the Killer Whale

A Song of Hope

Rebecca Chamberlain

> As Native people, our value system is based on our relationship to the land.
> Our environment is part of every aspect of our lives. The land will sing to
> you if you listen. It is the source of songs. Many have stopped listening,
> but the spirits are still there. We manifest our value system through music,
> dance, art, and legends of our elders. . . . As we explore our Native values,
> we ask these questions:
>
> > What is your relationship to land?
> > What is your relationship to exchange?
> > What is your relationship to others?
> > What is your relationship to work?
>
> —Pauline Hillaire, in Chamberlain, *Sharing the Circle*, 15

To know Pauline, Scälla, is to feel the love she has for the earth and
the hope that she has for tomorrow. In September of 2011 we visited
to discuss her two life works: *A Totem Pole History: The Work of Lummi
Carver Joe Hillaire* and *Rights Remembered: A Salish Grandmother Speaks
on American Indian History and the Future*. Written in the wisdom of her
elder years, these works are an offering of love to her family, ancestors,
and the new generations. The first is a testament to her Lummi heritage and the celebrated life of her father, Joseph Hillaire. The second
chronicles her personal and cultural odyssey. It celebrates the ability to
transform suffering and adapt to change. It speaks to restorative justice

for the earth and generations of the future. Pauline wrote these works parallel to each other, and they should be read together. *A Totem Pole History* includes a brief biography that I wrote about Pauline's training and family traditions, as well as her teaching, research, writing, and cultural work, emphasizing the earlier decades of her life.[1]

As Pauline and I travel around the Lummi Reservation and visit in her home, she brings to life familiar people and places through her stories. Always she claims nothing on her own merit. Coming from a linage of prominent leaders, Pauline was trained early in her life to do this work. Her father, Joe Hillaire (Kwul-kwul'tʷ) was a descendant of spiritual leaders, and her mother, Edna Price (Petoie) was of a chiefly lineage.[2] Pauline says, "My father taught me to have a well-rounded intelligence, to never forget beautiful logic or common sense. My mother taught me to maintain self-control. If you have self-control, you can go anywhere. What I share comes from the hours of thinking, reflecting their talent coming through me out of love." With kindness and deliberation her parents cultivated her photographic memory, imagination, sensory awareness, and attention to detail, planting the seeds of her life and writings. They trained her ability to tell stories, to recall genealogies, and to practice traditional arts. They taught her to observe and tend to the world around her. They shaped her sense of fairness, justice, and moral discernment. She has said, "All I am doing is fine-tuning the songs [and teachings] for this age. As I teach, I share the correct words, information and stories behind them. Now is the time to make sure they are passed on correctly. We work hard to pass on our traditions with integrity."[3]

Honored among the elders of the Salish Sea tribes, Pauline is one of the great cultural teachers of our age. She has received numerous awards and recognitions, including the Washington State Governor's Heritage Arts Award in 1996. In 2013, the National Endowment for the Arts gave her the lifetime honor of naming her a National Heritage Fellow.[4] The NEA also named her the 2013 Bess Lomax Hawes National Heritage Fellow, a special distinction for her contributions to heritage arts preservation in the nation. With dignity and clarity, Pauline passes on an unbroken linage of Lummi and Halkomelem Salish stories, songs, dances, material arts, genealogy, and cultural and ceremonial traditions. At tribal gatherings, schools, and Northwest Indian College, she has passed on traditional teachings to children and other members of the Lummi Nation. She has also shared teachings at schools, colleges and universities, museums, and cultural, arts, and environmental organizations throughout the Pacific Northwest.

Pauline is a master artist and teacher. She humbly embodies artistic integrity and generosity, teaching educators and young people how to learn from the past as they move forward into the future. Through a sophisticated understanding of the philosophic, historic, cultural, social, and political contexts of Native life, Pauline is able to embed cultural teachings in the minds and imaginations of all who learn from her. A dynamic and charismatic orator, storyteller, dancer, and singer, she holds audiences in attention as she uses traditional arts to explore such issues as sustainability, spirituality, cultural survival, tribal sovereignty, and colonization. Pauline is diverse intellectually, artistically, and culturally, as she blends traditional arts and ancient knowledge in modern contexts.

For over thirty years, Pauline supported the dream of her sister, Mary Ellen Hillaire, who founded the thriving Native American Studies program at the Evergreen State College in Olympia, Washington. Among the largest Indigenous studies programs in the nation, this program serves traditional communities locally, nationally, and globally. After Mary died in 1982 at age fifty-five, Pauline worked with the college to build the first longhouse or similar Native cultural center to exist on a U.S. campus. As an artist and cultural leader, she consulted with administrators and gave presentations that inspired faculty, staff, and students. The Longhouse Education and Cultural Center on the Evergreen campus was dedicated in 1995.

The core of Pauline's artistic and cultural practice celebrates a deep relationship to the natural world. She and other Salish elders, such as Vi Hilbert, taqʷšəblu, (Upper Skagit, 1918–2008), have often said, "The Earth is our first teacher." But what does this mean? I asked Pauline this question for an essay, "The Earth Is Our First Teacher: Discovering Language and Place." She replied, "How does one even address this? It is so comprehensive—it includes every part of life!" I respond, "When we try, modern people often feel severed from the past, from the earth, and from traditional teachings. How do we recover a sense of intimacy with the earth?"[5] In addressing these concerns, Pauline and I gave college courses and workshops on cultural, environmental, and arts education, starting in the 1980s. She begins her discussion of these issues with reference to her father, Joe, and her sister, Mary Ellen. To gain understanding, Pauline asks four fundamental questions: "What is your relationship to land? What is your relationship to work? What is your relationship to others? What is your relationship to exchange?"

These questions are keys that unlock individuals' understanding of their purpose in life. In answering them Pauline challenges persons of all ages and backgrounds to express the dynamic relationship among these questions, through imagination and the arts: music, dance, language, myth, story, poetry, and the visual arts. She uses these questions to relate a worldview of abundance and prosperity shared by traditional Northwest communities who lived sustainably and generously with the natural world. She encourages people to enhance their understanding and experience through disciplines of body, mind, emotion, and spirit. Pauline demonstrates how—by reflecting on these questions and by cultivating respect toward all of life—one not only can survive but can thrive amid challenges of transformation and change, on personal and global levels.

In the spring of 2009 I invited Pauline to the Evergreen State College to address these issues in a program, *Ecology of Language and Place*. She asked the students:

What challenges do you face? How do you solve problems? Be silent. Observe. Examine. Interact. Explore. Get acquainted with nature and the elements. Don't rush in recklessly or needlessly. Probe the core of your question. Use the vision of your imagination to see the inner dimension of your question. There are differences between people and cultures. We must respect those differences. When you can do as well with what is strange as you can with what is familiar, then you are a superior person. There are times when what seems superior is inferior. That is when you must come to terms with your spiritual self. From this understanding you develop your artwork [your life's work] and your partnership with nature.[6]

Pauline taught students several songs, including the "Song of Hope: Song of Tomorrow," which explores how to develop the confidence and courage to overcome seemingly insurmountable obstacles and adversity. Pauline's mother taught her this song in Chinook Jargon, and it comes with a story:

> Warriors from the north captured twins at Gooseberry Point and cruelly imprisoned them in a pen, far to the north. Each young man was gifted in a different way. The stronger brother began running up against the walls, trying to gain momentum to throw himself over. The weaker brother was crippled. He sat cross-legged on the ground, watching and learning from his brother's mistakes. He realized that he would have more leverage if he used the corners of the walls to throw himself over. The crippled brother quietly prepared himself by singing and breathing in a rhythmic way. When he was mentally ready, he leaped up, ran to a corner, threw himself over the walls, and gained his freedom. When he got out, he saved his brother and his people.[7]

As Pauline taught the song, she advised students, "No matter how difficult or impossible a situation seems, we must develop the inner resources to face the challenge. These very circumstances sometimes bring out our best." She teaches the words in Chinook Jargon and English: "Tomorrow, tomorrow, we will make it, you will see." Through song and dance, students pass beneath canoe paddles that are crossed in an arch and move symbolically into the future.

Pauline shares this song with groups of all ages; however, when speaking to teachers or college students, she goes into detail about the challenging circumstances of her people. Reciting her genealogy back seven generations, she describes how her family came to terms with the heavy history of colonialism and the suffering it caused. She says, "We had to live by laws that were made by the very people who were breaking laws they had made." Yet somehow each generation lovingly transformed their grief and pain, passing on their strength and insight. Life includes beauty along with suffering and loss. Both must be embraced. As Pauline and I visited in her home, she told me of her personal struggle to write *Rights Remembered*. Recovering from two strokes in 2007, at the age of seventy-eight, she began in earnest to complete her book. How could she reconcile what her family taught her with the deceptions shown in government documents? Pauline felt a strong sense of frustration at the injustice. How could she channel her feelings into something useful? She said:

> I was so angry at the government that I had to stop. I had to think harder than that. I began to ask deeper questions. What is the measure of unfairness? My father told me that we helped the newcomers, but where was that in the record? In the book, I put my research together with my father's teachings. Those years of talking with Mary Ellen also had a lot to do with how I understood these issues. My father taught me that we must work for change. We were born with the conditions to get along. How do we enhance, educate, and train our minds to do that?
>
> The first law of the Smokehouse is acceptance, and this was hard for me. I had to get through the pain. But if you understand the First Law of acceptance, it allows you to hold our relationship to the land in trust. Mother Earth is the common denominator. She will survive if we are kind to the land.
>
> We don't do anything to preserve Mother Earth. Yet it's common sense. We can't overrun her. Europeans were always running away. We didn't have to run away. We need to love where we are; our hope is that the coming generations can do the same. They must protect the land.
>
> My father knew that I would do this work, and that it would not be easy. He said he couldn't get into the ring with me, but he would stand on the sidelines and cheer. That's where he is now. The dead are not powerless. They are powerful.

Rights Remembered is painstakingly honest and practical. Grounded in the traditional education, sustainable practices, and spiritual insights of her ancestors, Pauline suggests how we can renew our present world by reestablishing bonds to the earth, developing sustainable economies, and cultivating healthy social relationships. Through her research into the records of the U.S. government, she challenges readers to look clearly at the systems of oppression that we have inherited and assess how they have gone wrong. In witnessing the wounds of the past, she asks readers to accept responsibility for helping to generate true change and to transform their lives in the present. Pauline goes beyond a historical and critical analysis of the past, as she unflinchingly explores cultural wounds to offer insight into potentials for social change and psychological healing. Pointing out systematic acts of injustice and inequity, she asks herself, and the reader, to take on the challenge of transformation and renewal. Where do the wounds end, and where does healing begin? By sitting in the fire of past wrongs, she guides us toward recognition of new cultural and social possibilities.

Rights Remembered offers a sensitive and thoughtful perspective into how we can acknowledge and begin to reverse generations of abuse and thoughtlessness against indigenous peoples and the ecological fabric of life on earth. What are the long-term consequences of historical inequity, appropriation, and abuse? Can social justice, psychological healing, and ecological restoration begin when we witness and heal the wounds of the past? Pauline asks us to join her and to begin a collective journey of understanding, renewal, and transformation. As we face coming challenges, we are reminded of the message in Pauline's Song of Hope: "Tomorrow, tomorrow, we will make it, you will see."

CHRONOLOGY

- c. 1832: Birth of Salaphalano, father of Pauline's grandfather Frank Hillaire.
- c. 1846: Birth of Frank Hillaire (Haeteluk), Pauline's paternal grandfather, on Orcas Island.

c. 1866: Frank Hillaire founds the Setting Sun Dance Group. Pauline's father, Joseph Hillaire, Joe Washington, and Jack Cagey continued the group well into the twentieth century. Pauline led the group from the late twentieth century into the twenty-first century.

1894: Birth of Pauline's parents, Joseph Hillaire (Kwul-kwul'tʷ) and Edna Price (Petoie) Hillaire Scott.

1929: Birth of Pauline Hillaire (1931, according to some records).

1937: Pauline begins attending the Lummi Tribal School.

1938: Joe and Edna separate. Joe moves to Suquamish.

1939: Pauline's family moves to Gooseberry Point.

1949: High school graduation, Ferndale (WA) High School.

1951: Associate of Arts, Business Law, Haskell Indian College, Lawrence, Kansas.

1951–58: Secretary to the tribal operations officer, Colville Confederated Tribes, Nespelem, Washington.

1960: Pauline moves to Seattle. She regularly visits her father on Blake Island, where he is carving and working at Tillicum Village.

1961: Joe Hillaire completes the Seattle-Kobe Sister-Cities totem pole and travels to Japan to complete the carving and for its dedication.

1962: Joe Hillaire completes two totem poles for Century 21, the World's Fair in Seattle: Man in Transition and Land in the Sky.

c. 1962–65: Secretary, Boeing Company, Electrical Engineering Department, Renton, Washington.

c. 1965–69: Secretary, Heath Sciences Personnel Department, University of Washington Hospital.

1966–67: Member, Human Rights Commission, University of Washington.

1967: Death of Joe Hillaire. Pauline begins her research in earnest.

1970: Begins working in the Lummi Tribal Archives and for the Lummi Indian Business Council (tribal council).

1970: Begins doing cultural work and teaching.

1973: President, American Indian Student Association, Seattle Central Community College.

1973: President, Minority Coalition, Seattle Central Community College.

1973: Associates of Applied Science, Legal Secretarial Science, Seattle Central Community College.

1973: Begins assisting her sister, Mary Ellen Hillaire, founder of the Native American Studies program at Evergreen State College, Olympia.

1974: Bachelor of Arts, Indian Education Administration, Evergreen State College.

1978: Publication of *Indian Policy: Crime or Reason?*, monograph by Pauline Hillaire, published by the *Omak (WA) Chronicle*, in connection with the Longest Walk I.

1982: Death of Mary Ellen Hillaire. Pauline works in consultation with Evergreen State College to continue Mary Ellen's work toward establishment of the Longhouse Education and Cultural Center.

1984–91: Cultural resource specialist, Lummi Tribe.

1985–88: Constitutional Revision Committee member, Lummi Indian Business Council.

1985–2002: Instructor, Northwest Indian Song and Dance I, II, III, and Genealogy I, II, Northwest Indian College.

1985–2002: Revives and for seventeen years leads the Lummi song and dance group Children of the Setting Sun, continuing into the twenty-first century the group begun by her grandfather in the nineteenth century.

1985–2008: Presentations, performances, teacher education workshops, and storytelling programs in the Pacific Northwest and locations nationally.

1989: Indian Health Issues Committee member, Lummi Indian Business Council.

1990: Oral History Project, Title III Grant, Lummi Tribe.

1990–2002: Instructor for Cultural Enrichment Programs, Bellingham School District.

1991: Preparation for the Salmon Ceremony at Lummi.

1992: Participation in the 1992 Northwest Folklife Festival.

1992–97: Washington State Arts Commission, Apprenticeship Grants, with grandson Benjamin Covington, 1992, 1996, 1997.

1994–95: Collaboration with Johnny Moses (Tulalip) and Kevin Paul (Swinomish/Colville) on the curriculum project *Sharing the Circle* (Evergreen State College; Artists in Residence Programs, Northwest Folk Arts; and the Shoreline School District).

1995: Participates in opening of Longhouse Education and Cultural Center at Evergreen State College.

1996: Washington Governor's Heritage Arts Award.

1999: Publication of *Spirit of the First People: Native American Music Traditions of Washington State*, edited by Willie Smyth and Esmé Ryan (Seattle: University of Washington Press), with audio CD including recordings by Pauline Hillaire (Seattle: Jack Straw Productions).

2000–2002: Washington State Arts Commission, Folk Arts Grants, 2000, 2002.

2003: Main organizer of the Grandmothers' Project Northwest, Whidbey Island Institute, Clinton, Washington.

2005: Recognized at the Day of Honoring (May 5, 2005), Seattle Art Museum.

2007–8: Artist in the Schools, Northwest Folklife.

2007–11: Recording of oral tradition, oral history, and songs at Northwest Heritage Resources, Jack Straw Productions, Southern Illinois University–Edwardsville, and SoundWise Studios, Bellingham.

2008: Release of audio CD *Lummi Legends: Legends Told by My Father, Kwul-kwul't*ᵘ, told by Pauline Hillaire (Mountlake WA: Northwest Heritage Resources).

2013: National Endowment for the Arts, National Heritage Award Fellowship and the Bess Lomax Hawes Award, for preservation of cultural heritage arts.

2013: Publication of *A Totem Pole History: The Work of Lummi Carver Joe Hillaire*, edited by Gregory P. Fields (University of Nebraska Press), with companion media "Coast Salish Totem Poles."

2016: Publication of *Rights Remembered: A Salish Grandmother Speaks on American Indian History and the Future*, edited by Gregory P. Fields (University of Nebraska Press), with companion media "A Century of Coast Salish History."

CHAPTER 11

Earth, Our First Teacher

ELDERS

My aunt Vi Hilbert (Upper Skagit, 1918–2008) taught me many important lessons of Indian Life. In addition to lessons from some of the most important elders in my life, I was very fortunate to be born early enough to live with elders and in times of old, and just as fortunate to be born a child who loved her elders. Older people, with the teachings of their own elders, fascinated me no end. Many times Aunt Vi acknowledged my fortune in being born of my mother and father; she knew them well. My teachers began with family elders, then community elders, and elders from other reservations.

My grandfather Frank Hillaire maintained a cultural bridge between the Indian world and the white man's world in our area. He acknowledged the times. He was born in or about 1846 and was present at the meetings of negotiation for the Point Elliott Treaty of 1855. His father, Salaphalano, the Priest, was a signer of that treaty. Grandpa Hillaire was a genius in his time for preserving our philosophy, values, songs, legends, and dance. He shared his memory with many of his descendants, relatives, and friends. One of Aunt Vi's favorite songs came from Gran'pa Hillaire; she requested that it be sung almost every time I had an opportunity to visit her, or when I shared legends at her historic birthday gatherings every year.

As I prepare you for my ultimate message in this chapter, I will continue to tell the qualifications of my teachers. My sister, Mary Ellen Hillaire, as a young girl of about eight years old, is pictured in the book *Lummi Indian How Stories*, with Grandpa Hillaire.[1] She is behind him to the left in the picture (fig. 10). She learned from him for years and used some of his teachings in the college-level Native American Studies program and classes that she developed. I am ever thankful to Grandpa Hillaire for his sharing.

There is a vastness, as in space, to the Indian world that only the Indian knows. Of course, our cultural practices were discouraged and were removed from our ancestors across the United States in an effort to give us white culture's form of civilization, while robbing us of ours. Their understanding of our cultural practices was that this type of "display" suggested hostility to white Americans, who interpreted it, or chose to regard it, as Indian "uprising."[2]

Haeteluk Frank Hillaire also taught his son, my father, Joe Hillaire, Kwul-kwul'tʷ (1894–1967), beginning with carving red cedar, carving totem poles, and telling legends for teaching. He also taught my father the songs and dances, philosophy, and art of the Setting Sun Dance Group, originally created by Grandpa Hillaire in the mid-nineteenth century. Grandpa traveled all over the United States with his dance group, sharing our culture in an effort to teach white America, especially dignitaries, that we were not hostile just because we sang songs of celebration or danced the legends to the songs—that we were harmless. He was a bridge between our two cultures for that valuable understanding. We were far removed from hostility in our family for all the generations of our family tree, and we know that genealogy back to the eighteenth century. Philosophy, as we know it today, and as I have examined in my deepest research, was a silent necessity in Grandpa Hillaire's time—as a matter of fact, in all Indian American ahistory. Philosophy is behind every legend, every song, every dance, and all value systems.

My father was lucky to have Grandfather Frank Hillaire as his father, just as I am blessed by having Joe Hillaire as my father. I learned so very much from him and from my mother. My father came from the Longhouse winter dance culture and my mother came from the original chief's line, not meaning chiefs that were appointed by the U.S. government or the church, but the leaders who were chosen by the membership of the community. My father, too, became a bridge in his time between the white culture and our Indian culture.[3] These two men passed on to their younger generations, friends, and relatives their philosophies and culture. After all, this was their mode of survival.

LEGENDS, PHILOSOPHY, AND VALUES

Legends were one of the most important teaching tools. We listened, and we calculated the behaviors of the characters and the intentions of the legends. We interacted with the environment in the place where the legend originated, and we had time to think through the philosophy used by the characters within the legends. We had the time, space, and opportunity to act out the legends we heard. There were no books, no televisions, no stages provided. Those contemporary things were not needed. Grandpa Hillaire had an orchard of nine to twelve fruit trees alongside a wheat field, where he taught his young ones how to dance the songs that he was teaching them. My father, Joe, taught the young ones of his time, also in fields, out in the open, or in houses owned by members of the community who were interested in the youth of our tribe learning the philosophy, songs, dances, and legends that go with the songs. I hope that the reader will understand our teachers' intents: they were not pushy, did not overtalk situations, laughed with the youth, and talked with the parents of their students. Panic is not a good ingredient of survival.

This form of learning was not of the secret society of the Longhouse tradition (what we call the Smokehouse). These were songs of celebration—not songs of a person's inner guardian spirit relationship. These are two different categories in Indian country. One has nothing to do with the other, except for the fact that both have songs, both have dance. One is of a celebration sense, the other of a spiritual sense. This is a lesson for you in itself. In our tradition, we are welcome to share the celebration sense of our culture, but not the spiritual sense. The spiritual sense of our culture is our own individual and cultural property.

Aunt Vi states the following in *Sharing the Circle*, a curriculum on Native Northwest Coast music created by Rebecca Chamberlain of the Evergreen State College and disseminated throughout public schools in the Seattle area:

> Each of these artists comes from a strong family, and has been given permission to pass on their traditions. For example, there is a story about Pauline Hillaire and her father. I visited Joe Hillaire at Messenger House after he had his stroke. As often as I could, I would bring him reel-to-reel tape recordings my dad [Charles Anderson] had left me. Because he knew my dad so well, I knew that he would be able to appreciate the songs my dad sang. I played him some of the old songs and we would reminisce about this or that owner, since my dad always identified whose song he was singing. Joe said, "You know, I'm going to leave a song here for the people to use. I'll sing it for you." So he sang for me "Tall Cedar Tree." It is the same song I heard Pauline sing with the children at Shoreline [public schools]. He told me, "I hope you have the chance to meet my daughter Pauline. She is going to carry on my work."[4]

And I danced with him in the 1940s as long as my classmates made me welcome. He said when I left that group, "I'll miss your voice, dear." No greater father ever lived. By the way, he and I did not verbally arrange at any time that I would carry on his work. I just did, and I did so with the greatest happiness.

In the same document, *Sharing the Circle*, Aunt Vi said the following in her introduction to this Native music curriculum:

> Songs that the artists have permitted to be videotaped for archival purposes can be used in social studies classes. This can be an important eye-opening experience for future students. For an hour they can be part of this one-time experience, especially if it is not repeated. Students from now into the future can have the opportunity to feel

the depth of the First People in a true and delightful way. This kind of teaching is still possible if teachers learn to use these materials in the classroom. Members of the families who have participated could be on record for public schools to access again. They could say, "Your grandparent, your parent, your relative did this for us. Can you come in and continue the legacy that was left by your relative?" This way, the material isn't just taken from the family and used. The door is open for any of them to come back, if that is what they would like to do.[5]

These quotations from Vi Hilbert cover tremendous territory, and I agree with her on every point she has made in them. She taught Lushootseed (Puget Sound Salish) language and legends at the University of Washington for years. My son, Bobby, took her class there. My connections with the university go back into my father's life; he contributed to an Indian language dictionary published there many years ago.

The background of our philosophy had to be mentioned before I can say more about the legends, songs, dance, and other aspects of Indian culture that kept us alive (for want of a better word: that made possible our *survival*). Indian American survival is a true blessing. Just how do Indians think, in order to have survived all that we survived? My sister, Mary Ellen Hillaire, organized the Native American Studies program in 1974 at Evergreen State College in Olympia, Washington. I graduated from that college that same year. I found it a powerful program. It gave a basis for Indian students not only to apply themselves to higher learning but also to update themselves on Indian Country activities throughout the nation. Our connecting with Indian initiatives nationally was a great motivating factor for us. The foundation of Mary Ellen's Native American Studies program was our Coast Salish value system. This system has nothing to do with money, power, sex, or any form of egotism. Evergreen's Native American Studies program flourished with greater numbers of students than any other college program of its kind at that time. It was a great success, and the college generously permits this program to carry on. The Native American Studies program and Evergreen's Longhouse Education and Cultural Center are the results of Mary Ellen Hillaire's vision for her friends and relatives in Indian Country. The Longhouse at Evergreen was a first of its kind for any college in the nation. Mary Ellen studied the Indian situation for years and participated in important state, college, human resources, and welfare committees as she established the curriculum. It was a struggle to get the college to understand and accept, but they did.

Our value system, because it has nothing to do with money, power, sex, or any form of egotism, is one method of realizing Indian America's philosophy of ages. My ancestors had a better chance to study Earth, our First Teacher, and I truly believe that our philosophy helped us to survive. This value system is manifested in Indian communities through songs, dance, legends, talk, games, art, and ceremonies. Education based on this type of philosophy builds individual powers of understanding of the past, present, and future of the Indian world, and of U.S., state, and county governments, through activities such as dialogue with visitors in the classroom—a great experience!

Some may find it a challenge to understand the philosophy of Indian Country for the sake of survival, because our current history books have not taught the full truth of our aboriginal history. In earlier decades and even today, it still happens that mockery and ridicule prevail. Too often, we are dragged across the stage as the joke of the day or as a mascot unworthy of playing the game.[6] My prayer now is that my reflections on philosophy from my family and from aboriginal value systems do not hinder anyone's natural growth in any way: mentally or spiritually. This philosophy is not to be pushed on a person in any way. No rules, regulations, or instructions go along with these reflections on our value system, only the truth.

My nephew, Gary Hillaire, a carver, orator, and teller of legends, once wrote an editorial in which he compared how teachings are conveyed through traditional arts, as distinct from how teachings are conveyed by words. He said of the totem pole carvers in the family:

> They were the writers of their times . . . the teachings didn't suffer with the burden of words, but were brought to us through symbology.

This manner of presentation allowed for the freedom of growth to meet the needs of the ever-advancing civilization of which we are an integral part. Words, on the other hand, have a certain limitation, which could conceivably stagnate after the passing of time. With this thought in mind, it can be readily understood why such emphasis must be put on the proper choice of the words, which shall serve our needs inadequately presenting the teachings. Hopefully, we can do without stifling those with progressive understanding and, at the same time, not cause those who are just beginning to develop an understanding to be lost in bewilderment.[7]

Carving and storytelling created fame for Gary Hillaire. He had his own style, different than any other carver's design (past or present), and that is the way it should be. The story never changes, only the design of the object of art. Gary suffered many years before he came out with his own technique in carving and storytelling.

MOTHER EARTH

Now, concerning Earth, our First Teacher, experience this for yourself: Wander out onto a trail you know well, in or near a forest or woods. Stop. Close your eyes. Listen to the quiet. Imagine the trees. Imagine their movements in the wind. Listen for the tones. Imagine the life of the trees with the accompaniment of the wind. You will hear tones — whirring, low, medium tones. Figure out the notes you must know as musical notes; connect them with the tones and tempos you hear from the trees' movements in the winds of all directions—strong wind, soft breeze, or anything in between. You can put together a song from the earth.

Or go to the beach; it does not matter where. It could be the tempestuous ocean, a bay, lake, or stream. Locate your body somewhere, comfortably. Close your eyes. Listen to the waters. Are they talking; are they singing? Are they fighting, or are they still? Open your eyes. Look out upon the water. What is it doing, as near and as far out as you can see? Is the wind blowing? Is the tide coming in? Or is the tide going out? Is the water shining? Twinkling? Sparkling? Glowing? Close your eyes again, for now you are familiar with your surroundings. Listen. Put tones to what you hear—musical tones. You will end up with a song from the earth.

Talk to an archaeologist; talk to a scientist. Ask them questions. If they dug into the earth—went underground for purposes of study, curiosity, or discovery of something—what did they see? Did they find what they were looking for at that time? Did they learn anything from Mother Earth? She always has something to teach. Go berry picking. As you search for the berries you want, listen to all the tones around you. You are not talking, not whistling, not singing, just walking and listening. You will see things that you never saw before, in the tiniest situation. After you find the berries you wanted, be thankful that Mother Earth provided them just for you. Do not take any rotten berries to that sacred place you call home.

The planet Earth keeps us from getting bored. Too many people spend every moment of their lives being bored and more bored; who can be more bored than the next person? Well, pay some attention to our planet, Earth. She tries to entertain us, every season of the year, every hour of the day. Every day there may be something new to see. If not, work with Mother Earth. If you farm or garden, plant something. If something is already planted, check it out to see how it is growing or if it has produced. Mother Earth is trying her very best to entertain us and help us, that we may not be bored, that we may always be able to accomplish something good. Being bored or helpless is a portion of the greatest nothingness. My father taught us that a person without a dream is nothing but a creature. We were discouraged from being bored; we always found something new to learn from Earth, our First Teacher.

Indian Songs were used by every Setting Sun Dance Group, led by Frank Hillaire, Joe Hillaire, Joe Washington (older son of Joe's sister, Veronica), Jack Cagey (youngest son of Veronica), and me. Songs from the environment played a major part in every presentation. With my Setting Sun Dance Group, I taught the men to "touch the Earth" with items they carried in their hands, because Mother Earth cares what they were doing. Touching the Earth is a moment of respect to her.

When they were older and in the military, I told them each to "touch the Earth" wherever they may be, and they have. Upon return home for special occasions, they have told me, "It worked, Grandma!" I had told them to touch the Earth, hold their hands there awhile, think of us at home and feel our presence, know that we are praying for them.

Today, I renew these words for the ones in the wars. May the Great Spirit of God bring them home safely, that they may be with their families, fully and securely. Love can be sent through Mother Earth if you and your loved ones agree on a time of the week to touch the Earth and think of each other for strength, courage, understanding, empowerment, and love. Our families know spirituality is powerful, sacred, and filled with love. Our prayers are for all those who are fighting wars: Bring them home safe, sound, and with the blessing of greater understanding. Fill their souls with the spirit of accomplishment.

Many poems have been written about Mother Earth. Indian America has many songs about Mother Earth. We do honor her. I have observed individuals who have jobs with the environment; to me they seem happier than those people with high-tension business jobs that keep them indoors.

Read the book *I Have Spoken: American History through the Voices of the Indians*.[8] Indian leaders across America speak of this land as sacred, and they speak steadfastly on her behalf. Their speeches, for me, are heartrending. The government is not programmed to listen to such speeches. In earlier history it appears that they looked down upon them as so much garble. There were but few government officials in the time leading up to and during treaty-making time who spoke well of Indian America and our relationship with the land. One of my favorite people in Indian American history is the Shawnee leader Tecumseh. I copied one of his speeches over forty years ago. He gave this speech to the territorial governor of Indiana, William Henry Harrison, in protest of the ceding of Indian lands in 1805–6:

> The way, the only way, to stop this evil is for all redmen to unite in
> claiming a common and equal right in the land, as it was at first, and

should be now—for it never was divided, but belongs to all. No tribe has a right to sell, even to each other, much less to strangers, who demand all and will take no less. Sell a country! Why not sell the air that surrounds us, the clouds and the great sea, as well as the earth?

Did not the Great Spirit make all these for the use of his children? How can we have confidence in the white people? When Jesus Christ came upon the earth, they killed Him. They nailed Him to a cross. You thought He was dead; but you were mistaken.

You have Shakers among you; and, you laugh and make light of their worship. The states have set the example of forming a union among all the fires [states]. Why should they censure the Indians for following the same? I shall be glad to know immediately what is your determination about the land.[9]

Chief Seattle's famous speech echoes the same lament, as does the speech of Chief Joseph of the Nez Perce. I hear these same laments from today's membership at Lummi as well as other local tribes. Our family has relatives all over Washington State. We meet at funerals, potlatches, winter dances, water festivals, canoe journeys, and meetings on behalf of our tribal governments. Anyone, I believe, can hear in the words of conversation or special speeches the controlled yearning for the land that was promised at the original treaty signings. And I believe the promises could be fulfilled, if only someone would hear these laments with their heart, spirit, and soul, get the idea, and do something about it in Washington DC. Individual Indians, like me, are quite powerless.

Mother Earth is the unsung hero of all time. She has provided so very much for us Indian people, and that is why we hold her in such reverence. She deserves one hundred percent of our respect and honor. Yet, we watch sadly as she is attacked. Mountains are actually moved. Timbered areas are clear-cut. If our trees are not caught on fire during a lightning storm, human beings destroy them by cutting them all down to the quick.

Natural disasters take their toll as well. At Sandy Point, during our winter storms, the ocean water causes suffering, because the waves wash over terraces, porches, lawns, and fences, destroying or damaging homes built on sand. Natural disasters in our area include windstorms, rainstorms, flooding, and snowstorms, with snow that builds up to dangerous heights, making travel difficult. We thank our Creator every day for the safety of our homeland, as compared to New Orleans and those regions where tornadoes sweep through, taking homes and lives. Our nearby islands protect us from the dreaded nightmare of tsunami. But earthquakes hit every ten years or so. And those are frightful; one never knows when they are going to hit or just how hard. Mother Earth seems to respond in these ways to our pollution, our disregard, and our ignoring of her work for us. We must be grateful to her, because nothing is any good at any time or anywhere without "thank you." Do something for Mother Earth that would benefit her.

Trees provide oxygen and give us the power to breathe, to speak, and to sing. They provide shade and shelter. Being grateful for these things in a spiritual sense may not make sense to many, but Indians have lived by this forever. Indians pruned trees along the routes they traveled through the great Northwest's Cascade Mountains. Tribes got game and gathered cedar, firewood, and berries of all kinds, with no end of benefits. They did not need stores; our environment provided all that was needed. Indian commissioners commented on the local Indian tribes as being fully supplied by their environment, not just for fishing, but for everything else, too.

But the Stone Age was a very slowly advancing age, compared to the Iron Age of the European cultures. We invented our necessities for gathering, hunting, and fishing, as well as clothing and shelter, by working with the environment. But white America used force against the environment to get what they wanted. In addition, they had a wealth of brainy inventors. Nevertheless, several records in the Indian Affairs documents show where Indians of specific areas helped white America survive, saved them from starvation with food from our environment, and traded with them. It was not all bad, as some movies make it out to be, in their debasing Indian America. I do not accept that distorted view, because I lived life as an Indian.

We still put a claim on this land, all of it, even though we understand fully that only a small picnic patch is officially reserved for us. When I look at the land, I think of when and how Indians lived there. I know many Indians in my age group who knew how to live strictly off the land. I admired them. I participated with them in their manners of survival, and I was grateful to learn how to live off the land, as they did. Today, it is quite impossible to gather, hunt, fish, and obtain medicine from the wild, as we used to do, and impossible to get the timbers needed to build the longhouses we once had. We are dependent on the white man's ways: going to the mall, going to the food market and clothing stores for what we need, hoping we have enough money to purchase our necessities. When we do not, we just look longingly at what we could make use of, if only we had enough money to buy it. Chinook Jargon uses the word *talla* (dollar) to mean money. *Owina* means "no." So we say *owina talla* or "no money," as we walk on by. But the longing stays, until we discover ways to make up for that loss with our own creative minds and hands. That creativity is still there too, thanks be to our Greater Powers.

Lately I have learned to admire the "environmentalist" population of our society. They are focused on peace, for which I am grateful. This is one of my strongest drives, also. Many of them have heard the lonesome cry of the rivers in our country and helped with restoring native flora and fauna. It is great to watch that group at work—so strong, so cool, so efficient. I do not know what they think of Indian America, but that does not take away any gratitude I feel toward them. If only we can turn around the members of gangs and cults—get them interested in saving Mother Earth. She is calling to everyone, anyone. She is in trouble and needs all the help she can get. My father used to say: "Everybody knows something!" I say: "Get everyone involved." My mother used to say: "Be good to everyone; you never know who you may depend on one of these days, if you have some kind of trouble they may know how to solve." I try to follow my elders' advice. Of course, the Great Spirit, God, or our higher power, has something to do with this.

Mother Earth provides for every single soul on her surface, underneath her surface, or who flies above her by whatever means. If they need her, we need her, too. Our continent will show us the way; our earth makes our stability or instability. If we work with Mother Earth, she will work with us. The gift of understanding Mother Earth is a sacred gift, a spiritual gift. Prepare yourself to hear her sacred teachings. She awaits your patience.

My father had followers from all walks of life. So did my sister, Mary Ellen Hillaire. One of her greatest admirers was a female student at Evergreen State College who testified at Mary Ellen's memorial how much Mary Ellen had helped her. On her first consultation with Professor Mary Ellen Hillaire, this student told Mary Ellen that all of her previous instructors had labeled her as "uneducable." Mary Ellen took this student under her wing, following her throughout the years to her graduation. I listened to this young lady as she spoke, admiring her mode of presentation. She sounded very professional and looked as presentable as anyone I have ever met in the higher echelons of modern society. I remember all this, and I feel grateful that we are all living at such a time that we can find reason to come together with one focus: Mother Earth, our First Teacher.

THE FIRST SALMON CEREMONY

Accounted in 2008 by Scälla, Pauline Hillaire (Lummi, b. 1929)

The First Salmon Ceremony is a most sacred ceremony for Coast Salish Indians. It guaranteed the return of the salmon every year. They put away food at the end of summer; they dry and smoke and wind-dry and sun-dry salmon, berries and roots, and all the fruit from the trees. We had wild potatoes; we had wild onions, wild carrots, wild strawberries, and berries, berries and berries, everywhere you looked. We were very fortunate for the food supply, and the people dried it for the winter. They dried it, preserved it, and stored it in something like a mound, but it's called a root house. It's just a frame building covered with dirt that's built in a side hill, and that's where we stored our meat and fish and vegetables.

The Salmon Ceremony was held at the end of winter when it was still cold, around the first day of spring. As winter ends and spring is upon us, the food supply is almost gone. So everyone is worried in the village. The holy men prayed; the fishermen tried harder. These people held a sacred covenant with the Salmon People.

Who is going to catch the first salmon this year? Where will it be caught this year? There are platforms all along the river, on one side of the river every short distance; then there's another platform on the other side. They kept these areas clean for the sake of the salmon. A fisherman went out to his platform early one morning. He saw the ice chips coming down the river and he thought to himself: This might be the day. The water is not that rough, and the chips are pretty small, so it gives room for the salmon to come down. The Spring Salmon, the Chinook salmon, the King Salmon, all the same thing, all the same fish, three names: spring, king, and chinook. They call it chinook because the south wind is the chinook wind. So this man, he knew it was going to be his day. He had his pole with the net at the bottom, and sure enough his fishing pole started to quiver, and he pulled it up and there was a great big spring salmon. Oh, he was happy: "I'm the one!" he said in his heart. He wasn't boasting; he just was proud that he was the one that caught the salmon. And his little boy who was watching him ran to the village and said, "My daddy caught the first salmon!"

Oh, everybody was happy. They started to prepare for this major ceremony, the First Salmon. We have to agree with each other, as well as have a covenant with the salmon population. Our covenant with the salmon population has to do with taking care of their habitat. We had no cows, we had no horses, we had no goats; so it was quite easy to maintain a good habitat system. The fisherman took his fish up a little hill to the shore, where the medicine men met him. They got red ochre, red earth; it's usually coming out of the mouth of Mother Earth somewhere near the bottom of a hill or mountain. The red earth comes out of her mouth, and they mixed it with deer fat, or seal oil, mixed with marrow from the deer, they mix it fine (that marrow, by the way, is good for wrinkles). It is put on the fisherman's face and he's marked; he's the one special fisherman who caught the fish. And so the medicine men escort him with their medicine songs to the village and everyone at the village is lined up and making a trail to the chief's house.

They held the potlatch in the chief's house because it was the richest and the biggest. And once they're in the chief's house, the people know where they're supposed to sit, because they've lived in the village for so long, all their lives perhaps. They know that this is their seat; this belongs to one family, this belongs to another. And so they'd come in, crowding the chief's house.

The wife of the fisherman readied herself in her best regalia. She had red ochre paint on her cheeks, just her cheeks. They had a special knife, some were made out of abalone—special beautiful knives—other knives were just made of stone, but it was an insult to the salmon population to carve it with just anything, so the people had special, well-cared-for butcher knives. They left the salmon's head on, they left the tail on, and they'd cut down the back of the salmon. The salmon's head was always to be pointing to the deep part of the water, where the currents flowed all the time. The people could see where the current flowed, because it shows on the surface of the water where it's deep and where it's not. People could read that river like it was a book.

The cooks prepared the feast while the holy men chose twins from the village. Twins were chosen to carry the salmon to the nearby water on a cedar-bough raft, prepared by village basket makers. They made a woven raft of cedar bow branches, leaving the greenery, and laid the salmon's head toward the water and the tail toward the land, with the backbone still on it. And the medicine men sang their song, carrying out their agreement with the Salmon People. "Go back home and tell your people, the Salmon People, that we treat every salmon carefully and we keep their homes safe. We as fishermen want you to come back again." The fishermen and the twins took a canoe out upon the water where it was deep enough that the current flowed strong. The twins placed the salmon headfirst into the onrushing current, and the current carried the salmon out to sea, where the salmon turned back into a whole salmon, to the magic music of the holy men's song. And so this ceremony took place. The salmon would come alive by the Indian doctors singing, and it swam back into the deep part of the ocean and told the Salmon People, "The Lummi people are really good; they've been good to us, let's be good to them." Every season we sing the Salmon Song. Before the feast began, youth served water to the elders, old ladies first. The holy men sang songs of thanks to the salmon. Then everyone enjoyed the salmon feast.

My mother remarried a man in La Connor on the Swinomish reservation, and he was the one who would bring us to their Smokehouse, Longhouse, for the Salmon Ceremony, when I was a child. He would take us there, and we young people would serve everybody water. I gave water to the women, and my classmate gave water to the men. The food was first placed before the old women, who showed everyone how to eat: not greedily. Eat nicely and don't get messy. The cooks who make that salmon are very particular about who eats first. They won't feed the children, they won't feed the men; they'll feed the old ladies who show how to eat: drink a little water; then eat the food. The old women were the teachers in my day. That was the way we did when I was a child in the Smokehouse.

When we were served, then we could eat. We never played at the table; we were not permitted. We couldn't sing or whistle at the table; you had to stay right there and eat in my day. I'm seventy-nine; I must have been seven, eight, nine, ten, eleven, twelve years old all those years that I went through this type of ceremony. It wasn't until after everyone had eaten that they had the potlatch of the chief, and he would give away baskets to everyone, for them to remember his generosity.

In order to be a chief you have to have honesty, you have to have the strength that comes with it—today's word for it is *integrity*—that courage, that withstanding, that ability to face any challenge and to complete whatever the transaction calls for. But you have to have honesty, integrity, and courage to face it. And then the last thing that you have to have is generosity. Only the chiefs had abundance for the people. Every family had abundance for their family, but the chief was different: he had to have honesty, integrity, courage, and generosity for the community people.

CHAPTER 12

Poems by Joseph R. Hillaire
and Pauline R. Hillaire

PROLOGUE
from "A Wedding in Lummi History," *plans for a play by Joseph Hillaire*

From the top of this great mountain,
Across the great and mighty water
A land I view of lakes and rivers.
Wooded hills of pine and cedar
Stretching over eastward
Toward the rising of the sun. Food is
there in great abundance, in the lakes
and in the rivers.

Broad the plains where game is plenty
In the hills are roots and berries,
cedar's there to build our houses.
Would that we might share the plenty,
With our brothers in that great land.

Must we stay here on this island—at the foot of this great
   mountain? As my
people grow more mighty, how can we enlarge our borders?
   Would we gain or

lose in war? A northland people have I heard of. Even now they're
   looking
toward us. With envying eyes at this
great land. Do we want them
here among us? Would they not make trouble always? If this
   tribe across the waters and my tribe could be united in a quiet
   peaceful manner.

Could we not drive back this people—when
our lands they try to conquer? A way there is
in peace and honor
Whereby tribes may be united.
Industrious and fair are their daughters
Young and brave are our sons.
Might we not make some agreement
whereby our young ones would be wedded?
Thus would our tribes be united
and become one mighty people
Strong enough to guard our loved ones
and drive back all who would harm us.

   Joseph R. Hillaire

RED, WHITE, AND BLUE

The flag of our country is Red, White, and Blue
Ever think, search, and wonder why?
Remove the Red
from the White and Blue.
Red is what the government tried to wipe out

White represents power, and blue
Who sings the blues?
History, politics, and school
overlook the Redman's red
but not the White and the Blue.

The forgotten Redman watches
the story unfold. All he wanted
was his treaty rights secured So he can survive
like all others here
in America, once called Mother Earth
still held dear.

> Pauline R. Hillaire

NOW

There flies an eagle with lofty wings,
He's sailing smoothly, and my heart sings
now.

Here comes my puppy with her friendly eyes,
we look at each other and it's paradise
now

But to the great city I will fly
and leave behind the earth and sky
now

I'll concentrate through the smoke and dust
hear urgent sounds, but who can I trust
now

> Pauline R. Hillaire

MOTHER EARTH, FATHER SEA

A memory of love has brought me here,
to these sands along the shore.
As I sift the sands of Mother Earth,
my arms reach out for more.

As always, she stands by Father Sea,
who also cares for his own.

They teach me, in loving kindness.
Here, I am never alone.

Pauline R. Hillaire

AN EPIC TO NOWHERE

The Indian!
From the bounds of his reservation
To a city's skid row.
Once, he was happy
now, he just carries a load.
Yet even under such a load,
He cannot successfully hide
'cause when we mention the Redman,
he struts with a certain pride.

Did he cause himself to stumble
When with school's merits
He was told to go back home and
dishonor his parents?
Teach them, was their command.
Where was the reverence? Now he
proves oblivion better in
his perseverance.

He turns his back on
the scorn, misunderstanding,
tips back the bottle
and cries, "Happy landing!"
Only to hear "Forget it kid. That's not
where it's at."

No matter what the people say
This Indian only lives
He lives and learns the hard way

But what he finds, he gives!
He'll give to the one that's needier
His compassion's at a peak.

He knows they'll laugh together
Going on with a cheerful air,
For once again they feel that
they have done their share.
He doesn't look important anymore
But he still wishes someone could hear.

    Pauline R. Hillaire

THE ETERNAL FAMILY

I am an Indian
I am proud!
The mountains are my brothers.
    The streams that tumble from them
    are my brothers' voices.
Lakes set high for safety
    are my little sisters.
    They're shy to make great noises.
Trees are our guardians, they guard us very well.
    Everything they do,
    they do perfectly.
Flowers are our visitors.
    Throughout every year
    they visit very often.
Mother Earth is kind to me, she feeds me.
    Her breasts are very full,
    herbs, roots, and berries are always in her basket.
Father Sea challenges me
    every season
    to hunt the fish he nurtures.

I am an Indian!
   I am proud.
   This is my family.

     Pauline R. Hillaire

THERE IS SOMEONE GREATER THAN I

There is Someone greater than I
   for this is where He's been.
There is Someone greater than I
   for this is what He's given me.

Behold, the forest of flowers that welcome every prayer.
Pick the red, juicy berry
   crush it with grateful lips.
Walk the cool earth with bare feet, feel its vital kindness
   as the scent of the sea and of rich soil.
Join us in the harvest.

There is Someone greater than I
   for this is where He's been.
There is Someone greater than I
   for this is what He's given me.

     Pauline R. Hillaire
     These words come from my father, Joe Hillaire. His words did turn into
     poetry.

CEDAR TREE

O Cedar Tree, where are you?
   my tears fall like rain
   from clouds that cover the day.
My heart pounds like thunders
   from many storms.
Where are you? You were once here.

O Cedar Tree, if we cannot find you
    how will our babies sleep
    without your comforting hands?
Their homes may never be blessed
    with the outpour of gifts from your bounty.

Cedar Tree, where are you?
    You were once right here.

Cedar Tree, your shadows we crave
    to hide our lonely hearts in coolness.
Please come back to heal our needs.
    Your people need you, like the sun needs sky.
Where are you? You were once right here.

Cedar Tree! *Sumewassintalh Siem.*
    Why was the circle broken,
    once more shattered?
Craft our lives and living
    together again
    with your strong arms
    and maidens in graceful lace.

O, Cedar Tree! Where are you?
You were once here, *Siem.*

    Pauline R. Hillaire

TO OUR FRIENDS, THE SALMON

O, Salmon People, bold and free
Swimmers, wise in the ways of the deep
Sharing faith

Coming to see the land of your friends
Friends vowing to do their best,
Sharing faith with each other

With thankful hearts and loving care
We open our arms and raise our hands to you
in welcome!

Pauline R. Hillaire

GREAT SPIRIT

What the Great Spirit means to me:
The essence of life of Mother Earth
life forces of Father Sea
my existence and life as their child
and the love that binds us together

Pauline R. Hillaire

I KNOW WHERE GOD LIVES

I know where God lives, son
echoing words of an elder mom
vision floating with the shade of
day's setting sun touching
into your soul, my son
a silent, gentle prayer. Hear
His voice in the stillest silence

from His heart as big as the sky,
scattered, shining dew drops
after the miracle of rain, His
blessings will show you where
God lives, my son

Pauline R. Hillaire

CHILDREN OF THE SETTING SUN

We are the children of the setting sun
Not by choice but fate's inevitable hand
The splendor of that day lingers still
We bask in its glory for Auld Lang Syne

Farewell to these sandy gray shores we knew
In reverent silence from skimming canoe
The hillsides we hunted from dawn 'til night
Tribal games we played in contests of might

The high leaping flame of ceremonial fire
The dance praying out spirit desire
Farewell and behind me, that web is spun
We are the Children of the Setting Sun

Joseph R. Hillaire

CHAPTER 13

History in the Time of the Treaty of Point Elliott

An Oration by Joseph R. Hillaire

My father, Joseph R. Hillaire, Kwul-kwul'tʷ, Spirit of the War Club (Lummi, 1894–1967), was a fine orator. He gave the following speech, about the history of the treaty period, at the Makah Reservation in northwest coastal Washington in the early 1960s. It was recorded by Mr. R. O. Bishop. This transcription is from the archives of Pauline Hillaire.

Once long ago when the great trees covered all this beautiful land, the waters of the *Whulge* (Puget Sound) swirled with salmon, numerous as the stars in the sky. For the most part, the wild animals moved about without fear as the Indian lived in peace with all nature. Nature was his protector, and the great white sentinels stood watch: Kulshan, Mt. Baker, guarded the approaches to the north; Tahoma and Mt. Rainier protected the south. It is said that their snows were so pure that gods used their vaulting slopes for play, and in doing so, their life force entered the snow to later melt and run off into the lower valleys. This is why old chiefs would sample water coming into camp and say, "Ah, there is life in this water."

Nature provided the salmon from the sea and the clams from the beach. The berries and herbs were his for the taking. The Black Bear shared not only the berries, but also his hide with the Indians. The deer was chased down for his skin and the meat he provided. Consequently, he killed only what was needed for food and furs. He fished just enough to supply sun-dried salmon to last his tribe through the long winters.

The great chiefs lived and died one after another. Life did not change much from year to year, as there was no necessity for change. The wave of the white men's future had not yet fallen on the shores of the Island called Ike, the foundation of that great lodge pole that everyone knows supports the arch of the sky. Beneath that inverted bowl, all was well. Our medicine was good. Our children were many. The Great Spirit was with us and had not forgotten his red children. Even the water-roaming Haidas, the fierce Vikings of the north, could not seriously upset the yearly pattern of our lives. The warriors from the east, the Yakamas, rarely came through the lands where lived the People of the Sky.

So, the young men of Suquamish raced their canoes. They wrestled, Indian style, leg to leg. They threw their spears at cedar stumps and plunked their arrows alongside for good measure. The young women were prepared for the time when they would take their places as wives and caretakers of the children. It was not uncommon to observe in the village a woman shredding cedar bark for mats and cloth. They learned to preserve and dry the berries, how to cut up salmon into strips for sun drying, how to make the leather goods, and in general, the cycle of village life did not change.

The ceremonial dances were taught by the elders, and the totems were carved. The young people were the same as any other group of young people in any society, anywhere. And they were of no small concern to their elders, who would yearn for the good old days as they worried for the tribe's future, while they watched the young braves wrestle and play with bones.

Slahál—Slahál. Gamble they must, but the roll of the bones held a secret from them that had been only dimly revealed by old men's tales that spoke of other people in other places, much like themselves, but with faces like that of the moon.

And so to a very notable person from the Skagit of Goliah's people, and to an equally important person from Suquamish, a baby was born. This young one was destined to live many years and to lead his people most of that time, bringing credit to the House of Skagit and to the longhouse of Suquamish. The seasons changed and much water made its way through Agate Pass. The baby developed into manhood. He became the greatest of the tribe, being feared and known as far north as the Queen Charlottes. It was he, along with Chief Schweabe, father of the future Chief Seattle, who was to lead a war party of almost two hundred canoes to Vancouver Island and inflict such damage to the Haidas that they stayed away for many years from the waters of Salmon Bay, where once lived the Shilshoe, and from the lower waters of the *Whulge*. Chief Kitsap had very strong medicine, and his mind soared to places his people could not follow. As some of the other Northwest Indians believed that the fire watch would allow their souls to travel to the farthest star, so did his mind travel over things that could and would happen during his future life.

Now, Kitsap had reason to meditate on his life. The vitality of his life was so great and his psychic forces too strong for his loved ones to endure, and he found himself in deep sorrow and grief over the death of his children. Yet he could not give way entirely, for he was the rock that made the Suquamish firm. He was immovable.

During this period of concentration, when he was examining his life and his thoughts, in a dream, if you please, it came to him that a great canoe with wings would come from the waters north of the *Whulge*. The people would be of pale skin and speak a language that only he, Chief Kitsap, would understand. At this the younger ones, who in every society are the doubters, would shake their heads and say, "Ha! These chiefs and their dreams. Pale faces and a canoe with wings! Chief Kitsap must have been flying with the Thunderbird!" Of course, they were careful not to let the great chief hear them say these words.

So, the elders watched the young, for they were always on the alert for exceptional children. When one was found, every effort was made to teach him all aspects of their culture before the child reached puberty. This applied to girls, also. So, it was not necessary to be a chief's son to become a leader, but when you were already a leader's son, how much better it was. This was how Schweabe's son, Seattle, came to the attention of Kitsap, who was like an uncle to him and let him stand near him at the tribal councils. So, in the game of time, the bets were made, the bones of the years rolled and moved the youth to old age. Kitsap's vision had been all but forgotten by his tribesmen.

So, on this day in May, nothing seemed out of the ordinary. Kitsap and some of his braves, young and old alike, were at Bemis Point near Blakely Rocks. Perhaps they were after clams or fish, but in any respect, there is nothing to indicate that this was anything but a normal day for them. Some of the younger braves were on the beach when it happened. They looked to the north and came running up to Kitsap. "Run! Run!" they cried. "Hat Island is loose and is drifting down the *Whulge*!" And they headed for the *Sla-lal* brush, but Kitsap stood his ground and remained calm, assuring them that no harm would come, that this was the fulfillment of his old dream.

After some time passed, a long boat came ashore and offered to take some of the Indians to the ship. The great canoe had come to rest, and Kitsap, along with Schweabe, circled the ship and made the magic circle so no evil could come. The next day, the story goes, Kitsap boarded the ship and was hired as a pilot to Captain Vancouver. He spent some time taking them up sound and returned. Of course, his prediction having come true raised his stature among his own people. But he probably observed enough from being with the white man to realize that the Indian had to live in peace with him if he were to live at all.

When Vancouver returned Kitsap to Agate Pass, it was a time of giving on the part of the white man. Some say it was three canoes of strange food, blankets and things of iron. Of course, there was that jug of "tagum" that the Indians tried to use as caulking material, like pitch, until they tasted it and found it good. Black strap molasses was never more appreciated. "See, my people," cried Kitsap. "This *tyee* [leader] doesn't just speak with his mouth but he gives with his hands, as befits one chief to another."

In the next season Kitsap recommended to the tribal council that Old Man House be built. For he was a man of pride and when the moonfaced ones returned, he wanted to impress them with the knowledge that the Suquamish could do big things, too. So a wide search was conducted to find the proper location for Old Man House. It had to meet many requirements. First it had to be where lookouts could see, not only up the inland sea, but also down the sound. It had to be where there was protection from the elements. There had to be fresh water, and the trees had to be available for the house itself. Probably the planning and construction took many years. But the history and the memory of our people has it that it was about 1816 when the structure was finally complete.

The building of the house was the biggest cooperative effort ever put forth by the Suquamish. Each family would bring planks or thongs, or give of time to help dig the foundation. A strong spirit of competition arose and everyone tried to outdo his neighbor. "When the whiteman comes again," said Kitsap, "this house will be our arms to receive him." Vancouver wasn't going to return; but the chief could not know this.

Finally, in order to complete the house, Chief Kitsap held a huge potlatch. Forty deer were chased down to provide meat for the expected guests. Many baskets of clams were dug and this was long before the time of Ivar. Berries were picked and salmon prepared for baking. Canoes were sent to Hyus Chuck (Lake Washington), to gather wapatoes. Perhaps some of them were harvested from the swampy area between Tenas Church, Lake Union, and Skookumchuck, Elliot Bay, which later became known as the site of largest potlatch ever: the Seattle World's Fair.

It was at this time that Kitsap became sure in his own mind that Seattle would be his successor. The Duwamish chief was given a special place in Old Man House so that he was host of all who came there and visited. After he was accorded this honor, instead of staying among his people at Duwamish, near Pidgeon Point in Seattle, he spent more and more time at Old Man House and became very familiar with the people in Suquamish. So now Seattle the man shared the honors with his mentor, Kitsap. Both chiefs had a larger view of the entire situation than the average brave. Both chiefs knew from the beginning that they must live in peace with the whiteman, for they realized that the white *tyees* had weapons the Indians could not match.

So, for thirty years, Kitsap and Seattle shared the honors of Old Man House and waited. The Oregon Territory was established and Lane became Governor. Lincoln refused the chance to be the second governor and went on to be president. The boundary dispute was semi-settled with Great Britain, and Chief Kitsap, that old warrior, before he took the long trip that has no return, expressed satisfaction that the King George man had withdrawn and that the Boston man had raised his flag high. Now Seattle was really alone; he had no wise old fighter to advise him. It was with heavy heart that he saw the body of his old and beloved teacher carried out of Old Man House, his arms folded, his spirit out ahead of him. There are those who say that the old chief was placed in a canoe and the caressing waters of the blue green *Whulge* lofted him away on the tide. But those who really know say that grandfather Kitsap was laid to rest behind a high boulder on the large Island, Bainbridge; and if you but find the rock, there will you find Kitsap.

Now the settlement on the Skookumchuck and the name of Du Wamps had been given them by some eastern mapmaker, so in January of 1853 they decided to use Chief Seattle's name for their settlement. This upset the chief for he knew there would be no rest for him in the spirit world if his name were forever being called. But in later years it was a source to him that the Boston man loved him enough to use his name for their village.

He, by this time was more sedate and dignified and he could be found either at Port Blakely or in Old Man House seated in his big chair, and the youths would bring water to take to their lodges and he would taste it. "Very good," he would say to each one. "There is life in this water." It was during this same important one half decade that the first missionary started to teach. The Indians were very pleased, for Father Chirouse taught in the Snohomish language and consequently, most every tribe on the Sound learned to pray and sing the church songs in a tongue they formerly could not understand.

But the time was when the people of the chiefs were to meet with the little man who talked so tall for the Great White Father. Governor Stevens was at Point Elliot, known now as Mukilteo, to await them and his fireboat was off the shore. "My Children, My Children," he said, "your wants are known to the Great White Father. Your heart is my heart and his heart. He will care for you on land of your own and pay you well for land that you sell to us."

Now, Governor Stevens was in a hurry. He had been to Washington and had pointed out that because of this Oregon Donation Act of 1850, many whitemen were already on reservation land; he knew this would lead to trouble, so he spoke as softly as the mist falling on the grass. He had learned with Leschi at Medicine Creek that the harsh words and preemptory orders would only arouse resentment.

The chief and his people listened as the Governor spelled out that this treaty would be the same as that with the Great Indian Nations beyond the shiny mountains. Schools would be built, carpenters sent and the Great White Father would look on them as his own children. The tribe was numbered and told that a large amount of money would be paid in annuities: $150,000 in annuities and $15,000 to improve the reservation. The tribes could hunt and fish where they had always done these things, as long as the sun should shine and as long as the grass was green.

Then Stevens asked the chiefs how they stood and the Indian leaders showed their hearts, having believed his words and made their marks on the treaty. And then it was the sign of the cross they made on themselves and the shout rang out of dusky throats. *Hip hip hooray! Hip hip hooray!*

Bits of ribbon and little squares torn of blankets were passed out in a symbolic potlatch. The little *tyee* with the sweet words left and went down sound to the Makahs to attempt further treaties. The circle of events was going faster and faster. And the cry of people seeking to understand shrilled in every village.

Then in the winter of that same year, Colonel Simmons told Seattle that if his people were to share in the payments, they must move to Old Man House or that area. The sad exodus began. Away from their beloved sweet flowing Duwamish, away from the Tenas Chuck. Apart from their dead who must stay behind to watch over strange whitemen, who lived in a way no red spirit could understand. And when they got to Agate Pass, they found only two sections of land awaiting them. But move they did, for Seattle's word was good. Dr. Maynard's purse was nearly empty before it was over. He paid for all the expenses, for no funds were forthcoming from the government for that purpose. Chief

Seattle was hurt by the treatment, for the Treaty at Point Elliott was not one dictated to a beaten foe, but an agreement where the five big counties that are now King, Kitsap, Whatcom, Island, and part of Snohomish were sold for certain conditions.

There came the dark times and through an interpretation of the treaty, the tribes were no longer allowed to sing their tribal songs, not allowed to do their ancient dances, denied the Indian custom of bewailing their dead. What they heretofore had been proud of, they now had to do in secret or not at all. It was a bad time to be an Indian.

The old chiefs were daily leaving this troubled land never to return and a decade passed. The Boston Man came each year to pay on the monies promised at Point Elliott. It seldom was money. Sometimes it would be in shoes, with copper toes. Or perhaps a man would receive a saddle, complete with bridle. He, who had never owned a horse. Would it fit his wife?

The years drummed by and the Whiteman's economy passed the Indian by. He could not sell his land and had little to work it with. In other parts of the territory the late Indian Wars raged but for the most part the Suquamish were able to stay out of it.

Chief Seattle was deeply troubled in his heart when Leschi threw his own words back at him, "Join with us or we all die." But Seattle was true to his heart, even though it was apparent that the Great White Father would be slow in keeping his word, if at all.

This was a lonely time for Seattle. Governor Stevens now looked through him instead of at him. The old chief must have thought the grass had ceased to be green. With trouble all about him and many of his former comrades now calling him to fight with them against the whites, Seattle remained firm. There was room for all. But six years passed and the old man weakened. He sickened and passed, loved by many; hated by some of his own people, unsure in his own mind if he had done well. No doubt he often thought how things might have been had he followed the counsel of Leschi or Pat Kanim. But for him, the roll of the bones was over. The whiteman and the redman laid him to rest in the little graveyard overlooking Agate Pass and the gulls of peace dipped and soared.

The news of the Civil War impelled Stevens to forego his possible election to Congress and he volunteered his services to the president. He with the soft tongue but with a mind like a snare now fought with guns instead of words. He fell in the Battle of Chantilly, a servant of the Union.

He, too, did not find peace, but he was in good company, for neither did Seattle, Leschi, Kitsap, Pat Kanim, Goliah, Schweabe, or Chief Joseph. The critics of these people continue to harp until this very day, but as another great American has said, "The critic is not the one who counts, not the one who points out how the strong man stumbles, or how the doer of good deeds could have done them better. The man the credit is due is he who is actually in the arena; his face covered with blood, sweat, and tears, for him after long effort comes the high feeling of achievement, or should he fail after trying time and time again, he shall at least know his place will never be with those poor souls who have never tried at all."

It was fitting that now Old Man House should now be all but gone. The army considered putting a fort there to guard the entrance to Agate Pass. The old chiefs were gone and their home was gone. The Indian Training Schools were in operation. The younger tribesmen were now reading of the history of the whole country, instead of knowing just a sectional view of it. The schools were run with a military type of discipline and the young ones, who had always been trained to respect authority, responded readily and in later years it was to stand them in good stead.

In 1911, the veil of silence that had the Indian Culture was broken up; no longer could an interpretation of the treaty be twisted to forbid the rituals. The damper was lifted by Chief William Shelton of the Snohomish, who managed to get congressional consent for elders of the tribe under the Point Elliot Treaty to celebrate the anniversary by the singing of the ancient songs and performance of the tribal dances. Now, I'm not positive if it were written in the treaty, but for long years the Suquamish were not allowed to sing their songs. Even the burial ceremonies were changed so that the Indian could not show his grief in the ways of his people from time immemorial. These restrictions contributed to the lack of development on the reservations. If the mind is shackled, it is hard for the body to perform. But after Chief Shelton made his successful appeal, the tribes began to recount the promises that had been made. They began again to be proud of being Indians. The original signers were gone but the children remembered what father had said and what grandfather had said. The treaty would do this, and, the treaty would do that. But we children do not see it done.

So at Lummi in 1912 a longhouse was built and the people gathered. At La Conner the longhouse went up and the people remembered. Finally, in 1915, a large longhouse was built at Tulalip by Chief Shelton and his people. Even the Yakamas attended the conclaves. The annual get-togethers and the yearly recounting of the wrongs of the treaty due to the non-performance by the government led to a yearning for redress and in 1914, Thomas Bishop, of the Chimakum Tribe, Hood Canal, organized the Northwest Federation of American Indians to speak for the desires of Indians of Puget Sound. The Federation encompassed all the tribes under the treaties made with Governor Stevens of the United States Government at Point Elliott (Mukilteo), Washington.

The first great World War was in progress, and in 1917 along with other Americans, the Indians all over this great land began to volunteer for the armed services. Of course, under the Indian Treaties, they were not supposed to bear arms, but the army looked the other way, and they rendered faithful and brave service. It is believed that their service and valor fighting for this country was a contributing factor in the decision to grant them the right to vote. On June 6, 1924, Calvin Coolidge signed the Proclamation giving the vote to the original American.

At long last, these, our people, who had lived so many centuries on and in this beautiful land, now had full and equal rights to vote and to carry on the duties of citizenship. So here we stand: Look about you, red man and white man. Is there so much difference? I have often said I do not think it was a mere accident the stripes of our flag are red and white. It was the close relationship between the two races, the red and the white, and together they choose their leaders to shine as stars in the blue field of service.

Afterword

And to My Father

There are no words left; my heart is filled with tears of love and gratitude to you, my father here on earth. I, your ignorant child, lay my heart before you, asking the Great Spirit to bless us both in our efforts. It was a long road for you long ago, and it remains a long road for us. Your portrait, gracing these four walls, brings such admiration. The artist did a fine job of painting you, and his vision of all that he painted around you is truly the best an artist could bring to view for the world to see.

God provided me with one of the finest role models in all history, you. Elders like you are rapidly disappearing from our world. Remembering all that you, and they, have taught us in those tense moments long ago, even when our culture was removed from us, I retained so much from you, and all the elders that God put into my life. Still, in this moment, you are taking care of me, for I tell the legends that you told to me. I tell the legends of your totem poles, which I see as messages for all time, and for all people. Your foresight, like the foresight of the great Chief Seattle, is beyond the reach of our poor minds. But the longer we remember you, the more we learn. And with each memory, angels are disguised as blessings in my midst, surrounding me.

I simply pray that God, the Great Spirit, our Creator, stay with us, guide and guard us, as we bring your message to the world of our friends everywhere.

APPENDIX 1

Treaty of Point Elliott, 1855

Articles of agreement and convention made and concluded at Múcklte-óh, or Point Elliott, in the Territory of Washington, this twenty-second day of January, eighteen hundred and fifty-five, by Isaac I. Stevens, governor and superintendent of Indian affairs for the said Territory, on the part of the United States, and the undersigned chiefs, head-men and delegates of the Dwámish, Suquámish, Sk-táhlmish, Sam-áhmish, Smalh-kamish, Skope-áhmish, St-káh-mish, Snoquálmoo, Skai-wha-mish, N'Quentl-má-mish, Sk-táh-le-jum, Stoluck-whá-mish, Sha-ho-mish, Skágit, Kik-i-állus, Swin-á-mish, Squin-áh-mish, Sah-ku-méhu, Noo-whá-ha, Nook-wa-cháh-mish, Mee-sée-qua-quilch, Cho-bah-áh-bish, and other allied and subordinate tribes and bands of Indians occupying certain lands situated in said Territory of Washington, on behalf of said tribes, and duly authorized by them.

ARTICLE 1.

The said tribes and bands of Indians hereby cede, relinquish, and convey to the United States all their right, title, and interest in and to the lands and country occupied by them, bounded and described as follows: Commencing at a point on the eastern side of Admiralty Inlet, known as Point Pully, about midway between Commencement and Elliott Bays; thence eastwardly, running along the north line of lands heretofore ceded to the United States by the Nisqually, Puyallup, and other Indians, to the summit of the Cascade range of mountains; thence northwardly, following the summit of said range to the 49th parallel of north latitude; thence west, along said parallel to the middle of the Gulf of Georgia; thence through the middle of said gulf and the main channel through the Canal de Arro to the Straits of Fuca, and crossing the same through the middle of Admiralty Inlet to Suquamish Head; thence southwesterly, through the peninsula, and following the divide between Hood's Canal and Admiralty Inlet to the portage known as Wilkes' Portage; thence northeastwardly, and following the line of lands heretofore ceded as aforesaid to Point Southworth, on the western side of Admiralty Inlet, and thence around the foot of Vashon's Island eastwardly and southeastwardly to the place of beginning, including all the islands comprised within said boundaries, and all the right, title, and interest of the said tribes and bands to any lands within the territory of the United States.

ARTICLE 2.

There is, however, reserved for the present use and occupation of the said tribes and bands the following tracts of land, viz: the amount of two sections, or twelve hundred and eighty acres, surrounding the small bight at the head of Port Madison, called by the Indians Noo-sohk-um; the amount of two sections, or twelve hundred and eighty acres, on the north side Hwhomish Bay and the creek emptying into the same called Kwilt-seh-da, the peninsula at the southeastern end of Perry's Island, called Shális-quihl, and the island called Chah-choo-sen, situated in the Lummi River at the point of separation of the mouths emptying respectively into Bellingham Bay and the Gulf of Georgia. All which tracts shall be set apart, and so far as necessary surveyed and marked out for their exclusive use; nor shall any white man be permitted to reside upon the same without permission of the said tribes or bands, and of the superintendent or agent, but, if necessary for the public convenience, roads may be run through the said reserves, the Indians being compensated for any damage thereby done them.

ARTICLE 3.

There is also reserved from out the lands hereby ceded the amount of thirty-six sections, or one township of land, on the northeastern shore of Port Gardner, and north of the mouth of Snohomish River, including Tulalip Bay and the before-mentioned Kwilt-seh-da Creek, for the purpose of establishing thereon an agricultural and industrial school, as hereinafter mentioned and agreed, and with a view of ultimately drawing thereto and settling thereon all the Indians living west of the Cascade Mountains in said Territory. Provided, however, that the President may establish the central agency and general reservation at such other point as he may deem for the benefit of the Indians.

ARTICLE 4.

The said tribes and bands agree to remove to and settle upon the said first above-mentioned reservations within one year after the ratification of this treaty, or sooner, if the means are furnished them. In the meantime it shall be lawful for them to reside upon any land not in the actual claim and occupation of citizens of the United States, and upon any land claimed or occupied, if with the permission of the owner.

ARTICLE 5.

The right of taking fish at usual and accustomed grounds and stations is further secured to said Indians in common with all citizens of the Territory, and of erecting temporary houses for the purposes of curing, together with the privilege of hunting and gathering roots and berries on open and unclaimed lands. Provided, however, that they shall not take shell-fish from any beds staked or cultivated by citizens.

ARTICLE 6.

In consideration of the above cession, the United States agree to pay to the said tribes and bands the sum of one hundred and fifty thousand dollars, in the following manner—that is to say: For the first year after the ratification hereof, fifteen thousand dollars; for the next two year, twelve thousand dollars each year; for the next three years, ten thousand dollars each year; for the next four years, seven thousand five hundred dollars each years; for the next five years, six thousand dollars each year; and for the last five years, four thousand two hundred and fifty dollars each year. All which said sums of money shall be applied to the use and benefit of the said Indians, under the direction of the President of the United States, who may, from time to time, determine at his discretion upon what beneficial objects to expend the same; and the superintendent of Indian affairs, or other proper officer, shall each year inform the President of the wishes of said Indians in respect thereto.

ARTICLE 7.

The President may hereafter, when in his opinion the interests of the Territory shall require and the welfare of the said Indians be promoted, remove them from either or all of the special reservations hereinbefore made to the said general reservation, or such other suitable place within said Territory as he may deem fit, on remunerating them for their improvements and the expenses of such removal, or may consolidate them with other friendly tribes or bands; and he may further at his discretion cause the whole or any portion of the lands hereby reserved, or of such other land as may be selected in lieu thereof, to be surveyed into lots, and assign the same to such individuals or families as are willing to avail themselves of the privilege, and will locate on the same as a permanent home on the same terms and subject to the same regulations as are provided in the sixth article of the treaty with the Omahas, so far as the same may be applicable. Any substantial improvements heretofore made by any Indian, and which he shall be compelled to abandon in consequence of this treaty, shall be valued under the direction of the President and payment made accordingly therefor.

ARTICLE 8.

The annuities of the aforesaid tribes and bands shall not be taken to pay the debts of individuals.

ARTICLE 9.

The said tribes and bands acknowledge their dependence on the Government of the United States, and promise to be friendly with all citizens thereof, and they pledge themselves to commit no depredations on the property of such citizens. Should any one or more of them violate this pledge, and the fact be satisfactorily proven before the agent, the property taken shall be returned, or in default thereof, of if injured or destroyed, compensation may be made by the Government out of their annuities. Nor will they make war on any other tribe except in self-defence, but will submit all matters of difference between them and the other Indians to the Government of the United States or its agent for decision, and abide thereby. And if any of the said Indians commit depredations on other Indians within the Territory the same rule shall prevail as that prescribed in this article in cases of depredations against citizens. And the said tribes agree not to shelter or conceal offenders against the laws of the United States, but to deliver them up to the authorities for trial.

ARTICLE 10.

The above tribes and bands are desirous to exclude from their reservations the use of ardent spirits, and to prevent their people from drinking the same, and therefore it is provided that any Indian belonging to said tribe who is guilty of bringing liquor into said reservations, or who drinks liquor, may have his or her proportion of the annuities withheld from him or her for such time as the President may determine.

ARTICLE 11.

The said tribes and bands agree to free all slaves now held by them and not to purchase or acquire others hereafter.

ARTICLE 12.

The said tribes and bands further agree not to trade at Vancouver's Island or elsewhere out of the dominions of the United States, nor shall foreign

Indians be permitted to reside in their reservations without consent of the superintendent or agent.

ARTICLE 13.

To enable the said Indians to remove to and settle upon their aforesaid reservations, and to clear, fence, and break up a sufficient quantity of land for cultivation, the United States further agree to pay the sum of fifteen thousand dollars to be laid out and expended under the direction of the President and in such manner as he shall approve.

ARTICLE 14.

The United States further agree to establish at the general agency for the district of Puget's Sound, within one year from the ratification hereof, and to support for a period of twenty years, an agricultural and industrial school, to be free to children of the said tribes and bands in common with those of the other tribes of said district, and to provide the said school with a suitable instructor or instructors, and also to provide a smithy and carpenter's shop, and furnish them with the necessary tools, and employ a blacksmith, carpenter, and farmer for the like term of twenty years to instruct the Indians in their respective occupations. And the United States finally agree to employ a physician to reside at the said central agency, who shall furnish medicine and advice to their sick, and shall vaccinate them; the expenses of said school, shops, persons employed, and medical attendance to be defrayed by the United States, and not deducted from the annuities.

ARTICLE 15.

This treaty shall be obligatory on the contracting parties as soon as the same shall be ratified by the President and Senate of the United States.

In testimony whereof, the said Isaac I. Stevens, governor and superintendent of Indian affairs, and the undersigned chiefs, headmen, and delegates of the aforesaid tribes and bands of Indians, have hereunto

set their hands and seals, at the place and on the day and year hereinbefore written:

*I. Stevens, Governor and Superintendent. [L. S. (locus sigilli, "place of
the seal")]*

Seattle, Chief of the Dwamish and Suquamish tribes, his x mark. [L. S.]

*Pat-ka-nam, Chief of the Snoqualmoo, Snohomish and other tribes, his x
mark. [L. S.]*

Chow-its-hoot, Chief of the Lummi and other tribes, his x mark. [L. S.]

Goliah, Chief of the Skagits and other allied tribes, his x mark. [L. S.]

*Kwallattum, or General Pierce, Subchief of the Skagit tribe, his x mark.
[L. S.]*

S'hootst-hoot, Subchief of Snohomish, his x mark. [L. S.]

Snah-talc, or Bonaparte, Subchief of Snohomish, his x mark. [L. S.]

Squush-um, or The Smoke, Subchief of the Snoqualmoo, his x mark. [L. S.]

See-alla-pa-han, or The Priest, Su-chief of Sk-tah-le-jum, his x mark. [L. S.]

*He-uch-ka-nam, or George Bonaparte, Subchief of Snohomish, his x mark.
[L. S.]*

Tse-nah-talc, or Joseph Bonaparte, Subchief of Snohomish, his x mark. [L. S.]

Ns'ski-oos, or Jackson, Subchief of Snohomish, his x mark. [L. S.]

*Wats-ka-lah-tchie, or John Hobtsthoot, Subchief of Snohomish, his x mark.
[L. S.]*

Smeh-mai-hu, Subchief of Skaiwha-mish, his x mark. [L. S.]

Slat-eah-ka-nam, Subchief of Snoqualmoo, his x mark. [L. S.]

St'hau-ai, Subchief of Snoqualmoo, his x mark. [L. S.]

Lugs-ken, Subchief of Skai-wha-mish, his x mark. [L. S.]

S'heht-soolt, or Peter, Subchief of Snohomish, his x mark. [L. S.]

Do-queh-oo-satl, Snoqualmoo tribe, his x mark. [L. S.]

John Kanam, Snoqualmoo subchief, his x mark. [L. S.]

Klemsh-ka-nam, Snoqualmoo, his x mark. [L. S.]

Ts'huahntl, Dwa-mish subchief, his x mark. [L. S.]

Kwuss-ka-nam, or George Snatelum, Sen., Skagit tribe, his x mark. [L. S.]

Hel-mits, or George Snatelum, Skagit subchief, his x mark. [L. S.]

S'kwai-kwi, Skagit tribe, subchief, his x mark. [L. S.]

Seh-lek-qu, Subchief Lummi tribe, his x mark. [L. S.]

S'h'-cheh-oos, or General Washington, Subchief of Lummi tribe, his x mark.
    [L. S.]

Whai-lan-hu, or Davy Crockett, Subchief of Lummi tribe, his x mark. [L. S.]

She-ah-delt-hu, Subchief of Lummi tribe, his x mark. [L. S.]

Kwult-seh, Subchief of Lummi tribe, his x mark. [L. S.]

Kwull-et-hu, Lummi tribe, his x mark. [L. S.]

Kleh-kent-soot, Skagit tribe, his x mark. [L. S.]

Sohn-heh-ovs, Skagit tribe, his x mark. [L. S.]

S'deh-ap-kan, or General Warren, Skagit tribe, his x mark. [L. S.]

Chul-whil-tan, Subchief of Suquamish tribe, his x mark. [L. S.]

Ske-eh-tum, Skagit tribe, his x mark. [L. S.]

Patchkanam, or Dome, Skagit tribe, his x mark. [L. S.]

Sats-Kanam, Squin-ah-nush tribe, his x mark. [L. S.]

Sd-zo-mahtl, Kik-ial-lus band, his x mark. [L. S.]

Dahtl-de-min, Subchief of Sah-ku-meh-hu, his x mark. [L. S.]

Sd'zek-du-num, Me-sek-wi-guilse subchief, his x mark. [L. S.]

Now-a-chais, Subchief of Dwamish, his x mark. [L. S.]

Mis-lo-tche, or Wah-hehl-tchoo, Subchief of Suquamish, his x mark. [L. S.]

Sloo-noksh-tan, or Jim, Suquamish tribe, his x mark. [L. S.]

Moo-whah-lad-hu, or Jack, Suquamish tribe, his x mark. [L. S.]

Too-leh-plan, Suquamish tribe, his x mark. [L. S.]

Ha-seh-doo-an, or Keo-kuck, Dwamish tribe, his x mark. [L. S.]

Hoovilt-meh-tum, Subchief of Suquamish, his x mark. [L. S.]

We-ai-pah, Skaiwhamish tribe, his x mark. [L. S.]

S'ah-an-hu, or Hallam, Snohomish tribe, his x mark. [L. S.]

She-hope, or General Pierce, Skagit tribe, his x mark. [L. S.]

Hwn-lah-lakq, or Thomas Jefferson, Lummi tribe, his x mark. [L. S.]

Cht-simpt, Lummi tribe, his x mark. [L. S.]

Tse-sum-ten, Lummi tribe, his x mark. [L. S.]

Klt-hahl-ten, Lummi tribe, his x mark. [L. S.]

Kut-ta-kanam, or John, Lummi tribe, his x mark. [L. S.]

Ch-lah-ben, Noo-qua-cha-mish band, his x mark. [L. S.]

Noo-heh-oos, Snoqualmoo tribe, his x mark. [L. S.]
Hweh-uk, Snoqualmoo tribe, his x mark. [L. S.]
Peh-nus, Skai-whamish tribe, his x mark. [L. S.]
Yim-ka-dam, Snoqualmoo tribe, his x mark. [L. S.]
Twooi-as-kut, Skaiwhamish tribe, his x mark. [L. S.]
Luch-al-kanam, Snoqualmoo tribe, his x mark. [L. S.]
S'hoot-kanam, Snoqualmoo tribe, his x mark. [L. S.]
Sme-a-kanam, Snoqualmoo tribe, his x mark. [L. S.]
Sad-zis-keh, Snoqualmoo, his x mark. [L. S.]
Heh-mahl, Skaiwhamish band, his x mark. [L. S.]
Charley, Skagit tribe, his x mark. [L. S.]
Sampson, Skagit tribe, his x mark. [L. S.]
John Taylor, Snohomish tribe, his x mark. [L. S.]
Hatch-kwentum, Skagit tribe, his x mark. [L. S.]
Yo-i-kum, Skagit tribe, his x mark. [L. S.]
T'kwa-ma-han, Skagit tribe, his x mark. [L. S.]
Sto-dum-kan, Swinamish band, his x mark. [L. S.]
Be-lole, Swinamish band, his x mark. [L. S.]
D'zo-lole-gwam-hu, Skagit tribe, his x mark. [L. S.]
Steh-shail, William, Skaiwhamish band, his x mark. [L. S.]
Kel-kahl-tsoot, Swinamish tribe, his x mark. [L. S.]
Pat-sen, Skagit tribe, his x mark. [L. S.]
Pat-teh-us, Noo-wha-ah subchief, his x mark. [L. S.]
S'hoolk-ka-nam, Lummi subchief, his x mark. [L. S.]
Ch-lok-suts, Lummi subchief, his x mark. [L. S.]

Executed in the presence of us—
M. T. Simmons, Indian agent.
C. H. Mason, Secretary of Washington Territory.
Benj. F. Shaw, Interpreter.
Chas. M. Hitchcock.
H. A. Goldsborough.
George Gibbs.
John H. Scranton.

Henry D. Cock.
S. S. Ford, Jr.
Orrington Cushman.
Ellis Barnes.
R. S. Bailey.
S. M. Collins.
Lafayetee Balch.
E. S. Fowler.
J. H. Hall.
Rob't Davis.

APPENDIX 2

United Nations Declaration on the Rights
of Indigenous Peoples, 2007

Resolution adopted by the General Assembly
[without reference to a Main Committee (A/61/L.67 and Add.1)]

61/295. UNITED NATIONS DECLARATION ON
THE RIGHTS OF INDIGENOUS PEOPLES

The General Assembly,

Taking note of the recommendation of the Human Rights Council contained in its resolution 1/2 of 29 June 2006,[1] by which the Council
adopted the text of the United Nations Declaration on the Rights of
Indigenous Peoples,

Recalling its resolution 61/178 of 20 December 2006, by which it decided
to defer consideration of and action on the Declaration to allow time for
further consultations thereon, and also decided to conclude its consideration before the end of the sixty-first session of the General Assembly,

Adopts the United Nations Declaration on the Rights of Indigenous
Peoples as contained in the annex to the present resolution.

107th plenary meeting
13 September 2007

ANNEX. UNITED NATIONS DECLARATION ON
THE RIGHTS OF INDIGENOUS PEOPLES

The General Assembly,

Guided by the purposes and principles of the Charter of the United Nations, and good faith in the fulfillment of the obligations assumed by States in accordance with the Charter,

Affirming that indigenous peoples are equal to all other peoples, while recognizing the right of all peoples to be different, to consider themselves different, and to be respected as such,

Affirming also that all peoples contribute to the diversity and richness of civilizations and cultures, which constitute the common heritage of humankind,

Affirming further that all doctrines, policies and practices based on or advocating superiority of peoples or individuals on the basis of national origin or racial, religious, ethnic or cultural differences are racist, scientifically false, legally invalid, morally condemnable and socially unjust,

Reaffirming that indigenous peoples, in the exercise of their rights, should be free from discrimination of any kind,

Concerned that indigenous peoples have suffered from historic injustices as a result of, inter alia, their colonization and dispossession of their lands, territories and resources, thus preventing them from exercising, in particular, their right to development in accordance with their own needs and interests,

Recognizing the urgent need to respect and promote the inherent rights of indigenous peoples which derive from their political, economic and social structures and from their cultures, spiritual traditions, histories and philosophies, especially their rights to their lands, territories and resources,

Recognizing also the urgent need to respect and promote the rights of indigenous peoples affirmed in treaties, agreements and other constructive arrangements with States,

Welcoming the fact that indigenous peoples are organizing themselves for political, economic, social and cultural enhancement and in order to bring to an end all forms of discrimination and oppression wherever they occur,

Convinced that control by indigenous peoples over developments affecting them and their lands, territories and resources will enable them to maintain and strengthen their institutions, cultures and traditions, and to promote their development in accordance with their aspirations and needs,

Recognizing that respect for indigenous knowledge, cultures and traditional practices contributes to sustainable and equitable development and proper management of the environment,

Emphasizing the contribution of the demilitarization of the lands and territories of indigenous peoples to peace, economic and social progress and development, understanding and friendly relations among nations and peoples of the world,

Recognizing in particular the right of indigenous families and communities to retain shared responsibility for the upbringing, training, education and well being of their children, consistent with the rights of the child,

Considering that the rights affirmed in treaties, agreements and other constructive arrangements between States and indigenous peoples are, in some situations, matters of international concern, interest, responsibility and character,

Considering also those treaties, agreements and other constructive arrangements, and the relationship they represent, are the basis for a strengthened partnership between indigenous peoples and States,

Acknowledging that the Charter of the United Nations, the International Covenant on Economic, Social and Cultural Rights[2] a and the International Covenant on Civil and Political Rights,[3] as well as the Vienna Declaration and Programme of Action,[4] affirm the fundamental importance of the right to self-determination of all peoples, by virtue of which they freely determine their political status and freely pursue their economic, social and cultural development,

Bearing in mind that nothing in this Declaration may be used to deny any peoples their right to self-determination, exercised in conformity with international law,

Convinced that the recognition of the rights of indigenous peoples in this Declaration will enhance harmonious and cooperative relations between the State and indigenous peoples, based on principles of justice, democracy, respect for human rights, non-discrimination and good faith,

Encouraging States to comply with and effectively implement all their obligations as they apply to indigenous peoples under international instruments, in particular those related to human rights, in consultation and cooperation with the peoples concerned,

Emphasizing that the United Nations has an important and continuing role to play in promoting and protecting the rights of indigenous peoples,

Believing that this Declaration is a further important step forward for the recognition, promotion and protection of the rights and freedoms of indigenous peoples and in the development of relevant activities of the United Nations system in this field,

Recognizing and reaffirming that indigenous individuals are entitled without discrimination to all human rights recognized in international law, and that indigenous peoples possess collective rights which are indispensable for their existence, well-being and integral development as peoples,

Recognizing that the situation of indigenous peoples varies from region to region and from country to country and that the significance of national and regional particularities and various historical and cultural backgrounds should be taken into consideration,

Solemnly proclaims the following United Nations Declaration on the Rights of Indigenous Peoples as a standard of achievement to be pursued in a spirit of partnership and mutual respect:

ARTICLE 1

Indigenous peoples have the right to the full enjoyment, as a collective or as individuals, of all human rights and fundamental freedoms as recognized in the Charter of the United Nations, the Universal Declaration of Human Rights[5] and international human rights law.

ARTICLE 2

Indigenous peoples and individuals are free and equal to all other peoples and individuals and have the right to be free from any kind of discrimination, in the exercise of their rights, in particular that based on their indigenous origin or identity.

ARTICLE 3

Indigenous peoples have the right to self-determination. By virtue of that right they freely determine their political status and freely pursue their economic, social and cultural development.

ARTICLE 4

Indigenous peoples, in exercising their right to self-determination, have the right to autonomy or self-government in matters relating to their internal and local affairs, as well as ways and means for financing their autonomous functions.

ARTICLE 5

Indigenous peoples have the right to maintain and strengthen their distinct political, legal, economic, social and cultural institutions, while retaining their right to participate fully, if they so choose, in the political, economic, social and cultural life of the State.

ARTICLE 6

Every indigenous individual has the right to a nationality.

ARTICLE 7

1. Indigenous individuals have the rights to life, physical and mental integrity, liberty and security of person.

2. Indigenous peoples have the collective right to live in freedom, peace and security as distinct peoples and shall not be subjected to any act of genocide or any other act of violence, including forcibly removing children of the group to another group.

ARTICLE 8

1. Indigenous peoples and individuals have the right not to be subjected to forced assimilation or destruction of their culture.

2. States shall provide effective mechanisms for prevention of, and redress for:

   (a) Any action which has the aim or effect of depriving them of their integrity as distinct peoples, or of their cultural values or ethnic identities;
   (b) Any action which has the aim or effect of dispossessing them of their lands, territories or resources;

(c) Any form of forced population transfer which has the aim or effect of violating or undermining any of their rights;

(d) Any form of forced assimilation or integration;

(e) Any form of propaganda designed to promote or incite racial or ethnic discrimination directed against them.

ARTICLE 9

Indigenous peoples and individuals have the right to belong to an indigenous community or nation, in accordance with the traditions and customs of the community or nation concerned. No discrimination of any kind may arise from the exercise of such a right.

ARTICLE 10

Indigenous peoples shall not be forcibly removed from their lands or territories. No relocation shall take place without the free, prior and informed consent of the indigenous peoples concerned and after agreement on just and fair compensation and, where possible, with the option of return.

ARTICLE 11

1. Indigenous peoples have the right to practise and revitalize their cultural traditions and customs. This includes the right to maintain, protect and develop the past, present and future manifestations of their cultures, such as archaeological and historical sites, artefacts, designs, ceremonies, technologies and visual and performing arts and literature.

2. States shall provide redress through effective mechanisms, which may include restitution, developed in conjunction with indigenous peoples, with respect to their cultural, intellectual, religious and spiritual property taken without their free, prior and informed consent or in violation of their laws, traditions and customs.

ARTICLE 12

1. Indigenous peoples have the right to manifest, practise, develop and teach their spiritual and religious traditions, customs and ceremonies; the right to maintain, protect, and have access in privacy to their religious and cultural sites; the right to the use and control of their ceremonial objects; and the right to the repatriation of their human remains.

2. States shall seek to enable the access and/or repatriation of ceremonial objects and human remains in their possession through fair, transparent and effective mechanisms developed in conjunction with indigenous peoples concerned.

ARTICLE 13

1. Indigenous peoples have the right to revitalize, use, develop and transmit to future generations their histories, languages, oral traditions, philosophies, writing systems and literatures, and to designate and retain their own names for communities, places and persons.

2. States shall take effective measures to ensure that this right is protected and also to ensure that indigenous peoples can understand and be understood in political, legal and administrative proceedings, where necessary through the provision of interpretation or by other appropriate means.

ARTICLE 14

1. Indigenous peoples have the right to establish and control their educational systems and institutions providing education in their own languages, in a manner appropriate to their cultural methods of teaching and learning.

2. Indigenous individuals, particularly children, have the right to all levels and forms of education of the State without discrimination.

3. States shall, in conjunction with indigenous peoples, take effective measures, in order for indigenous individuals, particularly children, including those living outside their communities, to have access, when possible, to an education in their own culture and provided in their own language.

ARTICLE 15

1. Indigenous peoples have the right to the dignity and diversity of their cultures, traditions, histories and aspirations which shall be appropriately reflected in education and public information.

2. States shall take effective measures, in consultation and cooperation with the indigenous peoples concerned, to combat prejudice and eliminate discrimination and to promote tolerance, understanding and good relations among indigenous peoples and all other segments of society.

ARTICLE 16

1. Indigenous peoples have the right to establish their own media in their own languages and to have access to all forms of non-indigenous media without discrimination.

2. States shall take effective measures to ensure that State-owned media duly reflect indigenous cultural diversity. States, without prejudice to ensuring full freedom of expression, should encourage privately owned media to adequately reflect indigenous cultural diversity.

ARTICLE 17

1. Indigenous individuals and peoples have the right to enjoy fully all rights established under applicable international and domestic labour law.

2. States shall in consultation and cooperation with indigenous peoples take specific measures to protect indigenous children from economic exploitation and from performing any work that is likely to be hazardous or to interfere with the child's education, or to be harmful to the

child's health or physical, mental, spiritual, moral or social development, taking into account their special vulnerability and the importance of education for their empowerment.

3. Indigenous individuals have the right not to be subjected to any discriminatory conditions of labour and, inter alia, employment or salary.

ARTICLE 18

Indigenous peoples have the right to participate in decision-making in matters which would affect their rights, through representatives chosen by themselves in accordance with their own procedures, as well as to maintain and develop their own indigenous decision-making institutions.

ARTICLE 19

States shall consult and cooperate in good faith with the indigenous peoples concerned through their own representative institutions in order to obtain their free, prior and informed consent before adopting and implementing legislative or administrative measures that may affect them.

ARTICLE 20

1. Indigenous peoples have the right to maintain and develop their political, economic and social systems or institutions, to be secure in the enjoyment of their own means of subsistence and development, and to engage freely in all their traditional and other economic activities.

2. Indigenous peoples deprived of their means of subsistence and development are entitled to just and fair redress.

ARTICLE 21

1. Indigenous peoples have the right, without discrimination, to the improvement of their economic and social conditions, including, inter alia, in the areas of education, employment, vocational training and retraining, housing, sanitation, health and social security.

2. States shall take effective measures and, where appropriate, special measures to ensure continuing improvement of their economic and social conditions. Particular attention shall be paid to the rights and special needs of indigenous elders, women, youth, children and persons with disabilities.

ARTICLE 22

1. Particular attention shall be paid to the rights and special needs of indigenous elders, women, youth, children and persons with disabilities in the implementation of this Declaration.

2. States shall take measures, in conjunction with indigenous peoples, to ensure that indigenous women and children enjoy the full protection and guarantees against all forms of violence and discrimination.

ARTICLE 23

Indigenous peoples have the right to determine and develop priorities and strategies for exercising their right to development. In particular, indigenous peoples have the right to be actively involved in developing and determining health, housing and other economic and social programmes affecting them and, as far as possible, to administer such programmes through their own institutions.

ARTICLE 24

1. Indigenous peoples have the right to their traditional medicines and to maintain their health practices, including the conservation of their vital medicinal plants, animals and minerals. Indigenous individuals also have the right to access, without any discrimination, to all social and health services.

2. Indigenous individuals have an equal right to the enjoyment of the highest attainable standard of physical and mental health. States shall

take the necessary steps with a view to achieving progressively the full realization of this right.

ARTICLE 25

Indigenous peoples have the right to maintain and strengthen their distinctive spiritual relationship with their traditionally owned or otherwise occupied and used lands, territories, waters and coastal seas and other resources and to uphold their responsibilities to future generations in this regard.

ARTICLE 26

1. Indigenous peoples have the right to the lands, territories and resources which they have traditionally owned, occupied or otherwise used or acquired.

2. Indigenous peoples have the right to own, use, develop and control the lands, territories and resources that they possess by reason of traditional ownership or other traditional occupation or use, as well as those which they have otherwise acquired.

3. States shall give legal recognition and protection to these lands, territories and resources. Such recognition shall be conducted with due respect to the customs, traditions and land tenure systems of the indigenous peoples concerned.

ARTICLE 27

States shall establish and implement, in conjunction with indigenous peoples concerned, a fair, independent, impartial, open and transparent process, giving due recognition to indigenous peoples' laws, traditions, customs and land tenure systems, to recognize and adjudicate the rights of indigenous peoples pertaining to their lands, territories and resources, including those which were traditionally owned or otherwise occupied or used. Indigenous peoples shall have the right to participate in this process.

ARTICLE 28

1. Indigenous peoples have the right to redress, by means that can include restitution or, when this is not possible, just, fair and equitable compensation, for the lands, territories and resources which they have traditionally owned or otherwise occupied or used, and which have been confiscated, taken, occupied, used or damaged without their free, prior and informed consent.

2. Unless otherwise freely agreed upon by the peoples concerned, compensation shall take the form of lands, territories and resources equal in quality, size and legal status or of monetary compensation or other appropriate redress.

ARTICLE 29

1. Indigenous peoples have the right to the conservation and protection of the environment and the productive capacity of their lands or territories and resources. States shall establish and implement assistance programmes for indigenous peoples for such conservation and protection, without discrimination.

2. States shall take effective measures to ensure that no storage or disposal of hazardous materials shall take place in the lands or territories of indigenous peoples without their free, prior and informed consent.

3. States shall also take effective measures to ensure as needed, that programmes for monitoring, maintaining and restoring the health of indigenous peoples, as developed and implemented by the peoples affected by such materials, are duly implemented.

ARTICLE 30

1. Military activities shall not take place in the lands or territories of indigenous peoples, unless justified by a relevant public interest or

otherwise freely agreed with or requested by the indigenous peoples concerned.

2. States shall undertake effective consultations with the indigenous peoples concerned, through appropriate procedures and in particular through their representative institutions, prior to using their lands or territories for military activities.

ARTICLE 31

1. Indigenous peoples have the right to maintain, control, protect and develop their cultural heritage, traditional knowledge and traditional cultural expressions, as well as the manifestations of their sciences, technologies and cultures, including human and genetic resources, seeds, medicines, knowledge of the properties of fauna and flora, oral traditions, literatures, designs, sports and traditional games and visual and performing arts. They also have the right to maintain, control, protect and develop their intellectual property over such cultural heritage, traditional knowledge, and traditional cultural expressions.

2. In conjunction with indigenous peoples, States shall take effective measures to recognize and protect the exercise of these rights.

ARTICLE 32

1. Indigenous peoples have the right to determine and develop priorities and strategies for the development or use of their lands or territories and other resources.

2. States shall consult and cooperate in good faith with the indigenous peoples concerned through their own representative institutions in order to obtain their free and informed consent prior to the approval of any project affecting their lands or territories and other resources, particularly in connection with the development, utilization or exploitation of mineral, water or other resources.

3. States shall provide effective mechanisms for just and fair redress for any such activities, and appropriate measures shall be taken to mitigate adverse environmental, economic, social, cultural or spiritual impact.

ARTICLE 33

1. Indigenous peoples have the right to determine their own identity or membership in accordance with their customs and traditions. This does not impair the right of indigenous individuals to obtain citizenship of the States in which they live.

2. Indigenous peoples have the right to determine the structures and to select the membership of their institutions in accordance with their own procedures.

ARTICLE 34

Indigenous peoples have the right to promote, develop and maintain their institutional structures and their distinctive customs, spirituality, traditions, procedures, practices and, in the cases where they exist, juridical systems or customs, in accordance with international human rights standards.

ARTICLE 35

Indigenous peoples have the right to determine the responsibilities of individuals to their communities.

ARTICLE 36

1. Indigenous peoples, in particular those divided by international borders, have the right to maintain and develop contacts, relations and cooperation, including activities for spiritual, cultural, political, economic and social purposes, with their own members as well as other peoples across borders.

2. States, in consultation and cooperation with indigenous peoples, shall take effective measures to facilitate the exercise and ensure the implementation of this right.

ARTICLE 37

1. Indigenous peoples have the right to the recognition, observance and enforcement of treaties, agreements and other constructive arrangements concluded with States or their successors and to have States honour and respect such treaties, agreements and other constructive arrangements.

2. Nothing in this Declaration may be interpreted as diminishing or eliminating the rights of indigenous peoples contained in treaties, agreements and other constructive arrangements.

ARTICLE 38

States in consultation and cooperation with indigenous peoples, shall take the appropriate measures, including legislative measures, to achieve the ends of this Declaration.

ARTICLE 39

Indigenous peoples have the right to have access to financial and technical assistance from States and through international cooperation, for the enjoyment of the rights contained in this Declaration.

ARTICLE 40

Indigenous peoples have the right to access to and prompt decision through just and fair procedures for the resolution of conflicts and disputes with States or other parties, as well as to effective remedies for all infringements of their individual and collective rights. Such a decision shall give due consideration to the customs, traditions, rules and legal systems of the indigenous peoples concerned and international human rights.

ARTICLE 41

The organs and specialized agencies of the United Nations system and other intergovernmental organizations shall contribute to the full realization of the provisions of this Declaration through the mobilization, inter alia, of financial cooperation and technical assistance. Ways and means of ensuring participation of indigenous peoples on issues affecting them shall be established.

ARTICLE 42

The United Nations, its bodies, including the Permanent Forum on Indigenous Issues, and specialized agencies, including at the country level, and States shall promote respect for and full application of the provisions of this Declaration and follow up the effectiveness of this Declaration.

ARTICLE 43

The rights recognized herein constitute the minimum standards for the survival, dignity and well-being of the indigenous peoples of the world.

ARTICLE 44

All the rights and freedoms recognized herein are equally guaranteed to male and female indigenous individuals.

ARTICLE 45

Nothing in this Declaration may be construed as diminishing or extinguishing the rights indigenous peoples have now or may acquire in the future.

ARTICLE 46

1. Nothing in this Declaration may be interpreted as implying for any State, people, group or person any right to engage in any activity or to perform any act contrary to the Charter of the United Nations or construed as authorizing or encouraging any action which would dismember or impair, totally or in part, the territorial integrity or political unity of sovereign and independent States.

2. In the exercise of the rights enunciated in the present Declaration, human rights and fundamental freedoms of all shall be respected. The

exercise of the rights set forth in this Declaration shall be subject only to such limitations as are determined by law and in accordance with international human rights obligations. Any such limitations shall be non-discriminatory and strictly necessary solely for the purpose of securing due recognition and respect for the rights and freedoms of others and for meeting the just and most compelling requirements of a democratic society.

3. The provisions set forth in this Declaration shall be interpreted in accordance with the principles of justice, democracy, respect for human rights, equality, non-discrimination, good governance and good faith.

NOTES

1. See *Official Records of the General Assembly*, Sixty-first Session, Supplement No. 53 (A/61/53), part one, chap. II, sect. A.
2. See resolution 2200 A (XXI), annex.
3. See resolution 2200 A (XXI), annex.
4. A/CONF.157/24 (Part I), chap. III.
5. Resolution 217 A (III).

APPENDIX 3

Events in U.S. Indian History and Policy,
Emphasizing the Point Elliott Treaty Tribes

Gregory P. Fields

ca. 10,000 BCE: The first Native camping sites and fishing settlements are established on the North Pacific Coast of the American
continent.[1]

ca. 1,000: Scandinavian explorers sail to Greenland and the Northeast
Coast of the American continent; some settlements are established
in Newfoundland. The Scandinavian colonists encounter and kill
Native inhabitants off the northeast of North America; the Norse
leader Thorvald (brother of Leif Erickson) is killed in the Native
counterattack.[2]

"DISCOVERY" AND COLONIZATION

15th C.: Papal bulls (authorizations) by Roman Catholic popes and
authorizations by European monarchs allow European explorers to
enslave, and to take the property of, non-Christian Native people
in the "New World" of Africa and the Americas.[3]

1492–1502: Columbus makes four voyages to the "New World." He
explores islands in the Caribbean and coastal regions of Central
and South America and brings Europe's attention to the American
continent. Columbus called the Native people *Indios*, since he had
been looking for a route to the East Indies. On his second journey
in 1493, he brought a cargo of domestic plants and animals and a
thousand settlers in seventeen ships.[4]

1520s: The first wave of epidemic smallpox, brought from Europe, begins to spread among Native Americans.[5]

16th C.: The first European colonies are founded in the future United States by the Spanish in present-day Florida (1565) and New Mexico (1598). French explorers begin arriving. While the Spanish were more conquest oriented, the French emphasis was trade. Both the French and the Spanish sent priests.[6]

17th C.: English immigrants found a settlement at Jamestown, Virginia (1607), and Pilgrims from England establish Plymouth Colony (1620); tens of thousands of immigrants arrive soon after. Robert de La Salle claims the Mississippi River basin for France under Louis XIV; it was called La Louisiane (1682). Europeans from various nations continue to found settlements; Native populations continue to be reduced by epidemic disease and other consequences of contact with Europeans.[7]

EARLY EUROPEAN CONTACT IN THE PACIFIC NORTHWEST

1542: Spanish explorers Juan Rodríguez Cabrillo and Bartolomé Ferrelo lead the first European expedition to explore the West Coast of North America, reaching the coast of what is now southern Oregon. They claim the West Coast for Spain and name it Las Californias.[8]

1579: British explorer and privateer/pirate Sir Francis Drake, seeking the treasure of Spanish ships and ports, sails north along the West Coast of North America, at least to present-day northern California. He claimed the sighted land for England, with the name New Albion (a reference to England's White Cliffs of Dover).[9]

1592: A Greek sea captain using the name Juan de Fuca, sent by the Spanish viceroy of Mexico, claimed to have sailed in 1592 the strait between present-day Vancouver Island, British Columbia, and Washington's Olympic Peninsula. The strait still bears his name, although it was not documented until the expedition of Barkley in 1787.[10]

1741: Dutch sea captain Vitus Bering, in the service of Russian ruler Peter the Great, succeeds, on his second attempt, to locate and explore the separation of the Eurasian and American continents (the Bering Strait), west of present-day Alaska.[11]

18th C.: The Russians establish trade and settlements in Alaska. At the same time, the Spanish consider that all Pacific Northwest coastal lands, including Alaska, are the Spanish territory Alta (Upper) California.[12]

1774: The viceroy of New Spain sends Juan Pérez to explore the Pacific coast in order to assess Russian and British settlements and to establish Spain's claim to the Pacific Northwest. The expedition trades with the Haida. Although Pérez is not able to go ashore to formally establish a claim, evidence of his expedition's Spanish presence influences the future placement of the U.S./Canada border at its present location (rather than at the Washington/Oregon border, on the basis of Great Britain's claim to the Oregon Country).[13]

1774–78: Captain James Cook of the British Royal Navy, an explorer, geographer, and trader, makes three scientific and commercial trips to the North Pacific. Cook, among others, seeks a "Northwest Passage": a route between the Pacific and Atlantic Oceans. Cook profitably trades for sea otter furs at Nootka Sound; his report leads to that location's becoming a busy trade port.[14]

1775: Spanish navigators Bruno de Hezeta (Heceta) and Juan Francisco de la Bodega y Quadra are sent to claim the Pacific Northwest (Nueva Galicia) for Spain. Seven Spanish sailors go ashore on the Olympic Peninsula in the Quinault area and die in an attack by Native residents.[15]

1770s: The first smallpox epidemic occurs on the Northwest Coast, as a result of contact with European explorers.[16]

1785: French naval officer Jean Franois de Galaup, comte de La Perousse, is sent to explore regions of the Northwest not previously explored by Captain Cook, for purposes of scientific inquiry and potential fur trade. He produces good maps of the outer islands of British Columbia, which are later recovered, after his ships are wrecked in the South Pacific.[17]

1787: English navigator and trader Charles Barkley, seeking furs and other items, confirms the existence of the Strait of Juan de Fuca. His crew is attacked at the Hoh River by people indigenous to the Quileute area.[18]

1788: John Meares, English navigator, trader, and former officer of the British Navy, explores the Strait of Juan de Fuca, the coasts of Vancouver Island, Haida Gwaii (the Queen Charlotte Islands), and the Alaska Coast. His business and cartographical claims contain some inaccuracies. Meares establishes a fur trading post on Nootka Sound. His first shipment of furs to China was the start of transoceanic trade in the Pacific Northwest.[19]

1788: American navigators and merchants John Kendrick and Robert Gray arrive at Nootka Sound. They trade with Indians on Vancouver Island for furs. The next year Gray sells the furs in China, where he buys tea to sell in Boston at great profit, initiating U.S. participation in the international fur trade in the Northwest.[20]

1788: Esteban José Martínez, representing the viceroy of New Spain, arrives at Nootka Sound to assert Spain's claim to the Pacific Northwest, with the intention of blocking British and Russian claims.[21]

1790: With England threatening war, Spain and England sign the Treaty of Nootka, affirming England's claims to the coastal Pacific Northwest.[22]

1790–91: Spanish naval captain Francisco de Eliza is sent by the viceroy of New Spain to reoccupy Nootka Sound on Vancouver Island. His expeditions explore regions including the Strait of Georgia, Rosario Strait, and the Strait of Juan de Fuca.[23]

1790: Manuel Quimper, a Spanish naval officer in the Eliza expedition, charts and names several geographical features in the regions of southern Vancouver Island, the Strait of Juan de Fuca, and the Olympic Peninsula.[24]

1791–92: George Vancouver, British naval officer and explorer, is sent to the Northwest to receive Spanish land and buildings in the name of Britain and to survey the coast and its inland waters. His expedition produces very accurate maps and reports. He names many geographical features, such as Puget Sound, named in honor of surveyor Peter Puget.[25]

1792: American navigator Robert Gray sails into the Columbia River and names it. The other navigators miss this large river, except for Hezeta, who had located and named it in 1775. Gray's navigation of the river becomes part of the basis of U.S. territorial claims to the Oregon Country.[26]

1800: A smallpox epidemic occurs among Native people of the Central Northwest Coast during the first decade of the nineteenth century.[27]

1841: U.S. naval commander Charles Wilkes arrives at Puget Sound as part of the five-year United States Exploring Expedition. He surveys Puget Sound, the Strait of Juan de Fuca, and the coast.[28]

THE COLONIAL PERIOD

1763: The first Treaty of Paris (1763) concludes the Seven Years' War; in North America this was the French and Indian War (1756–63). France's empire in North America ends; France cedes its North American land claims to Britain.[29]

1775–83: The American Revolution—American colonists fight for and win independence from British rule.[30]

1775: The Continental Congress establishes a Committee of Indian Affairs, headed by Benjamin Franklin.[31]

1776: The Declaration of Independence is adopted by the Continental Congress on July 4, 1776, declaring that the thirteen American colonies are independent states, no longer part of the British Empire.

1778: Ratification of the first U.S. treaty with American Indians— Treaty with the Delaware at Ft. Pitt, Pennsylvania.[32]

1783: A second Treaty of Paris (the Peace of Paris)—Britain recognizes the independence of the thirteen American colonies. Britain's Indian allies are left to the mercy of the new claimants of the lands: the Americans. Despite the formal lands claims exchanged among various European nations and Americans, most of the transferred lands are Indian homelands under Indian control.[33]

1787: The Northwest Ordinance, an Act of the Confederation Congress, is "an ordinance for the government of the territory of the United States, Northwest of the river Ohio. . . . The utmost good faith shall always be observed towards the Indians; their lands and properties shall never be taken from them without their consent; and in their property, rights and liberty, they never shall be invaded or disturbed, unless in just and lawful wars authorized by Congress."[34]

1789: The U.S. Constitution is adopted. The Commerce Clause (Article I, Sect. 8, Clause 3) affirms the sovereignty of U.S. Indian tribes. One of the powers of Congress enumerated in the Constitution is the sole power of Congress to regulate commerce "with foreign Nations, and among the several States, and with the Indian Tribes."[35]

1789: Under President George Washington, Congress assigns Indian Affairs to the newly established Department of War (1 Stat. 54).[36]

FEDERAL CONTROL AND TREATY MAKING

1790–1834: The Trade and Intercourse laws—President George Washington and Secretary of War Henry Knox advocate federal relations with Indian tribes, based not only on American military dominance and treaties but also on diplomacy. In 1790 Congress passes the first of a series of statutes (1 Stat. 137 [1790]) that gradually come to embody the general features of Indian policy until the 1830s, when policy shifts to Indian removal. A main feature of the Trade and Intercourse laws is that the transfer of Indian land requires approval of Congress; present-day law maintains the condition that Indian land cannot be sold without federal consent. Various prohibitions restrict the sale of liquor to Indians.[37] Whites continued to sell liquor to Indians for profit and to gain advantage.

1803: The Louisiana Purchase—Under President Thomas Jefferson, the United States acquires the Louisiana Territory from France, doubling its land area with the addition of these lands stretching from west of the Mississippi River to the Rocky Mountains. Jefferson believes that Indians must assimilate into white society.

The Louisiana Purchase paves the way for Indians to be removed to the trans-Mississippi West.[38]

1804–6: The Lewis and Clark Expedition—President Jefferson sends Meriwether Lewis and William Clark to explore the newly acquired land west of the Mississippi River. In 1805 they arrive at the Pacific Ocean at the mouth of the Columbia River, between present-day Oregon and Washington.[39]

1805–11: Affected by tremendous land losses from treaties such as Fort Stanwix (1768), Greenville (1795), and Fort Wayne (1809), the Shawnee brothers Tecumseh and Tenskwatawa labor to establish an intertribal confederacy from the Appalachian Mountains west to the Mississippi River, in order to block American expansion and to preserve Indian homelands.[40]

1812–14: The War of 1812, between the United States and Great Britain with its Indian allies—The United States declares war to settle issues remaining from the War of Independence, including American interests in annexing British North America (part of contemporary Canada). Neither side gains or loses territory in the war, but Indian allies of the British are greatly disadvantaged.[41]

1823: *Johnson v. McIntosh* (21 U.S. 543 [1823])—The first case in the "Marshall Trilogy." Supreme Court chief justice John Marshall applies the Doctrine of Discovery to serve the interests of the United States. On this interpretation, the right of European nations to hold title to North American lands, based on "discovery" of those lands, passes to the United States. Based on the interpretation that discovery implies rights of conquest, the court concludes that tribes retain title only in the sense of the right of occupancy, secondary to title in the sense of ownership, held by the United States.[42]

1817–29: During the presidencies of James Monroe and John Quincy Adams, Indian policy focuses on acquiring lands east of the Mississippi.[43]

1824: Secretary of War John C. Calhoun, without the authorization of Congress, establishes the Bureau of Indian Affairs, within the

Department of War. He appoints Thomas L. McKenney as the first superintendent.[44]

1830: Congress passes the Indian Removal Act (4 Stat. 411) under President Andrew Jackson. This law provides new lands west of the Mississippi for Indians in any state or territory, in exchange for their giving up their homelands to be used for white settlement. Indians are evicted against their will, by use of arms, and in violation of their treaty rights.

1831: *Cherokee Nation v. Georgia* (30 U.S. 1, 8 L. Ed. 25 [1831])—Second case in the "Marshall Trilogy." Supreme Court chief justice John Marshall characterizes Indian tribes as "domestic dependent nations" and describes their relationship to the federal government as like that of a ward to a guardian. On this interpretation land management and transactions are to be conducted only by the "guardian," because of the presumed limitations of the "wards."[45]

1832: *Worcester v. Georgia* (31 U.S. 515, 8 L. Ed. 483 483 [1832])—Third case in the "Marshall Trilogy." Supreme Court chief justice John Marshall writes for the court that tribes have sovereignty against state intrusion and that they have government-to-government relationships with the U.S. federal government on the basis of international law, ratified treaties, and the U.S. Constitution.[46]

1832: The Office of Indian Affairs is established by Act of Congress (50 Stat 4:564), which provides for a commissioner of Indian Affairs, under the direction of the secretary of war.

1835–36: A smallpox epidemic occurs among Native people of the northern and southern Northwest coasts.[47]

1835: Treaty of New Echota—A fraudulent treaty is signed by a group of Cherokee leaders, not including principal chief John Ross. It is ratified by the U.S. Senate and signed by President Andrew Jackson. The treaty establishes the basis of cession of Cherokee lands in the southeast and removal of the people to the West.

1838–39: *The Place Where We Cried/Trail of Tears*—Cherokee and other southeastern Native people leave their homelands and undergo an eight-hundred-mile forced relocation march to Oklahoma.[48]

1843: Settlers in wagon trains begin to arrive in large numbers the Pacific Northwest by means of the Oregon Trail. Immigrants in increasing numbers are drawn by opportunities for residential and farm land, business opportunities, and gold. They take over lands west of the Cascade Mountains without the government's first developing land policies or relationships with Indians. The immigrants displace Indians west of the Cascade Mountains, and as they travel, they violate the lands of those on the east, precipitating the Northwest wars of 1855–56.[49]

1843: Settlers in the region that will later be designated the Oregon Territory form the Oregon provisional government.

1845–48: During James Polk's presidency, the United States expands westward from the Rocky Mountains to the Pacific Ocean. The Republic of Texas is annexed as a state (1845). At the end of the Mexican-American War (1846–48), the United States acquires the lands that become California, Nevada, Utah, most of Arizona, and portions of Colorado, New Mexico, and Wyoming.

1846: The Oregon Treaty—Under President Polk, Britain cedes the disputed Oregon Country to the United States at the 49th parallel. The United States gains the lands that will become Oregon, Washington, and portions of Idaho, Montana, and Wyoming. The area remains unorganized territory until the formation of the Oregon Territory.

1846: The Bureau of Land Management is created within the Department of the Interior by merging the General Land Office with the Grazing Service.[50]

1848: The Oregon Territory is established by an Act of Congress.[51]

1849: The Bureau of Indian Affairs (BIA) is transferred from the Department of War to the newly established Department of the Interior, under the Bureau of Land Management. In subsequent years the BIA is known by various names: the Indian Office, the Indian Bureau, the Indian Department, and the Indian Service.[52]

1850: The Donation Land Claim Act (Oregon Land Donation Act) (9 Stat. 496), signed by President Millard Fillmore, provides for any U.S. male citizen at least eighteen years old to stake a claim to

320 acres, or 640 acres for a married couple (640 acres=1 square mile). The Donation Land Claim Act is in force for five years. Most claims are staked before any treaties have been signed; therefore, this is Indian land. About three million acres of land are granted, after the treaties are ratified, to non-Indian settlers in Washington and Oregon.

1850: Congress passes a resolution to establish treaties with the Indian tribes of the Pacific Northwest to extinguish Indian title to all lands west of the Cascade Mountains.[53]

1852: Captain Henry Roeder and Russell V. Peabody explore Bellingham Bay in the Lummi country and establish a sawmill there; white settlement begins in the area.[54]

1853: Washington Territory's population expands such that Congress establishes the Washington Territory, which is subdivided from the Oregon Territory in 1853.[55] The new Washington Territory covers present-day Washington State, plus northern Idaho and Wyoming, and portions of Montana west of the Rocky Mountains.

1853: The Donation Act Land Claim Act applies to the new Washington Territory (10 Stat. 305).

1853: The city of Seattle is founded. Plats are filed, and the city is named for the Duwamish and Suquamish leader Chief Siʔał (Seattle), known as a speaker for his people and the first signatory of the Treaty of Point Elliott.[56]

1853: A smallpox epidemic occurs among Native people of the inland waters of Puget Sound, the Olympic Peninsula, and the southern Northwest Coast.[57]

1853: Isaac I. Stevens is appointed governor of Washington Territory and superintendent of Indian Affairs. He negotiates ten treaties in the Pacific Northwest between December 1854 and January 1856.

1855: The Treaty of Point Elliott with the Duwamish, Suquamish, and Other Tribes (including the Lummi) is signed by representatives of twenty-two named tribes and bands, plus allied tribes and bands with homelands in the northern Puget Sound region. The treaty council was held at Mukilteo, Washington, near present-day Seattle, on January 22, 1855 (appendix 1).[58]

1855–56: Yakama War in Washington; Rogue River War in Oregon; Puget Sound War in Western Washington.[59]

1857: Catholic Father Casimir Chirouse arrives at Tulalip. Father Chirouse is assigned as Indian agent at Tulalip, and subagent in charge of the Tulalip, Swinomish, and Lummi Reservations. He builds a church at Tulalip and begins building the Indian mission school. He conducts missions also at Lummi, Swinomish, Port Madison, and Muckleshoot.[60]

1859: Oregon is admitted to the Union as the thirty-third state. James Buchanan is president at that time.

1859: Ratification of the Point Elliott Treaty and seven other Stevens treaties that are signed in 1854 and 1855, following ratification of Stevens's Treaty of Medicine Creek in 1855 and his Treaty with the Blackfeet in 1856.

1861: The first annuities (equivalent to a few dollars per person) are paid to members of the Point Elliott Treaty tribes, six years after the treaty was signed.[61]

1862: A smallpox epidemic occurs among Native people of the northern Northwest Coast.[62]

1861–65: American Civil War—Military men on the frontier were called to battle, so westward expansion slowed during the war. Tens of thousands of Indians fought in the Civil War, on both the Union and the Confederate sides.[63] The costs of war reduced funds allocated for Indian agencies. In 1862 the Indian superintendent for Washington Territory had no operating funds for the needs of treaty tribes for five months.[64]

1862: President Abraham Lincoln signs the Homestead Act (12 Stat. 392), allowing non-Indian citizens to lay claim to 160 acres of surveyed government land by building a dwelling and growing crops. After five years a homesteader could file for patent (deed) by submitting proof of residency and of improvements.

Along with raising revenue for the government, the Homestead Act transformed additional aboriginal lands into U.S. controlled lands.

1864: The Navajo Long Walk—A four-hundred-mile forced relocation march of Navajo people from present-day Arizona to Bosque Redondo, in eastern New Mexico.[65]

1867: In 1867 the United States purchases from Russia the land that would become the state of Alaska. In 1884 it is designated the District of Alaska, and Congress makes provision for its government. In 1912 Alaska is renamed a territory, and in 1959 it attains statehood.[66]

1868: The final treaty is transacted between the United States and an Indian nation, the Treaty with the Nez Perce, of northeastern Oregon and northern Idaho. The treaty is signed in Washington DC.[67]

1868: The Fourteenth Amendment (15 Stat. 706) is ratified, in response to issues concerning the citizenship and civil rights of former slaves after the Civil War. It does not grant citizenship to American Indians.

ALLOTMENT AND ASSIMILATION

1869: Congress establishes the Board of Indian Commissioners (16 Stat. 40) to investigate and reduce mismanagement by the Bureau of Indian Affairs.

1869: President Ulysses S. Grant accepts the proposal of a delegation of Quakers that Indian agencies should be administered by various Christian denominations. Although this feature of Grant's "Peace Policy" lasts only a decade, efforts continue to hire agents who are more just and competent than previous ones.[68]

1869: Appointment of the first commissioner of Indian Affairs who is Indian: Ely S. Parker (Seneca). The next Native commissioner of Indian Affairs is not appointed for nearly a century.[69]

1871: The Indian Appropriations Act (16 Stat. 566)—Under President Ulysses S. Grant, Congress terminates treaty making with U.S. Indian tribes. Further agreements between tribes and the U.S.

government are thereafter to be established by act of Congress or by executive (presidential) order.

1872: The San Juan Islands become part of the United States and the state of Washington after the bloodless "Pig War." The San Juans were left in dispute when Great Britain and the United States agreed in 1846 on their border at the 49th parallel (the border between present-day Washington State and mainland British Columbia).[70]

1877–85: President Rutherford B. Hayes limits the number of diplomatic visits by Native leaders to the White House.[71] Under Presidents James A. Garfield and Chester Alan Arthur, Indian policy focuses on the allotment of reservation lands.

1879: Carlisle (PA) Indian School is established, under the direction of retired Civil War army captain Richard Pratt. Its strict regimen was the model for two dozen more off-reservation boarding schools and many reservation schools.[72]

1880: The U.S. government bans the Sun Dance. Canada bans the potlatch and spirit dancing.[73]

1881: The Northern Pacific Railroad reaches Spokane; it reaches Seattle in 1893 (map 8). Rapid train travel largely replaces slow travel to the West Coast by wagon or ship. Transport of raw materials and goods by train further serves and stimulates business interests; the non-Indian population in the Northwest soars.

1881: Publication of *A Century of Dishonor: A Sketch of the United States Government's Dealings with Some of the Indian Tribes*. Author Helen Hunt Jackson sends a copy to each member of the U.S. Congress.[74]

1882: Under President Chester Arthur, Secretary of the Interior Henry M. Teller writes a letter to the commissioner of Indian Affairs instructing him that Indian agents must stop Indians' "heathenish practices" such as ceremonies, dances, and feasts. A Court of Indian Offences is established at each Indian agency to judge these and other infractions.[75]

1882: The Indian Rights Association is founded by white Christian reformers who wish to help Native communities. In general, it members think that the solution is assimilation. The group holds semi-annual meetings at Lake Mohonk, New York.[76] The group's policy ideas influence Indian policies enacted by Congress.

1884: Allotment begins on the Lummi Reservation. Lands are allotted on other Puget Sound reservations as early as a decade before the General Allotment Act of 1887.[77]

1887: Congress passes the General Allotment Act (Dawes Act or Dawes Severalty Act)—"An Act to Provide for the Allotment of Lands in Severalty to Indians on the Various Reservations" (24. Stat. 388).[78] The act is named for Senator Henry Dawes. Grover Cleveland is president when it is passed. Its main aims are (1) to eliminate Indian landholdings, which in turn would make more land available for non-Indian settlement and commercial ventures (including railroads) and (2) to break up Indian cultural and political units, in order to assimilate Indians according to white ideals of cultural life. Approximately 65 percent of 138 million acres of Native lands are lost before the Dawes Act is repealed in 1934.

1889: Washington is admitted to the Union as the forty-second state. Benjamin Harrison is president at that time.

1889: Indian lands that are not allotted are designated "surplus" by the government and are opened to non-Indian settlers.[79]

1890: Over two hundred Miniconjou Sioux children, women, and men are killed at Wounded Knee, South Dakota, by the Seventh Cavalry of the U.S. Army.[80]

1891: The amendment to the Dawes Act is passed (26 Stat. 794), permitting smaller land allotments; this further reduces Indian land holdings.[81]

1898: The Curtis Act (*Indians in Indian Territory*, 30 Stat. 495) forces the allotment of tribal lands of the Cherokee and other southeastern tribes, whose treaties provided for Indian land ownership in perpetuity. These tribes are not subject to the Dawes Act, which gives the U.S. president authority to sell "surplus" Indian lands to non-Indians. Congress wants these tribes to sell land, and to that end the Curtis Act violates treaty terms by extending the terms of the Dawes Act to those tribes. The Curtis Act also removes particular powers of self-government from tribes, such as by abolishing tribal courts. Its originator is Charles Curtis, a member of the House of Representatives from Kansas with Kaw and other Native ancestry, who advocates assimilation for Native Americans.[82]

1898: The Nation of Hawai'i is annexed by the United States.[83]

1901: President Theodore Roosevelt refers to the Dawes Act in his First Annual Message to Congress as "a mighty pulverizing machine to break up the tribal mass."[84]

1903: *Lone Wolf v. Hitchcock* (187 U.S. 553; 23 S. Ct. 216, 47 L.Ed 299 [1903])—In violation of the Treaty of Medicine Lodge, Congress approves the sale of post-allotment "excess" lands on the Kiowa-Comanche reservation, without tribal approval as stipulated by treaty. The Supreme Court rules that Congress has the power to abrogate its treaty commitments to tribes. The court did this by invoking a connotation of the word *plenary* that implies that Congress has complete power over tribes. The court rejects the principle that tribes have independent status, and asserts that tribes have always been subject to the plenary power (interpreted as "sole and complete") power of Congress.[85]

1905: *United States v. Winans* (198 U.S. 371; 25 S. Ct. 662, 49 L.Ed. 299 [1905])—The Supreme Court upholds the treaty-granted right of the Yakama and other tribes to fish in off-reservation areas. The court upholds treaty-rights in stating that "the treaty was not a grant to them [the Indians], but a grant of rights from them—a reservation of those [rights] not granted."[86]

1909–29: Under Presidents William Howard Taft, Woodrow Wilson, Warren G. Harding, and Calvin Coolidge the focus of Indian policy is allotment, assimilation, and education to acculturate Indians to white society.[87]

1911: The Society of American Indians (SAI) is formed. Educated Indian men and women of the early twentieth century (such as Sioux writer Gertrude Bonin, also known as Zitkala-Ša, and Seneca anthropologist Arthur S. Parker) hold conferences and give commentary on American Indian issues. The SAI pursues an ideal of combining the best of Indian and non-Indian cultures.[88]

1912: The Lummi Smokehouse (ceremonial longhouse) is rebuilt.

1913: William Shelton (Snohomish) successfully negotiates with Charles Buchanan, Indian agency superintendent at Tulalip, to allow the reconstruction of a smokehouse (ceremonial longhouse) on the Tulalip Reservation for potlatches and spirit dancing, in celebration of "Treaty Days." Shelton's work is an example of successful Native efforts to restore religious freedom and ceremonial life among Puget Sound tribes.[89]

1914–18: World War I—The United States is involved during 1917–18. After World War I, Native Americans who serve in the U.S. military become eligible for U.S. citizenship.[90]

1914: Thomas Bishop of the Chimakum organizes the Northwest Federation of American Indians, one of the nation's first regional organizations to work for Native rights.[91]

1921: Under President Woodrow Wilson the Snyder Act (42 Stat. 208) authorizes the Bureau of Indian Affairs to spend funds appropriated by Congress for the needs of Indians for purposes such as education, health, irrigation, and property improvements.

1924: Indian Citizenship Act (43 Stat. 253)—In 1924, under President Calvin Coolidge, all Indians become eligible for U.S. citizenship.

1927: *Duwamish, et al. Tribes of Indians v. the United States*, U.S. Court of Claims 79 Ct. Cl. 530, No. F-275 (decided 1934)—One hundred fifty-five members of tribes who are party to Puget Sound treaties, including ten Lummi, testify in a suit against the U.S. government in the Court of Claims for U.S. failures to honor treaties, and for Indian lands lost to settlers by means of the Oregon Land Donation Act before treaties had been signed and ratified.[92]

1928: Publication by the Institute for Government Research of the *Report on the Problem of Indian Administration* (Meriam Report).[93] This report to the secretary of the interior deals with the failures of the federal Indian policies of allotment and assimilation. Based on the findings of the Meriam Report, the Indian Reorganization

Act (Wheeler-Howard Act) of 1934 would give a new, more positive direction to Indian policy.

1929–33: Charles Curtis, of Kaw, Osage, Pottawatomie, and European ancestry, serves as U.S. vice president in the administration of Herbert Hoover.[94]

REORGANIZATION

1933: President Franklin D. Roosevelt's New Deal begins to counterbalance the U.S. economy during the Great Depression. The exceptional poverty and suffering of Indian people during the Depression is one factor that inclines Indian policy toward reform of the assimilation and allotment policies that left Native American in a state of economic deprivation and cultural loss.[95]

1934: Under Indian commissioner John Collier, the Indian Reorganization Act (IRA), known also as the Wheeler-Howard Act (48 Stat. 984), reverses policies of the General Allotment Act (Dawes Act), ending allotments on reservation lands and restoring some of the lands lost since 1887. It also authorizes tribes to be self-governing and to have their own constitutions, if a tribe so chooses. Jobs with the BIA are opened to Indians. The IRA aims to restore tribes' power to manage their lands and assets and includes a $10 million revolving credit fund for tribes.[96]

1934: The Johnson-O'Malley Act (48 Stat. 596) is passed in order to provide federal funds for American Indian agricultural development, health care, welfare, and education, including cooperation between state and federal governments for the education of Indian students.[97]

1939–45: World War II—Approximately 25,000 Native American men and women serve in the war.[98]

1944: The National Congress of American Indians is formed. It is the first national Native American organization with a focus on Native rights.[99]

1945: President Harry S. Truman takes office in 1945, the year that World War II ends. Indian policy changes course again. The nation's postwar prosperity moves Indian policy away from its post-Depression direction of greater self-determination for tribes toward termination of tribes' federal recognition and termination of the federal government's responsibilities to them. Truman supports this direction in policy.[100]

1946: Congress approves the Indian Claims Commission Act (60 Stat. 1049), so that Indian tribes and bands could bring suit against the United States in the U.S. Court of Claims and receive payment for lost lands. The Indian Claims Commission is terminated in 1978, and its cases are transferred to the U.S. Court of Claims (now the Federal Court of Claims).[101]

1947: The Department of the Interior formally adopts for the BIA the name Bureau of Indian Affairs.[102]

TERMINATION AND RELOCATION

1949: The *Hoover Commission Report* rejects the tribal independence emphasis of the 1934 Indian Reorganization Act and advocates assimilation as the basis of Indian policy.[103]

1951: *Lummi Tribe of Indians v. the United States*, Indian Claims Commission, Docket 110 (decided 1972)—The Lummi Tribe submits a claim to the Indian Claims Commission for $30 million, plus interest, for lands ceded to the United States by the Treaty of Point Elliot and for lands lost as a consequence of the Oregon Land Donation Act of 1850.[104]

1953: Under President Dwight D. Eisenhower the U.S. government seeks to terminate the federal relationship with tribes (House Concurrent Resolution 108).

1953: Under Public Law 280 (House Resolution 1063; 67 Stat. 588), jurisdiction over tribes in some states is extended to the state level, as well as the federal level (including criminal jurisdiction).

1953: Under House Concurrent Resolution 108 (67 Stat. B122), the federally recognized status of thirteen tribes is terminated; the largest were the Klamath in Oregon and the Menominee in Wisconsin (both were later reinstated). Over a hundred smaller tribes and bands lost their federal trust status and lost federal protections and services, including health care and education. Without trust status, some tribes had to sell off lands to pay property taxes.

1955: In the Supreme Court case *Tee-Hit-ton v. United States* (348 U.S. 272; S. Ct. 313, 99 L.Ed. 314 [1955]), the just compensation clause of the Fifth Amendment to the Constitution is at stake: "nor shall private property be taken for public use, without just compensation." The court drew a distinction between Indian title and "recognized" title, and held that, on the basis of unrecognized title, no compensation was due for lumber taken from land of the Tee-Hit-ton, a Tlingit subgroup in Alaska.[105]

1956: The Indian Vocational Training Act (Relocation Act, 70 Stat. 44) aims to achieve assimilation of Indians by offering vocational and housing assistance in selected urban areas. A large percentage of Indians who relocated to cities returned to their reservations, after finding offers inadequate or deceptive. Others stayed, establishing pan-Indian communities that were a force in the Red Power movement of the 1960s, when civil rights activity gained traction for African Americans and other disenfranchised groups.[106]

1961–63: The presidency of John F. Kennedy—The administration investigated the negative effects of termination, but tribes continued to be terminated during the Kennedy administration.[107]

SELF-DETERMINATION

1961: Indians from across the nation convene at the American Indian Chicago Conference and write a Declaration of Indian Purpose.[108]

1964: The Economic Opportunity Act of 1964 (70 Stat. 508) is part of President Lyndon B. Johnson's War on Poverty. For the first time American Indians are eligible for funds distributed by grant to benefit American citizens. The act allowed tribal grant recipients to administer for themselves the programs that they designed for their own communities.[109]

1966: Robert L. Bennett (Oneida) is appointed commissioner of Indian Affairs, the first Native American to hold the office since Ely Parker

(Seneca), who served from 1871 to 1873. Since 1968, the office has been held by Native Americans. In 2003 the title was changed to director of the Bureau of Indian Affairs.[110]

1968: President Lyndon B. Johnson advocates self-determination for Indian tribes in a Special Message to Congress, but the administration's Indian policy did not repudiate termination.[111]

1968: The Indian Civil Rights Act is passed (Pub. Law No. 90-284, Title II; 82 Stat. 77). The act provides for application of the provisions of the Bill of Rights for Indian citizens in their relations with their tribal governments.

1969: Indians of All Tribes occupy Alcatraz Island in San Francisco Bay and issue a proclamation of reclamation of the island, by Right of Discovery. The proclamation lists uses for the island: ecological, educational, and cultural resources for Indian people, especially the youth.[112]

1970: President Richard Nixon, in a Message to Congress (July 8, 1970), promotes Indian self-determination, rejects the termination policy, and calls for other measures, followed by reforms in BIA procedures.[113]

1970: Under President Nixon, Congress authorizes the return of Blue Lake and its adjacent lands (48,000 acres) to Taos Pueblo in New Mexico (84 Stat. 1437).

1972: The Indian Education Act of 1972 (86 Stat. 335) commits federal support and funding to education for Native youth and improvement of educational opportunities for adults.

1973: At Wounded Knee, South Dakota, the site of an 1890 massacre, Indian activists, supported by tribal leaders and with the help of leaders of the American Indian Movement (AIM), occupy the village for seventy-one days, during negotiations and armed conflict with the U.S. government.[114]

1973: The Native American Studies program begins at the Evergreen State College, Olympia, Washington.[115] Work begins to establish the Longhouse Education and Cultural Center at Evergreen, the first building of its kind on a public campus in the United States, with the mission of promoting indigenous arts and cultures. The Longhouse was dedicated in 1995.[116]

1973: Ada Deer (Menominee) and others succeed in their efforts for the restoration of the status of the Menominee Tribe as a federally recognized tribe, marking the end of the termination era. In 1993 Deer was appointed assistant secretary of Indian Affairs by President Bill Clinton.[117]

1974: *United States v. State of Washington* (384 F. Supp. 312, Western Dist. Wash., the Boldt Decision)—Federal judge George Boldt upholds the treaty right of fishing by ruling that the fishing tribes of Washington are entitled to 50 percent of harvestable fish and shellfish. The Boldt Decision follows a century-long struggle for treaty-reserved fishing rights in the Northwest, involving many cases in state courts and six U.S. Supreme Court cases. In the seventh, the Supreme Court upholds the Boldt decision in 1979.[118]

1975: The Indian Self-Determination and Education Assistance Act (88 Stat. 2203) was signed into law by President Gerald R. Ford. It replaced the termination policy with one of self-determination for tribes, so that tribes could administer federal programs on their reservations (such as health, education, law enforcement, and social services). This act also authorizes government agencies to make grants to Indian tribes and to participate in contracts with them. Ford's presidency employed diplomacy and negotiation to resolve issues with tribes, and under his administration, tribal lands were restored to a few Native communities.[119]

1976: The Indian Health Care Improvement Act (90 Stat. 1400) is enacted, based on evidence that the health status of American Indians ranked far below that of other Americans. The act declares the U.S. policy goal of raising the health status of the Indian population up to the level of the general U.S. population.

1978: Under President Jimmy Carter, the U.S. Congress passes the American Indian Religious Freedom Act (92 Stat. 469) (AIRFA), an act "to protect and preserve for Native Americans their inherent rights of freedom of belief, expression, and exercise of traditional religions . . . including but not limited to access to sites, use and possession of sacred objects, and the freedom to worship through ceremonials and traditional rites." As a joint resolution (Joint Resolution 102), AIRFA lacks the status of federal law and lacks provision for penalty. Amendments to the American Indian Religious Freedom Act are made in 1994.[120]

1978: The Indian Child Welfare Act is passed. The stated intent of the act is to "protect the best interests of Indian children and to promote the stability and security of Indian tribes and families" (92 Stat. 3069). The act resulted after a congressional investigation showing that more than 25 percent of Indian children are being removed by state welfare agencies and courts, with most of them placed in non-Indian homes.[121]

1978: The Tribally Controlled Community College Assistance Act (Public Law 95-471) provides grants to tribally controlled colleges, which offer education for livelihood and culturally relevant curricula for Native students.[122]

1978: The Longest Walk I—Indian leaders and people walk from California to Washington DC to bring attention to treaty, governance, and other Native rights.[123]

1980: *U.S. v. the Sioux Nation of Indians* (448 U.S. 371, 487 [1980])—Supreme Court associate justice Harry Blackmun delivers the opinion (with only William Rehnquist dissenting) that the U.S. government has acquired lands by dishonorable means and in violation of the 1868 Treaty of Fort Laramie, and that the Lakota Sioux are thus entitled to damages under the Fifth Amendment of the Constitution (the "just compensation" clause). The Lakota reject compensation (of hundreds of millions of dollars, including accrued interest). Accepting compensation would terminate their claim to the land and the sacred Black Hills.[124]

1980: President Jimmy Carter signs the Maine Indian Claims Settlement Act (94 Stat. 1785) to resolve a land claim by the Passamaquoddy and Penobscot, who ceded land in the nation's early history under terms that violate the Indian Trade and Intercourse Act of 1790, which requires congressional approval for transfer of Indian lands. The Act of 1980 provides, in exchange for the tribes' claims to the land, that they receive $81.5 million dollars to purchase three hundred thousand acres from the current owners. The tribes also receive federal recognition.

1982: The Indian Mineral Development Act (25 USC 2502) is enacted. This act permits tribes to undertake joint ventures with companies that have equipment and capital for exploration, extraction, processing, and sale of energy and mineral resources (e.g., oil, gas, uranium, coal, and geothermal energy).

1982: The Indian Tribal Government Tax Status Act of 1982 is enacted (Title II of Public Law No. 97-473; 96 Stat. 2607). In keeping with the Self-Determination Act of 1976, this act makes an effort to recognize tribal governments as similar to state governments and allows federal tax deductions for taxes paid to a tribe. However, the act restricts tribes' ability to issue tax-exempt bonds, such that they can be used only for essential government functions (like schools and roads), thereby limiting tribes' ability to raise revenue and to exercise their treaty-granted sovereignty rights.[125]

1983: President Ronald Reagan issues a major policy statement that formally rejects termination policy, reaffirms a government-to-government relationship of tribes with the U.S. government, and calls for efforts to develop reservation economies. However, severe cuts in federal funding during the Reagan administration create hardships for tribal programs and people.[126]

1983: The Indian Land Consolidation Act (96 Stat. 2515) is passed by Congress to address problems of land heirship and allotments that had become too small to use. The act authorized tribes to create plans for the sale and exchange of lands and to adopt their own probate codes for land inheritance.

1988: Congress passes the Indian Gaming Regulatory Act (102 Stat. 2467). The IGRA does not authorize gaming on Indian reservations (gaming was already recognized as an inherent right of tribes in the 1987 case *California v. Cabazon Band of Indians*, which went to the Supreme Court). The IGRA limits tribal powers in an effort to balance the allowing of tribes to exercise self-government in their economic development while allowing states some control of gaming enterprises within their borders.[127]

1988: *Lyng v. Northwest Indian Cemetery Protective Association* (485 U.S. 439, 1988)—Yurok, Tolowa, and Karok tribal members attempt unsuccessfully to invoke their right to freedom of religion regarding sacred sites and lands, in a Supreme Court case that concerns a logging road and federal land management.[128]

1989: President George H. W. Bush signs the National Museum of the American Indian Act (103 Stat. 1336), leading to the construction of the museum with the other Smithsonian museums near the U.S. Capitol. The following year President Bush signs legislation to designate 1992 as the Year of the American Indian and November as National American Indian Heritage Month (later expanded to include the heritage of Native Alaska).[129]

1990: Under President George H. W. Bush, Congress passes the Native American Graves and Repatriation Act (104 Stat. 1153). NAGPRA requires that federal and federally funded agencies attempt to identify the tribal origin of human remains and artifacts and to inform tribes who may reclaim them. NAGPRA also provides protections regarding excavation on federal and tribal lands.[130]

1990: The passage of the Indian Arts and Crafts Act (104 Stat. 4662) makes it a criminal offense to misrepresent oneself, or one's art, as "Indian."[131]

1992: Congress enacts the Native American Languages Act to protect and develop Indian languages (106 Stat. 3434). Only 13 percent (estimated) of the remaining (estimated) 155 Indian languages in the United States (approximately 20 languages) are being taught widely to Indian children.[132]

1994: President Bill Clinton invites the leaders of all federally recognized tribes to meet with him at the White House; it is the first invitation to Native leaders to a conference at the White House extended by a U.S. president in approximately 172 years. A total of 566 tribal leaders were invited, and 322 attended the meeting, which addressed issues such as religious freedom, economic development, and sovereignty.[133]

1994: The Self-Determination and Education Act Amendments of 1994 (H.R. 3508, S. 2036) become law and authorize tribes to redesign and administer programs and services formerly managed by the BIA and to administer their funds based on tribal priorities.[134]

1994: The American Indian Religious Freedom Act Amendments of 1994 (108 Stat. 3125) protect Native persons' right of religious use of peyote as a right of free exercise of religion.[135] The legislation that is proposed to protect religious use of sacred lands (House Resolution 4155) does not become law.

1996: President Bill Clinton signs an executive order authorizing a White House initiative on tribal colleges and universities, to ensure that they are accredited and recognized. During his terms in office, Clinton signs a number of executive orders that, for example, increase funding for the Indian Health Service and Indian Head Start, improve Internet access to remote Indian health and education facilities, and assist with the distribution of eagles for religious purposes.[136]

2004: President George W. Bush signs into law the American Indian Probate Reform Act (118 Stat. 1773). The act facilitates the passing of individual Indian land from one generation to the next, helping to resolve problems of fractionated heirship and loss of family lands.[137]

2007: The Northwest Indian Fisheries Commission (NWFC) reaches a settlement with commercial shellfish growers in Washington so that tribes can access a $33 million trust to buy and enhance tidelands exclusively for tribal use.[138]

2007: The United Nations General Assembly formally adopts its Declaration on the Rights of Indigenous Peoples, which recognizes human rights problems faced by indigenous peoples across the globe, owing to patterns of domination consequent upon colonization. The rights articulated in the Declaration are drawn from principles of democracy and international human rights law. The Declaration is an instrument that elucidates means of respecting indigenous cultures' self-determination and distinctive identities, of restoring and maintaining their rights, and means of reconciliation.[139]

2008: The Longest Walk II—Indian leaders and people walk across the country to Washington DC to bring attention to treaty, governance, and other Native rights issues.[140]

2009: Congress enacts an apology that remains undelivered. It appears on pages 45 and 46 of the sixty-seven-page document "Defense Department Appropriations Act, 2010" (H.R. 3326). Section 8113 is "Apology to the Native Peoples of the United States." Its sponsors are Senators Sam Brownback (R-KS), Byron Dorgan (D-ND), and Daniel K. Inouye (D-HI). The act is passed by Congress and signed by President Barack Obama.[141]

2010: The Patient Protection and Affordable Care Act is signed into law by President Barack Obama. With this act the Indian Health Care Improvement Act of 1976 no longer has to be periodically renewed; it has been made permanent.[142]

2010: On December 16, 2010, at a White House gathering of leaders of U.S. indigenous nations and tribes, President Barack Obama announces U.S. support for the United Nations Declaration on the Rights of Indigenous Peoples.[143]

Continuing: Indian communities continue to engage with issues concerning land rights, resource rights, treaties, justice, policy, law, health, education, business, energy, environmental sustainability, culture, language, and art.

NOTES

INTRODUCTION

1. Nabokov, *Forest of Time*, 214–15.
2. Timothy Montler's article "The Grammar of Traditional Personal Names in Klallam" shows that traditional Northwest Coast names are generally proper nouns, which do not literally translate the meanings that are associated with the names. Brent Galloway observes that the name *Scälla* may not have a literal translation, but he does not rule out that the name may concern membership in a society connected with the whale, and that it could have distant etymological associations with Straits Salish words such as *quénes*: "whale," or *q'elhólemechn*: "killer whale" in the Samish dialect, a dialect closely related to Lummi, also a Straits Salish language (Galloway, personal communication, July 17, 2012).
3. P. Hillaire, *Totem Pole History*, and its media companion, "Coast Salish Totem Poles."
4. Hoopes, *Indian Affairs*, 1–10.
5. Coan, "First Stage of the Federal Indian Policy," 46–48.
6. Utley, *Indian Frontier*, 39–40.
7. Josephy, Nagel, and Johnson, *Red Power*, 157.
8. Hoopes, *Indian Affairs*, 19.
9. Ruth A. Gallaher, "The Indian Agent in the United States before 1850," *Iowa Journal of History and Politics* 14, no. 1 (January 1916): 37, cited in Hoopes, *Indian Affairs*, 28, 28n49.
10. Hoopes, *Indian Affairs*, 16–22.
11. Utley, *Indian Frontier*, 41.
12. Bernholz and Carr, "Annual Reports of the Commissioner of Indian Affairs," 540.

13. U.S. Government Documents (hereafter USGD), 2008, U.S. Department of the Interior, Bureau of Indian Affairs, "Commissioners of Indian Affairs."
14. Utley and Washburn, *Indian Wars*, 163–65.
15. Harmon, *Indians in the Making*, 53–55, 70–71.
16. Hoopes, *Indian Affairs*, 93.
17. Harmon, *Indians in the Making*, 87–88.
18. Hoxie, *Final Promise*, 147–51, 186–87. See also Prucha, *Great Father*, 503, 510. Under President Ulysses S. Grant, a Board of Indian Commissioners was organized in 1869 to reduce mismanagement by the Indian Service and to exercise joint control with the secretary of the interior over Indian appropriations. Religious leaders had a dominant voice in the group, which advocated Christianization, cessation of cash annuities, and abrogation of treaties.
19. Thornton, *American Indian Holocaust*, 133.
20. Joseph de la Cruz (Quinault), "On Knowing What Is Good for the American Indian." De la Cruz's comments appear in an editorial exchange with Wilcomb E. Washburn of the Smithsonian Institution in a dispute concerning the Longest Walk in 1978. See Josephy, Nagel, and Johnson, *Red Power*, 58–59.
21. Echo-Hawk, *In the Light of Justice*, 102–4, citing research by Lance G. Echo-Hawk, www.ehcounseling.com.
22. Harmon, "Indian Treaty History," 358–73.
23. Hanke, *Aristotle and American Indians*; Poole, *In Defense of the Indians*.
24. Waters, *American Indian Thought*.
25. Pratt, "Influence of the Iroquois," 274–314.
26. See, for example, Thom, "Paradox of Boundaries," 179–205.
27. Turner, "Oral Traditions," 230, 237.
28. Echo-Hawk, *In the Light of Justice*, 3.
29. Echo-Hawk, *In the Light of Justice*, 8. Alexander Hamilton (1755–1804) wrote fifty-one of the eighty-five essays later known as *The Federalist Papers* (first published in 1788), a series of essays defending the proposed U.S. Constitution.
30. Duane Champagne (Turtle Mountain Band of Chippewa), "Rethinking Native Relations with Contemporary Nation-States," in *Indigenous Peoples and the Modern State*, edited by Duane Champagne, Karen Jo Torjeson, and Susan Steiner (Lanham MD: Alta Mira Press, 2005), 18–19, cited in Echo-Hawk, *In the Light of Justice*, 129, 311n83.
31. United Nations, "Declaration on the Rights of Indigenous Peoples."
32. S. James Anaya (Apache-Purepecha), United Nations special rapporteur on the rights of Indigenous peoples, foreword, Echo-Hawk, *In the Light of Justice*, x.

33. Echo-Hawk, *In the Light of Justice*, 3–4.
34. Echo-Hawk, *In the Light of Justice*, 34–35.
35. Echo-Hawk, *In the Light of Justice*, xiv.
36. Echo-Hawk, *In the Light of Justice*, xiv, 10.

PROLOGUE

1. USGD, 1858, U.S. Congress, Senate, *Annual Report of the Commissioner of Indian Affairs* (hereafter cited as *ARCIA*, Simmons to Nesmith, 578.
2. See Stewart, *Cedar*.
3. USGD, 1858, U.S. Congress, Senate, *ARCIA*, Simmons to Nesmith, 583.

1. FORGOTTEN GENOCIDE

1. Charles J. Kappler lists 369 ratified treaties in *Indian Affairs: Laws and Treaties*, vol. 2: *Treaties*. On Kappler's list some treaties were accidentally omitted or merged. Such errors also occurred on the list maintained by the U.S. Department of State, which contains a total of 374 treaties. See Deloria and DeMallie, *Documents of American Indian Diplomacy*, vol. 1, ch. 5, "Valid Treaties," 252. Analysis by Deloria and DeMallie shows that correction of Kappler's list would result in a count of 372 ratified treaties between the U.S. government and Indian tribes. Correction of the State Department's list, which contains different errors, would also result in 372. The total would be 379 if the count includes the seven pre-revolutionary treaties that were negotiated by American colonists under British authority.
2. See R. A. Williams Jr., *American Indian in Western Legal Thought*.
3. Bernholz and Carr, "Annual Reports of the Commissioner of Indian Affairs," 540–45.
4. United Nations, "Convention on the Prevention and Punishment."
5. Rutecki, "Forced Sterilization," 33–42; "Killing Our Future: Sterilization and Experiments," *Akwasasne Notes*, no. 1, 4, cited in R. A. Williams Jr., *American Indian in Western Legal Thought*, 329n9.
6. Emmerich de Vattel, *The Law of Nations*, ed. Joseph Chitty (Philadelphia: T. and J. W. Johnson, 1867), 290, 326, cited in Jackson, *Century of Dishonor*, 12–13.
7. Grace Gouveia, introduction to Jackson, *Century of Dishonor*, xiii.
   Major J. Thomas Turner, quoted in Thrush, *Native Seattle*, 139.
   ʾh Sanderson Redfield, quoted in Thrush, *Native Seattle*, 139–40.
     Native Seattle, 154.
       ʾive Seattle*, 158.
         ʾer, *History of Indian Policy*, 7.

13. USGD, 1977, *American Indian Policy Review Commission, Final Report*, vol. 1, Preamble to Public Law 93-580.

14. USGD, 1977, *American Indian Policy Review Commission, Final Report*, "Separate Dissenting Views of Congressman Lloyd Meeds," 571.

15. USGD, 1977, "Separate Dissenting Views of Congressman Lloyd Meeds," 571.

16. Nugent, *Schooling of the Lummi Indians*.

17. Child, *Boarding School Seasons*; Lomawaima, *They Called It Prairie Light*; Lesiak, *White Man's Way*.

18. USGD, 1931, U.S. Congress, Senate, *Survey of Conditions of Indians in the United States*, 11759–75.

19. "Honor Pacts with America's Natives," *Omak (WA) Chronicle*, guest comment, U.S. Representatives Patrick J. Kennedy (D-RI) and Dale Kildee (D-MI), December 17, 1997, 4.

20. The "Indies" was a fifteenth-century term denoting Japan, China, the Ryukyu Islands, Spice Islands, Indonesia, Thailand, and the sweep of eastern Asia and Southeast Asia to the west coast of India. Columbus's error led to islands in the Caribbean being named the West Indies. See R. A. Williams Jr., *American Indian in Western Legal Thought*, 111n63.

21. Watson, *Leaving Paradise*; Koppel, *Kanaka*.

22. USGD, 1924, Indian Citizenship Act.

23. USGD, 1919, "An Act Granting Citizenship to Certain Indians."

24. USGD, 1887, General Allotment Act (Dawes Act).

25. USGD, 1897, "An Act to Prohibit the Sale of Intoxicating Drinks to Indians." See also USGD, 1895, U.S. Congress, House, "Sale of Intoxicants to Indians."

26. Calloway, *First Peoples*, 445.

27. Martin, "'Greatest Evil,'" 35–53.

28. Zinn, *People's History*, 298.

29. According to U.S. census data for 2006–8 (http://factfinder.census.gov/), there were 1,982,261 American Indians, 108,052 Alaska Natives, and 150,899 Native Hawaiians in the U.S. population. These three groups together represented 0.74 percent of the U.S. population of 301,237,703 at that time. The number of citizens who identified themselves as "American Indian and Alaska Native alone or in combination with other races" was 4,560,735, equivalent to about 1.5 percent of the U.S. population; those who identified as "Native Hawaiian alone or in any combination" totaled 449,328, equivalent to about 0.15 percent. Therefore, the total percentage of American Indians, Alaska Natives, and Native Hawaiians totaled approximately 1.65 percent of the U.S. population, according to U.S. census

data for 2006–8. The U.S. census permits citizens to identify ethnicity as they choose; therefore, the increased number of Native citizens reflects not only the rebound of many Native populations in the United States but also the increased willingness to claim Indian identity and, in some cases, the claiming of Indian identity that is unverified. Another factor relevant to consideration of U.S. census data is that fact that not all Native individuals are counted in the census. A more accurate estimate of the number of Native people in the United States would be obtained by incorporating data from tribal membership rolls. The Bureau of Indian Affair's (BIA's) 2005 *American Indian Population and Labor Force Report* indicates that the total number of enrolled members of federally recognized tribes is 1,978,099: about 2 million persons, which is less than half the number indicated by the U.S. census. However, the BIA figure excludes Native people who do not belong to federally recognized tribes. On the topic of identifying individuals as Native, see Jaimes, "Federal Indian Identification Policy," 279–86. Regarding projections of the U.S. American Indian population, see USGD, 1986, U.S. Office of Technology Assessment, "Four Projections."

30. Boxberger, *To Fish in Common*, 9.
31. Tanner, "'Take These Tribes Down.'" This article outlines the positions and activities of two national anti-Indian groups, the Citizens Equal Rights Alliance (CERA) and the Citizens Equal Rights Foundation (CERF). CERA and CERF held forums in several U.S. cities in 2013, including Bellingham, Washington.
32. USGD, 1883, U.S. Congress, House, *Annual Report of the Secretary of the Interior*, x–xiii.
33. Cole and Chakin, *Iron Hand upon the People*.
34. P. Hillaire, "Lummi Legends." The media companion to *Rights Remembered* includes a DVD, "A Century of Coast Salish Life at Lummi," and two audio collections, "Lummi Traditional Songs" and "Children's Songs and Stories from the Lummi Coast Salish Indians."
35. "Coast Salish Totem Poles." The media companion to *A Totem Pole History* includes a DVD, "Interpretation of Totem Poles," and two audio CDs, "Lummi Songs Sung by Joe Hillaire" and "Totem Pole Stories told by Pauline Hillaire." Songs of Joe Hillaire are also included in *Music of the American Indian: Northwest (Puget Sound)* recorded by Willard Rhodes.
36. USGD, 1881, U.S. Congress, House, *Codification of Laws on Survey and Disposition of Public Land*, 727. See also Duthu, *American Indians and the Law*, 75–82.

37. Boxberger, "In and Out of the Labor Force," 167–68.
38. Lummi Natural Resources Department, *Lummi Nation Atlas*, 52.
39. International Labour Organization, "C169 Indigenous and Tribal Peoples Convention." See also Duthu, *American Indians and the Law*, 202.
40. The Longest Walk, 1978–2008, http://www.longestwalk.org.
41. P. Hillaire, *Indian Policy*. This monograph was published by the *Omak (WA) Chronicle* newspaper in conjunction with the Longest Walk I, 1978.
42. Organization of American States, "American Declaration of the Rights and Duties of Man."
43. *Idaho World* (Idaho City ID), February 24, 1866. The *Owyhee Avalanche* (Ruby City ID) on December 16, 1866, carried a front-page article noting that on November 17, 1866, citizens and soldiers in the Humboldt Country had "rendered some fifty-five Indians permanently friendly."
44. Utley and Washburn, *Indian Wars*, 56, 181.
45. Franklin, *Autobiography*, 199.
46. Jackson, *Century of Dishonor*, 243–75.
47. Thornton, *American Indian Holocaust*, 44–45.
48. USGD, 1957, *Lummi Tribe of Indians v. the United States*, 525–42.
49. USGD, 1974, *U.S. v. State of Washington*.
50. Prucha, *American Indian Treaties*, 1, 103. For the history and texts of treaties, including unratified and other categories of treaties, see Deloria and DeMallie, *Documents of American Indian Diplomacy*. The texts of ratified treaties are available in Kappler, *Indian Affairs*, vol. 2: *Treaties*.

2. THE BUILDING OF AMERICA

1. See R. A. Williams Jr., *American Indian in Western Legal Thought*.
2. Pope Nicholas V, *Romanus Pontifex*, 13–20.
3. Pope Alexander VI, *Inter caetera divinai*, 9–13.
4. Hanke, *Spanish Struggle for Justice*, 18–19.
5. Van Doren and Boyd, *Indian Treaties*, 78.
6. See Calloway, *Crown and Calumet*.
7. Mathes, *Helen Hunt Jackson*, 160.
8. Timothy Walker, *Introduction to American Law* (Cincinnati: Derby, 1846), 33, cited in Jackson, *Century of Dishonor*, 7–8.
9. Jackson, *Century of Dishonor*, 8.
10. Jackson, *Century of Dishonor*, 8.
11. Vattel, *Law of Nations*, cited in Jackson, *Century of Dishonor*, 9.
12. Jackson, *Century of Dishonor*, 10.

13. Jackson, *Century of Dishonor*, 382–85.
14. Jackson, *Century of Dishonor*, 298–335.
15. Zinn, *People's History*, 298.
16. Zinn, *People's History*, 299.
17. Zinn, *People's History*, 300.
18. Zinn, *People's History*, 316.
19. Lord Jeffrey Amherst to Colonel Henry Bouquet, July 16, 1763 (microfilmed copy of letter), University of Massachusetts–Amherst, Department of Legal Studies, British Manuscript Project, 1941–1945, http://www.umass.edu/legal /derrico/amherst/lord_jeff.html.
20. Vanderwerth, *Indian Oratory*.
21. Josephy, *Patriot Chiefs*.
22. Hudson, *Black Drink*.
23. Dowd, "Thinking outside the Circle," 30–52.
24. Zinn, *Howard Zinn on War*, 45.

3. CENTURIES OF INJUSTICE

1. P. Hillaire, *Totem Pole History*, 14.
2. See Suttles, "Central Coast Salish," 464; Suttles, "Affinal Ties, Subsistence, and Prestige," 16–17; Harmon, *Indians in the Making*, 85, 85n37. Harmon describes the Lummi in the treaty era as "a group of loosely affiliated and complex lineages, linked by marriages and grouped around various head-men who established large, multifamily houses in portions of the San Juan Islands and the Bellingham Bay area"; see "Performing Treaties" in *Power of Promises*, 161. Harmon's article "Indian Treaty History" examines notions of "tribe" and "chief" in the Northwest as U.S. constructions (366, 366n15). An article by Thom, "The Paradox of Boundaries in Coast Salish Territories," addresses permeable boundaries such as kin, travel, and sharing, which establish "borderless kin networks" that transcend regions delineated by occupancy and land use. See also Marian W. Smith, "The Coast Salish of Puget Sound," for a discussion of sociopolitical life in Coast Salish villages written in the mid-twentieth century (198).
3. USGD, 1787, Northwest Ordinance.
4. USGD, 1791, U.S. Congress, "Speech of President George Washington," 16.
5. Prucha, *Great Father*, 52–53.
6. USGD, 1911, *Checklist of United States Public Documents*, 493.
7. USGD, 1942, F. S. Cohen, *Handbook of Federal Indian Law*, "Commissioners of Indian Affairs, 1832–1933" (table), 12.

8. USGD, 1942, F. S. Cohen, *Handbook of Federal Indian Law*, 11.

9. Elbert Herring, *ARCIA* (1831), 172, cited in USGD, 1942, F. S. Cohen, *Handbook of Federal Indian Law*, 12, 12n65.

10. Herring, *ARCIA* (1831), 12, 12n65.

11. Herring, *ARCIA* (1832), 160, cited in USGD, 1942, F. S. Cohen, *Handbook of Federal Indian Law*, 13, 13n67.

12. Herring, *ARCIA* (1833), 186, cited in USGD, 1942, F. S. Cohen, *Handbook of Federal Indian Law*, 13, 13n68.

13. Presidents Monroe and Adams followed a policy of voluntary emigration by Indians, but President Jackson, even though no changes are evident in the U.S. statutes to warrant it, used military force. Laurence F. Schmeckebier, *The Office of Indian Affairs: Its History, Activities, and Organization* (Baltimore, 1927), cited in USGD, 1942, F. S. Cohen, *Handbook of Federal Indian Law*, 13n69.

14. USGD, 1852, U.S. Congress, Senate, *ARCIA*, Lea to Stuart, 294.

15. See R. A. Williams Jr., *American Indian in Western Legal Thought*. See also F. S. Cohen's *Handbook of Federal Indian Law* (2005 edition, 10–15) for an overview of early European legal theories on colonization.

16. USGD, 1856, U.S. Congress, House, *ARCIA*, Manypenny to McClelland, 572.

17. USGD, 1855, U.S. Congress, House, *ARCIA*, Manypenny to McClelland, 337–38.

18. USGD, 1830, Indian Removal Act, 411–12. See also Prucha, *Great Father*, 191–208.

19. USGD, 2013, U.S. Department of the Interior, National Park Service, *National Native American Graves and Repatriation Act*, map.

20. USGD, 1942, F. S. Cohen, *Handbook of Federal Indian Law*, Section C: "Indian Removal Westward, 1817 to 1846," 53–63.

21. Perdue and Green, *Cherokee Removal*.

22. Thompson, *Army and the Navajo*; Roessel, *Navajo Stories*.

23. USGD, 1842, U.S. Congress, House, *Annual Report of the Secretary of War*.

24. USGD, 1850, U.S. Congress, Senate, *ARCIA*, Loughery to Gaines, Skinner, and Allen.

25. USGD, 1850, U.S. Congress, Senate, *ARCIA*, Loughery to Gaines, Skinner, and Allen, 146.

26. USGD, 1852, U.S. Congress, Senate, *ARCIA*, Starling to Dart.

27. USGD, 1850, U.S. Congress, Senate, *ARCIA*, Loughery to Gaines, Skinner, and Allen, 146.

28. USGD, 1850, U.S. Congress, Senate, *ARCIA*, Loughery to Gaines, Skinner, and Allen, 146.

29. USGD, 1850, U.S. Congress, Senate, *ARCIA,* Loughery to Gaines, Skinner, and Allen, 146–47.

30. USGD, 1850, U.S. Congress, Senate, *ARCIA,* Loughery to Gaines, Skinner, and Allen, 147.

31. Edson, *Fourth Corner,* 74.

32. USGD, 1842, U.S. Congress, House, *Annual Report of the Secretary of War,* 189.

33. USGD, 1854, U.S. Congress, Senate, *ARCIA,* Palmer to Manypenny.

34. USGD, 1856, U.S. Congress, House, *ARCIA,* Manypenny to McClelland, 569.

35. USGD, 1856, U.S. Congress, House, *ARCIA,* Manypenny to McClelland, 572.

36. USGD, 1856, U.S. Congress, House, *ARCIA,* Manypenny to McClelland, 575.

37. A 2003 study by Northwest Economic Associates projected that the number of Indians living on the Lummi Reservation could increase from 2,346 in the year 2000 to 3,767 in 2010, to 15,451 in 2020. Lummi Natural Resources Department, *Lummi Nation Multi-Hazard Mitigation Plan,* 3.

4. RESERVATION CREATION

1. USGD, 1966, *Ratified Indian Treaties.* See Prucha, *American Indian Treaties.* See also Deloria and DeMallie, *Documents of American Indian Diplomacy,* which contains the texts of eighteen categories of treaties and agreements, including those rejected by Congress and those rejected by Indian nations.

2. USGD, 1848, U.S. Congress, House, Department of War, *General Orders.*

3. When the United States established the Oregon Territory (by the Act of August 14, 1848), Section 14 of that act extended the Northwest Ordinance to the Oregon Territory (1 Stat. 51, Note A).

4. USGD, 1848, U.S. Congress, House, Department of War, *General Orders,* 180.

5. Stevens, *Life of Isaac Ingalls Stevens,* vol. 1, ch. 24.

6. USGD, 1848, U.S. Congress, House, *Annual Message of the President.*

7. USGD, 1841, U.S. Congress, Senate, *Annual Report of the Secretary of War.*

8. USGD, 1934, U.S. Court of Claims, *Duwamish et al. v. U.S.*

9. USGD, 1850, U.S. Congress, Senate, *ARCIA,* Lane to Solmie, 165.

10. USGD, 1853, U.S. Congress, House, *Annual Report of the Secretary of War,* "Report on the Indian Tribes of the Territory of Washington," 419–66.

11. W. T. Tolmie was a physician and surgeon, ornithologist, and entrepreneur with the British Hudson's Bay Company. The HBC maintained a monopoly on the fur trade in the nineteenth-century Pacific Northwest. Founded in 1640, it is the oldest continuously operated company in North America, with operations in a range of industries, including finance, car rental, and

foods. It also operates the department store chain Lord & Taylor. Hudson's Bay Company, http://www3.hbc.com/.

12. USGD, 1850, U.S. Congress, Senate, *ARCIA*, Lane to Solmie, 157–63.

13. USGD, 1850, U.S. Congress, Senate, *ARCIA*, Lane to Solmie, 162.

14. USGD, 1852, U.S. Congress, Senate, *ARCIA*, Starling to Dart, 459.

15. USGD, 1852, U.S. Congress, Senate, *ARCIA*, Starling to Dart, 461–62.

16. USGD, 1850, U.S. Congress, Senate, *ARCIA*, Lea to Dart, 150.

17. USGD, 1853, U.S. Congress, Senate, *ARCIA*, Manypenny to Stevens, 454–55.

18. USGD, 1854, U.S. Congress, Senate, *ARCIA*, Stevens to Manypenny, 454.

19. USGD, 1854, U.S. Congress, Senate, *ARCIA*, Stevens to Manypenny, 458–59.

20. USGD, 1853, U.S. Congress, House, *Annual Report of the Secretary of War*, "Report on the Indian Tribes of the Territory of Washington."

21. USGD, 1853, U.S. Congress, House, *Annual Report of the Secretary of War*, "Report on the Indian Tribes of the Territory of Washington," 461.

22. USGD, 1853, U.S. Congress, House, *Annual Report of the Secretary of War*, "Report on the Indian Tribes of the Territory of Washington," 455.

23. USGD, 1853, U.S. Congress, House, *Annual Report of the Secretary of War*, "Report on the Indian Tribes of the Territory of Washington," 455.

24. USGD, 1850, U.S. Congress, Senate, *ARCIA*, Lea to Dart, 149.

25. USGD, 1850, U.S. Congress, Senate, *ARCIA*, Lea to Dart, 151.

26. USGD, 1853, U.S. Congress, Senate, *ARCIA*, Manypenny to Stevens.

27. USGD, 1852, U.S. Congress, Senate, *ARCIA*, Starling to Dart, 464–65.

28. USGD, 1852, U.S. Congress, Senate, *ARCIA*, Lea to Stuart, 293.

29. USGD, 1853, U.S. Congress, House, *Annual Report of the Secretary of War*, "Report on the Indian Tribes of the Territory of Washington," 452.

30. USGD, 1850, U.S. Congress, Senate, *ARCIA*, Lea to Dart, 167.

31. USGD, 1850, U.S. Congress, Senate, *ARCIA*, Lea to Dart, 167.

32. USGD, 1853, U.S. Congress, House, *Annual Report of the Secretary of War*, "Report on the Indian Tribes of the Territory of Washington," 453.

33. USGD, 1942, F. S. Cohen, *Handbook of Federal Indian Law*, "Indian Trade: History of Legislation," 348–51.

34. USGD, 1853, U.S. Congress, Senate, *ARCIA*, Manypenny to McClelland, 261.

35. A list of "Sources of Income" for the tribes is found in USGD, 1942, F. S. Cohen, *Handbook of Federal Indian Law*, 342.

36. Section 3 of the Act of June 22, 1874; in USGD, 1942, F. S. Cohen, *Handbook of Federal Indian Law*, 340.

37. USGD, 1942, F. S. Cohen, *Handbook of Federal Indian Law*, 340.

38. USGD, 1942, F. S. Cohen, *Handbook of Federal Indian Law*, 343–40.

39. USGD, 1850, Donation Land Claim Act.
40. Stephens, "Oregon's Courts under the Provisional Government."
41. USGD, 1934, U.S. Court of Claims, *Duwamish et al. v. U.S.*, Sects. XIII, XLVI.
42. USGD, 1952, *Lummi Tribe of Indians v. the United States.*
43. Thrush, *Native Seattle*, 45.
44. USGD, 1854, U.S. Congress, Senate, *ARCIA*, Manypenny to McClelland.
45. USGD, 1853, U.S. Congress, Senate, *ARCIA*, Manypenny to McClelland, 260.
46. USGD, 1934, U.S. Court of Claims, *Duwamish et al. v. U.S.*
47. USGD, 1873, U.S. Congress, Senate, *ARCIA*, Milroy to Smith.
48. USGD, 1944, U.S. Congress, House, Committee on Indian Affairs, *Investigate Indian Affairs.*
49. Deloria and DeMallie make the distinction that although the seven pre-revolutionary treaties were not produced by negotiators representing the United States and are not therefore treaties for which the U.S. government takes responsibility, these seven treaties should nevertheless be considered valid, absent evidence to the contrary. Deloria and DeMallie, *Documents of American Indian Diplomacy*, 201–2.
50. Clark, *Lone Wolf v. Hitchcock.*
51. Wilkins and Lomawaima, *Uneven Ground*, 15–16, 101–2, 110–11, 170–71.
52. Prucha, *American Indian Treaties*, 356–57.
53. See Bierwert, "Remembering Chief Seattle," 283, 301n14. Bierwert's article examines versions and interpretations of Seattle's speech, utilizing Native sources. Bierwert notes that Henry Smith, who transcribed the speech, states that it was given during Governor Stevens's first visit to the city of Seattle. Concerning the date of the speech, Bierwert also cites David Buerge's article "Seattle's King Arthur" in *Seattle Weekly* (January 17, 1991), 28.
54. Jefferson, *World of Chief Seattle*, 91.
55. USGD, 1855, Ratified Treaty No. 283. The proceedings of the Treaty of Point Elliott are available also from the U.S. government's Records of the Office of Indian Affairs, "Documents Relating to the Negotiation of Ratified and Unratified Treaties with Various Indian Tribes," *Records of the Proceedings of the Commission to Hold Treaties with the Indian Tribes in Washington Territory and the Blackfoot Country* (T494, reel 5, frames 205–6). A Native history of the treaty council, and the times that followed, is available in Hilbert, *Siastənu*, 18–30. Siastənu (Ruth Shelton) was born in 1857. Audio recordings of her relating oral history, which Vi Hilbert translated to produce the text, were made in the 1950s by Leon Metcalf.

56. USGD, 1853, U.S. Congress, Senate, *ARCIA*, Manypenny to McClelland, 261.
57. "Point Elliott, 1855," *Lummi Squol-quol* 1, no. 1 (November–December, 1973).
58. Nugent, *History of Lummi Fishing Rights*, 5.
59. USGD, 1854, U.S. Congress, Senate, *ARCIA*, Stevens to Manypenny, 455–56, 458.
60. USGD, 1855, U.S. Congress, House, *Report of the Secretary of the Commissioner of Indian Affairs*, Manypenny to McClelland, 339–40.
61. USGD, 1855, U.S. Congress, House, *ARCIA*, Manypenny to McClelland, 340.

5. AFTER THE TREATY

1. USGD, 1858, U.S. Congress, Senate, *ARCIA*, Simmons to Smith, 582–83.
2. USGD, 1858, U.S. Congress, Senate, *ARCIA*, Simmons to Smith, 583.
3. USGD, 1858, U.S. Congress, Senate, *ARCIA*, Nesmith to Mix, 574.
4. USGD, 1858, U.S. Congress, Senate, *ARCIA*, Fitzhugh to Simmons, 575.
5. USGD, 1858, U.S. Congress, Senate, *Annual Report of the Secretary of the Interior*, 580–81.
6. USGD, 1858, U.S. Congress, Senate, *Annual Report of the Secretary of the Interior*, 581.
7. USGD, 1858, U.S. Congress, Senate, *Annual Report of the Secretary of the Interior*, 580–82.
8. USGD, 1858, U.S. Congress, Senate, *Annual Report of the Secretary of the Interior*, 582.
9. See Boyd, *Coming of the Spirit of Pestilence*.
10. USGD, 1854, U.S. Congress, Senate, *ARCIA*, Stevens to Manypenny, 440.
11. USGD, 1853, U.S. Congress, House, *Annual Report of the Secretary of War*, "Medical Report," 125, 126; and "Report of the Indian Tribes of the Territory of Washington," 433, 454, 455–56. For evidence of smallpox in the years 1860 and 1869, see the National Archives census records, Seattle. See also the image of an 1872 handbill, warning of smallpox in Seattle (University of Washington Library Special Collections, image 4095) in Thrush, *Native Seattle*, 2007.
12. USGD, 1853, U.S. Congress, House, *Annual Report of the Secretary of War*, "Report on the Indian Tribes of the Territory of Washington," 454, 455–56.
13. USGD, 1854, U.S. Congress, Senate, *ARCIA*, Stevens to Manypenny, 439.
14. Richards, "Stevens Treaties of 1854–55," 6–7.
15. USGD, 1934, U.S. Court of Claims, *Duwamish et al. v. U.S.*; Department of Ecology, State of Washington, http://www.ecy.wa.gov; Washington Governor's Office of Indian Affairs, http://goia.wa.gov.
16. USGD, 1899, *Eighteenth Annual Report*, 868, 864.

17. USGD, 1899, *Eighteenth Annual Report*, 834.
18. USGD, 1859, U.S. Congress, Senate, *ARCIA*, Simmons to Geary, 766. The reservation areas, original and adjusted, are listed in USGD, 1934, U.S. Court of Claims, *Duwamish et al. v. U.S.*
19. USGD, 1899, *Eighteenth Annual Report*, 868; USGD, 1873, "Executive Orders Related to Indian Reserves," 917.
20. USGD, 1958, Public Law 85-612.
21. USGD, 1875, U.S. Congress, House, *Indians in Washington Territory*, 167.
22. Boxberger, "In and Out of the Labor Force," 165.
23. Suttles, "Post-Contact Culture Change," 71, 85.
24. USGD, 1867, U.S. Congress, Senate, *ARCIA*, Finkbonner to Elder, 58.
25. USGD, 1932, U.S. Congress, Senate, *Survey of Conditions of Indians in the United States*, Hearing before a Subcommittee on Indian Affairs, Hearings at Tacoma WA, 11794.
26. Richardson and Galloway, *Nooksack Place Names*, 22.
27. Swinomish Indian Tribal Community, "Swinomish Climate Change Initiative," 7.
28. USGD, 1887, General Allotment Act (Dawes Act).
29. Prucha, *Great Father*, 667–80.
30. Hoxie, *Final Promise*, 70–71, 76.
31. Prucha, *Great Father*, 864–65.
32. Boxberger, "In and Out of the Labor Force," 167–68.
33. Harmon, *Indians in the Making*, 113–14.
34. USGD, 1855, Treaty with the Dwamish, Suquamish, etc./Treaty of Point Elliott, Article 7.
35. Tribal Law and Policy Institute, *Tribal Court Clearinghouse*, "Fractionated Ownership of Indian Lands."
36. Kent, *Kent's Commentary on International Law*, 394.
37. USGD, 1942, F. S. Cohen, *Handbook of Federal Indian Law*, 12.
38. Morris, "Forest Fires," 313–39. The article documents a sawmill catching fire from a forest fire raging in the woods around Bellingham Bay; it was part of a series of fires that occurred in western Washington and western Oregon in 1868.
39. Lummi Natural Resources Department, *Lummi Nation Multi-Hazard Mitigation Plan*, 21, 146.
40. Nugent, *History of Lummi Legal Action*, 38–82.
41. USGD, 1857, U.S. Congress, House, *ARCIA*, 299.
42. USGD, 1855, U.S. Congress, House, *ARCIA*, Cain to Manypenny, 513.
43. USGD, 1855, U.S. Congress, House, *ARCIA*, Manypenny to McClelland, 334.

44. Stevens, *Life of Isaac Ingalls Stevens*, 479. See also Richards, *Isaac I. Stevens*.

45. Stevens, *Life of Isaac Ingalls Stevens*, 479.

46. Washington Secretary of State, "Northern Oregonians Vote to Split."

47. USGD, 1855, U.S. Congress, House, ARCIA, Cain to Manypenny, 513; and Palmer to Cain, 514–15.

48. See Ruby and Brown, *Indians of the Pacific Northwest*, 100–122, 145–54.

49. Northwest Digital Archives, *Cayuse, Yakima and Rogue River Wars Papers*, "Summary."

50. Northwest Digital Archives, *Cayuse, Yakima and Rogue River Wars Papers*, "Summary."

51. See Deloria and DeMallie, *Documents of American Indian Diplomacy*, vol. 1, ch. 8, "Railroad Agreements," 514–62.

52. See Harmon, *Power of Promises*. See also Haines, "Problems of Indian Policy," 205–7.

53. Following is a list of the ten treaties in the Pacific Northwest concluded by Isaac I. Stevens, Washington territorial governor and superintendent of Indian Affairs. Two of these treaties were concluded by Stevens and Joel Palmer, Oregon territorial governor and superintendent of Indian Affairs: the Treaty with the Wallawalla, etc. and the Treaty with the Nez Perce. Following the name of each treaty is a list of the current tribes that are party to that treaty and the page numbers of the treaty texts in Kappler, *Indian Affairs*, vol. 2: *Treaties*: (1) Treaty with the Nisqualli, etc./Treaty of Medicine Creek (Nisqually, Puyallup, Squaxin Island, and Muckleshoot, in the southern Puget Sound area), signed 12/12/1854, ratified 3/3/1855 [Kappler, 661–64]). (2) Treaty with the Dwamish, Suquamish, etc./Treaty of Point Elliott (Lummi, Nooksack, Samish, Upper Skagit, Swinomish, Tulalip, Suquamish, Sauk-Suiattle, Stillaguamish, Snoqualmie, and Muckleshoot), signed 1/22/1855, ratified 3/8/1859 [Kappler, 669–73]. (3) Treaty with the S'Klallam/Treaty of Point No Point (Jamestown S'Klallam, Port Gamble S'Klallam, and Lower Elwha S'Klallam, on the Strait of Jan de Fuca, and the Skokomish, on Hood Canal), signed 1/26/1855, ratified 3/8/1859 [Kappler, 674–77]. (4) Treaty with the Makah/Treaty of Neah Bay (Makah Tribe, Cape Flattery), signed 1/31/1855, ratified 3/8/1859 [Kappler, 682–85]. (5) Treaty with the Wallawalla, etc. (Walla Walla, Cayuse, and Umatilla tribes and bands in southeastern Washington and in Oregon), signed 6/9/1855, ratified 3/8/1859 [Kappler, 694–98]. (6) Treaty with the Yakima, etc. (Yakama and confederated tribes and bands in southcentral Washington), signed 6/9/1855, ratified 3/8/1859 [Kappler, 698–702]. (7) Treaty with the Nez Perce (Nez Perce, southeastern Washington, Oregon, and Idaho; now

in north central Idaho), signed 6/11/1855, ratified 3/8/1859. (8) Treaty of Quinaielt/Treaty of Olympia (Quinault, Hoh, and Quileute, on the Olympic Coast), signed 7/1/1855 and 1/25/1856, ratified 3/8/1859 [Kappler, 719–21]). Stevens also negotiated two treaties, one in Montana Territory and one in Nebraska Territory, which were important for opening railroad routes to the Northwest. (9) Treaty with the Flathead, etc./Treaty of Hell Gate, with the Bitter Root Salish, Kootenai, and Pend d'Oreille/Upper Kalispel (Confederated Salish and Kootenai Tribes of the Flathead Nation), signed 7/16/1855, ratified 3/8/1859 [Kappler, 722–25]. (10) Treaty with the Blackfeet, signed 10/17/1855, ratified 4/15/1856 [Kappler, 736–40]. Isaac Stevens and Colonel Alfred Cumming were the treaty commissioners representing the United States in the Treaty with the Blackfeet; it is the only one of Stevens's treaties that does not have provisions concerning fishing rights.

6. LEGAL AND LAND RIGHTS

1. USGD, 1968, Civil Rights Act. Titles II–VII deal with Indian matters. See Prucha, *Documents of United States Indian Policy*, 2nd ed., 249–52.
2. USGD, 1853, U.S. Congress, Senate, *ARCIA*, Manypenny to McClelland, 261.
3. *Black's Law Dictionary*; see under "laches."
4. USGD, 1942, F. S. Cohen, *Handbook of Federal Indian Law*, 163.
5. Getches, Wilkinson, and Williams, *Cases and Materials*; Pevar, *Rights of Indians and Tribes*; Wilkins and Lomawaima, *Uneven Ground*.
6. USGD, 1942, F. S. Cohen, *Handbook of Federal Indian Law*, 96.
7. Prucha, *Great Father*, 1017–18.
8. USGD, 1946, Indian Claims Commission Act.
9. Pevar, *Rights of Indians and Tribes*, 368–69.
10. Wilkins and Lomawaima, *Uneven Ground*, 100–116.
11. USGD, 1934, U.S. Court of Claims, *Duwamish et al. v. U.S.*
12. Nugent, *History of Lummi Legal Action*, Appendix A: "Testimony of Ten Lummi Elders at the Court Hearing of D'wamish et al. v. U.S., 1927," 38–83.
13. USGD, 1934, U.S. Court of Claims, *Duwamish et al. v. U.S.*, Sects. XVI, XLIII, XLVI.
14. USGD, 1919, *U.S. v. Romaine et al.*
15. USGD, 1931, *United States v. Stotts*; USGD, 1931, *United States v. Boynton*.
16. Deloria, *Indians of the Pacific Northwest*, 140, 177–89.
17. USGD, 1934, U.S. Court of Claims, *Duwamish et al. v. U.S.*, Sect. XLVI, see under "Counterclaims of the United States."
18. USGD, 1934, U.S. Court of Claims, *Duwamish et al. v. U.S.*, Sects. XLIII, XLVI.

19. Wilkins, *Hollow Justice*, 55.

20. USGD, 1952, *Lummi Tribe of Indians v. the United States*.

21. Indian Claims Commission Decisions, Oklahoma State University Library, OSU Digital Publishing Center, http:digital.library.okstate.edu/icc/.

22. USGD, 1952, *Lummi Tribe of Indians v. the United States*.

23. Nugent, *History of Lummi Legal Action*, 20; USGD, 1952, *Lummi Tribe of Indians v. the United States*.

24. Nugent, *History of Lummi Legal Action*, Appendix A, 40–41.

25. Nugent, *History of Lummi Legal Action*, 5–6.

26. Nugent, *History of Lummi Legal Action*, Appendix A, 40–41.

27. USGD, 1850, U.S. Congress, Senate, ARCIA, Loughery to Gaines, Skinner, and Allen, 146–47.

28. See Lazarus, *Black Hills/White Justice*; Josephy, Nagel, and Johnson, *Red Power*, 157–59.

29. USGD, 1934, U.S. Court of Claims, *Duwamish et al. v. U.S.*, Sect. XXII.

30. Lummi Natural Resources Department, *Lummi Nation Atlas*, 6.

31. Nugent, *History of Lummi Legal Action*, 5, Appendix A, 53.

32. Lummi Natural Resources Department, *Lummi Nation Atlas*, 52.

33. Lummi Natural Resources Department, *Lummi Nation Multi-Hazard Mitigation Plan*, 43–45.

34. Carpenter, Pascualy, and Hunter, *Nisqually Indian Tribe*.

35. *Bellingham (WA) Herald*, Letters to the Editor, Pauline Hillaire, "Dawson Misunderstands Lummi Nation, Treaty" (February 1, 2001); *Bellingham (WA) Herald*, Letters to the Editor, Marlene Dawson, "Federal Dollars Should Not Fund Separate Services" (May 20, 2002), "Cantwell, Others, Chose to Ignore Rule of Law" (March 31, 2003), "How Will Candidates Correct the Tribal Land Status Ruse?" (August 10, 2003); *Washington Post*, Editorial, Sen. Slade Gorton (R-WA), "Indians Are Getting a Fair Shake" (September 18, 1995, A-19); *New York Times*, Timothy Egan, "Indians Unite against a Senator, Despite His Grip on Tribal Funds" (August 25, 2000).

36. Hoig, *Sand Creek Massacre*, 180.

37. USGD, 2013, Violence against Women Reauthorization Act. This law "improves and expands legal tools and grant programs addressing domestic violence, dating violence, sexual assault, and stalking."

38. In *Cherokee Nation v. Georgia* (USGD, 1831), Chief Justice John Marshall designated Indian tribes "domestic dependent nations," whose relationship with the United States "resembles that of a ward to his guardian." See Deloria, *American Indian Policy*, ch. 11, "The Evolution of Federal Policy Making," 239–56.

39. Northwest Indian College, Bellingham WA, www.nwic.edu.

7. A SHRINKING LAND BASE

1. USGD, 1961, U.S. Congress, House, Committee of Interior and Insular Affairs, *Indian Heirship Land Study*, 1:1–2.
2. USGD, 1963, U.S. Congress, Senate, *Relating to the Indian Heirship Land Problem*.
3. USGD, 2004, American Indian Probate Reform Act (AIPRA). "Some allotment shares are as small as one nine-millionth of the original parcel; if the smallest shares could be physically partitioned, they would be smaller than a piece of paper; the average allotment has 17.4 owners; the number of allotment shares under 2 percent doubles every seven years; the number of fractional shares could increase from 1.5 million in 1994 to 11 million by 2030; the BIA estimates that 50–75 percent of its realty budget is spent managing fractionated interests" (American Indian Law Clinic, "What Will Happen to Your Land?"). When this presentation was given in 2007, only one tribe had an approved tribal probate code under AIPRA: the Lummi Nation.
4. See chapter 3 of Cole, *Captured Heritage* (48–69), for an account of museum collecting and research on the Northwest Coast in the late nineteenth century, including a tour by Bella Coola Salish people who gave performances in Germany in 1885–86, for both public and scholarly audiences. Nettl's *North American Indian Musical Styles* discusses findings in major studies (European and American) of Northwest Coast music (8–14). Densmore's "History of the Study of Indian Music" shows the prominence of both Northwest Coast music and of German scholars in early Anglo-European studies of Native music (115–23).
5. P. Hillaire, *Totem Pole History*, 59–61, 152–61.
6. USGD, 1855, U.S. Congress, House, *ARCIA*, Manypenny to McClelland, 340.
7. USGD, 1852, U.S. Congress, Senate, *ARCIA*, Lea to Stuart, 293.
8. USGD, 1883, U.S. Congress, House, *Annual Report of the Secretary of the Interior*, x–xiii.
9. "Kill the Indian, but save the Man" was originally stated in a paper read by Captain Richard B. Pratt, speaking at a convention about the Carlisle Indian School, a U.S. training and industrial school founded by Pratt in 1879 at Carlisle Barracks, Pennsylvania. The Carlisle Indian School was a model for about 150 U.S. Indian boarding schools in operation at the end of the nineteenth century to "civilize" and assimilate Indian youth. *Official Report of the Nineteenth Annual Conference of Charities and Correction*, 1892, 46–59, reprinted in Richard H. Pratt, "The Advantages of Mingling Indians

with Whites," in Prucha, *Americanizing the American Indians*, 260–71. Also available at the Center for Media and Learning, City University of New York, and the Roy Rosenzweig Center for History and New Media, George Mason University, "'Kill the Indian, and Save the Man': Capt. Richard H. Pratt on the Education of Native Americans," History Matters: The U.S. Survey Course on the Web, http://historymatters.gmu.edu/d/4929/.

10. Deloria, *Indians of the Pacific Northwest*, 135.
11. USGD, 1926, U.S. Congress, Senate, "For the purpose of reclaiming certain lands."

8. ABORIGINAL FISHERMEN

1. USGD, 1841, U.S Congress, Senate, *Annual Report of the Secretary of War*, 61–62.
2. USGD, 1850, "An Act for Removal of Western Washington Indians," 272. See Prucha, *Great Father,* 397–99, 398n42.
3. Ezra Meeker, *Pioneer Reminiscences of Puget Sound: The Tragedy of Leschi* (Seattle: Lowman and Hanford, 1905), cited in F. G. Cohen, *Treaties on Trial*, 30.
4. Garfield and Johnnie (Sts'aStelQuyd), "Revised Statement of Significance Concerning Nomination," 1. See Ames and Maschner, *Peoples of the Northwest Coast.*
5. Jenness, "Faith of a Coast Salish Indian," 21.
6. Jenness, "Faith of a Coast Salish Indian," 21–22; Wayne P. Suttles, 1988, correspondence to Bouchard, cited in Garfield and Johnnie, "Revised Statement of Significance," 5.
7. Garfield and Johnnie, "Revised Statement of Significance," 2.
8. Garfield and Johnnie, "Revised Statement of Significance," 1.
9. Stein, *Exploring Coast Salish Prehistory.*
10. Garfield and Johnnie, "Revised Statement of Significance," 1, 2.
11. Nugent, *Lummi Elders Speak.*
12. Lane, *Political and Economic Aspects*, 6, cited in Nugent, *History of Lummi Fishing Rights*, 3–4.
13. Olin D. Wheeler, *The Trail of Lewis of Clark, 1804-1904* (New York: Putnam, 1926), 2:139, cited in F. G. Cohen, *Treaties on Trial*, 30, 193n32.
14. Lane, *Political and Economic Aspects*, 9, cited in Nugent, *History of Lummi Fishing Rights*, 6.
15. F. G. Cohen, *Treaties on Trial*, 25.
16. Lane, *Political and Economic Aspects*, 18, cited in Nugent, *History of Lummi Fishing Rights*, 7.

17. Stein, *Exploring Coast Salish Prehistory*, 31–34. For details about reef netting and other types of fishing, see Boxberger, *To Fish in Common*; Stewart, *Indian Fishing*.
18. Deloria, *Indians of the Pacific Northwest*, 22–23.
19. Garfield and Johnnie, "Revised Statement of Significance," 2.
20. Coan, "First Stage of Federal Indian Policy," 46–47.
21. USGD, 1854, U.S. Congress, Senate, *ARCIA*, Stevens to Manypenny, 456.
22. F. G. Cohen, *Treaties on Trial*, 40–43.
23. Russel L. Barsh, *The Washington Fishing Rights Controversy: An Economic Critique*, 2nd ed. (Seattle: University of Washington, Graduate School of Business Administration, 1979), 23–24, cited in F. G. Cohen, *Treaties on Trial*, 44, 196n42.
24. William A. Wilcox, "Notes on the Fisheries of the Pacific Coast in 1895," in *Report of the Commissioner of Fish and Fisheries for 1896* (Washington DC: Government Printing Office, 1998), 592, cited in Boxberger, *To Fish in Common*, 49.
25. USGD, 1897, *U.S. v. Alaska Packers Association*.
26. Boxberger, *To Fish in Common*, 50–53.
27. Nugent, *History of Lummi Fishing Rights*, 18, 23.
28. Nugent, *History of Lummi Fishing Rights*, 28–29.
29. Deloria, *Indians of the Pacific Northwest*, 138–39.
30. Nugent, *History of Lummi Fishing Rights*, 23, 60n55.
31. F. G. Cohen, *Treaties on Trial*, 59.
32. F. G. Cohen, *Treaties on Trial*, 43.
33. Bureau of Indian Affairs, Portland, October 8, 1962, "Summary of Regular Monthly Staff Meeting," Sand Point 21524, report by George Dysart, Assistant Regional Solicitor, June 8, 1962, cited in Nugent, *History of Lummi Fishing Rights*, 49.
34. USGD, 1905, *U.S. v. Winans*.
35. USGD, 1916, *State of Washington v. Alexis*; Nugent, *History of Lummi Fishing Rights*, 24–26, 32–34.
36. Nugent, *History of Lummi Fishing Rights*, 34–35.
37. USGD, 1916, *State of Washington v. Towessnute*.
38. USGD, 1942, *Tulee v. State of Washington*.
39. F. G. Cohen, *Treaties on Trial*, 62–63; Boxberger, *To Fish in Common*, 109.
40. F. G. Cohen, *Treaties on Trial*, 59, 63–66.
41. American Friends Service Committee, *Uncommon Controversy*, 82–106.
42. Woods, "Who's in Charge of Fishing?," 423; Wilkinson, *Messages from Franks Landing*.

43. USGD, 1957, *State of Washington v. Satiacum*; Deloria, *Indians of the Pacific Northwest*, 160–76; Harmon, *Indians in the Making*, image and caption #23; Josephy, Nagel, and Johnson, *Red Power*, 22; Wilkinson, *Messages from Frank's Landing*, 40–46; Wilma, "State Supreme Court Issues."

44. U.S. Congress, Senate, Committee on Interior and Insular Affairs, Subcommittee on Indian Affairs, *Indian Fish Rights: Hearing on Senate Joint Resolution 170 and S.J.R. 171*, 88th Congress, 2nd Session (August 5–6, 1964), 80, cited in Cohen, *Treaties on Trial*, 72, 201n17.

45. Wilkinson, *Messages from Frank's Landing*, 54–55; F. G. Cohen, *Treaties on Trial*, 99, 137–38.

46. USGD, 1980, *U.S. v. Washington*, 196.

47. Woods, "Who's in Charge of Fishing?," 426. The case *U.S. v. Oregon* was led by attorney George D. Dysart of the Department of the Interior, an advocate of Indian rights.

48. Woods, "Who's in Charge of Fishing?," 426.

49. USGD, 1969, *Sohappy v. Smith*; Boxberger, *To Fish in Common*, 135–36.

50. Wilkinson, *Messages from Franks Landing*, 38.

51. F. G. Cohen, *Treaties on Trial*, 80.

52. USGD, 1974, *U.S. v. State of Washington*.

53. *Biographical Directory of the United States Congress*, s.v. "Gorton, Thomas Slade, III"; Slade Gorton and Co., www.sladegorton.com.

54. F. G. Cohen, *Treaties on Trial*, 7.

55. Wilkinson, *Messages from Franks Landing*, 51.

56. USGD, 1974, *U.S. v. State of Washington*, 349.

57. Woods, "Who's in Charge of Fishing?," 427.

58. F. G. Cohen, *Treaties on Trial*, 7–10.

59. Woods, "Who's in Charge of Fishing?," 420.

60. Deloria, *Indians of the Pacific Northwest*, 165–66.

61. F. G. Cohen, *Treaties on Trial*, 7–12.

62. Woods, "Who's in Charge of Fishing?," 430.

63. Northwest Indian Fisheries Commission, http://nwifc.org/; William Yardley, "Billy Frank Jr., 83, Defiant Fighter for Native Fishing Rights," *New York Times*, May 9, 2014, http://www.nytimes.com/2014/05/09/us/billy-frank-jr -fighter-for-native-fishing-rights-dies-at-83.html?_r=0.

64. USGD, 1979, *Washington v. Washington State Commercial Passenger Vessel Association*, 685–89; Woods, "Who's in Charge of Fishing?," 433. Woods's article provides a chronology and commentary on the history of Pacific Northwest fishing rights and policy for the years 1855 to 2005.

65. See Confederated Salish and Kootenai Tribes, *Explore the River Education Project.*
66. Regional Team of the Federal Task Force on Washington State Fisheries, John C. Merkel, Chairman, Dayton L. Alverson, and John D. Hough, *Settlement Plan for Washington State Salmon and Steelhead Fisheries*, June 1978.
67. Federal Task Force, *Settlement Plan*, xi.
68. Federal Task Force, *Settlement Plan*, xiv.
69. See Pinkerton, *Cooperative Management of Local Fisheries.*
70. Federal Task Force, *Settlement Plan*, xii.
71. Nugent, *History of Lummi Fishing Rights*, 4.
72. Nugent, *History of Lummi Fishing Rights*, 4–5.
73. Lane, *Political and Economic Aspects*, 26, 27, cited in Nugent, *History of Lummi Fishing Rights*, 5–6.
74. Sanders, "Damaging Indian Treaty Fisheries," 171.
75. Sanders, "Damaging Indian Treaty Fisheries," 172. Sanders's article describes legal theories for protection of Indian treaty fisheries from habitat degradation; in particular, the article elucidates the position that the treaty right of fishing is a property interest for which compensatory damages may be sought.
76. *Northwest Indian Fisheries Commission*, "Puget Sound Treaty Indian Tribes."

9. BREAK THROUGH AHISTORY

1. Poole, *In Defense of the Indians*. See R. A. Williams Jr., *American Indian in Western Legal Thought*; see also F. S. Cohen, *Cohen's Handbook of Federal Indian Law*, 2005 ed., 10–15, for an overview of early European legal theories on colonization.
2. See Kalter, *Benjamin Franklin*, for a discussion of Iroquois influences on the political formation of the United States. Kalter quotes Anishinaabe scholar Gerald Vizenor, who has written that the privileging of textual evidence over oral tradition, and the accepting of solely Western-dominated standards of reasoning and evidence, amount to "a euphemism for colonization of oral tradition" (Kalter, *Benjamin Franklin*, 26). Even more important than whether textual traces exist, Vizenor writes, are questions concerning *why* particular textual traces may not exist, a theme that is addressed in the present work: past and current conditions for the ahistorical nature of Indian history. See Vizenor, "Socioacupuncture," 180–91. Regarding the issue of potential Iroquois influence on American philosophy in general, see S. L. Pratt, "Influence of the Iroquois," 274–314.

3. In the landmark cases *Johnson v. McIntosh* (USGD, 1823) and *Worcester v. Georgia* (USGD, 1832) Chief Justice John Marshall applied principles of the Doctrine of Discovery to justify U.S. rights to Indian lands; Marshall's articulations have remained influential in U.S. Indian law and policy. See Deloria, *Behind the Trail of Broken Treaties*, ch. 5, "The Doctrine of Discovery." See also Newcomb, "Five Hundred Years of Injustice."

4. *International Council of Thirteen Indigenous Grandmothers*, "Petition to the Vatican."

5. Toensing, "Quaker Committee Disavows Doctrine."

6. Council for a Parliament of the World's Religions, "Indigenous Peoples' Statement to the World."

7. USGD, 1942, F. S. Cohen, *Handbook of Federal Indian Law*, ch. 4, "Federal Indian Legislation"; see especially section 16, "Legislation from 1930–1939."

8. USGD, 1928, *Report on the Problem of Indian Administration.*

9. *American Indian Life*, "Review of the Meriam Report," 6.

10. USGD, 1942, F. S. Cohen, *Handbook of Federal Indian Law*, 83.

11. Prucha, *Great Father*, 948, 948n16. See also Szasz, *Education and the American Indian*, 91–105.

12. USGD, 1978, American Indian Religious Freedom Act.

13. USGD, 1883, *Annual Report of the Secretary of the Interior*, x–xiii.

14. Fassett, *Giving Our Hearts Away,* 3.

15. M. E. Hillaire, "Meeting Human and Social Needs," 11.

16. M. E. Hillaire, "Meeting Human and Social Needs," 11.

17. "Tribal Climate Change Profile: The Lumi Nation." University of Oregon Environmental Studies Program and USDA Forest Service Pacific Northwest Research Station.

10. SCÄLLA—OF THE KILLER WHALE

Rebecca Chamberlain is a Northwest writer, storyteller, scholar, and educator. Her work with elders includes Salish language and storytelling traditions that explore culture and place. She has a fascination with cosmology and star stories and teaches interdisciplinary programs—focused on writing, literature, myth, oral narratives, and natural history—at the Evergreen State College.

1. Rebecca Chamberlain, "Pauline Hillaire: Scälla, Of the Killer Whale: A Brief Biography," in P. Hillaire, *Totem Pole History*, xxxix–lxi.

2. Pauline's mother's ancestral family name, Petoie, was anglicized as Price.

3. Hillaire in Chamberlain, *Sharing the Circle*, 14.

4. National Endowment for the Arts, "NEA National Heritage Fellowships: Pauline Hillaire."

5. Chamberlain, "Earth Is Our First Teacher," 2.
6. Pauline Hillaire, quoted in Chamberlain, "Pauline Hillaire, Scälla, Of the Killer Whale," lii.
7. Story adapted from P. Hillaire in *Sharing the Circle*, 29.

11. EARTH, OUR FIRST TEACHER

1. Beck, *Lummi Indian How Stories*, frontispiece.
2. USGD, 1883, U.S. Congress, House, *Annual Report of the Secretary of the Interior*, x–xiii.
3. See P. Hillaire, *Totem Pole History.*
4. Vi Hilbert (Upper Skagit) in Chamberlain, *Sharing the Circle*, 2.
5. Hilbert, quoted in Chamberlain, *Sharing the Circle*, 3.
6. See Rosenstein, *In Whose Honor?*
7. Editorial by Gary Hillaire, *Lummi Squol-quol* 1, no. 1 (November–December, 1973): 3.
8. Armstrong, *I Have Spoken.*
9. Tecumseh (Shawnee), Speech to the Territorial Governor of Indiana, William Henry Harrison (1810), to protest the ceding of Indian land that took place in 1805–6, in Armstrong, *I Have Spoken*, 51.

APPENDIX 1

Source: Kappler, *Indian Affairs*, vol. 2: *Treaties.*

APPENDIX 2

Source: United Nations, "Declaration on the Rights of Indigenous Peoples."

APPENDIX 3

1. Ames and Maschner, *Peoples of the Northwest Coast*, 64–86.
2. Thornton, *American Indian Holocaust*, 11–12.
3. R. A. Williams Jr., *American Indian in Western Legal Thought*, 71–81.
4. Calloway, *First Peoples*, 76–81.
5. Thornton, *American Indian Holocaust*, 45.
6. Calloway, *First Peoples*, 76–79.
7. Calloway, *First Peoples*, 87–88, 92–101.
8. Bolton, "Relation of the Voyage," 6.
9. Gunther, *Indian Life*, 18. Gunther cites primary source accounts by European explorers of the American West Coast, which provide information about Indian cultures and Indian/European interactions.
10. Hayes, *Historical Atlas*, 16.

11. Gunther, *Indian Life*, 3–4; Hayes, *Historical Atlas*, 20, 22.

12. Gunther, *Indian Life*, 5; Hayes, *Historical Atlas*, 108–9.

13. Gunther, *Indian Life*, 6–8; Hayes, *Historical Atlas*, 35–36.

14. Gunther, *Indian Life*, 5, 15, 17; Hayes, *Historical Atlas*, 43–45.

15. Gunther, *Indian Life*, 12–14; Hayes, *Historical Atlas*, 37–40.

16. Boyd, *Coming of the Spirit of Pestilence*, 49, 266: table 4.

17. Hayes, *Historical Atlas*, 65.

18. Gunther, *Indian Life*, 55, 56; Hayes, *Historical Atlas*, 16, 62; Sanchez, "Spanish Exploration."

19. Gunther, *Indian Life*, 56–60, Hayes, *Historical Atlas*, 59–61.

20. Gunther, *Indian Life*, 59, 72; Hayes, *Historical Atlas*, 82.

21. Hayes, *Historical Atlas*, 67.

22. Hayes, *Historical Atlas*, 68.

23. Hayes, *Historical Atlas*, 69.

24. Hayes, *Historical Atlas*, 70.

25. Hayes, *Historical Atlas*, 85–93.

26. Gunther, *Indian Life*, 74, 85; Hayes, *Historical Atlas*, 38–39, 82.

27. Boyd, *Coming of the Spirit of Pestilence*, 49, 266: table 4.

28. Hayes, *Historical Atlas*, 119–20.

29. Calloway, *First Peoples*, 164–75, 175–80.

30. Calloway, "Continuing Revolution," 3–33.

31. USGD, 2014, U.S. Department of the Interior, Bureau of Indian Affairs, "Frequently Asked Questions."

32. USGD, 1778, Treaty with the Delawares.

33. Calloway, *First Peoples*, 179–80.

34. USGD, 1787, Northwest Ordinance.

35. USGD, 1789, Constitution of the United States, Article 1, Sect. 8. See Wilkins and Lomawaima, *Uneven Ground*, 9.

36. USGD, 1911, *Checklist of United States Public Documents*, 493.

37. Prucha, *Great Father*, 89–114.

38. Prucha, *Great Father*, 71, 94–95.

39. Ronda, *Lewis and Clark*.

40. Dowd, "Thinking outside the Circle," 30–52.

41. Prucha, *Great Father*, 76–80.

42. Wilkins and Lomawaima, *Uneven Ground*, 53–54.

43. Trafzer, *American Indians/American Presidents*, 63–69, 73.

44. USGD, 1826, Superintendency of Indian Affairs, "A Bill for the Establishment of a General Superintendency," 6.

45. Wilkins and Lomawaima, *Uneven Ground*, 24–25.

46. Wilkins and Lomawaima, *Uneven Ground*, 60–61.
47. Boyd, *Coming of the Spirit of Pestilence*, 49ff, 266: table 4.
48. Perdue and Green, *Cherokee Removal*.
49. Coan, "First Stage of the Federal Indian Policy," 48.
50. USGD, 2012, U.S. Department of the Interior, Bureau of Land Management, "Our Heritage, Our Future."
51. USGD, 1848, "An Act to Establish the Territorial Government of Oregon."
52. USGD, 2014, U.S. Department of the Interior, Bureau of Indian Affairs, "Frequently Asked Questions."
53. Prucha, *Great Father*, 397–99.
54. Lieb, "Bellingham."
55. USGD, 1853, "An Act to Establish the Territorial Government of Washington."
56. Thrush, *Native Seattle*, 37–38.
57. Boyd, *Coming of the Spirit of Pestilence*, 49, 266: table 4.
58. USGD, 1855, Treaty with the Dwamish, Suquamish, etc.
59. Utley and Washburn, *Indian Wars*, 159–65, 179–85; Harmon, *Indians in the Making*, 85–96.
60. Riddle, "Chirouse, Father Eugene Casimir."
61. Harmon, *Indians in the Making*, 96–97.
62. Boyd, *Coming of the Spirit of Pestilence*, 49, 266: table 4.
63. Nichols, *Lincoln and the Indians*.
64. Harmon, *Indians in the Making*, 96–97.
65. Roessel, *Navajo Stories*; Thompson, *Army and the Navajo*.
66. Alaska Public Lands Information Centers, "Timeline of Alaska's History."
67. USGD, 1868, Treaty with the Nez Percés.
68. Harmon, *Indians in the Making*, 108.
69. USGD, 2008, U.S. Department of the Interior, Bureau of Indian Affairs, "Commissioners of Indian Affairs."
70. Stein, *Exploring Coast Salish Prehistory*, 7–8.
71. Trafzer, *American Indians/American Presidents*, 21.
72. Hoxie, *Final Promise*, 54–60.
73. O'Brien, "Legal Analysis," 28; Cole and Chakin, *Iron Hand upon the People*, 14.
74. Mathes, *Helen Hunt Jackson*.
75. USGD, 1883, U.S. Congress, House, *Annual Report of the Secretary of the Interior*, x–xiii.
76. Mathes, *Helen Hunt Jackson*.
77. Boxberger, "In and Out of the Labor Force," 167–68; Harmon, *Indians in the Making*, 113–14.
78. USGD, 1887, General Allotment Act (Dawes Act).

79. Prucha, *Great Father*, 668–69.
80. Calloway, *First Peoples*, 315–16, 392–93.
81. USGD, 1891, Amendment to the General Allotment Act.
82. Pevar. *Rights of Indians and Tribes*, 305–6.
83. Silva, *Aloha Betrayed*. Silva examines historical documents in the Hawaiian language in an analysis of Native resistance to colonization.
84. Roosevelt actually borrowed this phrase from Merrill E. Gates, president of the Lake Mohonk (NY) Conference, an annual gathering of white reform groups concerned with Indian causes, whose approaches toward policy reform and influence on public thought emphasized Indians' becoming assimilated and Christianized.
85. Deloria, *Behind the Trail of Broken Treaties*, 215.
86. Boxberger, *To Fish in Common*, 88, 134–35.
87. Trafzer, *American Indians/American Presidents*, 26, 138–43.
88. Coolige, "Function of the Society of American Indians."
89. Brotherton, "Joseph Raymond Hillaire," 47–48.
90. Calloway, *First Peoples*, 402–3.
91. Harmon, *Indians in the Making*, 178–86, 227.
92. USGD, 1934, U.S. Court of Claims, *Duwamish et al. v. U.S.*
93. USGD, 1928, *Report on the Problem of Indian Administration*.
94. Trafzer, *American Indians/American Presidents*, 147–48, 149–50.
95. Calloway, *First Peoples*, 439–42.
96. Calloway, *First Peoples*, 442–45.
97. Prucha, *Great Father*, 948, 948n16. See also Szasz, *Education and the American Indian*, 91–105.
98. Calloway, *First Peoples*, 445–46.
99. Josephy, Nagel, and Johnson, *Red Power*, 13.
100. Trafzer, *American Indians/American Presidents*, 160–61.
101. Pevar, *Rights of Indians and Tribes*, 368–69.
102. USGD, 2014, U.S. Department of the Interior, Bureau of Indian Affairs, "Frequently Asked Questions."
103. Trafzer, *American Indians/American Presidents*, 161.
104. USGD, 1957, *Lummi Tribe of Indians v. United States*.
105. Duthu, *American Indians and the Law*, 72.
106. Pevar, *Rights of Indians and Tribes*, 12.
107. "Indian Statement on Policy and Legislation" (1967), in Josephy, Nagel, and Johnson, *Red Power*, 75.
108. "Declaration of Indian Purpose," American Indian Chicago Conference (June 13–20, 1961), in Josephy, Nagel, and Johnson, *Red Power*, 13–15.

109. "American Indian Capital Conference on Poverty" (1946), in Josephy, Nagel, and Johnson, *Red Power*, 143–46.
110. USGD, 2008, U.S. Department of the Interior, Bureau of Indian Affairs, "Commissioners of Indian Affairs."
111. "Indian Statement on Policy and Legislation," in Josephy, Nagel, and Johnson, *Red Power*, 75–77.
112. Johnson, *Occupation of Alcatraz Island*.
113. "Message to Congress on Indian Affairs," President Richard Nixon (July 8, 1970), in Josephy, Nagel, and Johnson, *Red Power*, 101–18.
114. Jensen, Paul, and Carter, *Eyewitness at Wounded Knee*.
115. Evergreen State College, "Native Programs."
116. Evergreen State College, "Longhouse Education and Cultural Center."
117. "Statement of Ada Deer before the Senate Committee on Indian Affairs" (July 15, 1993), in Josephy, Nagel, and Johnson, *Red Power*, 136–39; Trafzer, *American Indians/American Presidents*, 212.
118. USGD, 1974, *U.S. v. State of Washington*.
119. Trafzer, *American Indians/American Presidents*, 192–93.
120. Pevar, *Rights of Indians and Tribes*, 263–65; Trafzer, *American Indians/American Presidents*, 209–10, 251–52.
121. "The Indian Child Welfare Act," in Pevar, *Rights of Indians and Tribes*, 333–52.
122. "Tribally Controlled Community College Assistance Act," in Josephy, Nagel, and Johnson, *Red Power*, 196–98.
123. "The Longest Walk, Washington DC, 1978," in Josephy, Nagel, and Johnson, *Red Power*, 75–77.
124. Lazarus, *Black Hills/White Justice*.
125. USGD, 2004, Internal Revenue Service, *Report of Recommendations*; R. A. Williams, "Small Steps," 335–97.
126. "Statement on Indian Policy," President Ronald Reagan (January 24, 1983), in Josephy, Nagel, and Johnson, *Red Power*, 126–35.
127. Pevar, *Rights of Indians and Tribes*, 319–20; USGD, 1987, *California v. Cabazon Band of Mission Indians*.
128. Duthu, *American Indians and the Law*, 109–12.
129. Trafzer, *American Indians/American Presidents*, 206, 208.
130. Native American Graves and Repatriation Act, 104 Stat. 3048 (1990), in Josephy, Nagel, and Johnson, *Red Power*, 233–44.
131. Indian Arts and Crafts Act, 104 Stat. 4662 (1990), in Josephy, Nagel, and Johnson, *Red Power*, 245–50.
132. Native American Languages Act, 104 Stat. 1153 (1992), in Josephy, Nagel, and Johnson, *Red Power*, 199–201.

133. Trafzer, *American Indians/American Presidents*, 212–15.
134. Trafzer, *American Indians/American Presidents*, 216.
135. Josephy, Nagel, and Johnson, *Red Power*, 251–52.
136. Trafzer, *American Indians/American Presidents*, 212–15; "American Indian Tribal Colleges and Universities," Executive Order of President Bill Clinton, October 21, 1996, in Josephy, Nagel, and Johnson, *Red Power*, 202–4.
137. USGD, 2004, American Indian Probate Reform Act.
138. Northwest Indian Fisheries Commission, "Puget Sound Treaty Indian Tribes."
139. United Nations, "Declaration on the Rights of Indigenous Peoples."
140. Longest Walk, 1978–2008.
141. USGD, 2010, U.S. Congress, Defense Department Appropriations Act. See also Echo-Hawk, *In the Light of Justice*. 275–78.
142. USGD, 2010, U.S. Congress, Patient Protection and Affordable Care Act.
143. USGD, 2014, U.S. Department of State, *United Nations Declaration on the Rights of Indigenous Peoples Review*. See also Echo-Hawk, *In the Light of Justice*, xii, 34.

BIBLIOGRAPHY

U.S. GOVERNMENT DOCUMENTS

1778

Treaty with the Delawares (September 17). Kappler, *Indian Affairs*, vol. 2: *Treaties*. http://digital.library.okstate.edu/kappler/Vol2/treaties/del0003.htm.

1787

Northwest Ordinance: "An Ordinance for the Government of the Territory of the United States, Northwest of the River Ohio." *Journals of the Continental Congress* 32: 340–41. In Prucha, *Documents of United States Indian Policy*, 9–10.

1789

Constitution of the United States. Available at Cornell University School of Law. http://www.law.cornell.edu/anncon/.

1791

U.S. Congress. "Speech of President George Washington," delivered October 25, 1791. *American State Papers* 01 Foreign Relations 4: 16–17.

1823

Johnson v. McIntosh, 21 U.S. 543.

1826

Superintendency of Indian Affairs. "A Bill for the Establishment of a General Superintendency of Indian Affairs in the Department of War." J. C. Calhoun, U.S. Secretary of War, to Thomas L. McKenney, appointed first Superintendent of Indian Affairs. House Doc. No. 146. 19th Congress, 1st Session (Serial Set 138).

1830

Indian Removal Act: "An Act to provide for an exchange of lands with the Indians residing in any of the states or territories, and for their removal west of the river Mississippi." 4 Stat. 411 (May 28).

1831

Cherokee Nation v. Georgia, 30 U.S. (5 Pet.) 1.

1832

"An Act to Provide for the Appointment of a Commissioner of Indian Affairs, and for Other Purposes." 4 Stat. 4: 564 (July 9).
Worcester v. Georgia, 31 U.S. 515.

1841

U.S. Congress, Senate. *Annual Report of the Secretary of War*. John C. Spencer to President John Tyler. 27th Congress, 2nd Session, S. Exec. Doc. 1, Session Vol. 1 (Serial Set 395).

1842

U.S. Congress, House. *Annual Report of the Secretary of War*. John C. Spencer to President John Tyler. 27th Congress, 3rd Session, H. Exec. Doc. 2, Session Vol. 1 (Serial Set 418.).

1848

"An Act to Establish the Territorial Government of Oregon." Statutes at Large 177: 323–34 (August 14). 30th Congress, 1st Session.
U.S. Congress, House. *Annual Message of the President of the United States to the Two Houses of Congress*. President James K. Polk. 30th Congress, 2nd Session, H. Exec. Doc. 1, Session Vol. 1 (Serial Set 537).
U.S. Congress, House. Department of War. *General Orders* No. 49. R. Jones, Adjutant General. 30th Congress, 2nd Session, H. Exec. Doc. 1 (Serial Set 537).

1850

"An Act for Removal of Western Washington Indians to East of the Cascade Mountains." 9 Stat. 437 (February 1).
Donation Land Claim Act: "An Act to Create the Office of Surveyor-General of the Public Lands in Oregon, and to Provide for the Survey, and to Make Donations to Settlers of the Said Public Lands." 9 Stat. 496. Center for Columbia River History. www.ccrh.org/comm/cottage/primary/claim.htm.
U.S. Congress, Senate. *Annual Report of the Commissioner of Indian Affairs*. A. S. Loughery, Acting Commissioner, to J. P. Gaines, Alonzo Skinner, and Beverly S. Allen. 31st Congress, 2nd Session, S. Exec. Doc. 1, Session Vol. 1 (Serial Set 587).

U.S. Congress, Senate. *Annual Report of the Commissioner of Indian Affairs.* Joseph Lane, Governor and Superintendent of Indian Affairs, Territory of Oregon, to Williams F. Solmie, esq., Office of the Superintendent of Indian Affairs, Territory of Oregon. 31st Congress, 2nd Session, S. Exec. Doc. 1, Session Vol. 1 (Serial Set 587).

U.S. Congress, Senate. *Annual Report of the Commissioner of Indian Affairs.* Luke Lea, Commissioner of Indian Affairs, to Anson Dart, Superintendent of Indian Affairs, O.T. 31st Congress, 2nd Session, S. Exec. Doc. 1, Session Vol. 1 (Serial Set 587).

U.S. Congress, Senate. *Report of the Indian Agent for the District of Puget Sound.* E. A. Starling to Anson Dart, Superintendent of Indian Affairs, O.T. 32nd Congress, 2nd Session, S. Exec. Doc. 1 pt. 1, Session Vol. 1 (Serial Set 658).

U.S. Congress. U.S. Statutes 437. Removal of Western Washington Indians to East of the Cascade Mountains, 5 June 1850. *Congressional Globe,* 31st Congress, 1st Session, 272: 9.

1852

U.S. Congress, Senate. *Annual Report of the Commissioner of Indian Affairs.* Luke Lea to A. H. H. Stuart, Secretary of the Interior. 32nd Congress, 2nd Session, S. Exec. Doc. 1 pt. 1, Session Vol. 1 (Serial Set 658).

U.S. Congress, Senate. *Annual Report of the Commissioner of Indian Affairs,* No. 71. E. A. Starling, Agent for the District of Puget Sound, to Anson Dart, Superintendent of Indian Affairs, O.T. 32nd Congress, 2nd Session, S. Exec. Doc. 1 pt. 1, Session Vol. 1 (Serial Set 658).

1853

"An Act to Establish the Territorial Government of Washington." H.R. 348, 32nd Congress, 2nd Session.

U.S. Congress, House. *Annual Report of the Secretary of War Communicating the Several Pacific Railroad Explorations.* "Medical Report of the Assistant Surgeon (George Suckley) and the Surgeon of the Exploration (Dr. J. G. Cooper)." 33rd Congress, 1st Session, H. Exec. Doc. 129, Session Vol. 1 (Serial Set 736).

U.S. Congress, House. *Annual Report of the Secretary of War Communicating the Several Pacific Railroad Explorations.* "Report on the Indian Tribes of the Territory of Washington." George Gibbs to George B. McClellan, Commanding the Western Division of the Pacific Railroad Exploration. 33rd Congress, 1st Session, H. Exec. Doc. 129, Session Vol. 1 (Serial Set 736).

U.S. Congress, Senate. *Annual Report of the Commissioner of Indian Affairs.* George W. Manypenny, Commissioner, to Isaac I. Stevens, Governor and Superintendent of Indian Affairs, W.T. 33rd Congress, 1st Session, S. Exec. Doc. 1 pt. 1, Session Vol. 1 (Serial Set 690).

U.S. Congress, Senate. *Annual Report of the Commissioner of Indian Affairs*. George W. Manypenny, Commissioner, to R. McClelland, Secretary of the Interior. 33rd Congress, 1st Session, S. Exec. Doc. 1 pt. 1, Session Vol. 1 (Serial Set 690).

1854

U.S. Congress, Senate. *Annual Report of the Commissioner of Indian Affairs*. George W. Manypenny, Commissioner, to R. McClelland, Secretary of the Interior. 33rd Congress, 2nd Session, S. Exec. Doc. 1 pt. 1. Session Vol. 1 (Serial Set 746).

U.S. Congress, Senate. *Annual Report of the Commissioner of Indian Affairs*, No. 86. Isaac I. Stevens, Governor and Superintendent of Indian Affairs, W.T., to George W. Manypenny, Commissioner. 33rd Congress, 2nd Session, S. Exec. Doc. 1 pt. 1, Session Vol. 1 (Serial Set 746).

U.S. Congress, Senate. *Annual Report of the Commissioner of Indian Affairs*, No. 87. Joel Palmer, Superintendent of Indian Affairs, O.T., to George W. Manypenny, Commissioner. 33rd Congress, 2nd Session, S. Exec. Doc. 1 pt. 1, Session Vol. 1 (Serial Set 746).

1855

Ratified Treaty No. 283. Documents Relating to the Negotiation of the Treaty of January 22, 1855, with the Dwamish, Suquamish, and other Indians (Treaty of Point Elliott). A transcription of the treaty and handwritten notes of the treaty proceedings are available at "Documents Relating to Indian Affairs," University of Wisconsin Madison, Digital Collections Center. http://digicoll.library.wisc.edu/History; http://digital.library.wisc.edu/1711.di/History.IT1855no283.

Records of the Proceedings of the Commission to Hold Treaties with the Indian Tribes in Washington Territory and the Blackfoot Country (T494, reel 5, frames 205–6). "Documents Relating to the Negotiation of Ratified and Unratified Treaties with Various Indian Tribes." Washington DC: U.S. Records of the Office of Indian Affairs, 1855.

Treaty with the Dwamish, Suquamish, etc./Treaty of Point Elliott (January 22). Kappler, *Indian Affairs*, vol. 2: *Treaties*. http://digital.library.okstate.edu/kappler/Vol2/treaties/dwa0669.htm.

U.S. Congress, House. *Annual Report of the Commissioner of Indian Affairs*, No. 97. J. Cain, Acting Superintendent of Indian Affairs, W.T., to George W. Manypenny, Commissioner. 34th Congress, 1st Session, H. Exec. Doc. 1 pt. 1, Session Vol. 1 (Serial Set 840).

U.S. Congress, House. *Annual Report of the Commissioner of Indian Affairs*, No. 98. Joel Palmer, Superintendent of Indian Affairs, O.T., to Capt. J. Cain, Indian

Agent, W.T. 34th Congress, 1st Session, H. Exec. Doc. 1 pt. 1, Session Vol. 1 (Serial Set 840).

U.S. Congress, House. *Report of the Secretary of the Commissioner of Indian Affairs.* George W. Manypenny, Commissioner, to R. McClelland, Secretary of the Interior. 34th Congress, 1st Session, H. Exec. Doc. 1 pt. 1, Session Vol. 1 (Serial Set 840).

U.S. Congress, Senate. *Annual Report of the Commissioner of Indian Affairs.* George W. Manypenny, Commissioner, to R. McClelland, Secretary of the Interior. 34th Congress, 1st Session, S. Exec. Doc. 1 pt. 1, Session Vol. 1 (Serial Set 810).

1856

U.S. Congress, House. *Annual Report of the Commissioner of Indian Affairs.* George W. Manypenny, Commissioner, to R. McClelland, Secretary of the Interior. 34th Congress, 3rd Session, H. Exec. Doc. 1 pt. 1, Session Vol. 1 (Serial Set 893).

U.S. Congress, Senate. *Annual Report of the Commissioner of Indian Affairs.* George W. Manypenny, Commissioner, to R. McClelland, Secretary of the Interior. 34th Congress, 3rd Session, S. Exec. Doc. 5 pt. 1, Session Vol. 2 (Serial Set 875).

1857

U.S. Congress, House. *Annual Report of the Secretary of the Interior.* J. W. Denver, Commissioner of Indian Affairs, to J. Thompson, Secretary of the Interior. 35th Congress, 1st Session, H. Exec. Doc. 2 pt. 1, Session Vol. 2 (Serial Set 942).

1858

U.S. Congress, Senate. *Annual Report of the Commissioner of Indian Affairs.* E. C. Fitzhugh, Bellingham Bay Agency, W.T., to Col. M. T. Simmons, Indian Agent, Puget Sound District. 35th Congress, 2nd Session, S. Exec. Doc., Session Vol. 1, No. 80 (Serial Set 974).

U.S. Congress, Senate. *Annual Report of the Commissioner of Indian Affairs.* J. W. Nesmith, Superintendent of Indian Affairs, O.T. and W.T., to Charles E. Mix, Commissioner of Indian Affairs. 35th Congress, 2nd Session, S. Exec. Doc. 1, Session Vol. 1 (Serial Set 974).

U.S. Congress, Senate. *Annual Report of the Commissioner of Indian Affairs.* M. T. Simmons, Indian Agent, W.T., to Isaac W. Smith, Special Agent of the Light House, W.T. 35th Congress, 2nd Session, S. Exec. Doc. 1 pt. 1, Session Vol. 1, No. 81 (Serial Set 974).

U.S. Congress, Senate. *Annual Report of the Secretary of the Interior.* M. T. Simmons, Indian Agent, Puget Sound District, W.T., to Col. J. W. Nesmith, Superintendent of Indian Affairs, W.T. and O.T. 35th Congress, 2nd Session, S. Exec. Doc. 1 pt. 1, Session Vol. 1 (Serial Set 974).

1859

U.S. Congress, Senate. *Annual Report of the Commissioner of Indian Affairs.* M. T. Simmons, Indian Agent, Puget Sound District, W.T., to Edwards R. Geary, Superintendent of Indian Affairs, W.T. and O.T. 36th Congress, 2nd Session, S. Exec. Doc. 2 pt. 1, Session Vol. 1 (Serial Set 1023).

1862

Homestead Act. Public Law 37-64; 12 Stat. 392 (May 20).

1867

U.S. Congress, House. *Annual Report of the Commissioner of Indian Affairs.* C. C. Finkbonner, Agent in Charge, Lummi Reservation, to A. R. Elder, Indian Agent, Olympia WA. 40th Congress, 2nd Session, H. Exec. Doc. 1 pt. 3, Session Vol. 3 (Serial Set 1326).

1868

Treaty with the Nez Percés (August 13). Kappler, *Indian Affairs,* vol. 2: *Treaties.* http://digital.library.okstate.edu/kappler/Vol2/treaties/nez1024.htm.

1869

An Act to Appoint a Board of Indian Commissioners. 16 Stat. 4 (April 10).

1873

"Executive Orders Related to Indian Reserves, Washington: Lummi Reserve." 12 Stat. 928 (November 22). Kappler, *Indian Affairs,* vol. 1: *Laws.* http://digital .library.okstate.edu/kappler/Vol1/HTML_files/WAS0901.html.

U.S. Congress, Senate. *Annual Report of the Commissioner of Indian Affairs.* R. H. Milroy, Superintendent of Indian Affairs, W.T., to George W. Manypenny, Commissioner. 43rd Congress, 1st Session, H. Exec. Doc. 1 pt. 5, vol. 1, Session Vol. 4 (Serial Set 1601).

1874

U.S. Congress, House. *Annual Report of the Secretary of the Interior.* J. D. Lang and F. H. Smith to C. B. Fisk, Chairman, Board of Indian Commissioners. 43rd Congress, 2nd session. H. Ex. Doc. 1 pt. 5 (Serial Set 1639).

1875

U.S. Congress, House. *Indians in Washington Territory.* Ex. Doc. No. 87, to accompany H.R. 4874, 43rd Congress, 2nd Session.

1881

U.S. Congress, House. *Codification of Laws on Survey and Disposition of Public Land.* 47th Congress, 2nd Session, House Misc. Doc. 45 pt. 4 (Serial Set 2158).

1883

U.S. Congress, House. *Annual Report of the Secretary of the Interior.* Henry
M. Teller, Secretary of the Interior, to U.S. President Chester Alan Arthur.
48th Congress, 1st Session, H. Exec. Doc. 1 pt. 5, Session Vol. 1 (Serial Set
2190).

1887

General Allotment Act (Dawes Act or Dawes Severalty Act): "An Act to provide
for the allotment of lands in severalty to Indians on the various reservations."
24 Stat. 390 (February 8). Kappler, *Indian Affairs,* vol. 1: *Laws.* http://digital
.library.okstate.edu/kappler/vol1/html_files/ses0033.html.

1891

Amendment to the General Allotment Act. 26 Stat. 794 (February 28). Kappler,
Indian Affairs, vol. 1: *Laws.* http://digital.library.okstate.edu/kappler/Vol1
/HTML_files/SES0056.html.

1895

U.S. Congress, House. Committee on Indian Affairs. "Sale of Intoxicants to Indians." 53rd Congress, 3rd Session, House Report No. 1791, to accompany House
Resolution 6657 (Serial Set 3346).

1896

U.S. Congress. Committee on Indian Affairs. 54th Congress, 3rd Session, House
Report No. 1781, Session Vol. 2 (Serial Set 3346).

1897

"An Act to Prohibit the Sale of Intoxicating Drinks to Indians." 29 Stat. 506 (January 30).
U.S. v. Alaska Packers Association, Circuit Court Washington 79 F. 152.

1898

Indians in Indian Country (Curtis Act). 30 Stat. 495 (June 28).

1899

*Eighteenth Annual Report of the Bureau of American Ethnology to the Secretary
of the Smithsonian Institution,* 1896–97, J. W. Powell, Director. Part 2 of 2:
"Indian Land Cessions in the United States," compiled by Charles C. Royce.
56th Congress, 1st Session, House Exec. Doc. 736 (Serial Set 4015).

1903

Lone Wolf v. Hitchcock, 187 U.S. 553.

1904

Kappler, Charles J., comp. and ed. *Indian Affairs: Laws and Treaties*. Vols. 1, 3, 4, 5, 6, and 7: *Laws*. Washington DC: Government Printing Office. Available at Oklahoma State University Library, OSU Library Electronic Publishing Center. http://digital.library.okstate.edu/kappler/index.htm.

———, comp. and ed. *Indian Affairs: Laws and Treaties*. Vol. 2: *Treaties*. Washington DC: Government Printing Office. Available at Oklahoma State University Library, OSU Library Electronic Publishing Center. http://digital.library.okstate.edu /kappler/Vol2/toc.htm.

1905

U.S. v. Winans, 198 U.S. 371.

1911

Checklist of United States Public Documents, 1789–1909, 3rd ed. Vol. 1, *Lists of Congressional and Departmental Publications*, Section I-20: "Indian Affairs Office." Washington DC: Government Printing Office. Reprinted by Kraus Reprint Corporation, 1962.

1916

State v. Alexis, 89 Wash. 492.
State v. Towessnute, 89 Wash. 478.

1919

"An Act Granting Citizenship to Certain Indians" (upon honorable discharge from service in World War I). 41 Stat. 350 (November 6). In Prucha, *Documents of United States Indian Policy*, 215.

U.S. v. Romaine et al., 255 F. 253, 9th Cir. *United States Circuit Courts of Appeals Report, with key-number annotations, with table of cases in the United States Circuit Courts of Appeals, which have been passed upon by the Supreme Court of the United States*, vol. 166 (St. Paul: West Publishing, 1919).

1921

Snyder Act: "An Act Authorizing appropriations and expenditures for the administration of Indian affairs, and for other purposes." 42. Stat. 208.

1924

Indian Citizenship Act: "An Act to authorize the Secretary of the Interior to issue certificates of citizenship to Indians." 43 Stat. 253 (June 2). In Prucha, *Documents of United States Indian Policy*, 218.

1926

U.S. Congress, Senate. "For the purpose of reclaiming certain lands in Indian and private ownership within and immediately adjacent to the Lummi Indian Reservation." 69th Congress, 1st Session, Report No. 354.

1928

Report on the Problem of Indian Administration (Meriam Report), Lewis M. Meriam, technical director. Baltimore: Johns Hopkins University Press, for the Institute for Government Research (Brookings Institute). Available at National Indian Law Library, *Native American Rights Fund.* http://www.narf.org/nill/resources/meriam.htm.

1931

United States v. Boynton, 49 F. 2d 810.

United States v. Stotts, 49 F. 2d 619.

U.S. Congress, Senate. *Survey of Conditions of Indians in the United States.* Hearing before a Subcommittee on Indian Affairs. 71st Congress, 3rd Session, Pursuant to S. Res. 79 and 308 (70th Congress) and S. Res. 263 and 416 (71st Congress), Part 21, Hearings at Tacoma WA, June 1, 1931.

1932

U.S. Congress, Senate. *Survey of Conditions of Indians in the United States.* Hearing before a Subcommittee on Indian Affairs. 71st Congress, 3rd Session, Pursuant to S. Res. 79 and 308 (70th Congress) and S. Res. 263 and 416 (71st Congress), Part 21, Hearings at Riverside CA, April 13, 1932.

1934

Indian Reorganization Act (Wheeler-Howard Act): "An Act to conserve and develop Indian lands and resources; to extend to Indians the right to form business and other organizations; to establish a credit system for Indians; to grant certain rights of home rule to Indians; to provide for vocational education for Indians; and for other purposes." 48 Stat. 984 (June 18).

Johnson-O'Malley Act: "An Act Authorizing the Secretary of the Interior to arrange with States or Territories for the education, medical attention, relief of distress, and social welfare of Indians, and for other purposes." 48 Stat. 596 (April 16).

U.S. Court of Claims. *The Duwamish, Lummi, Whidby Island Skagit, Upper Skagit, Swinomish, Kikiallus, Snohomish, Snoqualmie, Stillaguamish, Suquamish, Samish, Puyallup, Squaxin, Skokomish, Upper Chehalis, Muckleshoot, Nooksack, Chinook, and San Juan Tribes of Indians v. the United States*, 79 Ct. Cl. 530, F-275. LexisNexisAcademic, www.lexisnexis.com.

1942

Cohen, Felix S. *Handbook of Federal Indian Law*. Washington DC: Department of the Interior.

Tulee v. State of Washington, 315 U.S. 681.

1944

U.S. Congress, House. Committee on Indian Affairs. *Investigate Indian Affairs, Part 3: Hearings in the Field*. HRG-1944-INH-0003. La Conner WA, October 1.

1945

U.S. Congress, House. Committee on Indian Affairs. *Investigate Indian Affairs: Hearings pursuant to H. Res. 166. Part 3: Hearings in the Field*, July 22 to August 8; October 1–3 and November 9–22, 1944. 78th Congress, 2nd Session.

1946

Indian Claims Commission Act. 60 Stat. 1049.

1952

Lummi Tribe of Indians v. the United States, Indian Claims Commission Decisions, Docket 110 (decided 1972). Vol. 2, "Opinion" (January 30, 1952). Oklahoma State University Library, OSU Digital Publishing Center. http://digital.library .okstate.edu/icc/v02/iccv02p001.pdf.

1953

House Concurrent Resolution 108 (termination of federal recognition of, and assistance to, particular tribes). 67 Stat. B122.

Public Law 280, Ch. 505; 67 Stat. 588 (August 15): "An Act to confer jurisdiction on the States of California, Minnesota, Nebraska, Oregon, and Wisconsin, with respect to criminal offenses and civil causes of action committed or arising on Indian reservations within such States."

1955

Tee-hit-ton v. U.S., 348 U.S. 272.

1956

The Indian Vocational Training Act (Relocation Act): "An Act relative to employment for certain adult Indians on or near Indian reservations." Public Law 959, Ch. 930; 70 Stat. 986 (August 3).

1957

Lummi Tribe of Indians v. the United States, Indian Claims Commission Decisions, Docket 110 (decided 1972). Vol. 5, "Findings of Fact" (October 30, 1957).

Oklahoma State University Library, OSU Digital Publishing Center. http://digital
.library.okstate.edu/icc/v05/iccv05p525.pdf.

State of Washington v. Satiacum, 314 P.2d 400.

1958

Public Law 85-612 (August 8). [House Resolution 7681] 72 Stat. 543, "An Act to
authorize the Secretary of the Interior to convey certain land with the improvements located thereon to the Lummi Indian Tribe for the use and benefit of
the Lummi Tribe." http://digital.library.okstate.edu/kappler/vol6/html_files
/v6p0819.html#p819a.

1961

U.S. Congress, House. Committee of Interior and Insular Affairs. *Indian Heirship
Land Study.* Vol. 1: *An Analysis of Indian Opinion as Expressed in Questionnaires.*
House Committee Print no. 27.

1963

U.S. Senate. *Relating to the Indian Heirship Land Problem.* 88th Congress, 1st Session, Senate Report No. 479.

1966

Ratified Indian Treaties, 1722–1869. Washington DC: National Archives and Records
Service, Publication No. 668, Cabinet No. 26.

1967

U.S. Court of Claims. *Lummi Tribe of Indians v. U.S.,* 181 Ct. Cl. 753 (the Indian
Claims Commission decision reversed and remanded the decision of the Indian
Claims Commission on December 15, 1967). See under "Indian Claims Com-
mission Decisions."

1968

Civil Rights Act. Public Law 90–284; 82 Stat. 73. http://legcounsel.house.gov/Comps
/civil68.pdf.

1969

Sohappy v. Smith, 302 F. Supp. 899.

1970

"An Act providing for the protection of the watershed within the Carson National
Forest for the Pueblo de Taos Indians in New Mexico." Public Law 91-550; 84
Stat. 1437 (December 15).

1972

U.S. Court of Claims. *Lummi Tribe of Indians v. U.S.*, 197 Ct. Cl. 780 (affirmed March 17, 1972). See under "Indian Claims Commission Decisions."

1973

Tyler, Lyman S. *History of Indian Policy*. Washington DC: Department of the Interior, Bureau of Indian Affairs.

1974

U.S. v. State of Washington (Boldt Decision), 384 F. Supp. 312. U.S. District Court for the Western District of Washington at Tacoma. Available at Washington Department of Fish and Wildlife. http://wdfw.wa.gov/fishing/salmon/Boldt Decision8.5x11layoutforweb.pdf.

1975

American Indian Policy Review Commission Act. Public Law 93-580 (January 2).
Indian Self-Determination and Education Assistance Act. Public Law 93-638; 88 Stat. 2203.

1976

Indian Health Care Improvement Act. Public Law 437.

1977

American Indian Policy Review Commission, Final Report, "Separate Dissenting Views of Congressman Lloyd Meeds (D-WA), Vice-Chairman of the Commission."
American Indian Policy Review Commission, Final Report, submitted to Congress May 17, 1977, vol. 1 of 2. Preamble to Public Law 93-580 (1975).

1978

American Indian Religious Freedom Act. 92 Stat. 469.
Indian Child Welfare Act. 92 Stat. 3069.
Settlement Plan for Washington State Salmon and Steelhead Fisheries (June). Regional Team of the Federal Task Force on Washington State Fisheries, John C. Merkel, Chairman, Dayton L. Alverson, and John D. Hough.
Tribally Controlled Community College Act. Public Law 95-471.

1979

Washington v. Washington State Commercial Passenger Vessel Association, 443 U.S. 658.

1980

U.S. v. Sioux Nation of Indians, 601 F. 2d 1157, Ct. Cl. (1979); affirmed 448 U.S. 371, 487 (1980).

U.S. v. Washington, Phase II, 506 F. Supp. 187.

1982

Indian Mineral Development Act. 25 USC 2502.

Indian Tribal Government Tax Status Act. Title II of Public Law No. 97-473; 96 Stat. 2607.

Maine Indian Claims Settlement Act. 94 Stat. 1785.

1986

U.S. Office of Technology Assessment. "Four Projections of the Effect of Intermarriage on the Number of Indian Descendants." In Josephy, Nagel, and Johnson, *Red Power*, 279–86.

1987

California v. Cabazon Band of Mission Indians, 480 U.S. 202.

1988

Indian Gaming Regulatory Act. 102 Stat. 2467.

Lyng v. Northwest Indian Cemetery Protective Association, 485 U.S. 439.

1989

National Museum of the American Indian Act. 103 Stat. 1336.

1990

Indian Arts and Crafts Act. 104 Stat. 4662.

Native American Graves and Repatriation Act. 104 Stat. 3048.

1992

Native American Languages Act. 104 Stat. 1153.

1994

American Indian Religious Freedom Act Amendments. 108 Stat. 3125.

Indian Self-Determination and Education Assistance Act Amendments. 104 Stat. 4665.

2004

American Indian Probate Reform Act (AIPRA). Public Law 108-374; 118 Stat. 1773. Available at Indian Land Tenure Foundation. https://www.iltf.org/sites/default/files/AIPRA_2004.pdf.

Internal Revenue Service, Advisory Committee on Tax Exempt and Government Entities (ACT). *Report of Recommendations*. "II: Tribal Advice and Guidance Policy." Raymond C. Etcitty (Navajo), Project Leader (June 9). Washington DC: Internal Revenue Service Document No. 5-2004, Catalog No. 38578D. Available at http://www.irs.gov/pub/irs-tege/tege_act_rpt3.pdf.

2005

U.S. Department of the Interior, Bureau of Indian Affairs. "2005 American Indian Population and Labor Force Report." http://www.bia.gov/cs/groups/public /documents/text/idc-001719.pdf.

2008

U.S. Department of Commerce, U.S. Census Bureau. *U.S. Census*, 2006–2008. http://factfinder.census.gov/.

U.S. Department of the Interior, Bureau of Indian Affairs. "The Commissioners of Indian Affairs, 1824–1981" (January 5). http://www.bia.gov/cs/groups/public /documents/text/idc-001881.pdf.

2010

U.S. Congress. Defense Department Appropriations Act. Section 8113, "Apology to the Native Peoples of the United States," 45–46. 111th Congress, 1st Session, House Res. 3326. http://www.gpo.gov/fdsys/pkg/BILLS-111hr3326enr/pdf/BILLS -111hr3326enr.pdf.

U.S. Congress. Patient Protection and Affordable Care Act. 111th Congress, 2nd Session, House Doc. 3590. https://www.govtrack.us/congress/bills/111/hr3590 /text.

2012

U.S. Department of the Interior, Bureau of Land Management (August 14). "Our Heritage, Our Future." http://www.blm.gov/wo/st/en/info/history.html.

2013

U.S. Department of the Interior, National Park Service. *National Native American Graves and Repatriation Act* (NAGPRA). Map: "Indian Reservations in the Continental United States." www.nps.gov/nagpra/DOCUMENTS/RESERV.PDF.

Violence against Women Reauthorization Act. Public Law No. 113-4. http://www .govtrack.us/congress/bills/113/s47/text.

2014

U.S. Department of State. *United Nations Declaration on the Rights of Indigenous Peoples Review.* www.state.gov/s/tribalconsultation/declaration/.

U.S. Department of the Interior, Bureau of Indian Affairs. "Frequently Asked Questions" (February 27). www.bia.gov/FAQs/index.htm.

PUBLISHED SOURCES

Alaska Public Lands Information Centers. "Timeline of Alaska's History." 2014. http:www.alaskacenters.gov/alaska-timeline.cfm.

Alexander VI (pope). *Inter caetera divinai,* a papal bull issued in 1493. English translation in *European Treaties Bearing on the History of the United States and Its Dependencies to 1648,* edited by Francis Gardiner Davenport. Washington DC: Carnegie Institution of Washington, 1917.

American Friends Service Committee. *Uncommon Controversy: Fishing Rights of the Muckleshoot, Puyallup, and Nisqually Indians.* Seattle: University of Washington Press, 1970.

American Indian Law Clinic, University of Colorado School of Law, Boulder. "What Will Happen to Your Land When You Pass On? The American Indian Probate Reform Act and What It Means for You" (presentation, April 27, 2007).

American Indian Life. "Review of the Meriam Report." Bulletin No. 12 (June 1928): 6–11.

Ames, Kenneth M., and Herbert D. G. Maschner. *Peoples of the Northwest Coast: Their Archaeology and Prehistory.* London: Thames and Hudson, 1999.

Armstrong, Virginia I., ed. *I Have Spoken: American History through the Voices of the Indians.* Athens: University of Ohio Press/Swallow Press, 1971.

Beck, Ethel Fyles. *Lummi Indian How Stories.* Caldwell ID: Caxton Printers, 1955.

Bernholz, Charles D., and Anthony G. Carr (Laguna Pueblo). "The Annual Reports of the Commissioner of Indian Affairs: Revisiting the Key to the United States Congressional Serial Set, 1824–1920." *Government Information Quarterly* 26, no. 3 (July 2009): 540–45.

Bierwert, Crisca. "Remembering Chief Seattle: Revising Cultural Studies of a Vanishing Native American." *American Indian Quarterly* 22, no. 3 (Summer 1998): 280–304.

Biographical Directory of the United States Congress. "Gorton, Thomas Slade, III (Slade), (1928–)." http://bioguide.congress.gov/scripts/biodisplay.pl?index =g000333.

Black's Law Dictionary. 9th ed. Eagan MN: West Publishing, 2009.

Bolton, Herbert Eugene, ed. "Relation of the Voyage of Juan Rodriguez Cabrillo, 1542–1543." In *Spanish Exploration in the Southwest, 1542–1706,* 3–39. New York: Charles Scribner's Sons, 1916. Available at Wisconsin Historical Society, *American Journeys,* http:www.americanjourneys.org/aj-001/.

Boxberger, Daniel L. "In and Out of the Labor Force: The Lummi Indians and the Development of the Commercial Fishery of North Puget Sound." *Ethnohistory* 35, no. 2 (Spring 1988): 161–90.

———. *To Fish in Common: The Ethnohistory of Lummi Indian Salmon Fishing.* Seattle: University of Washington Press, 2000.

Boyd, Robert. *The Coming of the Spirit of Pestilence: Introduced Infectious Diseases and Population Decline among Northwest Coast Indians, 1774–1874.* Vancouver:

University of British Columbia Press, 1999; Seattle: University of Washington Press, 1999.

Braund, Kathryn E. Holland, ed. *Tohopeka: Rethinking the Creek War and the War of 1812.* Tuscaloosa: University of Alabama Press, 2012.

Brotherton, Barbara. "Joseph Raymond Hillaire: Lummi Artist-Diplomat." In P. Hillaire, *A Totem Pole History*, 44–67.

Calloway, Colin G. "The Continuing Revolution in Indian Country." In *Native Americans and the Early Republic*, edited by Frederick E. Hoxie, Ronald Hoffman, and Peter J. Albert, 3–33. Charlottesville: Published by the University Press of Virginia for the United States Capitol Historical Society, 1999.

———. *Crown and Calumet: British-Indian Relations, 1783–1815.* Norman: University of Oklahoma Press, 1987.

———. *First Peoples: A Documentary Survey of American Indian History.* 3rd ed. Boston: Bedford/St. Martin's, 2008.

Carpenter, Cecelia Smith (Nisqually), Maria Pascualy, and Trisha Hunter. *The Nisqually Indian Tribe.* Images of America series. Charleston NC: Arcadia, 2008.

Chamberlain, Rebecca. "The Earth Is Our First Teacher." Evergreen State College, 2006. http://academic.evergreen.edu/c/chambreb/articles.htm.

———, ed. *Sharing the Circle: A Resource Guide and Classroom Curriculum on Native American Music of the Northwest.* Contributions by Vi Hilbert (Upper Skagit), Pauline Hillaire (Lummi), Johnny Moses (Nuu-chah-nulth/Tulalip), Kevin Paul (Swinomish/Colville), and Loran Olsen. CD-ROM. Part of the "Northwest Native American Reading Curriculum." Olympia WA: Evergreen State College Center for Educational Improvement, 1994.

Chavers, Dean. *Racism in Indian Country.* New York: Peter Lang, 2009.

Child, Brenda J. (Red Lake Ojibwe). *Boarding School Seasons: American Indian Families, 1900–1940.* Lincoln: University of Nebraska Press, 2000.

Clark, Blue. *Lone Wolf v. Hitchcock: Treaty Rights and Indian Law at the End of the Nineteenth Century.* Lincoln: University of Nebraska Press, 1994.

Coan, C. F. "The First Stage of the Federal Indian Policy in the Pacific Northwest, 1849–1852." *Oregon Historical Quarterly* 22, no. 1 (March 1921): 46–89.

Cohen, Fay G. *Treaties on Trial: The Continuing Controversy over Northwest Indian Fishing Rights.* Seattle: University of Washington Press, 1986.

Cohen, Felix S. *Handbook of Federal Indian Law.* Newark NJ: LexisNexis, 2005.

Cole, Douglas. *Captured Heritage: The Scramble for Northwest Coast Artifacts.* Norman: University of Oklahoma Press, 1985.

Cole, Douglas, and Ira Chakin. *An Iron Hand upon the People: The Law against the Potlatch on the Northwest Coast.* Vancouver: Douglas and McIntyre; Seattle: University of Washington Press, 1990.

Confederated Salish and Kootenai Tribes (Pablo MT). *Explore the River Education Project. Bull Trout, Tribal People, and the Jocko River* (an interactive multi-media CD produced by the Confederated Salish and Kootenai Tribes); *Field Journal*—Snqeymintn; and *Bull Trout's Gift: A Salish Story about the Value of Reciprocity*. Lincoln: University of Nebraska Press, 2011.

Coolige, Sherman. "The Function of the Society of American Indians." In *The Elders Wrote: An Anthology of Early Prose by North American Indians 1768–1931*, edited by Bernd Peyer. Berlin: Dietrich Reimer, 1982.

Council for a Parliament of the World's Religions. "An Indigenous Peoples' Statement to the World." 2009 Parliament of the World's Religions, December 9, 2009, Berkeley Center for Religion, Peace, and Justice, Georgetown University. http://berkleycenter.georgetown.edu/publications/an-indigenous-peoples-statement-to-the-world.

Deloria, Vine, Jr. (Standing Rock Sioux), ed. *American Indian Policy in the Twentieth Century*. Norman: University of Oklahoma Press, 1985.

———. *Behind the Trail of Broken Treaties*. Austin: University of Texas Press, 1974, 1985.

———. *Indians of the Pacific Northwest: From the Coming of the White Man to the Present Day*. Garden City NY: Doubleday, 1977.

Deloria, Vine, Jr., and Raymond J. DeMallie. *Documents of American Indian Diplomacy: Treaties, Agreements and Conventions, 1775–1979*. 2 vols. Legal History of North America 4. Norman: University of Oklahoma Press, 1999.

Densmore, Frances. "History of the Study of Indian Music." In *The American Indians and Their Music*, 115–23. New York: Woman's Press, 1926.

Dowd, Gregory E. "Thinking outside the Circle: Tecumseh's 1811 Mission." In Braund, *Tohopeka*, 30–52.

Duthu, N. Bruce (Houma). *American Indians and the Law*. Penguin Library of American Indian History. New York: Penguin Books, 2008.

Echo-Hawk, Walter R. (Pawnee). *In the Light of Justice: The Rise of Human Rights in Native America and the UN Declaration on the Rights of Indigenous Peoples*. Golden CO: Fulcrum Press, 2013.

Edson, Leah Jackson. *The Fourth Corner*. Bellingham WA: Whatcom Museum of History and Art, 1968.

Evergreen State College. "Longhouse Education and Cultural Center." 2015. http://www.evergreen.edu/longhouse/.

———. "Native Programs." 2015. http:www.evergreen.edu/nativeprograms/.

Evers, Larry, and Barry Toelken. *Native American Oral Traditions: Collaboration and Interpretation*. Logan: Utah State University Press, 2001.

Fassett, Thom White Wolf (Seneca). *Giving Our Hearts Away: Native American Survival*. New York: General Board of Global Ministries, United Methodist Church, 2008.

Franklin, Benjamin. *The Autobiography of Benjamin Franklin*. Edited by Leonard W. Labaree et al. 1789. Reprint, New Haven: Yale University Press, 1964.

Garfield, Leonard, and Al Scott Johnnie—Sts'aStelQuyd (Lummi). "Revised Statement of Significance Concerning Nomination of the Chelhtenem Site for the Washington State Registry of Historic Places." April 16, 1992. Bellingham WA: Lummi Tribe Culture Department.

Getches, David H., Charles F. Wilkinson, and Robert A. Williams. *Cases and Materials on Federal Indian Law*. American Casebooks series. Eagan MN: West, 2005.

Gunther, Erna. *Indian Life on the Northwest Coast of North American, as seen by the Early Explorers and Fur Traders during the Last Decades of the Eighteenth Century*. Chicago: University of Chicago Press, 1972.

Haines, Francis. "Problems of Indian Policy." *Pacific Northwest Quarterly* 41, no. 3 (July 1950): 203–12.

Hanke, Lewis. *Aristotle and American Indians: A Study in Race Prejudice in the Modern World*. London: Hollis and Carter, 1959.

——. *The Spanish Struggle for Justice in the Conquest of America*. Philadelphia: University of Pennsylvania Press, 1949.

Harmon, Alexandra. *Indians in the Making: Ethnic Relations and Indian Identities around Puget Sound*. Berkeley: University of California Press, 1998.

——. "Indian Treaty History: A Subject for Agile Minds." *Oregon Historical Quarterly* 106, no. 3 (Fall 2005): 358–73.

——. *The Power of Promises: Rethinking Indian Treaties in the Pacific Northwest*. Seattle: University of Washington Press, 2008.

Hayes, Derek. *Historical Atlas of the Pacific Northwest: Maps of Exploration and Discovery*. Seattle: Sasquatch Books, 2000.

Hilbert, Vi (Upper Skagit), and Jay Miller, trans. *Siastənu: Gram Ruth Sehome Shelton, the Wisdom of a Skagit Elder*. Seattle: Lushootseed Press, 1995.

Hillaire, Joseph (Lummi). Songs in *Music of the American Indian: Northwest (Puget Sound)*. Recorded in 1950 by Willard Rhodes. Washington DC: Library of Congress, Archive of Folk Culture, AFS L34, audio cassette, 1954 with booklet revised in 1984.

Hillaire, Mary Ellen (Lummi). "Meeting Human and Social Needs in Planning Educational Programs in Indian Communities." *Coalition on Indian Controlled School Boards Special Issue*. N.d.

Hillaire, Pauline (Lummi). "A Century of Coast Salish History." Media companion to *Rights Remembered*, produced by Gregory P. Fields. DVD and two audio CDs. 2016.

———. "Coast Salish Totem Poles." Media companion to *A Totem Pole History*, produced by Gregory P. Fields. DVD and two audio CDs. 2013. Distributed by the University of Nebraska Press.

———. *Indian Policy: Crime or Reason?* Published in conjunction with the Longest Walk I. Omak WA: *Omak Chronicle*, 1978.

———. *Lummi Legends: Legends Told by My Father, Kwul-kwul't".* Produced by Jill Linzee. Audio CD. Mountlake WA: Northwest Heritage Resources, 2008. http://www.northwestheritageresources.org.

———. *A Totem Pole History: The Work of Lummi Carver Joe Hillaire*. Edited by Gregory P. Fields. Lincoln: University of Nebraska Press, 2013.

Hoig, Stan. *The Sand Creek Massacre*. Norman: University of Oklahoma Press, 1961.

Hoopes, Alban W. *Indian Affairs and Their Administration, with Special Reference to the Far West, 1849–60*. Philadelphia: University of Pennsylvania Press, 1932.

Hoxie, Frederick E. *A Final Promise: The Campaign to Assimilate the Indians, 1880–1920*. Lincoln: University of Nebraska Press, 1984.

Hudson, Charles M. *Black Drink: A Native American Tea*. Athens: University of Georgia Press, 2004.

Indian Claims Commission. Indian Claims Commission Decisions. *Lummi Tribe of Indians v. the United States*, Docket 110. Vol. 2 (1952, 1953), vol. 5 (1957), vol. 10 (1962), vol. 13 (1964), vol. 16 (1966), vol. 21 (1969), and vol. 24 (1970). Oklahoma State University Library, OSU Digital Publishing Center. http://digital.library.okstate.edu/icc/.

International Council of Thirteen Indigenous Grandmothers. "Petition to the Vatican." October 2005. http://www.grandmotherscouncil.org/major-accomplishments-a-prayer-unfolding.

International Labour Organization. "C169—Indigenous and Tribal Peoples Convention, 1989 (No. 169)." June 27, 1989. http://www.ilo.org/dyn/normlex/en/f?p=NORMLEXPUB:12100:0::NO::P12100_ILO_CODE:C169.

Jackson, Helen Hunt. *A Century of Dishonor: A Sketch of the United States Government's Dealings with Some of the Indian Tribes*. New York: Harper & Brothers, 1881; Boston: Roberts Brothers, 1885. Reprint, with introduction by Grace Gouveia, New York: Barnes & Noble, 2006.

Jaimes, M. Annette. "Federal Indian Identification Policy: A Usurpation of Indigenous Sovereignty in North America." In Josephy, Nagel, and Johnson, *Red Power*, 279–86.

Jefferson, Warren. *The World of Chief Seattle: How Can One Sell the Air?* Summertown TN: Native Voices, produced in cooperation with the Suquamish Tribe, 2001.

Jenness, Diamond. "The Faith of a Coast Salish Indian." *British Columbia Provincial Museum Memoirs*, no. 3 (1955).

Jensen, Richard E., R. Eli Paul, and John E. Carter. *Eyewitness at Wounded Knee.* Lincoln: University of Nebraska Press, 1997.

Johnson, Troy. *The Occupation of Alcatraz Island: Indian Self-Determination and the Rise of Indian Activism.* Urbana: University of Illinois Press, 1997.

Josephy, Alvin M. *The Patriot Chiefs: A Chronicle of American Indian Leadership.* New York: Viking Press, 1958, 1961.

Josephy, Alvin M., Jr., Joan Nagel, and Troy Johnson. *Red Power: The American Indians' Fight for Freedom.* 2nd ed. Lincoln: University of Nebraska Press, 1971, 1999.

Kalter, Susan. *Benjamin Franklin, Pennsylvania, and the First Nations.* Urbana: University of Illinois Press, 2006.

Kappler, Charles J., comp. and ed. *Indian Affairs: Laws and Treaties.* Vols. 1, 3, 4, 5, 6, and 7: *Laws.* Washington DC: Government Printing Office, 1904. Available at Oklahoma State University Library, OSU Library Electronic Publishing Center. http://digital.library.okstate.edu/kappler/index.htm.

──────, comp. and ed. *Indian Affairs: Laws and Treaties.* Vol. 2: *Treaties.* Washington DC: Government Printing Office, 1904. Available at Oklahoma State University Library, OSU Library Electronic Publishing Center. http://digital.library.okstate.edu/kappler/Vol2/toc.htm.

Kent, James. *Kent's Commentary on International Law.* Edited by J. T. Abby. Cambridge: Deighton, Dell, printed by C. J. Clay at the University Press, 1878.

Koppel, Tom. *Kanaka: The Untold Story of Hawaiian Pioneers in British Columbia and the Pacific Northwest.* North Vancouver: Whitecap Books, 1995.

Lane, Barbara. *Political and Economic Aspects of Indian-White Culture Contact in Western Washington in the Mid-Nineteenth Century.* Anthropological report submitted to *U.S. v. State of Washington.* May 10, 1973.

Lazarus, Edward. *Black Hills/White Justice: The Sioux Nation v. the United States, 1775 to the Present.* New York: HarperCollins, 1991.

Lesiak, Christine, producer. *White Man's Way: Genoa Indian School.* Native American Public Broadcasting Consortium, distributed by the Nebraska Educational Television Network, Lincoln. Documentary. 1986.

Lieb, Emily. "Bellingham: Thumbnail History." HistoryLink Essay 7904. August 20, 2006. http://www.historylink.org/index.cfm?DisplayPage=output.cfm&file_id=7904.

Lomawaima, K. Tsianina (Mvskoke Creek). *They Called It Prairie Light: The Story of Chilocco Indian School*. Lincoln: University of Nebraska Press, 1994.

Lummi Natural Resources Department. *Lummi Nation Atlas*. Prepared by Ann Stark, GIS Manager. Lummi Nation, Bellingham WA. February 2008. http://www.lummi-nsn.gov/NR/GIS/PDF/LummiAtlasFeb2008.pdf.

———. *Lummi Nation Multi-Hazard Mitigation Plan*. Funded by the Federal Emergency Management Agency. Prepared by the Water Resources Division, Steve Heywood et al. Bellingham WA: Lummi Indian Business Council, 2004, 2007. http://www.lummi-nsn.gov/NR/Water/PDF/LN%20MHMP_2007%20update.pdf.

Martin, Jill E. "'The Greatest Evil': Interpretations of Indian Prohibition Laws, 1832–1953." *Great Plains Quarterly* 23 (Winter 2003): 35–53.

Mathes, Valerie Sherer. *Helen Hunt Jackson and Her Indian Reform Legacy*. Austin: University of Texas Press, 1992.

Miller, Bruce Granville. *Be of Good Mind: Essays on the Coast Salish*. Vancouver: University of British Columbia Press, 2007.

———. *The Problem of Justice: Tradition and Law in the Coast Salish World*. With maps by Brian Thom. Lincoln: University of Nebraska Press, 2001.

Montler, Timothy. "The Grammar of Traditional Personal Names in Klallam." *Anthropological Linguistics*, forthcoming.

Morris, William G. "Forest Fires in Western Oregon and Western Washington." *Oregon Historical Quarterly* 35, no. 4 (December 1934): 313–39.

Nabokov, Peter. *A Forest of Time: Native Ways of History*. New York: Cambridge University Press, 2012.

National Archives (Pacific Northwest Region). "The National Archives at Seattle." http://www.archives.gov/seattle/public/#historical.

National Endowment for the Arts. "NEA National Heritage Fellowships, 2013: Pauline Hillaire." http://arts.gov/honors/heritage/fellows/pauline-hillaire.

Nettl, Bruno. *North American Indian Musical Styles*. Philadelphia: American Folklore Society, 1954.

Newcomb, Steven (Shawnee Lenape). "Five Hundred Years of Injustice: The Legacy of Fifteenth Century Religious Prejudice." Indigenous Law Institute. http://ili.nativeweb.org/index.html.

Newton, Nell Jessup, Robert Anderson, et al. *Handbook of Federal Indian Law*. Raleigh NC: LexisNexis, 2005.

Nicholas V. (pope). *Romanus Pontifex*, a papal bull issued in 1455. English translation in *European Treaties Bearing on the History of the United States and Its Dependencies to 1648*, edited by Francis Gardiner Davenport. Washington DC: Carnegie Institution of Washington, 1917.

Nichols, David A. *Lincoln and the Indians: Civil War Policy and Politics*. St. Paul: Minnesota Historical Society Press, 2012.

Northwest Digital Archives. University of Oregon Libraries, Special Collections and University Archives. *Cayuse, Yakima, and Rogue River Wars Papers*, Box 047. nwda.orbiscascade.org/ark:/80444/xv85849.

Northwest Indian Fisheries Commission. "Puget Sound Treaty Indian Tribes, Shellfish Growers Reach Pact." May 18, 2007. http://nwtreatytribes.org/puget -sound-treaty-indian-tribes-shellfish-growers-reach-pact/.

Nugent, Ann. *The History of Lummi Fishing Rights*. Bellingham WA: Lummi Communications, 1979.

——. *The History of Lummi Legal Action against the United States*. Bellingham WA: Lummi Communications, 1980.

——. *Lummi Elders Speak*. Bellingham WA: Lummi Historical Publications, 1982.

——. *Regulation of the Lummi Indians by Government Officials between 1900–1920*. Bellingham WA: Lummi Communications, 1977.

——. *Schooling of the Lummi Indians between 1885–1956*. Bellingham WA: Lummi Historical Publications, 1981.

O'Brien, Sharon. "A Legal Analysis of the American Indian Religious Freedom Act." In *Handbook of American Indian Religious Freedom*, edited by Christopher Vecsey, 27–43. New York: Crossroad, 1991.

Organization of American States, Department of International Legal Affairs, Office of Legal Cooperation. "American Declaration of the Rights and Duties of Man." Resolution adopted June 2, 1998. http://www.oas.org/juridico/english /ga-res98/eres1591.htm.

Parker, A. C. (Seneca), trans. and ed. *The Constitution of the Five Nations*. New York State Museum Bulletin no. 184. Albany: University of the State of New York, 1916.

Perdue, Theda, and Michael D. Green. *The Cherokee Removal: A Brief History with Documents*. Boston: Bedford/St. Martins, 2005.

Pevar, Stephen L. *The Rights of Indians and Tribes*. Carbondale: Southern Illinois University Press, 2002.

Pinkerton, Evelyn, ed. *Cooperative Management of Local Fisheries*. Vancouver: University of British Columbia Press, 1989.

Poole, Stafford, trans., ed., and annotator. *In Defense of the Indians: The Defense of the Most Reverend Lord, Don Fray Bartolomé de las Casas, of the Order of Preachers, Late Bishop of Chiapa, against the Persecutors and Slanderers of the Peoples of the New World Discovered across the Seas*. Dekalb: Northern Illinois University Press, 1974.

Pratt, Scott. "The Influence of the Iroquois on Early American Philosophy." *Transactions of the Charles S. Peirce Society* 32, no. 2 (Spring 1996): 274–314.

Prucha, Francis Paul. *American Indian Treaties: The History of a Political Anomaly.* Berkeley: University of California Press, 1994.

———, ed. *Americanizing the American Indians: Writings by the "Friends of the Indian," 1880–1900.* Cambridge MA: Harvard University Press, 1973.

———, ed. *Documents of United States Indian Policy.* 2nd ed. Lincoln: University of Nebraska Press, 1975, 1990.

———. *The Great Father: The United States Government and the American Indians.* Lincoln: University of Nebraska Press, 1984.

Richards, Kent D. *Isaac I. Stevens: Young Man in a Hurry.* Provo UT: Brigham Young University Press, 1979.

———. "The Stevens Treaties of 1854–55: An Introduction." *Oregon Historical Quarterly* 106, no. 3 (Fall 2005): 1–9.

Richardson, Allan, and Brent Galloway. *Nooksack Place Names: Geography, Culture, and Language.* Vancouver: University of British Columbia Press, 2011.

Riddle, Margaret. "Chirouse, Father Eugene Casimir (1821–1892)." HistoryLink Essay 9033. June 5, 2009. http://www.historylink.org/index.cfm?DisplayPage=output.cfm&file_id=9033.

Roessel, Ruth, ed., *Navajo Stories of the Long Walk Period.* Tsaile AZ: Navajo Community College Press, 1973.

Ronda, James P. *Lewis and Clark among the Indians.* Lincoln: University of Nebraska Press, 1984.

Rosenstein, Jay, writer and director. *In Whose Honor? American Indian Mascots in Sports.* Documentary. Champaign IL: New Day Films, 1997.

Ruby, Robert H., and John A. Brown. *Indians of the Pacific Northwest: A History.* Norman: University of Oklahoma Press, 1981, 1988.

Rutecki, Gregory. "Forced Sterilization of Native Americans: Later Twentieth Century Physician Cooperation with National Eugenic Policies." *Ethics and Medicine: An International Journal of Bioethics* 27, no. 1 (Spring 2011): 33–42.

Sanchez, Antonio. "Spanish Exploration: Juan Perez Expedition of 1774—First European Discovery and Exploration of Washington State Coast and Nueva Galicia (the Pacific Northwest)." HistoryLink Essay 5677. April 7, 2004. http://www.historylink.org/index.cfm?DisplayPage=output.cfm&file_id=5677.

Sanders, Allen, H. "Damaging Indian Treaty Fisheries: A Violation of Tribal Property Rights?" *Public Land and Resources Law Review* 17, no. 153 (1996): 153–75.

Silva, Noenoe K. (Kanaka Maoli). *Aloha Betrayed: Native Hawaiian Resistance to American Colonialism.* Durham NC: Duke University Press 2004.

Smith, Harlan Ingersoll. "Archaeology of the Gulf of Georgia and Puget Sound." *Memoirs of the American Museum of Natural History*, vol. 2, pt. 6. Jesup North Pacific Expedition. Leiden: E. J. Brill, 1907.

Smith, Harlan Ingersoll, and Gerard Fowke. "Cairns of British Columbia and Washington." *Memoirs of the American Museum of Natural History*, vol. 2, pt. 2. Jesup North Pacific Expedition. New York: Knickerbocker Press, January 1901.

Smith, Marian W. "The Coast Salish of Puget Sound." *American Anthropologist*, n.s., 43, no. 2 (April–June 1941): 197–211.

Stein, Julie K. *Exploring Coast Salish Prehistory: The Archaeology of San Juan Island*. Seattle: University of Washington Press, 2000.

Stephens, Joe K. "Oregon's Courts under the Provisional Government." Oregon Judicial Department History, State of Oregon Law Library. N.d. http://www.oregon.gov/soll/pages/ojd_history/historyojdpart1.aspx.

Stevens, Hazard. *The Life of Isaac Ingalls Stevens*. 2 vols. Boston: Houghton, Mifflin, 1900.

Stewart, Hillary. *Cedar: Tree of Life to the Northwest Coast Indians*. Seattle: University of Washington Press, 1984.

———. *Indian Fishing: Early Methods on the Northwest Coast*. Seattle: University of Washington Press, 1977.

Stover, John A. *The Routledge Historical Atlas of American Railroads*. New York: Routledge, 1999.

Suttles, Wayne P. "Affinal Ties, Subsistence, and Prestige among the Coast Salish." In *Coast Salish Essays*, 15–25. Seattle: University of Washington Press, 1987.

———. "Central Coast Salish." In *Handbook of North American Indians*, vol. 7: *Northwest Coast*, edited by Wayne Suttles, 453–76. General ed., William C. Sturtevant. Washington DC: Smithsonian Institution, 1990.

———. "Post-Contact Culture Change among the Lummi Indians." *British Columbia Historical Quarterly* 18, nos. 1 and 2 (January and April 1954): 29–102.

Swinomish Indian Tribal Community, Office of Planning and Community Development. "Swinomish Climate Change Initiative: Climate Adaptation Action Plan." La Conner WA: Swinomish Indian Tribal Community, October 2010. http://www.swinomish.org/climate_change/Docs/SITC_CC_AdaptationActionPlan_complete.pdf.

Szasz, Margaret. *Education and the American Indian*. Albuquerque: University of New Mexico Press, 1974.

Tanner, Charles, Jr. "'Take These Tribes Down': The Anti-Indian Movement Comes to Washington State." Institute for Research and Education on

Human Rights (IREHR). April 6, 2013. www.irehr.org/issue-areas/treaty
-rights-and-tribal-sovereignty/item/478-take-these-tribes-down.

Thom, Brian. "The Paradox of Boundaries in Coast Salish Territories." *Cultural Geographies* 16, no. 2 (2009): 179–205.

Thompson, Gerald. *The Army and the Navajo: The Bosque Redondo Reservation Experiment, 1863–1868*. Tucson: University of Arizona Press, 1976.

Thornton, Russell. *American Indian Holocaust and Survival: A Population History since 1492*. Norman: University of Oklahoma Press, 1987.

Thrush, Coll. *Native Seattle: Histories from the Crossing-Over Place*. Seattle: University of Washington Press, 2007.

Toensing, Gale Courey. "Quaker Committee Disavows Doctrine of Discovery, Affirms Declaration." *Indian Country Today*. December 17, 2009. http:// indiancountrytodaymedianetwork.com/ictarchives/2009/12/14/quaker -indian-committee-disavows-doctrine-of-discovery-affirms-declaration-82504.

Trafzer, Clifford E. (Wyandot), gen. ed. *American Indians/American Presidents: A History*. Washington DC: Smithsonian Institution in association with the National Museum of the American Indian, 2009.

Tribal Climate Change Project. University of Oregon Environmental Studies Program and USDA Forest Service Pacific Northwest Research Station. Tribal Profiles. "The Lummi Nation: Pursuing Clean Renewable Energy." http:// tribalclimate.uoregon.edu/tribal-profiles/.

Tribal Law and Policy Institute. *Tribal Court Clearinghouse*. "Fractionated Ownership of Indian Lands." http://www.tribal-institute.org/lists/fractionated _ownership.htm.

Trump, Matthew. "Oregon and Washington Territories in 1853." Wikimedia Commons file. 2004. File:Wpdms_oregon_washington_territories_1853.png.

———. "The State of Oregon and the Washington Territory in 1848." Wikimedia Commons file. 2006. File:Wpdms oregon territory 1848.png.

———. "The State of Oregon and the Washington Territory in 1859." Wikimedia Commons file. 2004. File:Wpdms_oregon_washington_territory_1859.png.

Turner, Dale (Teme-Augama Anishnaabe). "Oral Traditions and the Politics of (Mis)Recognition." In Waters, *American Indian Thought*, 229–38.

United Nations. "Convention on the Prevention and Punishment of the Crime of Genocide." Resolution 260 (III) A, adopted by the General Assembly of the United Nations on December 9, 1948. http://www.un.org/en/ga/search/view _doc.asp?symbol=A/RES/260(III) .

———. "Declaration on the Rights of Indigenous Peoples." Resolution 63/295 UN Document A/61/167, adopted by the General Assembly of the United Nations on September 13, 2007. http://www.un.org/esa/socdev/unpfii/documents/DRIPS_en.pdf.

Utley, Robert M. *The Indian Frontier of the American West, 1846–1890*. Albuquerque: University of New Mexico Press, 1984.

Utley, Robert M., and Wilcomb E. Washburn. *Indian Wars*. Boston: Houghton Mifflin, 1977.

Vanderwerth, W. C., ed. *Indian Oratory: Famous Speeches by Noted Indian Chieftains*. Norman: University of Oklahoma Press, 1971.

Van Doren, Carl, and Julian P. Boyd, eds. *Indian Treaties Printed by Benjamin Franklin, 1736–1762*. Philadelphia: Historical Society of Pennsylvania, 1938.

Vizenor, Gerald (Anishinaabe). "Socioacupuncture: Mythic Reversals and the Striptease in Four Scenes." In *The American Indian and the Problem of History*, edited by Calvin Martin, 180–91. New York: Oxford University Press, 1987.

Walker, Timothy. *Introduction to American Law*. Cincinnati: Derby, 1846.

Washington Secretary of State. Washington Territorial Timeline. "Northern Oregonians Vote to Split, 1851–1855." https://www.sos.wa.gov/legacy/timeline/default.aspx.

Waters, Anne (Seminole), ed. *American Indian Thought: Philosophical Essays*. Malden MA: Oxford Blackwell, 2004.

Watson, Bruce McIntyre. *Leaving Paradise: Indigenous Hawaiians in the Pacific Northwest, 1787–1898*. Honolulu: University of Hawai'i Press, 2006.

Wilkins, David E. *Hollow Justice: A History of Indigenous Claims in the U.S.* New Haven: Yale University Press, 2013.

Wilkins, David E., and K. Tsianina Lomawaima (Mvskoke/Creek). *Uneven Ground: American Sovereignty and Federal Law*. Norman: University of Oklahoma Press, 2001.

Wilkinson, Charles, with photo essay by Hank Adams (Assiniboine/Sioux). *Messages from Franks Landing: A Story of Salmon, Treaties, and the Indian Way*. Seattle: University of Washington Press, 2000.

Williams, G. Morris. "Forest Fires in Western Oregon and Western Washington." *Oregon Historical Quarterly* 35, no. 4 (December 1934): 313–39.

Williams, Robert A., Jr. (Lumbee). *The American Indian in Western Legal Thought: The Discourses of Conquest*. New York: Oxford University Press, 1990.

———. "Small Steps on the Long Road to Self-Sufficiency for Indian Nations: The Indian Tribal Governmental Tax Status Act of 1982." *Harvard Journal on Legislation* 22 (1985): 335–97.

Wilma, David. "State Supreme Court Issues Confusing Ruling in *Washington v. Satiacum* on Treaty Fishing Rights on July 1, 1957." HistoryLink Essay 2650. September 7, 2000. http://www.historylink.org/index.cfm?DisplayPage=output.cfm&file_id=2650.

Woods, Fronda. "Who's in Charge of Fishing?" *Oregon History Quarterly* 106, no. 3 (2005): 412–41.

Zinn, Howard. *Howard Zinn on War*. New York: Seven Stories Press, 2001, 2014.

———. *A People's History of the United States: 1492 to Present*. New York: HarperCollins, 2003, 2014.

INDEX

acculturation policy, 54, 152, 343
Adams, Hank, 214, 218
Adams, John Quincy, 335, 362n13
ahistory of Indian America, 22, 49–56,
    227–47; and ancestral dreams,
    227–29; and cultural and environ-
    mental cooperation, 245–47; and
    education, 243–45; and fairness
    and unity, 229–31; and immigration
    and the American Dream, 234–35;
    Indian contributions to, 240–42;
    and justice for the Earth and her
    children, 235–36; and righted
    wrongs, 236–40; and subjugation,
    231–33; and substance abuse pro-
    grams, 242–43; and tribal arts and
    marketing, 245; and United States
    of the World, 233–34
Alaska Packers, 206
alcohol and alcoholism, 21, 58, 62, 64,
    114–15, 137–43, 148, 188, 242–43.
    See also liquor; whiskey
Alexander VI, Pope, 76; Inter caetera
    divinai, 74
Alexis, John, 212
allotment policy: and assimilation,
    340–45; and citizenship, 58; and

George Manypenny, 144; and heir-
    ship policy, 185–87, 351; Helen Hunt
    Jackson on, 79; at Lummi Reserva-
    tion, 68, 152–54, 171–73, 185–87;
    overview of, 19–20, 53, 150–54; and
    sale of surplus land, 126. See also
    Dawes Act (General Allotment Act)
    (1887)
Alphonso V, King of Portugal, 74
America: building of, 73–88; class
    divide in, 84–86; official violence
    in, 82–84; precolonial, 75–77; and
    Tecumseh's vision of an Indian
    confederacy, 86–88
"American Declaration of the Rights
    and Duties of Man," 69–70
American Dream, 234–35
American Friends Service Committee,
    214
American Fur Company, 204
American Indian Defense Association,
    237
American Indian history timeline,
    329–54; and allotment and assimi-
    lation, 340–45; colonial period of,
    333–34; and "discovery" and coloni-
    zation, 329–30; and early European

inheritance policies, 103; as middle-
men for Indians, 119; stereotypes
and racism in, 191; transferal of, to
Department of the Interior, 13, 16,
61, 92, 337; and white settlement on
Lummi Reservation, 54
Bureau of Land Management, 337
Bush, George W., 150, 353

Cagey, Jack, 35, 269
Cain, J., 159
Calhoun, John C., 335
Campbell, Ben Nighthorse, 187
Canasatego, 76, 228
Carpenter, Cecelia Svinth: *The
Nisqually Indian Tribe*, 180
Casas, Bartolomé de las, 23
cash annuities, 356n18
Cayuga Nation, 76
Cayuse Tribe, 13–15, 181
Cayuse War, 14
cedar trees, 36–37
"Census of Various Indian Tribes Living
on or Near Puget's Sound" (Tolmie),
110
A Century of Dishonor (Jackson), 50–
51, 77–82, 153, 341
Chamberlain, Rebecca, 22, 251, 265, 376
Champagne, Duane, 27
Chavers, Dean: *Racism in Indian Coun-
try*, 65
Chelhtenem. *See* Lily Point
Cher, 242
Cherokee Nation v. Georgia, 181, 336
Cherokee Trail of Tears, 96, 336
Chicone, Audrey, 6
child binding, 118
Children of the Setting Sun, 6, 35, 57,
64, 143, 197, 258–59, 263, 269, 287
Chirouse, E. C., 147

Chowitsut, Chief, 2, 128, 136
Christianity, 73, 103. *See also*
missionaries
citizenship, U.S., 54, 57–58, 64, 81, 235,
297, 325, 340, 344
Civilian Conservation Corps (CCC),
238
Civil War, 296, 339
Clark, William, 140, 142, 148, 203, 335
class divide, 84–86
Classet Tribe, 141
Clinton, Bill, 150, 349, 352–53
Coalition of Indian Controlled School
Boards, 244
Coast Salish tribes, 98, 109–15, 124,
128, 138–39, 198–202, 266, 361n2.
See also specific tribes
Code Talkers, 189
*Codification of Laws on Survey and
Disposition of Public Land*, 68
Cohen, Felix S.: *Handbook of Federal
Indian Law*, 92, 119–20, 154, 167–68,
236
Collier, John, 20, 93, 345
Columbus, 8, 20, 48, 56, 59, 73–75, 247,
329, 358n20
Colville Confederated Tribes, 32, 142,
198, 237
Colville Indian Reservation, 32, 237,
242
Committee on Indians Affairs, 125, 146
commodities, government, 156, 170,
194, 224. *See also* annuity goods and
services
concentration policy, 53
Confederacy of the Five Nations, 76,
229–30
Constitution of the Five Nations, 230
Constitution of the United States. *See*
U.S. Constitution

Old Man House, 291–94, 296
Old Pierre, 200
Oliver, Emmett, 33
Omaha Treaty, 16, 46, 144, 171, 173
Onieda Nation, 76
Onondaga Nation, 76
oral history: of boarding school conditions, 54; and dances, 264–66; and drumming, 249–50; and Earth, Our First Teacher, 262–78; and elders, 262–64; and First Salmon Ceremony, 66, 200, 259, 274–78; and image of warlike tribes, 18, 160; and legends, philosophy, and values, 264–68; and Mother Earth, 268–74; and Pauline Hillaire, 251–61; of Point Roberts, 202; recording of, 260, 365n56; and songs, 251–57, 264–66, 269, 276–77
"Oral Traditions and the Politics of (Mis)Recognition" (D. Turner), 25
Oregon Land Donation Act (1850), 13, 121–24, 150, 160, 170–74, 294, 337–38, 344, 346
Oregon Organic Act (1843), 122
Oregon Treaty (1846), 10, 100, 337
Organization of American States (OAS), 69–70
Orrick, William, 216

Pacific Northwest, 36–41
Palmer, Joel, 14–16, 101–2, 159, 225, 368n53
Pandosy, Father, 160
papal bulls, 46, 74, 329
Pascualy, Maria, 180
Patient Protection and Affordable Care Act (2010), 354
Patkanim, 128
Paul, Debra Covington, xiii

Peace of Paris Treaty, 76
Penn, William, 232
Peo-peo-mox-mox, 70
persecution of Indians by Indians, 187–88
Pevar, Steven L.: *The Rights of Indian Tribes*, 167
Pierce, Franklin, 47
Pierre, Martha, 200
Plaster, Marina, 245
Plaster, Ted, 245
plenary power, 21, 67, 69, 126, 167–69, 343
Point Roberts, 199, 201–2, 204, 206–7
Polk, James K., 10, 15, 47, 92, 107, 337
population: of American Indians (1854), 113; of American Indians (2006–8), 358n29; of Lummi Tribe, 110, 113, 131
Port Madison/Suquamish Reservation. See Suquamish/Port Madison Reservation
potlatch gatherings, 25, 39, 63, 66, 97, 119, 276–77, 292, 341, 344
poverty: and the American class divide, 85; and employment opportunity, 244; escape from, 182; during Great Depression, 345; and Indian policy, 69, 101, 110, 167, 181, 239; and prejudice, 61–65
Pratt, Richard, 192, 341, 371n9
Pratt, Scott, 24
prejudice, 49, 64–65, 69, 86, 135, 182–83, 188, 191, 319
Price, Edna Scott Hillaire. See Scott, Edna Price Hillaire
Price, Harry, 140
probate reform, 153, 185, 187, 351, 353, 371n3
The Problem of Justice (Miller), 24

violence (*cont.*)
221; historical context of, 232; Joel Palmer on, 102; in nineteenth-century America, 82–84, 86–88, 94–95, 104; and Oregon Land Donation Act, 121; results of, 162; and United Nations Declaration on the Rights of Indigenous Peoples, 316, 321; against women, 181

Violence against Women Reauthorization Act (2013), 181, 370n37

Vitoria, Francisco de, 229

Walker, Timothy: *Introduction to American Law*, 79–80

Wallace, Leander, 117

Warm Springs Tribe, 216

War of 1812, 77, 82, 230, 335

wars to protect U.S. interests, 82–84

Washington, George, 20, 90, 334

Washington, Joe, 35, 200, 258, 269

Washington Department of Fisheries, 219, 221

Washington Department of Game, 219

Washington v. Washington State Commercial Fishing Vessel Association, 211

Washington v. Washington State Commercial Passenger Vessel Association, 221

Waters, Anne, 24

"Welfare Department," 184

Wheeler-Howard Act. *See* Indian Reorganization Act (IRA)

whiskey, 100–101, 122, 137, 148. *See also* alcohol and alcoholism; liquor

White, Elijah, 13

Whitman, Marcus, 14

Whitman, Narcissa, 14

Wilkes, Charles: "Tribal Member Census of 1841," 110

Wilkins, David E., 174; *Uneven Ground*, 126, 167, 169

Wilkinson, Charles F., 167; *Messages from Frank's Landing*, 217

Williams, John Andrew, 176

Williams, Robert A., 167

Willowpah Tribe, 141

Wilson, John Andrew, 178

Worcester v. Georgia, 55, 336

"Word Warriors," 25

World Parliament of Religions, 232

World War II, 40, 58, 189–90, 241, 345

Wounded Knee, 342, 348

Yakama Tribe, 17, 141–42, 159–61, 198, 211–13, 216, 219, 289, 297, 343

Yakama War, 17–18, 159–60, 339

Yaryan, John, 215

yaupon holly, 87

Young, James, 214

Zinn, Howard, 87

Printed in the USA
CPSIA information can be obtained
at www.ICGtesting.com
CBHW021324201124
17726CB00005B/49/J

9 780803 245846